OVER LORD

OVER LORD

General Pete Quesada and the

Triumph of Tactical Air Power

in World War II

THOMAS ALEXANDER HUGHES

THE FREE PRESS

New York   London   Toronto   Sydney   Tokyo   Singapore

The Free Press
A Division of Simon & Schuster Inc.
866 Third Avenue, New York, N.Y. 10022

Printed in the United States of America

printing number

1 2 3 4 5 6 7 8 9 10

Text design by Carla Bolte

Library of Congress Cataloging-In-Publication Data

Hughes, Thomas
    Over lord: General Pete Quesada and the triumph of tactical air power in World War II / Thomas Hughes.
        p.   cm.
    Includes bibliographical references and index.
    ISBN 0-02-915351-4
    1. Quesada, Elwood R. (Elwood Richard), 1904–   . 2. World War, 1939–1945—Campaigns—France—Normandy. 3. World War, 1939–1945—Aerial operations. 4. Normandy (France)—History. 5. Operation Overlord. I. Title.
D756.5.N6H84   1995
940.54'214—dc20   95–13614
                                                                                    CIP

For my parents

KEVIN AND JOANNE

Contents

Preface

THIS BOOK IS BOTH AN EFFORT TO RECOVER THE LOST MEMORY OF GEN-
eral Elwood R. (Pete) Quesada's tactical innovations in World War II
and an attempt to add insight to the modern-day debates on air policy
in the Department of Defense. It uses Quesada's career to trace the development of tactical aviation, or the close support of ground troops, in
World War II. Part biography, part campaign history, and part combat
analysis, it recounts how tactical air doctrine grew from battlefield experience. It also seeks to understand the limits of tactical air power, especially as they manifested themselves during the stalemated campaign
of autumn 1944.

This work cuts across traditional conceptions of World War II and
raises important questions about twentieth-century warfare. Most
World War II biographies either portray senior leaders in the last
years of their careers or they look back at junior officers who went on
to achieve great things after the war. The effect is to present the conflict as the culmination of an era or the start of a new epoch. Through
the eyes of a midlevel command general like Quesada, however, the
war seems less like an end or a beginning and more like a transition.
As both an old and a new war, World War II can provide important insight into the interplay between doctrine and strategy, and their combined influence on tactics; on the role of technology in war; on
battlefield innovation; and on the sociology and psychology of tactical
command.

What follows is a lost story of American tactical air power in World

War II and Pete Quesada's place in that story. It is a story as pertinent to the Army and Air Force today as it was for the flyers and soldiers of yesterday.

I incurred debts I cannot repay while working on this book. A dissertation-year fellowship from the Office of Air Force History, an advanced-research support grant from the Army Military History Institute, and a post-doctoral fellowship from The Ohio State University allowed me to pursue this topic for three years. Herbert Pankratz at the Eisenhower Library, Wilbert Mahoney and Timothy Nenninger at the National Archives, Archie DiFante at the Air Force Historical Research Center, and David Keogh and Richard Summers at the Army War College deserve special praise for their insight and help. Along the corridors of all these archives, Sharron Graves became my great friend and my noble research assistant. She typed letters, took notes, tracked expenses, and supported my temperamental ego. I thank her for all that, and for only those things she and I can know.

At the University of Houston, Professors James H. Jones, Carl Ittman, Frank L. Holt, and Arthur Stemmermann read all or parts of the manuscript and offered keen suggestions. Professor James Kirby Martin did all this and more; his enthusiasm for my work kept me going when I felt like quitting. Professor Joseph T. Glatthaar directed this project as a dissertation, and his hand is everywhere in it. From start to finish, he has been a perfect mentor.

At The Free Press, Joyce Seltzer and then Bruce Nichols, Norah Vincent, and Bob Harrington made this book possible.

In addition to this scholarly help, General Quesada himself granted me a number of interviews. So did hundreds of war veterans of every rank and branch of service. Together, these men in the twilight of their lives helped me to flesh out a complicated and subtle story. After Quesada died, his wife Kate Davis and his son Peter extended to me every imaginable kindness and trust. For that I am forever grateful.

This book is for my Mom and Dad. Kevin and Joanne Hughes have been my steadfast supporters for thirty years. At every point along the way, they have been everything parents could and should be. I have tried to make them proud of each word, each sentence, each paragraph, and each chapter. Although the mistakes in this book are mine alone, my parents are responsible for any merit it may have.

T.A.H.
Columbus, Ohio
Houston, Texas

OVER LORD

Introduction

History May Show They Saved the Day

The time will come when thou shalt lift thine eyes
To long-drawn battles in the skies,
While aged peasants, too amazed for words,
Stare at the flying fleets of wondrous birds.
Thomas Gray, 1737

SOUTHWICK HOUSE, PORTSMOUTH, ENGLAND. 3 JUNE 1944. 2030 HOURS. Major General Elwood R. "Pete" Quesada slumped in the staff car, wishing he were already back at IX Fighter Command headquarters at Middle Wallop. As his driver pulled away from the Allied command center, his aide-de-camp noted a difference in the general; normally well-groomed and almost fastidious about his appearance, he now looked frazzled and tired. A youthful forty, Quesada was the product of Chief of Staff George Marshall's determination to raise able and vigorous officers from the junior ranks early in the war. But months of feverish preparations had taken a toll on even his stamina, and he shouldered a large

1

burden this spring night. In just days, he and his 1,500 fighter planes would provide air support for the American soldiers of Operation OVER-LORD, the long-awaited invasion of Europe. Now only the uncertain path of storm clouds could derail a million men from their appointed tasks. At Southwick House, Allied Commander Dwight Eisenhower had just solicited Quesada's counsel about the weather, and motoring through the blacked-out night of wartime England, Quesada did not envy the burden and isolation of the Supreme Command. "It's entirely in Ike's hands," he thought.[1]

It was a lousy, chilly evening. Quesada bound his jacket closer. The driver, the aide, and the general did not speak. Their silence was broken only by sentries at innumerable checkpoints. Even those disruptions faded from Quesada's mind, and soon he was sleeping.

That was just as well, his aide thought. The endless days of meetings, maneuvers, and planning sessions that stretched back into 1943 were over. There was nothing left to do but wait for Eisenhower's decision. Even then, if all went according to plan, Quesada would be a mere spectator in the show. Now, in early June, Allied fate no longer rested in the hands of generals, admirals, and marshals. By now, D-Day was the responsibility of rifle brigades, assault battalions, naval gunnery crews, and pilots. Indeed, only an emergency would make Quesada change the plans for the close air support of American soldiers. Across the Channel the rigors of field command awaited him, and what Quesada needed most was rest.

When the car finally lurched to a stop at his headquarters in the village of Middle Wallop, he checked the weather forecast, wrote to his mother that when the time came "nobody will be able to say we weren't in the thick of things," and went to bed, sleeping the good sleep.[2]

In the morning, Eisenhower postponed the assault for at least twenty-four hours. At Middle Wallop, Quesada filled the day with last-minute preparations. He talked to aides serving as senior air controllers on ships already afloat beyond the white cliffs of Dover. He checked with subordinates at Uxbridge, the Allied Combined Air Control Center south of London. He conducted inspections of airfield construction teams and communications squadrons bound for Normandy on D-Day. He restricted all personnel at his eleven airstrips. To facilitate identification, his ground crews painted white stripes on P-38, P-47, and P-51 fighters.[3]

Eisenhower's delay increased the discomfort of nearly 100,000 infantry troops crowded aboard landing craft. The waiting greatly increased their mental and physical strain. Some played cards incessantly or chatted quietly. Many simply lay in their bunks and hammocks, gazing into the air.

Quesada thought mainly of them, the ground forces, on this day of delay. Weeks of air strikes against Nazi-occupied French rail and roadways, beach defenses, and marshaling yards were important, he knew, "but it was preliminary. If we failed now the army might fail." One of his representatives at Uxbridge, Colonel James Ferguson, noticed the strain on Quesada's face. "He was really on pins and needles." So were others. Aboard his command ship, the cruiser USS *Augusta*, First Army Commander Omar Bradley paced restlessly, a prisoner of a dark and windy day. Inevitably, the delay drained optimism from the hearts of the men, and even Eisenhower drafted a message announcing the invasion's failure—just in case.[4]

The attack was not postponed again. On 5 June the Supreme Commander committed to an invasion early the next day. Like most who knew the operation was going forward, Quesada retired early that night. He was up at 0230 hours, traveling to Uxbridge hours before the first Americans waded onto the Continent. Above, the skies of southern England filled with a thousand C-47s carrying airborne troops to France. Everywhere people awoke to the planes' thunder. Near Ashford, pilot William Dunn lay in bed and listened to the drone. At the 366th Fighter Group outside Thruxton, Group Commander Colonel Harold Holt interrupted his own briefing to watch the planes pass overhead. "There are thousands of them," he mused. "Our own lads—the first ones over." To one staffer at Middle Wallop, the black sky became a "carnival, a melange of colored lights, a giant brilliant Christmas tree." On the road to Uxbridge, Quesada also watched the planes. The entire machinery of the attack was now inexorably pledged.[5]

Quesada jumped from his car as it wheeled into the Uxbridge compound. Of all the command centers for D-Day, Uxbridge was perhaps the most important. Used by the Royal Air Force since the early days of the war, it had been the nerve center for fighter control during the Battle of Britain. For D-Day, most pilots had carefully scheduled missions, but from here Allied leaders could swiftly change the plans of some five thousand planes if the need arose. Befitting its value, the Uxbridge operations room was deep in the bowels of the earth, safe from even the most direct bombing.

Quesada went down eighty-seven steps, through two sets of steel doors, past a whole company of military police, through another steel door, past one final sentry, and at last into a huge room. For a moment the bright lights blinded him. A thirty-foot square table map dominated the space. Everywhere people moved in all directions, like tiny cogs in a vast machine. Radar operators, their eyes glued to a bank of oscilloscopes, reported aircraft positions to Royal Air Force WAAFs, who in turned moved symbols about the map to reflect the tactical situation. Sector operators and flight controllers viewed the whole panorama from an elevated balcony, and issued the actual movement orders for the attack.

The place was teeming with Allied top brass. Eisenhower and the senior air and sea commanders were there. In just a few hours, Chief of the Imperial Staff Sir Alan Brooke and Prime Minister Winston Churchill would arrive. On this day, it was nothing to be a mere general in that room.[6]

Reaching the IX Fighter Command desk along the balcony, Quesada greeted Ferguson and his other senior controller, Colonel Jim Howard. They were all nervous. Quesada gulped coffee and smoked cigars in a feeble attempt to while away the time. Watching the small ship symbols move closer to France on the map, he was surprised to see no real signs of German air activity. Navies are most vulnerable to air attack at the peak of amphibious operations, when they are not free to take evasive action, and over 500 of Quesada's planes—and hundreds of others— were covering the armada. It was a good omen that the Luftwaffe did not challenge them.[7]

Nothing much had changed when the first troops hit the shores around 0600 hours. As it turned out, the Allies enjoyed an overwhelming air superiority on 6 June. The German Luftwaffe managed less than 200 aerial forays against over 15,000 Anglo-American sorties. "For all the air that ventured out against us on the Channel," General Omar Bradley remembered, the vast air-control room on his command ship "might better have been converted into a pool hall."[8]

Most of the other operations along the Normandy coast also portended well for the Allies. Despite the presence of an elite Panzer division in the area, British Commonwealth forces stormed ashore on three beaches with limited difficulty. They fell short of important D-Day objectives, but by nightfall they had a secure foothold, which in places extended inland five miles. Their leader, Field Marshal Bernard Montgomery, judged the day a success.

The story was similar at UTAH, the westernmost U.S. beach. There, an attack by 360 medium bombers greatly assisted the invaders. The air strike wiped out entire German units before Americans even stepped from their landing craft. In one sector, the defenders had but a single 88mm gun, an old Renault tank turret dug into the sands, and a handful of machine guns by the time the aerial blitz ended. Seizing such an advantage, the U.S. Fourth Division landed 23,000 men at a cost of under 200 casualties. As the day passed, a combination of effective naval gunfire, aerial bombardment, and swift infantry movements overwhelmed the sparse defenders, who had expected an assault to the north near Calais. With few exceptions, here and in the British zone the landings had been a remarkable piece of good fortune and good judgment.[9]

It was very different with OMAHA, the American beach landing between UTAH and Montgomery's men. There, where two thirds of the U.S. D-Day effort was concentrated, the First and Twenty-ninth Divisions were enduring ten times as many losses as the Fourth, and very many times their fear and confusion. Before the first men set foot on the beach, over a thousand heavy bombers with 6,000,000 pounds of bombs had blasted the coast. But these pilots were unaccustomed to their task and were bombing through a thick cloud cover. Predictably, most of them missed their targets by as much as three miles. The effort disgusted Twenty-ninth Division commander Charles Gerhardt. "Very few of the bombs fell on the beach or the fortifications commanding it," he complained. Gerhardt's boss at V Corps, Major General Leonard Gerow, added that "the failure cost heavily in men and material." On top of the poor air show, naval guns were ineffective in blasting enemy batteries perched on cliffs overlooking the shore. As a result, when Allied landing craft crawled onto Omaha Beach, many German strongpoints remained unscratched.[10]

Not that anyone had to tell that to the attackers. The heavy surf played havoc with them. The sea swallowed the entire field artillery battalion of the Twenty-ninth Division. Of the first fifty-five tanks headed to shore, only five reached solid ground. The sea fouled rifles and pistols and compelled many soldiers to discard their equipment or drown. Once out of the water, many men fell easy prey to a hail of machine-gun fire.[11]

Army Ranger Mike Rehm and his ten men were among the first to land. Two of them were killed and three wounded in the first hundred yards of advance. Within sixty minutes, two thirds of his entire Ranger company were casualties. A survivor believed that the "invasion had been a failure." By midday some German officers agreed with this hapless soul when they reported that the invasion had been stopped on the beaches. For the few fortunate Americans who reached the relative safety of brush beyond the sand, the unexpected presence of a German attack division created yet another predicament.[12]

All this was unknown to Pete Quesada at Uxbridge in the early hours of D-Day, but his own men in the assault waves knew of the turmoil soon enough. Air-support liaison officers, slated to direct air missions, landed right behind the first infantry troops. One of them remembered groping to the shore from eight feet of water only to be greeted by "burning tanks, jeeps, abandoned vehicles, a terrific crossfire." By dusk his unit had suffered eight killed and thirty-five wounded, and had lost twenty-eight of its thirty-five vehicles.[13]

Colonel Blair Garland, IX Fighter Command's signals officer and a key Quesada subordinate, reached the coast with two truck-mounted radars and radios. The equipment was immediately knocked out and a British wing commander with him was wounded. His little band of warriors then sought refuge in a beach draw and waited for a backup radar set. It arrived, but its dish was ruined and most of the men badly shot up. "Scared green" and with no equipment, Garland could do nothing but stay in the draw all day and into the night.[14]

Elsewhere, Sergeant Andy Hertz and the 922nd Aviation Engineer Regiment battled ashore at about noon, ready to construct an emergency landing strip on the high ground behind the beach. Almost immediately, a desperate beachmaster ran up to him. "Who are you people?" Engineers, Hertz replied. "Good, we've got wires to clear. You got bangalores?" No, Hertz said, his men were aviation engineers. "Who the hell sent you in?" the beach master barked. "Some sonofabitch," Hertz shrugged. So he and his men took refuge with other stranded Americans, hiding behind what shelter the flat sandy terrain offered.[15]

Whatever else was certain, there could be few aircraft directed by American soldiers from Omaha Beach that morning, and no advance landing grounds to service Quesada's fighter planes. Already, the commander of the 101st Airborne Division, who had parachuted into Normandy before dawn, felt the pinch of ineffective air support. "Air-ground cooperation," he remembered, "produced virtually nothing in support of this Division."[16]

As these small dramas of humanity played out, Pete Quesada and other commanders grew anxious. On the cruiser *Augusta*, Omar Bradley's "worries deepened over the alarming and fragmentary reports we picked up . . . we could piece together only an incoherent account of sinkings, swampings, heavy enemy fire, and chaos on the beaches." By midmorning, Gerow's V Corps staff on the USS *Ancon* was in dismay, and one officer who had raced closer to the shore in a PT boat told of landing craft ranging about aimlessly like a "stampeding herd of cattle." The situation was desperate at 1200 hours. As General Heubner of the First Division succinctly explained it, "those goddamm Boche just won't stop fighting."[17]

At that point, Bernard Montgomery and Omar Bradley seriously considered diverting all subsequent OMAHA landings to other beaches, in effect abandoning OMAHA and throwing the entire Allied plan to the winds. Some, like Bradley's chief of staff Bill Kean, were somewhat calmer, though even he urgently demanded "some air support to help clear the beaches." Back at Uxbridge, radar operators, WAAFs, flight controllers and generals alike struggled to make any sense of the disjointed messages from the far shore. By midday the only certainty was that the OMAHA landings were in immediate danger of failure.[18]

Like others, Pete Quesada searched for ways to alleviate the crisis. He tried to redirect planes. He ordered aircraft already above the convoys to range over the beaches and attack any target that may appear.

He sent messages repeatedly to Blair Garland on the beach. But these efforts and more were in vain. The elaborate signals plan to direct air support had, by then, collapsed under what the German war philosopher Karl von Clausewitz once called "the fog of war." Well over half the American air liaison parties on Omaha Beach were now knocked out. There was precious little radio contact between the support parties ashore and their comrades afloat. The communications net, which had called for a series of relay points stretching from the beach to fighter-direction tenders offshore, to headquarters ships, and finally to the Combined Control Center at Uxbridge, was too cumbersome for the fast-paced battle.[19]

The vaunted efficiency of Uxbridge broke down under the weight of confusion. What pleas were received for air support only served to exacerbate a massive communications gridlock. At one point, it took a general on the *Augusta* thirty minutes just to contact Uxbridge, much less get approval for any missions. To one observer, the center's performance was "entirely inexcusable." For any company commander on the beach who needed fighters overhead quickly, the multistage signals net meant only frustration—and sometimes death.[20]

By 1315 hours Pete Quesada had had enough. Never one to enjoy a spectator's role, he believed that the situation demanded extraordinary action. After a fifteen-minute conference with his immediate boss, Ninth Air Force commander Lewis Brereton, he shifted his 1,500 planes from the Uxbridge communications net to his smaller yet more efficient signals setup at Middle Wallop. Before D-Day he and Blair Garland, his signals officer presently stuck on the beach, had developed an alternative communications scheme for close support once the Allies were firmly on the Continent. This net originated at Middle Wallop and ran directly to giant radio towers on the Isle of Wight, where direct contact was possible with headquarters ships, fighter-direction tenders, air officers on the far shore, and even individual pilots in the air. Racing back from Uxbridge to Middle Wallop, he delegated full command prerogatives to Colonels Lorry Tindal and John Taylor on headquarters ships, streamlining the system even further. He then placed his four reserve fighter groups on operational alert, ready to fly at ten minutes' notice. Meanwhile, back at Uxbridge, air officers of the British forces were making similar adjustments in their own chain of command.[21]

Quesada did all this with some trepidation. He believed that war was "nothing more than organized chaos and switching gears in mid-stream always gives the chaos an edge over the organization." But he had no other option. The massive maneuver that was D-Day had been choreographed to the last detail, and communications were the sinews that bound the complex campaign together. Without communications, the assault would surely fail. Already, the Americans were learning a fundamental lesson of the war that awaited them on the far shore. Bulky command channels were poorly suited to support a fluid ground battle. Such systems were fine for planned long-range bomber missions deep into Germany, which were just the kind of operations that had marked the air war up to D-Day. But the close-air-support war now dawning in Normandy would require new arrangements, sometimes new assumptions of command, certainly different doctrinal foundations, and probably distinct equipment and resources. In short, battle leaders would have to develop an entirely new method of air war.[22]

At the 358th Fighter Group, Quesada's operational alert caught Captain Robert Biggers munching a sandwich. Rushing to his P-47 Thunderbolt, he and fifteen others taxied their planes to the end of the runway, ready for immediate takeoff. "During our rotations we sat in our aircraft ready to go, feeling an excitement we could not explain. Conjecture was all we had." Biggers and others did not wait long for action. In mid-afternoon his squadron scrambled to Isigny, three miles behind Omaha Beach. There, part of the German Sixth Parachute Regiment was moving toward the estuaries between Utah and Omaha Beaches. Biggers and his flyers stopped more than four fifths of those defenders dead in their tracks.[23]

An hour later the Eighty-second Airborne Division, which had dropped near Ste. Mère Église before dawn, pressed Middle Wallop for help repelling a counter attack by Hitler's 243d Division. At the 366th Group, Colonel Harry Holt gunned his plane down the runway and into the air. Over the English Channel, his pilots were mesmerized by the thousands of ships below. Landing craft were spewing men at an astonishing rate, Holt remembered, "scattering like kids from school." In a way, the invasion took on a surreal quality from 20,000 feet; it was distant and somehow disconnected from the pilots. But the crackling radio jolted the flyers' attention back to their mission. Searching an area west of Ste. Mère Église, they failed to locate the Germans arrayed against the paratroops. A call back to Colonel Lorry Tindal on the *Ancon* did not help, and the controller feebly told Holt to "seek out targets of opportunity."[24]

Splitting into groups of four, the Thunderbolts fell to 2,000 feet and scoured the lush Norman terrain. They saw nothing until a bank of hedgerows spit tracer ammunition skyward. Still unable to see specific targets, the entire squadron merely sprayed the hedgerows with cannon and machine-gun fire until "no more tracers came out." Satisfied and low on fuel, Holt pointed his pilots home. This aid from the air helped the Eighty-second Division consolidate its position and added to German confusion as the Allies pushed ashore.[25]

So it went late on D-Day. All together, the Middle Wallop signal net directed six missions as night drew near. Squadrons from the 368th Group raided gun positions in the vicinity of Colleville that had pinned Americans down for hours. Later, fighter-bombers attacked German elements near Trévières, directly behind the heart of OMAHA, where the German 352nd Division was rushing to the beachhead.[26]

Meanwhile, medium and heavy bombers, which were not under Quesada's command, steadily pounded transportation centers farther inland from the beaches in a bid to cut off German reinforcements from the battle. Missions to Caen, St. Lô, Argentan, and Granville rained a million pounds of explosives on the defenders. Pound for pound less effective than Quesada's fighter-bomber efforts, the sheer weight of these attacks nonetheless slowed German movements into the coastal plain. As the sun set, only one bridge remained intact over the Orne, derailing the counterattack of the crack Twenty-first Panzer Division. On the American side, engineers at last managed to carve a 2,000-foot emergency airstrip from the grassland behind UTAH. All in all, at dusk the situation was markedly better than it had been just twelve hours before.[27]

Yet the danger had not passed. Late in the day the German commander, Gerd von Rundstedt, won Hitler's permission to commit two more Panzer divisions to the fray. Even more menacing, a huge traffic jam in the English Channel was already preventing any Allied reinforcements from reaching the beach in good time. Although the Anglo-Americans could count on supporting naval gunfire throughout the night, the ragged coastline in effect was shielding many German strongpoints, making the floating batteries relatively ineffective. The men of OMAHA badly needed twenty-four hours to consolidate their position before the German reinforcements arrived, and now air power seemed the only asset that might buy enough time for the doughboys huddled on the sand.[28]

Quesada survived on a few meager moments of rest that night. Up before dawn on 7 June, he again placed fighter groups on tactical alert. At first light Thunderbolts roared into the English sky and pointed toward the French coast. But for the second straight day cloud cover aided the Germans. Relying less and less on the signals net, Quesada directed most squadron leaders to duck underneath the soup and seek targets of opportunity. Missions to Cérisy and Balleroy forests trapped German reinforcements of armor. Another raid dismantled three troublesome gun positions near Maisy. In one of only two missions directed by a forward controller, planes from the 365th Group knocked out a battery holding up U.S. Rangers just thirteen minutes after their initial call for help. For the fighter-bombers, it had been a masterful day.[29]

Together, Quesada's fighter pilots sortied 1,742 times in direct support of the ground forces on 7 June, bringing their two-day total to 3,303 sorties. Collectively, they destroyed eight bridges and forty-two vehicles. They damaged, bombed, or strafed countless German columns moving toward the sea. At times, the air was literally choked with Quesada's planes. One pilot felt as if he "had to put his hand out to make a turn." Such effort was not without cost, of course, but the thirteen aircraft lost and Lieutenant Joe Miller's crash landing near Grandcamp seemed a small price to pay. In total, the casualty rate among Allied air forces for the two days was less than 1 percent.[30]

When darkness came once again to Normandy, OMAHA was no longer in immediate danger. Still far short of D-Day objectives and facing yet more toil and death, its soldiers nevertheless ceased to worry about utter failure. There was even light banter on Bradley's command ship *Augusta*. "Things were sticky," the Army commander admitted, "but they are clearing up." The next day he reported to Eisenhower that "everything is well in hand," although he confided to another that "someday I'll tell General Ike just how close it was." Back at Middle Wallop, Quesada surveyed the day's work and was pleased. He would go to Omaha Beach himself early the next morning.[31]

Others were happy with Quesada's planes, too. Bradley believed that "the fighter-bomber operations against road traffic played a major part in the success of the invasion." From UTAH, VII Corps commander J. Lawton Collins reported that fighter-bombers "reduced almost to zero enemy air attacks on the beaches." On Omaha Beach, V Corps' Gerow said that Quesada had delivered "the most beneficial effects of air support." On the shore itself, soldiers busy ducking Germans cheered their friends in the air.[32]

Hitler's men had a different perspective, but agreed that Allied air power was crucial to the invasion's success. Germans marching toward the invasion area quickly learned to move with eyes turned skyward, and one Panzer commander described highways to the Allied beaches as "*Jabo Rennstrecke*" (fighter-bomber race courses). The efficiency with which Quesada's planes attacked soon ruined German defense schemes. "Our predetermined battle plan is to a great extent eliminated because of the enemy's great control of the air," recounted one report to the high command in Berlin. Von Rundstedt felt that heavy bomber attacks were "decidedly disagreeable," and thought that fighter raids had "critically delayed" his reinforcements at the precise moment his beach defenses were crumbling. With timely replacements, he believed, OMAHA might have been a great victory for the Third Reich. As it was, the Allied success along the Norman coast was "all a question of air force, air force, and again air force."[33]

Quesada had ample reason to smile, then, when he awoke on 8 June. The close air support of his pilots had combined with naval fire and truly heroic close-order combat on the beaches to save OMAHA. Given the difficulties that the Americans had suffered against the defenders, it is hard to imagine that they could have bested them at all had they been without exceptional air support. On this, the third day of OVERLORD, the Allies were finally firmly ashore—though they were still gasping to regain their breath after the vast strain of getting there.

That evening Quesada wired congratulations and praise to his fighter-bomber groups. "The spirit with which these groups accepted and performed their mission reflects great credit to them and I am most grateful for their efforts. It is possible if not probable that their efforts were in large part responsible for the attack on Omaha Beach continuing. History may show they saved the day."[34]

If Quesada's words reflected the typical hyperbole of such communiqués, they revealed also the fervent promise of D-Day. Until then, airmen assigned to support ground forces had been weak cousins to the glamorous bomber pilots winging deep into Germany on strategic raids. Now, however, it seemed that the war in France and Germany would put a high premium on close air support of the doughboys. Perhaps at last the men of the tactical air forces would receive their due.

Instead, history quickly and easily forgot the contributions of Pete Quesada and others associated with tactical air power in World War II. In the decades since the war, the strategic efforts of American bombers above Germany and Japan became legendary while the achievements of this "other air war" faded into obscurity, even though the close air support of ground forces did indeed constitute an increasingly important element of Allied victory in North Africa, Italy, and France. At the end of the war, most commanders acknowledged the critical part that air power had played in land campaigns from the Sahara to the Rhineland. But soon after the fighting stopped, the newly independent U.S. Air Force stressed strategic bombardment at the expense of tactical accomplishments in an effort to carve a role for air power in the nuclear age. As Air Force leaders let their tactical aviation wither, the ground Army was forced to develop its own air arm. By the 1950s, the result was a duplication of weapon systems and a dichotomy of air-power doctrine in the armed forces.

This in turn profoundly influenced the American military experience in the Korean and Vietnam Wars. Neither of these conflicts became the swift nuclear holocausts envisioned by the Air Force, and both placed a premium on the more conventional role of close air support. But by then Army and Air Force officers had very different capabilities, and worked within very different systems, to assist ground troops from the air. On these two Asian peninsulas, confusion was often the only common denominator, and unnecessary American blood on the ground was often the only result.

Today, after the Cold War, officers of all branches are once again struggling to reconstruct their services, searching for the right relationship of strategic and tactical deterrents. In their endeavor, they would do well to remember the lessons of World War II and the policy choices made following that seminal event.

Quesada's story has its roots in the Great War. World War I lasted long enough to promise many things for military aviation, but it ended too soon to fulfill any single hope. Aerial dogfighting dominated the struggle in the air until bombing operations late in the war convinced many pilots that bombardment was the way of the future. As a result, before World War II air enthusiasts theorized that bombing could destroy an adversary's war-making potential and terrorize its citizenry into submission on its own, without ground or sea warfare. American pilots, under the control of the Army, pushed this independent-strategic-bombardment theory in part because they truly believed in the new doctrine. But they also hoped it would give them autonomy, independent of the ground generals.

The General Staff, on the other hand, remained skeptical of such notions throughout the 1920s and 1930s. In time, the relationships between ground and air advocates became strained to the breaking point. In acrimonious disputes, flyers stood steadfast against what they saw as a Civil War-bound and orthodox Army moving backward into the future. The charge was partly accurate, yet it was ironic that the assumptions of the airmen were far more conservative than those of the General Staff. After all, the tenets of strategic air power rested on coercion and terror, and these are among war's oldest stratagems.

This bitter Army infighting colored every aspect of the Air Corps before World War II, including its theory and practice of close air support. The wartime air chief, General Henry "Hap" Arnold, once complained that the "very word 'support' always makes people think of air power as an ancillary weapon of the Army or the Navy." Because it did not advance the cause of an independent Air Force, pilots neglected this "tactical" aviation in the years before Pearl Harbor. At the outset of the Second World War, Arnold placed close air support sixth on a list of the top ten air tasks demanded by the war. No detailed tactical doctrine even existed until well into the conflict. There were few tactical planes, and up to that point there had been few joint exercises using both air and ground forces. What the U.S. Army Air Corps did have, however, was an articulated theory of bombardment and the big planes to accomplish it.[35]

Then the real war got in the way of the flyers' dreams. The conflict's first major land campaign in North Africa was poorly suited for strategic air operations. No basic bombardment theories applied in the desert. There was no enemy civilian population to bomb, and no intricate supply lines or vast industries to destroy. When early fighting in Tunisia went poorly for the Americans, most war leaders at last concluded that there was a need for air operations coordinated with those of ground units. Within six months, a makeshift tactical doctrine emerged. When the Allies left the Mediterranean for Britain to prepare for the invasion of France, the United States had at least the foundations of a tactical air force.

Meanwhile, in England, the mighty and strategic Eighth Air Force had struggled with the vaunted notions of bombardment since shortly after Pearl Harbor. Its B-17 Flying Fortresses had proved more vulnerable to enemy flak and planes than the theorists had guessed. German industry had weathered aerial onslaughts remarkably well, and the people of Germany were more resilient in the face of air terror than the Allies had imagined they would be.

All this revealed that the big-bomber enthusiasts had committed a grave error: they had presumed that, in war, all people under all political systems will employ rational and universal logic to choose whether or not to fight. The truth can run to the contrary. What one population under democratic rule is willing to endure in war might be very different from what another population under a totalitarian regime can absorb, especially when its national survival is at stake. Even if strategic bombardment could have delivered all it promised in World War II, it is doubtful whether Adolf Hitler would have chosen to surrender and save the Third Reich from utter destruction. The Allies would still have been forced to invade occupied Europe.

At the outset of 1944, then, it was clear that strategic bombing alone would not end the war any time soon. The Americans needed large-scale tactical aviation and Hap Arnold finally directed his staff to "do anything and everything necessary to help the ground forces." By the Normandy invasion in June 1944 the largest numbered air force in the world was a purely tactical one. Even the strategic air forces became more tactical. The Eighth Air Force, for example, committed 84 percent of its missions to the ground assault in the weeks surrounding D-Day. For the rest of the war, only 34 percent of its sorties would be against classic strategic targets. By the Army Air Force's own estimation, just 24 percent of its entire wartime resources had been dedicated to strategic operations by 1945.[36]

Indeed, tactical operations were central to the air war in the last years of combat. Most American air forces engaged in them. The Fifth Air Force supported ground troops in Southeast Asia, the Tenth Air Force did so in the India-Burma theater, and both the Ninth Air Force in England and the Twelfth Air Force in Italy played important roles in the European ground war. Among the traditional strategic air forces, the Eighth Air Force in England and the Fifteenth Air Force in Italy regularly carried out tactical missions in addition to long-range bombardment. Only one, the Twentieth Air Force scattered throughout the Pacific, was committed solely to strategic operations. Even there, geography rather then the integrity of big-bomber theory compelled that strategy, for there could not be any major land campaigns to support in the middle of an ocean.

When the war ended, the outstanding lesson of the air conflict was clear. Warfare had muddied the distinctions between tactical and strategic air power. They may have had separate identities in peacetime, but the pressure of war inexorably molded them, as it does all forces, into a single weapon. In the words of one officer on the eve of D-Day, "forgotten now were differences between strategic and tactical, between ground and air, between Army and Navy, between Americans and their Allies. All were welded into one compact, devastating fist, set to deliver the Sunday punch."[37]

In the immediate postwar world these lessons governed military organization. In 1946, the Army Air Forces established a Tactical Air Command (TAC), equal in size and prestige to its Strategic Air Command (SAC). The next year, leading air officers promised to provide adequate close air support for ground forces if the Army would agree to the creation of a separate Air Force. And after the airmen finally won their coveted independence, pilots did indeed provide air support for the Army.

But this cooperation evaporated as the contours of the Cold War emerged in the late 1940s. A new emphasis on nuclear weapons and strategic deterrence combined with a shrinking defense budget to intensify competition for funding among the Army, Navy, and Air Force. As Air Force bombers were then the only way to carry nuclear warheads, the Strategic Air Command became more important and gained influential supporters in and out of the Air Force. The Tactical Air Command, on the other hand, shrank until it became a mere paper headquarters. In this way, Air Force leaders abdicated to the Army their responsibility to provide air support, forcing the ground leaders to establish their own air fleets, first of planes and later of helicopters.

By 1950, the structure of America's armed forces bore little resemblance to the paradigm established during World War II. The lessons of integrated and combined operations were lost. By then, too, the equipment and planes for close support were obsolete and had not been replaced. Perhaps worst of all, as the men of the tactical-air war retired or re-entered civilian life, the human expertise of tactical aviation left the Army and Air Force altogether. Very little tactical capacity and experience remained at the beginning of the Korean War. There, as well as in Vietnam and beyond, men paid in blood for the lack of efficient and adequate close air support.

In retrospect 1947 to 1949 were the critical years, the time when the lessons of World War II were lost. Memories of the war, so clear immediately after it ended, were now conditioned by atomic weapons and the Cold War. As is often the case, by 1950 memory had more to do with the present than the past.[38]

More than any other American general, Elwood "Pete" Quesada personified the rise and fall of tactical air power in the years before and after World War II. Born in 1904, he entered the Army as a private in 1924, earned his wings in 1925, and won a commission in 1926. He spent the bulk of his prewar service in nonoperational billets, often as aide or flying officer to senior officers or government officials. He learned about strategic bombardment theory at the Air Corps Tactical School, but his prewar service prevented him from adopting any single view of warfare. As a result, he went to North Africa in early 1943 with an open mind. He was a new and young brigadier general eager to learn.

The desert taught Quesada a great deal about warfare and combat leadership. When he arrived in France in October 1943 to establish the IX Fighter Command, he was ready. In the absence of any prewar tactical doctrine, he spent the spring before D-Day straining to develop a fighter force to support Lieutenant General Omar Bradley's First U.S. Army in France. He did a masterful job, and his flyers rendered great aid to American ground troops after D-Day. In the heyday of summer campaigning in 1944, he and Bradley enjoyed a close friendship. Years later the ground general remembered Quesada as a "young, imaginative officer unencumbered by the prejudices of so many of his air seniors regarding the prosecution of the war."[39]

To be sure, not everyone liked Quesada. At times, he was egotistical and petty, at other moments he exercised poor judgment and little tact or patience. But he was usually fair with subordinates, and always had the courage of his convictions. As one former staffer put it, "His friends liked to say he had a strong personality; his enemies said he was a son-of-a-bitch of the first order." Prima donna or prophet? Pete Quesada was probably a little of both. He probably needed both qualities to carry the torch of tactical air power at mid-century.[40]

From June 1944 to April 1945 his command, then known as the IX Tactical Air Command, was responsible for most of the major innovations in the tactical air war. His men designed the complicated signals system required for effective close support. His fighter groups developed the standard operating procedures for both bomb selection and fuse length. His fighter-control squadrons were the first to direct small planes on blind-bombing missions near the front lines. His training programs taught the pilots of other commands the complexities of dive-bombing. More often than not, when tactical precepts evolved— whether from changes in weapons, from German defensive measures, or from ground force requirements—Quesada and the IX Tactical Air Command played a leading role. Other units made contributions, but none were as old, big, or influential as Quesada's command. Major General O. P. Weyland, the wartime leader of the XIX Tactical Air Command and himself instrumental in the tactical air war, believed that most other tactical air commands "pretty much pattern themselves after the IX TAC, and I'm sure we operate much like them, too."[41]

Quesada's achievements made him the Air Force's leading expert on

tactical air power after the war. Predictably, he became the first commander of the Tactical Air Command in 1947. There, he developed li-
aisons with ground commands and worked to preserve the tactical
lessons of the war. He became increasingly frustrated in this role, however, as the Air Staff in Washington pulled more and more resources
from TAC, only to allocate them to SAC instead. In 1948, his superiors
removed him from TAC and swiftly gutted the command of its operational units. While working a series of difficult desk jobs, Quesada became a private critic of the trend away from close air support. He soon
realized that his career was at a dead end, and in 1951 he retired from
the Air Force a lieutenant general. He was forty-seven years old, he
was the foremost tactical-air-power expert in the United States, and he
was gone.

Big bombers made important, even critical, contributions in World
War II, but this is the story of another air war, one which was waged
with as much intensity as the bomber offensive, if not more, and one
which has been in large part ignored in air-power histories. Since that
war, the Air Force has grappled with the proper balance of its strategic
and tactical forces while the Army of necessity has struggled to meet its
own aviation needs. In 1991, as the Cold War faded into history and the
Persian Gulf War ended, Secretary of the Air Force Donald Rice announced a sweeping reorganization of his service. Both the Strategic
and Tactical Air Commands were eliminated, and all combat aircraft
were placed under a new Air Combat Command. "Desert Storm
demonstrated that the line between strategic and tactical air power has
become blurred," his report announced to the world. "The organization
needs to catch up."[42]

For forty-five years after World War II, Pete Quesada could have told
anyone the same thing. The sad fact was that too few were willing to
listen.

Chapter One

Unusual, Offbeat Assignments

WASHINGTON, D.C. 11 JUNE 1924. AFTERNOON. Twenty-year old Elwood R. Quesada gently rowed a small boat across the Tidal Basin. The little estuary of the Potomac was a popular swimming hole in Washington, and Quesada had snared a summer job as a lifeguard. It paid poorly, but the work was easy and the sights were good. The roaring twenties were at high tide, and the capital was awash with speakeasies, movie houses, dance halls, and flappers. With each passing year the Great War had faded ever more from memory, and now the days drifted by to the age-old beat of summer. All in all, it was a good time to be young.

The rowboat rocked when a swimmer climbed aboard without warning. "What the hell are you doing?" Quesada demanded, "I'm working."[1]

The stranger only smiled and whipped the water from his face. "What are you going to do next year?" he asked.

The man and his question perplexed Quesada. "I'll be a sophomore at Maryland," he replied at last.

"I know, but how about joining the Air Service instead?"

Millard "Tiny" Harmon then pitched his proposal. He was a full-time Army pilot stationed at Washington's Bolling Air Field and a part-time football referee. The previous fall he had worked a game between perennial power Penn State and a hapless Maryland team quarter-backed by Quesada. Maryland squeezed out an upset win that autumn day, Quesada became a brief hero, and Harmon remembered. To grab attention and attract stout recruits, the Air Service had for a few years sponsored its own team at Brooks Field, the Army's primary flight school in San Antonio. The military had chafed under tight budgets since World War I, and approving publicity and reliable enlistees were two ways to weather the lean years. Harmon figured Quesada could not only help the team but also pass the flight course. "Why don't you come over to Bolling tomorrow?" Harmon concluded. "We'll go for a fly and see what you think."

It was an odd way to entice enlistment, but the proposition intrigued Quesada. The idea buzzed about in his head for the rest of the day and into the evening. Until then, he and an older brother and sister had en-joyed a mildly affluent youth at the dawn of America's century. The only rough period came in 1914 when his parents, a Spanish banker and a naturalized Irish immigrant, divorced. Theirs was an amicable rift, and Lope Lopez Quesada continued to provide for Helen Quesada and his children. Still, such events bred trauma, and after the split Quesada rarely saw his father and did not even know when he died, remember-ing only that it was in the 1930s.

Save that, the years had sped by in Washington public schools and at Wyoming Seminary Preparatory in Pennsylvania. The quiet life of study held little interest for him, and sports, fishing, and swimming filled school afternoons and the glorious days of vacation. John Sirica, who later gained fame as the "Watergate" trial judge, was a steadfast chum. Together, they passed through the glory of youth not predis-posed to reflection or introspection. Yet, by 1924 the morrow called. "I had," Quesada remembered in the twilight of his life, "grown appre-hensive about the future."

It was now night, and the idea of flight absorbed Quesada as he lay in bed. He recalled running into the streets as a kid to watch novel flying contraptions cross the sky. Although he did not know it then, those planes were the Army's first aircraft, operating from a makeshift field in College Park, Maryland, and piloted by the Signal Corps's first flight instructors, Tommy Milling and Hap Arnold. Later as a teenager Quesada had been enthralled by the tales of Eddie Rickenbacker and the Red Baron, but so had tens and perhaps hundreds of thousands of other boys. As he tossed and turned in the darkness, Quesada knew he had never harbored deep dreams of being a pilot. Besides, his mother would surely be against such shenanigans. Why, then, did Harmon's invitation captivate him into the dawn?[2]

Morning saved him at last. With curiosity as his guide, he went to Bolling Field, telling his mother he was going to the beach and would return by dinner. It was a great day to fly the fragile canvas contraptions of the era. A little before noon, Harmon and Quesada hopped into a plane, faced into a mild breeze, and climbed into the sky. Piloting the ship straight and level, Harmon offered few words and let the experience of flight speak its own language. The simple trip charmed Quesada and delighted his youthful sense of adventure. When Harmon rolled the plane to a stop, Quesada walked to the base hangar and signed enlistment papers. In another forty-eight hours he left for Texas.

As the train moved down through the Carolinas and across the deep South toward San Antonio, Quesada must have reflected on the strange turn of events. Little in his early years had foreshadowed his recruitment into the military. His family had scant history as Americans and even less tradition of military service. He had never thought to attend a service academy. He did not share that sense of destiny and mission which, from a young age, drove so many other military leaders. Mostly, a confluence of time and circumstance made for his enlistment. It was an accident. Like others attracted to the nation's air arm in the 1920s, Quesada was exhilarated by flying; that became reason enough to join the Army. Like them, he was a breed apart from the conservative line and staff officers who dominated the old military. Yet, in a way, the very unorthodoxy of his enlistment presaged his later military accomplishments.

While his passenger car rolled over the Sabine River and into Texas, Quesada's thoughts were interrupted only by intermittent conversations with three other recruits. When he introduced himself as Elwood Richard Quesada, one of them declared: "The hell with that, you're

Pete!" Quesada carried the nickname until the day he died. Silent again as the train rumbled through Houston, the four boys wondered what lay ahead.

To a degree, Quesada was right: the Air Service did offer a brand of heroic adventure. But for its pilots the 1920s were a far cry from the exotic life promised by the Great War. Existence was austere, and the air arm was locked in a struggle for its very being in an age of neglect and interservice rivalry.

Less than a decade before, World War I had hinted of great things for military aviation. In a period of only three years the Army's air arm had grown from 1,200 men and a couple of hundred planes to over 190,000 men and some 11,000 aircraft. Young air pioneers, usually in their twenties or thirties, moved up through the ranks with meteoric speed. Benjamin Foulois and Billy Mitchell were mere captains in 1916; both wore stars by 1918. Hap Arnold was embarrassed when promoted to colonel at twenty-eight. The commander of the Ninety-first Aero Squadron rose from private to major in a year.[3]

These dramatic increases in size and rises in seniority reflected a new place for air power in both the panoply of weaponry and the organization of war. Early in World War I, planes were used mainly for observation and air-to-air combat. Three years of weary trench fighting encouraged a bolder role for aircraft by 1917, however, and some began advocating aerial bombardment to break the stalemate. In the summer of 1918, Brigadier General Billy Mitchell led bomber strikes in the Saint-Mihiel and Meuse-Argonne offensives. Although the results were ambiguous, the experiments worked well enough to foster optimism among flyers.

On top of that, pilots won a small measure of autonomy from the broader Army with the creation of the Air Service, which freed them from Signal Corps control. Quasi-independence for pilots proved a bit unorthodox, highly problematic, and absolutely necessary—for if no one knew how best to employ air power, everyone agreed that it had ceased to be a pure auxiliary service. With growth, promotions, new roles, and their own organization, pilots had every reason for confidence in the fall of 1918.[4]

Then the trouble began. Abruptly and without warning, Germany capitulated in November 1918 before bombardment could be adequately evaluated as a war tool. Flyers nonetheless believed that bombs were the key to their future, and they insisted that peacetime doctrine reflect this new dimension of air power. Ground officers begged to differ. Most of them urged a more traditional employment of planes, some even supporting a move to return the Air Service to the Signal Corps now that the national emergency had passed. Flyers vigorously opposed such a move, fighting to maintain some freedom to advance their notions of air power. To buttress their arguments, they pointed to the British, who had granted the Royal Air Force full autonomy from the British Army, and to Italian air theorist Giulio Douchet, who had maintained that air power alone could bring an adversary to its knees. In the years before Quesada enlisted, these opposing viewpoints fostered a great debate in the Army over air-power doctrine and military organization.

Demobilization only exacerbated the feud. Slogans like "Bring the Boys Home" reflected a strong national desire to shrink the military, and the Army experienced spectacular reductions in expenditures and manpower. In the proud American tradition of citizen-soldiers, most of those discharged happily returned to civilian life. But not the pilots. The Air Service had attracted a different type of man, certainly patriotic but also addicted to flight. Pioneers by disposition, innovators by mentality, and adventurers by temperament, they disliked the quiet life and had created an unusually strong esprit de corps within the Air Service. With little chance of an aviation career outside the military, they wanted to remain in uniform. Instead, they were discharged by the tens of thousands. The few that did manage to stay in the Army soon found their pay returned to prewar levels and in line with that of ground officers. When peacetime flying proved only marginally safer than wartime service, pilots declared that the General Staff did not fathom life in the air. "They wouldn't admit there was even such a thing as air power," one World War II air general bitterly remembered.[5]

Increasingly frustrated, flyers in the early 1920s circumvented the chain of command and carried their doctrine of bombardment and their case for a separate service to Congress and the American public. Brigadier General Billy Mitchell led this campaign, becoming an increasingly vocal critic of the General Staff and its attitudes toward air power. By mid-decade he had become overtly insubordinate, and the Army leadership court-martialed him in a very public and divisive proceeding.

Like most enduring debates, both sides had legitimate grounds for argument. On one hand, infantry, artillery, and cavalry officers were justly skeptical of bold claims that air power could win wars alone, without ground action. On the other hand, flyers rightly disdained the Army's narrow and conservative view in the face of the new technology of flight. Pilots held the General Staff in particular contempt, for the Army leadership had allowed the air arm to fall to a pathetic force level of just 396 modern, serviceable aircraft by 1924. Whatever else was true in this complicated dispute, this much was undeniable: the Air Service, being almost entirely a child of the Great War, suffered more than other Army branches in the postwar years.[6]

It had been quite a fall since the glory days of the Saint-Mihiel and Meuse-Argonne offensives. By the mid-1920s, the feud over doctrine and organization was inexorably entrenched in the institutions and culture of the Army. Men on the ground and in the air refused to subordinate or even accommodate their differing views on the future of war. In time, the dispute influenced everything about the military. For Pete Quesada, the fracas would affect his entire life.[7]

Quesada was, of course, oblivious to all that as his train rolled to a stop in San Antonio. He had only seen the novel winged machines as a boy and read of the wartime exploits of colorful aces as a teenager. He arrived at Brooks Field that summer, at the front end of his twentieth year, anxious to play some football and looking forward to flight instruction. If all went well, he would spend five months in the preliminary flight training course at Brooks and then move on to any number of fields for advanced training in pursuit, attack, or bombardment aviation.

Its status as the air arm's primary flight school had spared Brooks Field the decay that befell most military installations after the war. In fact, the post had even managed to grow. There was ample housing, sixteen hangars, and numerous equipment and sports facilities. Together, the buildings bordered a huge grass pasture where the wheels of planes had etched dirt runways into the earth. In the middle of the field a huge barn stood empty, a homestead relic from a bygone era. But Brooks was no frontier outpost. Although it was a world away from cosmopolitan Washington, the base's proximity to San Antonio supplied adequate social diversions.[8]

The dilapidated Curtiss "Jennies" that served as aircraft trainers punctured the illusion of a modern base. Cadets disparaged the slight biplanes. The cockpit was sparse; the fuselage was merely a canvas tarp tacked tautly to a wooden frame. Even under ideal conditions the birds barely reached 80 miles per hour. They were relics from the last war, and they looked like it.[9]

Quesada and his classmates began their educational program after three days of physicals and paperwork. Those recruits with no military experience—the bulk of the class—underwent an abbreviated basic training and spent the early weeks in drill. Luckily for some, football practice was an excused absence and players spent as much time on the gridiron as possible, managing to "march around damn little." But if the football workouts were numerous, they were not very effective. That fall, the team won just one game and Harmon's brainchild attempt to draw favorable attention to the Air Service ended in almost comic anticlimax.[10]

Almost. Quesada broke a leg playing against the University of Texas. With ground instruction nearing completion and actual flying slated to begin in days, the accident could not have come at a worse time. He watched helplessly as his classmates took their initial instruction in the Jennies. In the following weeks his spirits fell, and even the ground-school work became a struggle. He soon appeared to be one of the early washouts of the class. When at last the cast came off seven weeks later, Quesada's fellow cadets had completed nearly half their instruction in the air.

A flight instructor rescued Quesada from his predicament. First Lieutenant Nathan Twining, a former football star at West Point, liked Quesada and offered to help the cadet make up lost time. Together, the two remained at Brooks over the Christmas holiday for a crash course in flying. Day One was exciting. "After we drew helmets, goggles, and leather flight coats from the quartermaster," Quesada recalled, "Nate headed straight to the fastest Jenny. He got in the front seat and explained all the instruments to me and then told the ground crew to swing the propeller." Sputtering, the engine quickly came alive. Twining taxied to the end of the field. As they turned into a stout Texas breeze, Quesada's heartbeat quickened.[11]

For all cadets, the first lesson marked a significant rite of passage and was always a challenge. Quesada was no different. As soon as he grasped the controls, the plane banked violently to the left and pitched steeply downward. But within ten minutes Quesada managed straight and level flight, and in another twenty minutes he was executing constant-altitude turns. Sixty minutes after taking off, Quesada made his first assisted landing.

He learned quickly in the fourteen days he and Nate Twining flew above San Antonio. He became proficient in takeoffs, landings, figure eights, spirals, and other maneuvers. He soloed after six hours of instruction. His performance steadily impressed Twining, who years later became the Air Force Chief of Staff. In time, the two forged a friendship, foretelling Quesada's uncanny knack for forming important associations. When his classmates reconvened after the New Year, Quesada had made good the time lost after his fall and was on schedule to finish with the rest of the group. It had been a productive holiday break.[12]

In February of 1925 Quesada graduated from primary flight school and received orders to attend the half-year pursuit course at Kelly Field, just across town. The planes there were sleek and quick compared to the Jenny. To the cadets, the Sopwith SE-5 and Boeing VE-9 seemed to gallop across the sky with their large engines. Like most performance planes, however, these birds were temperamental. Limited visibility, high wing loading, and finicky flight characteristics all made for poor handling. They were not as forgiving as the Jennies. Still, Quesada thought the plane had "more pizzazz and zip than anything, and, in a perverse kind of way, was a delight to fly."[13]

The flying curriculum at Kelly sought to produce confident, accurate flyers with quick and keen judgement. In the early months, the students practiced formation flying, stunting, and simulated combat with camera guns. To produce well-rounded pilots, they also rehearsed simple observation tactics and basic elements of bombing. After covering the fundamentals, the class finally turned to gunnery practice with live ammunition.

To break the monotony and rigor of training, Quesada joined with other cadets and some instructors to form a baseball team in a San Antonio city league. They were a ragtag lot, but natural ability made up for any lack of practice and the squad finished toward the top of the standings. They also played a couple of exhibitions with the St. Louis Cardinals, who took their spring training in the area. Though they did not win a game from the pros, the contests did help promote a camaraderie among teachers and students.

Thomas White, like Twining an instructor and future Air Force Chief of Staff, became Quesada's lifelong friend. Another instructor later headed the Civil Aviation Authority in the 1930s, and two more served under Quesada in North Africa and France during World War II. Although Quesada did not know him well, Charles Lindbergh was at Kelly Field as well. In fact, of the twenty men who graduated there in that year, eight held positions of authority during World War II. The Air Service in the 1920s was a small fraternity of men, and anyone then serving was certain to cross paths with many of his brothers who were destined for prominence in the sky.[14]

As a grand finale to their training, the cadets staged a gunnery tournament on Galveston Island in July. Each day for a week they lifted into the air and chased a drone towed across the horizon by another plane. Bullet holes in the target determined each flyer's score. It may have been a primitive method, but in 1925 it was the best way to teach the art of aerial warfare. Quesada finished fifth in the competition, hardly outstanding but quite respectable.

He also discovered the hazards of early aviation as he returned from the Texas coast on 14 July. Bucking a strong head wind, his plane ran too hard for too long; eventually the radiator water boiled away and the engine failed. Spiraling downward, the craft hit telegraph wires and slammed against a large oak tree before thumping to the hard ground. Thrown from the wreck somewhere between the wires and the tree, Quesada escaped serious injury, though superficial wounds badly bloodied his face. After clearing his head, he hiked a few miles to the small town of Vienna and hopped a ride to San Antonio, leaving behind a thoroughly wrecked aircraft.[15]

This was the first of eight crackups for Quesada. Some, like this earliest accident, were serious. Others were not, like the next one just a month later as training drew to a close. In that incident, Quesada moved too swiftly down the taxiway and "ran up the ass of the commander's plane." Still, Quesada developed a reputation as a marvelous pilot. Whether in peace or war, flying was exceedingly dangerous in those early years, and a crash here or there did not end a career. Instead, the constant risk of flying helped to separate pilots from ground officers and contributed to a distinct culture of airmen, which fueled the interservice tensions dating from the Great War.[16]

Continuing budget and manpower constraints meant that Quesada did not receive a regular commission after his advanced training. Officer slots were extremely limited, and only those cadets with prior military service remained on active duty following graduation. Although many thought it was irresponsible to first recruit and then discharge pilots, Quesada was only mildly disappointed as he left Kelly Field in the fall of 1925. He had come to Texas on a whim anyway. The experience had offered exposure to a different part of the nation, new friends, and the chance to fly. That was enough for now.

Besides, Quesada thought, a new adventure lay ahead. His baseball play had impressed the St. Louis Cardinals, and the day after graduating from Kelly he left for a tryout with the club. To his surprise, he and one other hopeful, Dizzy Dean, made the team. It was the start of a Hall of Fame career for Dean and one of life's small byways for Quesada, who did not perform well enough to predict a distinguished baseball career. After three weeks he returned his $1000.00 signing bonus to the manager, Branch Rickey, and left the team of his own accord. "I'd have just ended up running a poolroom in Peoria," Quesada mused years later, "like most baseball players that didn't make the grade."[17]

Next he traveled to Florida, where his older brother Buddy ran a charter fishing service, but within months he grew restless with that life, too. He then took a job with the Criminal Investigation Division of the Treasury Department. He liked working out of its Detroit office in the fall of 1926. "It was great fun, and sometimes I got to carry a tommy gun." He even participated in one sting operation involving local bootleggers with connections to Al Capone's Chicago syndicate.[18]

But Quesada missed the Air Service. One Saturday in early December he wandered over to Selfridge Field, an Army installation just outside Detroit. From the perimeter fence, Quesada noticed a familiar face across the landing area. Tommy White saw Quesada at the same time and trotted over. After back-slapping greetings, they agreed to meet that night with Nathan Twining, who was also at Selfridge. The three caught up on lost time, and by evening's end Quesada promised to return the next Saturday for a ride in a Curtiss PW-8, the air arm's newest pursuit plane. Other visits followed, and in the spring of 1927 Quesada resolved to return to the air arm one way or another.[19]

He could not have known it, but events in Washington and within the Army were turning in the air arm's favor and conspiring to help Quesada back into uniform. Congress had finally awakened to dangerous deficiencies in America's air arm and, with broad political support, had passed the Air Corps Act of 1926. The law changed the name of the Air Service to the Air Corps and called for a twofold increase in manpower and a net addition of 1,800 planes by 1932. More than a mere blueprint for growth, the law also gave the Air Corps a greater degree of autonomy from the General Staff, a goal of pilots since the Great War. Although they would remain a part of the Army, flyers nevertheless gained direct access to political power with a new Assistant Secretary of War for Air. The legislation portended an ambitious program, and the nation poured some $100 million into aviation through the plan. As the aerial exploits of Charles Lindbergh and others captivated the nation, the expansion program propelled air-arm morale to heights not reached since the heyday of the war. In fact, the late 1920s were the best days for flyers since they had left a smoldering France ten years before.[20]

Quesada was one of the earliest applicants for the first "Army Air Corps Competitive Examination" to fill the new officer vacancies. He quit his job, moved back to his mother's house in Washington, D.C., and mapped out an education regimen. He studied hard, enrolling in a preparatory course at nearby Emerson Technical School to buttress his chances. Early on 24 March, about a hundred men arrived at the War Department Building to vie for eighteen Air Corps commissions. Quesada finished the exam confident of his showing, and ten days later his name was among the successful candidates. In April 1927, he donned again the cloth of an Army pilot.[21]

Quesada's first assignment was the engineering billet at Bolling Field, site of his original airplane ride with Tiny Harmon. Such jobs were not taxing in peacetime, especially at Bolling, where a choice array of aircraft provided service for Washington's dignitaries and not much else. To fill the days Quesada often did woodwork in the shops and, in a time before strict rules governed the use of equipment, he spent many an afternoon and most weekends flying assorted planes above Washington. He reveled in the machines, mastering the Army's first all-steel monoplanes and still others fitted with water-cooled engines. Years later, Quesada believed that his duty at Bolling was "the best job I ever had in my life. I'll never forget it, I was in seventh heaven."[22]

He especially liked two Loening Amphibians, nicknamed "air yachts." Their bulky hulls and inverted Liberty engines made them difficult to fly, which only enticed the young engineering officer. Using the Potomac River as his airstrip, he flew them every chance he got and soon earned a reputation as a junior officer with flying talent. Captain Ira Eaker, then one of the best-known pilots in the service and later an important general in his own right, came to "like Quesada's spirit, his pleasing personality, and his enthusiasm for flying." Even Quesada's third wreck, on 15 March 1928, failed to dim his growing status as a good pilot.[23]

Facility in flying was crucial to any air officer in those years. The fragile craft made piloting difficult under the best of circumstances, and many commanders regarded "air skills" as the most important check in a pilot's officer efficiency rating. The chief of the Air Corps, Major General James Fechet, was not a good pilot himself and particularly admired adept flyers. For young airmen like Quesada, expertise in the air could create opportunities and open new vistas. Though Quesada's job was not professionally demanding, it did offer him a chance to fly the newest planes and nurture important skills.

His penchant for the amphibious Loenings led to his participation in a dramatic rescue effort soon after he crashed into the Bolling turf. In early May, the German embassy in Washington asked the Air Corps to help recover an aircraft that had been used in an attempted east-to-west crossing of the Atlantic and that was now stranded on Greely Island. The tiny island off the Labrador coast was a long way from Bolling, and conditions in the North Atlantic would surely work against any attempt to reach the plane. Yet Fechet, sensing a chance to show off his rejuvenated air arm, agreed and hastily organized an expedition using the two air yachts.[24]

Fechet, Ira Eaker, First Lieutenant Sandy Fairchild, and Fred Melchoer, a German representative of the Bremen aircraft manufacturer, took off from Washington on Saturday 11 May. Making good progress, they reached St. John's, New Brunswick, by nightfall. Fairchild developed appendicitis on Sunday morning, however, and the expedition stalled. Eaker reminded Fechet that Quesada "had more experience with the amphibian than anyone" and suggested he be brought up. Fechet concurred. Quesada left Washington for St. John's on the morning of the thirteenth, and met the rescue expedition that night.[25]

The next day the reconstituted party resumed the flight north. Eaker, with Melchoer, flew the lead plane while Quesada, with Fechet, navigated off his wing. Everybody expected the weather to turn sour, and it did over the Bay of Fundy. "The weather got bad, then it got worse, and then it got extremely bad," Quesada recalled. By 1400 hours, the four men abandoned hope of reaching their refueling stop at Pictou, Nova Scotia, and set down at South Maitland. An hour later a gale-force wind convinced them to find better refuge. Eaker managed to get airborne amid the whitecaps, but Quesada had trouble with the growing swells. The Bay of Fundy has one of the world's greatest tidal differentials and, as Quesada and Fechet struggled against the brewing storm, the tide swept out to sea, stranding the two men and their plane on a sand bar.

Borrowing a shovel from a local fisherman, the general and the lieutenant dug the amphibian out of the sand and extended her landing gear. Quesada carefully taxied the groaning Loening out of its hole and took off. With better weather they reached Pictou by evening. Eaker was not there, however, and the two spent a restless night amid the gear of a ship's store worried about the other plane.

On Tuesday Quesada patched the damaged plane. He spent most of the day on his back sewing up the ripped canvas hull. General Fechet sat beside him, huddled against the cold and searching the sky for signs of Eaker. Basic repairs were complete by dusk, and Fechet resolved to press on to Greely Island the next day. Eaker, he sadly concluded, was probably dead.

Fred Melchoer strolled into the small village at 0300 hours on Wednesday. "Where have you been?" Quesada asked. "Where the hell is Ira?" barked Fechet. "We landed in the hills," the German replied.

The storm had forced Eaker down on top of a gentle slope the previous day. On Tuesday he and Melchoer had worked to lighten their craft and construct a makeshift ramp at the foot of the rise to catapult the plane into the air. When they had finished, Melchoer came to town to find Fechet and Quesada. Now, on Wednesday, the men at Pictou anxiously waited for Eaker. At 1500 hours Eaker flew out of the misty sky, and the trip resumed once again.[26]

At last the men reached Greely Island and the Bremen plane. All told, the journey took nearly a week of frantic and dangerous flying. Although they failed to salvage the stranded craft, when the four men returned to Bolling Field on 25 May they were greeted by a throng of reporters. In the following days, newspapers carried front-page accounts of the daring flight. Just as Fechet had hoped, the rescue had garnered important publicity for the air arm, and no doubt the public show of support added to the flyers' good morale in the late 1920s.

For Pete Quesada the Bremen plane rescue was an introduction into the power circles of the Army. He had spent whole days alone with the ranking member of the Air Corps, and he had made the most of it. Fechet, in Ira Eaker's estimation, developed "a marked preference for the young Quesada" after the flight. Among the air arm's small cadre of officers, exposure to senior leaders often shaped careers, and Quesada recognized the importance of this. "There I was, barely out of flight school, and spending a week in close quarters with the Chief of the Air Corps!"[27]

A few months later Quesada became Fechet's flying aide. For almost a year the two winged across the country in a state-of-the-art two-seat pursuit ship, inspecting various Air Corps bases. A fourth crash outside Worcester, Massachusetts—this one with Fechet in the passenger seat—failed to temper the chief's confidence in Quesada. Hours spent crowded together in a tiny cockpit created an uncommon bond between a general and a second lieutenant. In 1948, as Fechet lay dying in a Washington hospital, Eaker urged Quesada to visit the "old man" because "you and I owe him a great deal, which we should never forget." Quesada needed no prompting. "Don't think for a moment," he wrote Eaker, "that I do not recognize the great debt that is owed to good old General Fechet. I am more grateful to him than I think I could ever express."[28]

In late 1928, Eaker conceived an experiment to test the feasibility of midair refueling and the mechanical endurance of aircraft. With Carl

"Tooey" Spaatz, then a highly-respected major, and later the ranking American airman in World War II in Europe, he planned a marathon flight circling southern California. In part because Eaker liked Quesada, and in part to garner Fechet's support for the trial, Eaker and Spaatz asked Quesada to serve on the crew. "Maybe," Eaker remembered telling Spaatz, "we will have a better chance to get the thing approved with the Chief if we picked his aide." Fechet wholeheartedly sanctioned the flight, and in late December Spaatz, Eaker, Quesada, First Lieutenant Harry Halverson, and Sergeant Roy Hooe left Washington for Los Angeles in a modified Fokker trimotor dubbed the *Question Mark*.[29]

The flight west took three days. The four officers were quartered in a single large room in Atlanta at the end of the first day. Before bed, Quesada knelt in prayer, a habit from his Catholic upbringing that touched the others. "He did not allow our presence to prevent him from showing his religious teaching and conviction," Eaker recalled. "I know this courage in the youngster impressed us all very much." Throughout his career, Quesada again and again strongly displayed the courage of his convictions.[30]

At 0726 hours on the first day of 1929 the *Question Mark* climbed away from a Van Nuys airport and, with five men aboard, lifted heavily into the air. A refueling plane followed shortly thereafter and positioned itself twelve feet above and slightly ahead of the experimental ship. At 0815 hours the tanker played a line to the outstretched arm of Spaatz, who grabbed the hose and fed 100 gallons of gas to the *Question Mark* in a delicate and primitive maneuver. "Lieutenants Woodring and Strickland lowered the hose from the fuselage," remembered the refueling plane pilot, "and Major Spaatz fit it into the funnel. My only signals came from Woodring by a rope attached to my arm. One long pull meant slow up, two pulls, speed up. A constant jiggle meant the refueling was over."[31]

A second refueling that day took place directly above a packed California–Georgia Tech Rose Bowl game, a reminder of the great potential for publicity in the golden age of flight. After taking on an additional 255 gallons and some oil, the *Question Mark* banked toward San Diego, where it spent the night circling Rockwell Field.[32]

So it went for days, the four pilots rotating at the controls, shuttling between Los Angeles and San Diego. Messages written on the sides of refueling planes, chalked on a blackboard, or simply dropped to the ground served as a crude communications system. With each passing hour, the trial gained more attention. The *Question Mark* flyers surpassed the U.S. record for refueled flight at the thirty-eighth hour, the world record for sustained flight by a heavier-than-air craft at the sixtyfifth hour, and the record for continuous flight at the one hundred eleventh hour.[33]

Soon, fan mail reached the crew with their food, and the Air Corps rushed to print special stationery so the flyers might respond in style. "We are pleased with the mail we are getting," a buoyant Spaatz wrote on the fifth day, "especially Lieutenant Quesada, who is kept busy answering fan letters." One note Quesada wrote to his mother was published in the *Los Angeles Examiner*. "We are going strong is what I mean. No trouble at all. . . . Now I will have something to bounce off Lindy [Charles Lindbergh] whenever he boasts too much about that little hop he made."[34]

Despite the crew's exuberance, all was not well. Night refuelings were hairy at best, the noise was deafening, the quarters were close, and on the third day the engines began to exhibit stress. Roy Hooe worked wonders with the three power plants. But when, on 6 January, oil started spilling from one engine, everyone knew the end was near. "I think man will outlast machine," Quesada remarked to Halverson.[35]

The wheels of the *Question Mark* touched the earth at 1407 hours on 7 January, after 150 hours, 40 minutes of flight. Forty-three midair contacts had sustained the plane, transferring 5,660 gallons of gas, 245 gallons of oil, seventeen meals, water, batteries, and other supplies with an aggregate weight of nearly forty tons. By traveling 7,360 miles, the *Question Mark* had shattered all previous aviation records for distance. The crew were tired, sweaty, nearly deaf, and sick of cold-cut sandwiches, but ecstatic. "We have found that mechanical [limits] rather than the condition of man is the only limiting factor in sustained flight," Spaatz wrote in his report to Fechet. "After the first day or so the longest period any man slept was four hours. No one got on another's nerves. In cramped quarters, with parachutes on, we knocked each other about, but there was always a smile."[36]

Newspapermen and 2,000 others surrounded the plane as it came to rest. The flight became world famous, and for a time the crew were as well known as Charles Lindbergh. Headlines shouted the achievement, governors sent laudatory telegrams, Congress issued a proclamation of congratulation, and President Coolidge awarded the pilots the Distinguished Flying Cross, a rare peacetime achievement. The flight's fame followed Quesada into World War II, when some of his staff officers were "just thrilled to serve with someone who actually flew on the *Question Mark*."[37]

In the afterglow of success, everyone championed the technological progress of the day without thinking much about its implications for air doctrine. In the years to come the advancement of technology helped to foster the development of independent bomber theory, as well as the ongoing dispute between air and ground officers. Though for the Air Corps the *Question Mark* was a shining achievement, for other branches of the Army the flight was a reason to contemplate ebbing notions of traditional warfare.

Quesada's reputation as a superb pilot led him on to several billets as an aide to major public figures. When Fechet retired, the new commander of the air arm, Major General Benjamin Foulois, assigned Quesada to Cuba for a tour as assistant military attaché and flying officer for the U.S. Ambassador, Harry Guggenheim.

Major Red O'Hare, the chief attaché in Havana, was happy to have Quesada report for duty in October, 1930. "Okay, Pete," he said at their first meeting, "you know you don't have to be formal here. There are only two of us and a certain amount of work to be done and we will share and share alike. The fact that I am a major and you are a lieutenant will not cause one of us to bear the larger burden. We start on a fifty-fifty basis right now. I have been OD [Officer of the Day] for two years, now you be OD for two years." From the start, Quesada liked O'Hare, and this Cuban connection paid dividends when O'Hare became Omar Bradley's chief administrative officer in World War II. During the battle of France in 1944, this association contributed to a close air–ground organization.[38]

Quesada did not develop as intimate a friendship with Harry Guggenheim, but their dealings were cordial and consistent with relationships between aides and senior officials. Guggenheim was an early air-power enthusiast, and had already established the Guggenheim Foundation for the Promotion of Aeronautics, which funded such centers of aviation research as the aeronautical departments at the Massachusetts and California Institutes of Technology. He of course knew about the *Question Mark* flight, and was pleased to have a pilot from the famed trial.[39]

When Quesada arrived in Cuba, the life of an attaché was shifting from one of quiet duty to one of political turmoil. American interests had dominated the island since the dawn of the twentieth century, but in the late 1920s nationalist groups had risen to challenge the status quo. Now the U.S.-backed administration was in imminent danger of collapse. As the crisis worsened, Guggenheim and Quesada raced from one hot spot to another while O'Hare manned the embassy and helped to compile the daily diplomatic and military reports.

This basic pattern held for two years, until Franklin Roosevelt's 1932 presidential campaign foreshadowed a change in the American political landscape. As the election season reached high tide and Roosevelt seemed on the verge of a landslide success, Guggenheim prepared to vacate his ambassadorship. In Washington, Foulois decided to detail Quesada back to the States as well. As he left Cuba for the United States in the summer of 1932, Quesada's mind turned toward the future. His stint in Cuba had removed him from the Army's regular tour rotation and he had no idea of what his next job would be. One thing was certain. On the heels of the daring Bremen-plane rescue mission, the *Question Mark* flight, and a personal assignment to Fechet, the Cuban billet had established Quesada as an outstanding junior officer, pilot, and aide.

Foulois reaffirmed that judgment by making Quesada the personal pilot for the Assistant Secretary of War for Air, Trubee Davison. The wealthy son of a J. P. Morgan investment partner, Davison had gained his job under the auspices of the Air Corps Act of 1926. For five years he had supervised the air arm's expansion and, though his job was designed to bolster flyers in their feud with ground officers, he had worked hard to "heal the wounds left by the Mitchell court-martial and to bring the airmen and Army back together again." Quesada's assignment to Davison kept him near the apex of the Air Corps. Like Army connections, associations with politicos could help a career along. If he performed well, Quesada would be able to point to yet another important patron.[40]

As luck had it, Quesada assumed his post just as Davison was preparing to leave the War Department. The five-year expansion program was nearly over and Roosevelt, now the President-elect, had targeted assistant secretary positions for elimination in his Depression-era austerity program. It was no surprise, then, when the president eliminated Davison's job, giving him sixty days to complete any official business. As a result, the last half of Quesada's duty with Davison consisted of a sort of farewell tour. Over a two-month period the pair visited every major air-arm installation in the forty-eight United States.[41]

The cross-country trip revealed the growth of the Air Corps since its inception in 1926. Many bases had new or improved facilities. Modern runways, better housing, and increased recreational facilities all carried the stamp of the Air Corps Act. In fact, during the expansion the air arm had acquired new and better equipment in larger quantities than at any point dating to the Great War. Reliability had risen in every type of plane. All-metal low-wing monoplanes rolled off assembly lines for the first time. Pursuit planes showed remarkable gains in speed, climb, and handling. The range and altitude ceiling of bombers increased fourfold. Engineers pioneered the adjustable-pitch propeller. Even the plane Quesada now flew, a new Curtiss Condor complete with enclosed cockpit and pressurized fuselage, reflected the fruits of the spending spree.

For six years, from 1926 to 1931, aviation procurement had vastly outpaced expenditures in other military branches, a fact not lost on artillery, infantry, and cavalry officers. By 1933 if not earlier, startling differences among the various branches had become a new point of severe contention among military men. As the Great Depression shrank defense-budget dollars, other branches of the Army regarded the growing air arm with increasing frustration. Ironically, if Davidson had hoped to ease ill will in the nation's armed forces, the expansion program he supervised had instead exacerbated such tensions.[42]

After a busman's holiday flying to Africa with Davidson to collect elephants for an exhibition at the American Museum of Natural History in New York City, Quesada reported back to the War Department in the autumn of 1933. Despite the inherent advantages of aide assignments, he knew that extended time away from operational billets could derail a career and he pined for more traditional duty. He was happy, therefore, when new orders sent him to an advanced navigation course at Langley Field, Virginia. The rapid changes in avionics demanded more sophisticated flight skills, and the Langley course was one of many established during the five-year Air Corps program to keep pace with the growing need for better pilot training.[43]

The course was easy for Quesada. "I was for so long a glorified chauffeur for the Washington brass that flying in various types of weather over unfamiliar terrain was not unusual." The instructors soon recognized Quesada's experience, and he became a quasi-lecturer in certain navigational techniques. On weekends, he enjoyed visiting his mother and old friends in Washington. All in all, the posting proved to be a pleasure and he looked forward to an assignment with a pursuit group after graduation.[44]

Events then unfolding in the high halls of power interfered with these idyllic plans, however, and Quesada soon found himself in the middle of a growing Air Corps–Army ruckus. On 9 February 1934 President Roosevelt canceled air-mail contracts with civilian carriers after learning of virtual monopolies and possible fraud in their business. He then asked Benny Foulois if the Army's air arm could deliver the mails while the government awarded new contracts on a more open and competitive basis. Like his predecessors, Foulois jumped at the chance to show off the air arm. He figured that if the task was done well he could parlay it into increased autonomy for flyers. For this reason, he thought air-mail delivery was "an ideal peacetime test of the Army Air Corps' organization, equipment, and training." Reassured by Foulois' confidence, Roosevelt gave the air arm just ten days to prepare its pilots and planes to deliver the mail.[45]

Despite Foulois' optimism, delivering the nation's correspondence was a huge job. Some experts questioned the air arm's suitability for the task. "Either the Army is going to pile up ships all across the continent," World War I ace and airline executive Eddie Rickenbacker said, "or they are not going to fly the mail on schedule." He had a point. Air Corps pilots and planes were fashioned for wartime operations. Formation pursuit and bombardment techniques in good weather were their stock in trade, not the solitary nighttime cross-country flights of the mail carriers. Most Army planes had just a fraction of the 600-pound payload of civilian planes, and the vast majority of military pilots had less than twenty-five hours of night instrument flying to their credit. In a national radio broadcast, Will Rogers, humorist and air power enthusiast, probably cut to the heart of the matter best. "Mr. President, you are going to lose some fine boys in these army flyers. I hope your conscience is up to the impending torture coming its way."[46]

Foulois ignored these doubts and swiftly devised a plan to meet the challenge. With his assistant, Oscar Westover, he divided the nation into three regions and tapped Major Bryon Q. Jones, Lieutenant Colonel Horace Hickman, and Lieutenant Colonel Hap Arnold to run the Eastern, Central, and Western Zones respectively. On 15 February, Foulois officially allocated 269 pilots, 340 enlisted men, and 146 planes to the task. The next day he cut orders sending men around the country, and Pete Quesada had just twenty-four hours to get to the Eastern-Zone hub at Newark, New Jersey.[47]

An ominous winter storm swirled over much of the nation, making the normal puddle-jump flight from Washington to Newark out of the question. With four others, Quesada piled blankets and coffee into a car and headed up the coast. Everyone talked of the weather. Quesada knew from experience that flying the mails required a kind of skill that most of his fellow pilots lacked. Only nine Army pilots had more total flight time than his 3,200-plus hours, and just one had as much night-flying experience. In the past weeks he had lectured at Langley on beam flying, the primary method of instrument navigation in the 1930s, and he now delivered it from the rear seat of a cramped 1933 Packard. When he finished, the others realized that this flying could get rugged. But these fellows were young and full of enthusiasm. None of them lacked confidence. For them, there were no questions about the merits of the Air Corps' task, only the knowledge that it was theirs to do, and neither rain nor snow nor gloom of night would stay them from their appointed rounds.[48]

That was exactly the attitude B. Q. Jones wanted. Jones was a hotshot renegade pilot straight out of the legends of World War I. Years earlier, he had been the first pilot to intentionally experiment with flat spins; he deemed the air-mail task a grand opportunity to return the air arm to the serious business of dangerous flight. He made an indelible impression on his Eastern-Zone pilots during his initial briefing on 18 February. Speaking from a makeshift rostrum in a commandeered hangar, he barked, "Be seated, men. My name is B. Q. Jones, and if you wonder what B. Q. means, it means 'be quick.' We've got a job to do, men, and I don't give a rat's ass what the press says, we'll do it all the same." In Washington, Foulois echoed the gung-ho sentiment, telling reporters the air arm was "ready to hop on the dot."[49]

The first day seemed to make these men prophets. February 19 dawned with a break in the storms, and throughout the country the novice postmen crossed the skies without incident. They navigated all the checkpoints, collected all the letters, and made all the connections. When darkness came, Roosevelt sent Foulois a laudatory telegram and called the critics naysayers.

That night, Quesada left Newark on the first of his many evening runs. His was the major route in the Eastern Zone, Newark to Cleveland. The line's large volume of mail was too great for small planes, so Jones had assigned Quesada one of the modern Curtiss Condors. With its enclosed cockpit, bigger payload, and good instruments, the luxury plane rendered his nightly trip to Cleveland far less arduous than it was for those who had to fly in the open air.[50]

At 2300 hours, he and his crew chief, Roy Hooe, loaded the plane with mail and left Newark. Hooe, whom Quesada knew from the *Question Mark* flight, was that special kind of noncommissioned officer the Army could not have functioned without. He knew aircraft and a great deal more. A square-jawed career man to his grease-stained fingertips, he could handle a stubborn camshaft as well as the stuffiest brass. For Quesada, having Hooe along on the nightly runs was like having money in the bank.[51]

Heading toward Cleveland, the two made one fueling stop at Bellefonte, Pennsylvania. They came down out of the frozen sky and onto the empty prairie with nothing but the whip of the wind all around them. The mercury registered twenty degrees below zero, and the two shuddered against the cold while the airfield tender dutifully gassed up the plane. They were glad to lift again into the air. Landing at Cleveland, Quesada napped while Hooe loaded return mail from Ohio. Three hours later the two were off again, arriving in Newark about 0800 hours. And so the next twelve weeks passed for Quesada, with hardly a variation to break the monotony of the night.[52]

If only the other pilots had been so lucky. Notwithstanding the first day's good luck, to maintain the routes the airmen had to fly some 41,000 miles each day, and the weather would not cooperate forever. Many people felt that it was only a matter of time before something bad happened.[53]

It soon did. On 22 February Lieutenant Durwood Lowry strayed fifty miles off course in heavy fog and died in a crash near Deshler, Ohio. Another airman perished in Texas, and a third narrowly escaped death on a run from Newark to Richmond. The next day a pilot crashed and drowned in the Chesapeake Bay. Within a week, the Air Corps had lost six men in a dozen mishaps. Pundits pounced on the tragedies, and the accidents made the front pages of at least nine national newspapers. A scandal with wide repercussions was born.[54]

The critics came out of the woodwork from every direction. Roosevelt, facing Congressional scrutiny of New Deal programs, refused to spend any political capital defending the air arm. In a remarkable turnaround, he declared himself betrayed. Had he known how unprepared the Air Corps was for the job, he intimated in a letter to Secretary of War George Dern, he never would have canceled civilian contracts for the mails. "The continuation of deaths in the Army Air Corps must stop," he declared.[55]

Others moved to wash their hands of the growing fiasco as well. Dern and Army Chief of Staff Douglas MacArthur feared for the 1935 Army budget, then in Congressional committee, and wondered aloud how airmen could have received the lion's share of Army money for five years without making better use of it. Even the traditional air-power supporters on Capitol Hill (generally Republicans) used the fiasco to criticize Roosevelt, and indirectly the flyers. Whatever Benny Foulois had hoped the air mail might mean for the air arm, by early March the stakes were becoming higher than he had ever imagined.[56]

He and his lieutenants tried to quench the firestorm. In the Western Zone, Hap Arnold believed that better press could blunt the worst criticism. "I don't care what you do," he told his public-relations officer. "Cover a bathing beauty with air-mail stamps and send her to the Governor of California if you want to, but I want favorable publicity for a change." Foulois tackled the issue of safety more seriously. He forbade flying in conditions that were known to be icy, required more pilot rest between flights, grounded planes that did not have full instrumentation, canceled some of the most hazardous routes, and relaxed the schedules on most other runs. In the Eastern Zone, B. Q. Jones became an ardent partisan for the pilots and eagerly complied with Foulois' new restrictions.[57]

These policies did reduce tragedy, although they also decreased the number of routes flown from over sixty to around a dozen. Just one additional pilot died from late March to 1 June, when the Army formally ceased air-mail operations. By then, the air arm had flown one and a half million miles, carried close to a million pounds of mail, and completed nearly three quarters of its scheduled flights. The task had cost nearly three million dollars, fifty-seven accidents, and twelve deaths. To be sure, the Army pilots had hauled only 40 percent of the total civilian air-mail payload, but they had done so admirably. In the end, they could claim, unlike their civilian counterparts, that they had not lost a single letter.[58]

In May, the air arm even managed a public-relations coup. In an effort to salvage some favorable headlines, Foulois ordered that a modern B-10 bomber be loaded with mail in California and be flown at breakneck speed to New York in an effort to break the transcontinental speed record. On 8 May the plane lifted from a field in Burbank and, throttles to the wall, headed east. The pilot fell ill over Indiana, however, and landed in Cleveland, well ahead of the record pace, but unable to continue. Pete Quesada and other pilots in Cleveland, none of whom had any experience with the B-10, huddled to see who might take it on to New York. They quickly agreed on Quesada. Foulois breathed easy when informed of the decision by telegraph. "Quesada," he told an aide, "can fly anything."[59]

Quesada and Hooe warily approached the bomber. They climbed aboard and glanced around. Quesada recognized most of the instruments, and, to a degree, flying was flying. Still, he did not know its takeoff speed, its climb rate, its cruise speed, or its landing procedures. "I'll tell you what," he told Hooe, "you start it and I'll steer it. We'll fly it together." They arrived in New York alive, finishing the coast-to-coast trip in fourteen hours and eight minutes, a new record for a flight across the nation's northern states. At last, Foulois could point to something when asked what the five-year program had accomplished.[60]

There was little else left to rescue from the air-mail affair. Congress bore down hard on the airmen, temporarily abandoned by most of their political patrons. On 10 May, the House Committee on Military Affairs convened a special subcommittee under the joint chairmanship of John McSwain and William Rogers. Ostensibly a "careful inquiry into the air-mail affair and other related Air Corps topics," the panel was actually little more than a kangaroo court. Some members had already passed judgment, with one describing the early mail-related deaths as murder. McSwain, an Air Corps supporter in Congress for ten years, demanded explanations. Foulois and the Air Corps were in for a rough ride.[61]

The panel heard from a score of witnesses in the summer of 1934. Foulois was first to testify, and from the outset he recognized the stakes and set out an aggressive defense. "I am ready and willing at any time to meet my accusers in open court." All the talk in Congress about legalized murder, he added, was a "lot of political claptrap." Some of the worst weather in memory was the real culprit and, if truth be told, the Army pilots had done a decent job under difficult circumstances.[62]

Subsequent witnesses felt otherwise. Army Deputy Chief of Staff Major General Hugh Drum, never a friend of the air arm, was the most critical. "Foulois knowingly misrepresented the readiness of his force for the mission to the President from the outset," he said, adding that the air leader was "not a fit officer to be Chief of the Air Corps; and I come to that opinion not only in view of the misrepresentations that have been made, but from the state of affairs in the Air Corps." It was damning testimony from a ranking officer, and the remarks transformed the investigation from a narrow look into the air-mail episode to a scrutiny of Foulois' leadership and a general review of the Air Corps. Media reports dramatized the new twist, and overnight the inquiry boiled up into a political maelstrom.[63]

Years of pent-up frustrations, dating back to the earliest doctrinal debates about bombardment, fueled an ugly and public argument between ground and air officers. The committee took depositions from dozens of witnesses, which identified certain procurement irregularities and some sloppy bookkeeping under Foulois. Still, investigators uncovered no systematic abuse or outright fraud, and most disinterested observers anticipated at worst a sound rebuke of the air arm. Instead, the panel's report was so critical of Foulois that some politicians called for the chief's ouster.[64]

At first, MacArthur and Secretary of War George Dern refused to fire Foulois. Admittedly, his managerial skills were poor—everyone knew he was best as a soldier—but he was no crook. Incessant Congressional pressure, however, eventually forced MacArthur to ask for Foulois' resignation. Foulois agreed to step down for the greater good of the service, retiring from the Army on 17 September. The next day, his assistant, Oscar Westover, an unassuming pilot usually loyal to the General Staff, became the air-arm commander. Benny Foulois cleared out his office and left Washington, feeling betrayed by the Army he had served for thirty-three years.[65]

This turn of events left the pilots dazed and enraged. They aimed their fury at Dern and MacArthur, men they thought should have better protected Foulois from the political tempest. In years to come, the incident would rank with the Billy Mitchell court-martial as evidence of Army subversion of air-arm interests. "The Foulois business stayed like a bitter pill in our mouths for a long time," remembered Ira Eaker. "The General Staff would have liked nothing better than to fractionalize the Army Air Corps and, therefore, make it impotent, destroy it piecemeal." Pete Quesada agreed. "Kicking General Foulois from service was pure stupidity and it only reaffirmed how narrow the Army was when it came to air power." Fostering great hopes at the outset, in the end the air mails only served to escalate the tensions among ground and air officers and swell the ranks of a disenchanted military.[66]

The air-mail fiasco officially and mercifully ended in September when all participating units submitted official reports. The cover page for the Eastern Zone's summary served as a poignant postscript to the whole affair:

Conceived (in sin) February 10
Born (prematurely) February 19
Paralyzed (officially) March 9
Quartered (by order) March 30
Died (unmourned) June 1
Requiescant en Pace[67]

Larger lessons went unnoticed in all the bickering. No other air maneuvers that occurred between the World Wars would come close to
the size and scope of the air-mail operation, and the difficulties encountered in negotiating vast stretches of unfamiliar terrain in bad weather
should have indicated to pilots that there were serious flaws in their developing doctrine of strategic bombardment. For ground officers, the
extent to which flyers did carry the mail—especially in the later
weeks—should have led to a fuller recognition of air power's potential.
As it was, the atmosphere of malice prevailing in 1934 worked against
any broad understanding of air power's strengths and weaknesses. Instead, both ground and air officers closed their minds to the air-mail
lessons. For his part, Pete Quesada was only glad to depart Newark and
"leave that mess behind." For Benjamin Foulois, of course, the cost had
been even more personal and immediate.[68]

For the next year Quesada filled a swift and varied succession of aide
billets. He was the flight officer for Hugh Johnson, administrator of the
New Deal's National Recovery Administration, until the U.S. Supreme
Court ruled that organization unconstitutional. Then he ferried Secretary of War George Dern across the country, a dicey assignment given
the recent Foulois fracas.

Quesada next traveled to Fort Benning, Georgia, for more of the
same. Benning was the home of the Infantry School and personified the
very culture of the ground Army. On the heels of the air-mail incident,
Quesada figured it "wasn't the best place for a pilot." Still, there was little else to do save report to his new boss, the school's commandant,
Colonel George C. Marshall.[69]

Marshall was to become the finest American soldier of the twentieth
century. An infantryman to his very core, he nonetheless exhibited none
of the knee-jerk service parochialism so common to the period. "General Marshall," Quesada recalled, "was the fairest, most open-minded
person I ever met in my life. I felt soon after I met him that he was a
man who could rise above all the petty feelings between air and ground
officers." Unlike many line officers, Marshall harbored no innate skepticism about air power, and actually liked to fly. Marshall was constantly
"making excuses to fly somewhere or another," and Quesada spent

more time in the cockpit per day at Benning than at any other time in his life. Together in a cramped observation plane they traveled the American Southeast and made countless jaunts up to the War Department in Washington.[70]

Everywhere they went, Quesada was amazed at the poor state of affairs at infantry posts. Years of neglect had left many buildings dilapidated. Equipment was obsolete, armories were filled with World War I-era weapons, and soldiers were forced to drill with fake guns. Fort Benning even rationed pencils, as Quesada learned when he lost one and had to replace it himself.[71]

The disrepair revealed a stark reality. While airmen had continually carped about lack of support, other branches had actually suffered outright reductions in the name of Air Corps growth. During the five-year program authorized by the Air Corps Act of 1926, air expenditures had totaled nearly 35 percent of the entire Army budget. Flyers had siphoned 5,867 officer and enlisted slots from other services, swelling the ranks of pilots by 50 percent, and airplanes had increased from 903 to 1646. The expansion had yielded two generations of bombers and initiated a third. In contrast, during the same period, the Cavalry had received exactly forty-seven tanks, while more than half its officers were still on horseback. The Infantry had not purchased a single rifle. It was little wonder that, by the time of the air-mail episode, line officers had grown weary of pilot complaints. For many of them, the air arm was terribly spoiled by the Air Corps Act of 1926, and pilots had little conception of the severe economic cuts that had been endured by other branches to sustain their growth.[72]

At Fort Benning, Quesada gradually recognized the larger context within which the Army worked. Far from miserly in its treatment of the Air Corps, the General Staff had merely hoped to preserve a balanced fighting force as the Depression sank the nation into a deep economic morass. As MacArthur had written in his annual report for 1934, "An Army overstrong in the air would be like an Army overstrong in Cavalry, able to strike suddenly and with great effect, but powerless to hold objectives thus gained." He was right, and air officers were wrong to carp about its treatment by the General Staff. Thanks to his service to Marshall, Quesada become one of the few junior officers on the ground or in the air who understood this complex and nuanced relationship between the Army and its branches.[73]

Quesada spent only three months at Fort Benning, but the time was invaluable. Beyond offering a ground perspective on interservice animosity, the job exposed Quesada to the man who later ran the American war effort in World War II. In the years ahead, George Marshall acted as his benefactor on more than one occasion. Other men of destiny were at Benning, too. It was there that Quesada met Omar Bradley, then an Infantry School instructor and later the man with whom Quesada would forge an American tactical-air doctrine in France and Germany.

So Pete Quesada could chalk up another set of important associations when he returned to Washington. By then, after nearly a decade of aide billets, he yearned for an operational posting. Young officers with such broad experience were hard to come by, however, and the new Air Corps chief, Oscar Westover, sent Quesada to Major General Frank Andrews and the just-established General Headquarters Air Force (GHQ). Andrews needed a competent assistant to help get the paper organization off the ground, and Pete Quesada fit the bill.[74]

As far as airmen were concerned, the GHQ Air Force was the only positive outcome of the air-mail debacle. Partly as a result of the managerial quirks uncovered in testimony during the summer of 1934, Congress had recommended a semiautonomous unit, comprised of bomber, pursuit, and observation aircraft, to act as America's first line of defense. The Air Corps had advocated such an idea for years, but the General Staff feared its independent status and had never implemented the force. Now, with a political mandate, the Army generals had no choice but to comply, so they established the GHQ Air Force. In late 1934, Secretary of War Dern gave the command to Andrews, a sensible and highly regarded air officer.[75]

Quesada joined Andrews on 1 January, the second officer assigned to the command. In the early weeks, Andrews concentrated on getting a core of staff officers assembled while Quesada handled the mundane red tape associated with any new unit. By February, Andrews had assembled his personnel cadre, and Quesada took advantage of a corresponding lull in his duties to request a posting beyond the aide roles the Army had seemed to cast for him. At lunch one afternoon Quesada told Andrews that he feared too much attaché duty could derail his career. "Don't worry about that," Andrews replied, "you're getting great experience right here. It will someday make you a better officer. I need you right now, but maybe after all the initial work is complete I'll think about it."[76]

Whatever Quesada's concerns, Andrews was absolutely right. By mid-decade Quesada's unusual entry into the Army and his extensive aide duty had combined to produce an uncommonly broad officer. Quesada had not attended West Point, and he wore the uniform free of the timeless inter-Army rivalries that had helped fuel air–ground tensions. As a result, his basic impressions of service life took shape in his years as an aide, jobs that sheltered him from at least the harshest parochial infighting. Indeed, until the day he retired he never understood the "intensity of service rivalries." Looking back on it all, he recognized the value of such duty. "I think all those experiences made for a more rounded officer. Anybody can be a squadron adjutant, anybody can be a supply officer. But unusual, off-beat assignments often contribute to successful military careers." They certainly did for Pete Quesada.[77]

No officer escaped completely the interservice squabbles in the years between the World Wars. But at a time when tensions between ground and air officers reached a climax with the air-mail fiasco, Quesada's own duty preserved his essential intellectual balance. He had left his air-mail post as alienated from the General Staff as any flyer, but subsequent service with Dern and Marshall moderated his views on the whole episode. Quesada's formative experiences allowed him a bird's-eye view of Army disputes and forever after provided a perspective that placed the Air Corps in context against a larger backdrop. Such outlooks were rare indeed in the 1930s, and they became the hallmark of Quesada's career.

Besides all that, Andrews had left the door open for a transfer after the GHQ Air Force completed its move to Langley. Quesada did not let his boss forget that as winter turned to spring in 1935.

Chapter Two

They Allowed Their Doctrine
to Become Their Strategy

MONTGOMERY, ALABAMA. 17 AUGUST 1935. LATE MORNING. Hot and humid weather greeted First Lieutenant Pete Quesada as he left the train station. In contrast to the turmoil over civil rights that catapulted the small city to prominence in the 1960s, Montgomery in the mid-1930s was just one of many sleepy Southern communities. To casual observers, it was a place where everyone knew everyone else, and the Depression had merely accentuated its slow and silent existence.[1]

Whatever Montgomery's profound racial inequities, Quesada was happy to be in town. Just west of the city sat Maxwell Air Field, home of the Air Corps Tactical School (ACTS) and his destination that sultry day. After countless attempts, Quesada had finally won permission to leave aide service behind and enter what he now considered the real air arm. His old boss, Frank Andrews, had even hinted that if Quesada did well at the one-year Maxwell course, a stint at the prestigious Command and General Staff School in Kansas might follow.[2]

Attendance at service schools was a good way to compensate for extended aide duty. Begun in the late 1880s, the Army's school system had steadily grown in importance since the turn of the century. In the period between World Wars I and II, with no battlefield performances to order promotions, the schools offered a way to identify worthy junior officers and were important stepping-stones in any career.

In fact, attendance at the ACTS probably convinced Quesada that he had not yet ruined his career. To the contrary, his contacts with senior officers had, if anything, helped him gain admission before most of his peers. Of the sixty-one Air Corps students in his class, three were majors, fifty-five were captains, and only two others wore the same lieutenant bars as Quesada. Moreover, some of his former bosses were now, at least temporarily, his academic equals. This group included Major Ira Eaker and Captain Harry Halverson from the *Question Mark* flight, and Captain Nathan Twining, the man who nearly a decade before had taught Quesada to fly. Because the Air Corps was so small, many other future generals were in Quesada's class as well: Benjamin Chidlaw, William Kepner, William Old, and John Cannon, the wartime commander of the Twelfth Air Force and a great tactical air leader in his own right.[3]

Befitting the importance of the ACTS, Maxwell Field was a large and growing base when Quesada passed through its gates for the first time. It had its own power plant and thirty-bed hospital, over ninety sets of officer and NCO quarters, enlisted barracks for five hundred, two swimming pools, volleyball and tennis courts, a track and baseball field, a skeet range, a squash court, and fine officers' and enlisted clubs. Seventy additional sets of officers' quarters, a bowling alley, a football field, additional tennis courts, a golf course, and a theater for three hundred were under construction. To any careful observer, the grounds were a graphic illustration of the Air Corps's prosperity while other Army branches had languished during the past half-dozen years.[4]

However, if Quesada thought he could escape the atmosphere of interservice bickering with this new posting, he was sadly mistaken. Although persons and personalities drove much of the Army–Air Corps dispute at the highest leadership levels, competing notions of tactics and strategy were probably at the core of the controversy for lesser military men—and in the early 1930s these officers had institutionalized these differences in various service schools. The ACTS, as the "highest educational establishment [and] the doctrinal center of the Air Corps,"

naturally acted as a lightning rod in this fight. In the years before Quesada arrived there, the Tactical School had ardently advocated independent-bombardment theories as opposed to air power's more traditional
support functions, and the school's dogged adherence to such notions
had been yet another thorn stabbing harmonious relations with the
General Staff. So, for Quesada, there would be no respite from this infighting. Maxwell's school, he remembered, was a "hotbed of the controversy."[5]

He and his fellow students learned quickly that the curriculum
would directly advocate doctrines of strategic bombardment. At an orientation session, Major Harold George, a director and senior instructor
at Maxwell, outlined the essential theme of the year. "We are not concerned with fighting the last war," he began, "that was done eighteen
years ago. We are concerned, however, in determining how air power
shall be employed in the next war and what constitutes the principles
governing its employment." Finishing, he argued that aviation had revolutionized the art of war and had "given to air forces a strategic objective of their own independent of either land or naval forces which can,
in itself, accomplish the purpose of war."[6]

It was a bold statement from one of the Air Corps' strongest supporters of bombardment theory. An early Billy Mitchell disciple, George
had been among the few officers to risk testifying on Mitchell's behalf
at his court-martial. After Mitchell's dismissal from the Army, George's
bright and articulate mind had made him a leading spokesman for independent military aviation. Indeed, in the interwar years he was the
clearest thinker among all those who extolled the merits of bombardment for air power. By virtue of his position at the ACTS, he wielded
enormous influence because most of the eventual air commanders of
World War II would pass through the school's portals. For these reasons
and more, Harold George, more than anyone else, provided the intellectual groundwork for what became a fully-articulated independent-
strategic-air theory.[7]

From his first day at the Tactical School in 1929, George and other
like-minded instructors had pushed their theories to the near exclusion of other ideas. The appearance of technologically advanced
bombers like the B-10 in 1931 and B-12 in 1932 spurred them on,
eliminating in George's mind the need for fighter escort and air superi-

ority. The bombers apparently could do it all, and subjects like pursuit
and the close air support of ground troops virtually disappeared in the
curriculum.

With the potential for independent bombardment firmly established
to his satisfaction, George set out in the year Quesada attended the
ACTS to raise the theory to a new level. Two years earlier, a colleague
named Major Donald Wilson had broached the concept of selective
bombardment. A railroad engineer by training, Wilson had clearly understood that the destruction of vital transportation centers could disrupt an entire rail system and thus inflict severe damage on a national
economy. George swiftly saw the importance of Wilson's work to his
own, and linked the two ideas together in lectures that stressed the in-
terdependence of any industrialized economy. Through a careful examination of producer–consumer relationships, George identified
transportation, steel, iron ore, and electric-power complexes as the
most "strategic" points in an economy. Destruction of these industries,
he told Quesada's class, could destroy enemy morale, collapse critical
war industries, and ensure victory. Reflecting the air enthusiasts' almost
unlimited faith in bombardment, George argued that aircraft could "immediately reach the economic and political heart of a nation and there-
by defeat that nation."[8]

Selective bombardment made old notions of nighttime strikes obsolete, and placed a new premium on operations in the daytime, when
bombardiers can see their targets better. But it also meant that enemy
fighters might easily intercept the raiding planes, which created a new
hurdle for the war theorists at Maxwell. One of George's disciples, Captain Haywood Hansell (who as a general later directed the World War
II air offensive against Japan) tackled this problem by telling students
that the new bombers could fend off an entire swarm of little planes. Yet
another teacher, Lieutenant Kenneth Walker, confidently asserted:
"Military airmen of all nations agree that a determined air attack, once
launched, is most difficult, if not impossible, to stop."[9]

Together, these arguments reflected what became a central assumption of interwar strategic-air theory: that smaller aircraft could not
match the technological advances of bombers. Indeed, to Quesada's
class Hansell and George time and again stressed the prowess of
bombers and the inherent technological limits of fighters. "Their wing-

load ratio and weight restrictions make them unlikely candidates for dramatic improvement," George wrote of pursuit planes. Big planes, these men believed, would always fly higher and faster and would carry more armament and guns.

This special faith in bomber technology was more than curious; it was in direct contradiction to even the earliest understanding of airplanes. Before the Great War, and before *fighter* and *bomber* had even entered the lexicon of the day, Wilbur and Orville Wright knew that "large airplanes built with the same shape and relative dimensions as small ones will not have the same relative performance." Still, the airmen of the interwar years pushed, forced, and fought for advances in bombers and neglected fighter development. Their efforts begot the Air Corps' newest big plane in 1936 and gave it its popular moniker: the B-17 "Flying Fortress."[10]

Although George, Hansell, and other men made significant contributions to bombardment theory, and although bombers did play a critical role in World War II and beyond, the ACTS's prewar concentration on bombardment teachings helped to produce a lopsided Air Corps, with profound implications for the future. Twenty years after his ardent support of strategic operations at Maxwell, Haywood Hansell acknowledged as much. "I think we did get carried away somewhat with the very thesis that I did my utmost to espouse. I think we got carried away so far on this strategic thing . . . that we have decimated, we've emasculated our own force."[11]

Not surprisingly, the ascendancy of bombardment at the ACTS shunted other instruction to the periphery. By Quesada's year, pursuit education had fallen to an all-time low, receiving just 56 hours of class time to bombardment's 310 hours—though as late as 1930 pursuit tactics had accounted for nearly 50 per cent of total instruction. In fact, if not for the dogged efforts of a single teacher, the study and prestige of pursuit aviation might well have dwindled even further.

Claire Chennault, a West Texas cowboy turned fighter pilot, was a contentious figure who seemed to relish a good fight. A loner by nature and intention, he was well suited to the part of pursuit instructor at the ACTS. He had first taught there in 1930 and, as bomber theories had gained credence, his relationships with colleagues and air-arm leaders had deteriorated. He had criticized the Air Corps' emphasis on bombardment following war maneuvers in 1933, and had accused Colonel Hap Arnold, the ranking flyer during World War II and already an ardent bombardment enthusiast, of skewing the result of the exercises by pitting modern bombers against outmoded fighters. If the General Staff favored ground action in war games—a common complaint among air officers—then Chennault believed the Air Corps was committing the same sin vis-à-vis bombers and fighters. His protests were in vain, however, and Air Corps umpires continued to adopt the party line at subsequent exercises. In fact, after another war game that same year one official went so far as to write that "Due to increased speeds and limitless space it is impossible for fighters to intercept bombers and therefore it is inconsistent with the employment of air forces to develop fighters."[12]

Essentially ignored by the Air Corps hierarchy, Chennault turned to his classroom and to his published writings as one-man pulpits for his ideas. Day after day during Quesada's year Chennault blasted bombardment notions. With uncanny foresight, he predicted that an extensive ground-warning and fighter-deployment network could cancel out bombers' speed, armor, and guns. Moreover, if only the air arm would better balance its research and development, Chennault argued, pursuit planes could surely attain the performance of the bigger planes that were then in existence.[13]

In the middle of the 1935–1936 academic year, Chennault codified his ideas in three articles for the *Coast Artillery Journal*. The words were familiar to students, but their stark bitterness stunned Chennault's colleagues and sent vibrations through the school. Almost overnight, the pursuit advocate became a virtual outcast at Maxwell. He eventually moved his family off the base, and ate alone or with small groups of enlisted personnel during the day.[14]

Haywood Hansell later recalled the personal attacks which dominated faculty relations in the mid-1930s. "A strong rift developed between bombardment and pursuit sections, which created an impasse and resulted in a stubborn blindness that denied the need for mutual assistance. Without complete cooperation, the whole air doctrine before the war suffered, and it took until 1943 to straighten it all out." As Quesada saw it, Chennault's quarrels with other faculty members highlighted just how contentious flyers could be, not only with the General Staff, but also among their own who did not share an enthusiasm for bombardment theory.[15]

Try as he might, Chennault never reached many students. His quarrelsome nature alienated some of them and his course, only twenty-six hours, counted little toward their grades. Even Quesada did not buy into Chennault's notions and found the clean thought and internal logic of bomber ideas more sound. Sadly, in part because of his own bombastic personality, Chennault gained few allies and made many enemies in his paper-clip combat. When real war came, the Army paid a price for his and his colleagues' failure to work together toward a balanced and integrated air doctrine.[16]

While Chennault fought his losing battle for air pursuit, other subjects suffered even greater atrophy. In the antiaircraft and observation courses, Quesada heard essentially the same lectures and used the same text that students had used a full decade earlier. "Anti-Aircraft fire," Harold George opined to his students, "is expected to be exactly what it is, a very troublesome thing to the inexperienced, a source of mild annoyance to the veteran, never a formidable enemy." Later, after World War II, one student believed the air arm had "missed the boat" with such casual indifference: "Too little attention was given to developments in A.A. Artillery. I have always had the feeling that we treated the A.A. people too much like we ourselves had been treated by the General Staff."[17]

Between the school's stress on bombardment and Chennault's vigorous defense of pursuit, there was little room for development of any other ideas. In lectures, class time, and graded material, no topic suffered more than instruction in air–ground operations. At once between and beyond the pursuit–bombardment debates, combined operations had no champion in the interwar years. The ACTS's only course on the subject while Quesada attended Maxwell, "Aviation in Support of Ground Forces," required a mere day and counted as only one fortieth of the final grade. Even at that, bomber theory pervaded the class text. "The most valuable contribution the air force can make to the ground campaign," it stated, "is the successful destruction of targets deep inside enemy territory." The text authors went on to write that targets in range of field artillery were not legitimate objectives for air power, except in extreme circumstances. Time would prove both premises wrong. In one of those ironies of history, the subject in which Quesada

received the least formal training was the one he later worked to revolutionize in World War II.[18]

Everything about the ACTS underscored the importance of inde-
pendent-bomber theories and reflected the essentially inbred views of
its instructors. This was true right down to the student composition of
Quesada's class. Only four of his classmates came from other branches.
In fact, a whopping 916 of the 1,092 students that the ACTS graduated
in the interwar years hailed from the Air Corps, a proportion far above
the norm in other service schools of the era.[19]

With one important exception, the faculty during Quesada's year
shunned any formal interaction with other services. That one was
Major Herbert Dargue, a graduate of the Naval War College, who inaugurated a brilliant eighteen-hour seminar on naval operations in 1935.
Using a large map room, he illustrated aerial fleet dispositions and
over-water operations, always juxtaposing Air Corps notions of air
power with evolving ideas of naval aviation. With clarity and astuteness,
Dargue attributed doctrinal differences between the two services to
differences in Army and Navy objectives. "Whereas in land campaigns
the defense or acquisition of territory remains the primary objective,"
he said, "at sea the successful destruction of an enemy's fleet is sought."
For most students, Dargue's class provided the first exposure to air-
craft-carrier tactics, which later turned naval warfare on its head in the
Pacific. For Quesada, Dargue's lectures helped frame a particular perspective on the fighting in North Africa in 1943—for the Sahara Desert
was like a sea, where land mattered little and the only tangible prizes
were concentrations of armor and men.[20]

Perhaps because of Dargue, or perhaps as a result of his own varied
service background, Pete Quesada retained and in some ways widened
his own views of warfare throughout an otherwise parochial experience at Maxwell. Although he believed in the revolutionary character
of air power, he never shared the ardent convictions with which other
airmen adopted those notions. The ACTS became increasingly "orien-
tated toward strategic bombardment while I was there," he remembered. "I thought it was overstated then, but it didn't result to me
getting in any debate at Maxwell. I did not become a jealous advocate
of it either way."[21]

While most of his classmates buttressed bomber theory in their year-end theses, Quesada's paper, on the growing military turmoil in Europe, reflected this broad-mindedness. Not surprisingly, such a topic failed to garner high praise from the partisan faculty at Maxwell, but Quesada nevertheless finished in the top third of his class. In the spring of 1936, he left the Tactical School in good standing. If nothing else, his year there had given him his first break from aide duty in years.[22]

After he left Montgomery, the air arm's chief, Oscar Westover, delivered a speech at the ACTS that challenged its ardent teachers and teachings. Quesada later read it, and it stayed forever in his mind. "Whatever we may think of air power," Westover said,

> we as soldiers must always be in line with our superiors. Without that loyalty which makes our profession a profession, we cannot accomplish a fraction of what we might otherwise do. The fact is that nobody knows what the potential for independent air operations is, but I do know what the damage to Army solidarity can be if we persist in our public disputes with the Army. As soldiers, we must always submit everything to our loyalty up and down the ranks, it is the only thing that makes an effective fighting force.[23]

Even if Quesada had not been predisposed by disposition and experience to place Army–Air Corps squabbles against a large canvas, his next assignment would have helped him keep a moderate view on the whole affair. True to his word, Major General Frank Andrews now had his former aide sent to Fort Leavenworth and the Command and General Staff School (CGSS). Started in 1881 on the Kansas frontier, the Leavenworth school was a watershed in any military career. Between the wars, only a small percentage of officers from all branches attended that school, and graduation was regarded as a stepping-stone to command. George Marshall, Dwight Eisenhower, Omar Bradley, George Patton, and most of the rest of America's World War II military leadership were alumni. With this assignment, Quesada's superiors were clearly marking the perennial aide as a promising officer. His promotion to captain added to the prestige of the new posting, although a crash on the way to Kansas temporarily dampened his enthusiasm. No doubt, whatever Quesada's own feelings about aide duty, his recent close associations with many senior officers were paying off.[24]

The Leavenworth instructors and the composition of his class under-scored the point. Quesada's wartime superior, Lewis Brereton, as well as Wade Haislip, George Stratemeyer, and Lucius Truscott all taught at the CGSS during Quesada's year. Among the students, Quesada was again one of the most junior. Just one out of 237 was a lieutenant, most were senior captains or majors, a few were lieutenant colonels. Nathan Twining and Joe Cannon were again fellow students, as was Harold George, the old ACTS guru. Lieutenant Colonel Bill Kepner, fresh from staff duty in Washington and later the wartime commander of the VIII Fighter Command, was one of the few lieutenant colonels in the class. Quesada knew him well by reputation, and Kepner's presence at Leavenworth reminded Quesada of his fast rise through the Army school system.[25]

The CGSS was different from the Tactical School. Both the curriculum and the student body were broader. Here, education centered on the tactical and operational subjects of all the Army branches. These subjects were taught by the case method, with instructors outlining hypothetical war situations and students executing orders as if they were division or corps staff officers. Leavenworth lectures were highly structured in style and delivery, and teachers usually favored the "school solution" over student creativity in dealing with supposed problems. Some pupils found fault with such rigidity, but the method was suited to military education.

Leavenworth drew its students from all branches and services, creating a nice mix of Infantry, Cavalry, Air Corps, and Artillery officers. The school even had officers from the Chinese, French, British, and Norwegian armed forces during Quesada's year. Because its concerns went beyond military tactics, the CGSS required courses in foreign languages, law, engineering, logistics, and military history. Within that framework, each academic section emphasized a specific area of General Staff duty. Hence, courses concentrated on logistics, tactical and strategic precepts, economic mobilization, or war planning. Unlike Maxwell and the tactical schools of other Army branches, Leavenworth placed a high premium on exposure to many different aspects of service in the armed forces. In the end, it aimed to produce officers qualified for General Staff duty and to positions on division and corps staffs.

Despite such goals, many airmen viewed the CGSS as the ground army's agent in various doctrinal feuds. To be sure, the school's instructors were notoriously conservative in their thinking and very few of them liked the idea of air power independent of ground forces. While Quesada attended Leavenworth, there were only two days of instruction and one real map exercise on air power, at least as airmen would have defined it. For this reason, air-arm chief Oscar Westover had asked the General Staff for more instruction on aviation "other than in direct support of ground elements." His request had been denied, an action that air officers could neatly fit into their estimation of the Army as unfit to command air forces.[26]

All this plus the years of infighting contributed to a besieged mentality among pilots at Leavenworth, and they courted this isolation with a determined insistence upon their own ideas. The school commandant, for example, had to rebuke Harold George for persistently ridiculing the rest of the faculty to the point of outright insubordination. The airmen's sense of segregation was so strong that fifty years later Quesada mistakenly recalled that "There were only four or five of us pilots at Leavenworth that year, and some of them stayed pretty much to themselves." In fact, there were thirty-seven flyers in Quesada's class; only the contingents of Infantry and Artillery officers at the CGSS were more numerous.[27]

As with most abiding debates, the controversy over war teachings had two sides, and the pilots' criticism of the Leavenworth curriculum actually showed a poor understanding of the CGSS and its place in the Army's school hierarchy. By intention, the Kansas course concentrated on division and corps maneuvers, leaving the larger issues of national strategy and mobilization to the next school in the system, the War College. At Leavenworth's level of war gaming, then, independent strategic-air campaigns had little impact compared to close-air-support operations. As one observer noted, the reasons why the school downplayed strategic aviation were pedagogical, not political. In fact, as early as 1929 the school text on air power had granted the Air Corps its hallowed place in future wars, declaring that "the strategic employment of bombardment aviation forms the basis for the employment of the air forces as a whole." But the school was primarily concerned with the workings of corps and division ground operations, and necessarily dealt only with tactical aviation when it dealt with air power at all.[28]

Only the most perceptive of the air-oriented students saw this, and still fewer were able to differentiate between training and education or to recognize that Leavenworth constituted an important experience in uniform. "While I learned little I could use, I learned how to learn," George Marshall once remarked of his own time at Leavenworth. "My habits of thought were being trained. Leavenworth was immensely instructive, not so much because the course was perfect—because it was not—but because [of] the association with the officers, the reading we did and the discussion and the leadership."[29]

Gradually, Quesada came to the same conclusion, shedding the views prevalent among the air officers and seeing a certain value in the course. Among other things, his duty in Kansas introduced the young captain to officers in other branches. He shared a dormitory hallway with Captain Maurice Rose, a cavalry officer and an early convert to the concept of mobile warfare dominated by tanks. Like Quesada, Rose came to Leavenworth with extensive experience as an aide. He had just graduated from the armor school at Fort Knox, and later commanded his own armored division in World War II. The two men became close friends, and often went to Kansas City for a movie or museum visit in their spare time.[30]

With Rose, Quesada first thought of the ideas of close air support for which both men would later gain renown. For nearly half the year, most of the map exercises had not interested either man. "We went out to a field and we were given a problem," Quesada remembered of one typical drill. "I read the problem in five minutes and had my answer, which was to envelop the right flank the next morning. The instructor was annoyed that it took me only five minutes and it turned out to be the right answer. He asked me why I chose that answer and I said because that's the way the trucks were pointed." He and Rose laughed about that teacher's consternation until the day Rose died at the hands of a German gunner in 1945.[31]

But the Leavenworth map problems grabbed the attention of both men when, toward the end of instruction, the drills began concentrating on combined-arms operations. One exercise contemplated a fictitious corps attack against an enemy retreating toward a river, and advocated using airplanes to cut off the crossing points. In a crude yet elemental way the text foresaw the use of air power to isolate a battlefield, much as Allied aircraft were to do in Normandy in the summer of 1944.[32]

Yet another exercise hoped to illustrate the importance of air support to armor deployed far ahead of a main corps body. "Although not organically a part of a mechanized cavalry brigade," the school text stated, "air service is of such great assistance in executing reconnaissance for the advance and for flank security, for use in maintaining control of the columns . . . and for executing battle missions, that it should be considered an essential part of the mechanized combat team."[33]

Such talk came close to placing air power under ground control, of course, and struck fear into those pilots who dreamed of autonomy from the Army. But Quesada and Rose were young captains, free of old thinking. They worked together on the problem, and saw real merit in Leavenworth's "school solution." In a small notebook, Quesada scribbled that, although his fellow flyers would disagree with him, he thought that "future war will require all sorts of arrangements between the air and the ground, and the two will have to work closer than a lot of people think or want." He was right, and this particular Leavenworth exercise foresaw the European battles of World War II with remarkable clarity.[34]

Unfortunately, this was the kind of thinking contested by senior airmen, and Quesada was not yet a crusader for tactical air power. Perhaps because he did not have any clear convictions of his own, he remained largely silent about his notions of war. He finished the CGSS course just as he had at Maxwell, nowhere near the top but far from the bottom. Attendance at both the Air Corps Tactical School and the Command and General Staff School provided benefits in ways beyond grades, however, and for Pete Quesada the courses had been a systematic exposure to the prevailing theories of war, including the men and the ideas of bombardment aviation. He had not yet committed himself to any single principle of military aviation, but in an era marked by vast changes in the machines and concepts of combat, his open-mindedness was an asset in the preparation for war.

Quesada left Leavenworth in the spring of 1937 for his first truly operational billet since his initial assignment to Bolling Field a decade before. For the next year, he served under Major C. E. Duncan as a flight commander in the First Bombardment Squadron at Mitchell Field on Long Island, New York. After wishing so long for just such a field job, he found that service away from the corridors of power had its own pitfalls. The Martin B-10 bombers that the squadron flew were outdated, especially for someone used to flying the Air Corps' best and newest planes. Beyond that, the daily minutiae of duty dragged in comparison to the fast-paced world of senior commanders.[35]

In time, Quesada grew tired of the routine and the constraints of a standard chain of command, a fact not lost on Duncan. In his officer-efficiency rating of Quesada, Duncan noted that the captain was "a very capable officer with a wide range of varied experience," but hastened to add: "Due to much of his service having been on duties where he worked independently or directly in charge of the activity, he is used to acting on his own decisions. Increased service in tactical units is believed desirable to develop a greater sense of cooperation and teamwork." Duncan's reference to Quesada's independent streak was the first significant hint of what his critics later labeled his impulsive, aloof nature and his admirers called traits of self-reliance and innovation.[36]

Long Island was not always boring. On the contrary, in the spring of 1938 the First Bombardment Squadron found itself embroiled in a long-standing jurisdictional skirmish with the Navy over the coastal defense of New York. Before airplanes existed, the Navy had been mostly responsible for defending the nation's water line. Aviation had added another dimension, however, and in the 1920s a new War Department policy allowed the Army to conduct offshore air operations while the Navy retained responsibility for convoy escort, reconnaissance, and patrol. The rise of bombardment theory in the Army and the development of aircraft carriers in the Navy muddied the issue again, and in 1931 a revamped policy granted the Navy a seaborne air arm. From the beginning, however, these accords revealed the difficulty of integrating novel types of weaponry—like aircraft—into existing force structures. The policies were too restrictive of Army aviation and virtually prohibited joint operations, something any real emergency would certainly require.[37]

The stakes in the debate grew to huge proportions as the Depression deepened and the services competed for scarce federal dollars. Official

American military policy in the interwar years was based on defensive precepts, and the coastal-defense mission was the only sanctioned rationale for bombers in the air arm and aircraft carriers in the Navy. Indeed, air leaders initially had to sell Congress the B-17 and the B-29—the basic tools of the bomber offensive in World War II—on the basis of their coastal-defense roles. When in 1934 the Navy embarked on a program to corral for itself the whole coastal-defense mission, Army air leaders feared for the very existence of their bombardment programs. Relationships between Naval and Army air partisans quickly deteriorated, and the president, the Congress, and the secretary of war did nothing, despite pleas for help. There the issue sat until early 1938.[38]

The First Bombardment Squadron, responsible for offshore defense at a major Air Corps installation on the Northeast coast, was a prime place for the dispute to erupt. Without the coastal-defense mission, Quesada and the entire First Bombardment Squadron might as well have packed up and gone home. So when the unit received its first three operational B-17s, air-arm leaders hatched a plan to confirm their ability to defend the nation while undercutting the Navy's efforts to retain control over coastal defense. In May 1938 they authorized a highly-publicized patrol search to find the Italian passenger liner *Rex*, then crossing the Atlantic on a route not disclosed to the participating airmen. A year earlier, B-17s had located a Navy battleship off California in highly-controlled maneuvers, but now the planes would get a realistic test of their ability.[39]

May 12th was a lousy day: rainy, foggy, and windy; but that was the day a crack young navigator named Lieutenant Curtis LeMay had judged the best for finding the *Rex*. At about 0830 hours the B-17s took to the air. As their engines chewed on the turbulent air, hail pock-marked each plane and induced bone-jarring gyrations. LeMay remembered the morning flight as one of his worst ever—and not just because of the bucking craft. A lot was riding on his compass and protractor, and if he missed the target he might just as well try to swim home.[40]

The planes eventually broke through the towering cold front. With a clear horizon, the odds of locating the 900-foot liner in the immensity of an empty ocean immeasurably improved. Sure enough, the flyers spied the ship around noon. As they circled the *Rex*, Americans on its deck waved and sang "The Star Spangled Banner." The ship's captain invited the flyers for lunch when he reached port.

Back on land, the National Broadcasting Corporation radioed the triumph while newspapers headlined the success. A picture of two B-17s above the ship, which appeared in a *New York Herald Tribune* story, was reprinted on the front pages of more than eighteen hundred newspapers, magazines, and periodicals. Later that year, Congress appropriated additional money for the bombers. For LeMay, the junior officer on whose shoulders the whole affair had rested, the moment seemed "like a movie or dream. It was happening to someone else, it wasn't real, wasn't happening to us."[41]

The good publicity backfired on the airmen within days. To Naval leaders, coastal-defense feuds were one thing, but the Army Air Corps had just flown over 600 miles out to sea. The admirals threatened to complain to President Roosevelt—who had a marked preference for the Navy anyway—if Army Chief of Staff Malin Craig did not rein in his air arm. Craig swiftly complied, as Hap Arnold bitterly recalled: "Somebody in the Navy apparently got in quick touch with somebody on the General Staff, and in less time than it takes to tell about it, the War Department had sent down an order limiting all activities of the Army Air Corps to within 100 miles from the shoreline of the United States." Almost immediately, the 100-mile order became a rallying cry among Army pilots, ensuring that the Navy–Army jurisdictional feud would continue to smolder well into the early 1940s.[42]

The interservice dispute carried heavy consequences when the United States entered World War II, for the Navy could have taught the air arm much about modern war if relations between the two branches had been better. From their interwar experience fighting in the Caribbean, Navy and Marine Corps leaders understood the importance of combined-arms combat, and their doctrine placed a premium on cooperative efforts. Such foresight prepared sailors for their campaigns in the Central Pacific, just years away, and it might well have helped the Air Corps deal better with the problems of command and doctrine that plagued the Allied effort in North Africa. As it was, however, both services proceeded with plans remarkably independent of one another. Even Quesada, who had some idea of naval air precepts from his days in Herbert Dargue's class at the Tactical School, failed to recognize the value of amphibious doctrine. This failure to learn to work together was perhaps the greatest casualty of the war that raged among American military men in the 1920s and 1930s.[43]

It was probably a good thing when new orders sent Quesada far from New York and the whole sordid episode. In June 1938 he was assigned again to the Army diplomatic corps and boarded a steamer bound for Buenos Aires with nine other airmen. There, the small contingent led by Lieutenant Colonel John Cannon was to help Argentina develop a modern air force around its 152 American bombers and fighters. For more than two years, Quesada worked to install maintenance and supply systems and taught at a school for instrument flying. The assignment suited him well, and Cannon noted that Quesada was "an officer of engaging personality, is self-confident and capable of taking a definite stand." In his free time, Quesada enjoyed the country's European flavor, and the job gave him an opportunity to brush up his Spanish, which he had not spoken since his days in Cuba.[44]

At times, the U.S. Navy's presence was the only negative aspect of the Buenos Aires tour. Although the Air Corps had a tiny complement in the South American nation, the Navy maintained a sizeable presence up and down the coast of Argentina. But in South America, far from the parochial concerns of U.S. coastal defense, Quesada came to see the value of cooperation for both Army and Navy tasks. He actually grew to like many of the Naval officers in town, and the Navy shore commander threw a farewell party for Quesada when Quesada received orders to return to the United States in August 1940. It was quite a party; local police had to halt the drinking at about 0430 hours.[45]

Somewhere in the midst of the festivities, Quesada promised to fly an old Navy Grumman amphibian back to the United States. Just three hours after he had fallen asleep, sailors roused him from bed and drove him to the harbor and the waiting craft. Quesada had never been in a Grumman amphibian, though he figured it was better than the slow steamship he had been scheduled to take home. With only a few five-gallon tins of gasoline, a screwdriver, a pair of diagonals, and some safety wire on board, he took off, flying over the Andes to the Pacific and up the west coast to Panama.[46]

His arrival at the tightly-guarded American Naval Air Station in Panama caused quite an uproar. As he climbed from the plane, sailors trained rifles on him as the airdrome officer asked him for identification. Unable to locate a Captain Quesada on the Navy's register of officers, the Navy lieutenant summoned the station's commanding admiral. It took some time for the impish Quesada to clear up the suspicions naturally aroused by an Army officer with a Spanish name flying a U.S. Navy plane up from Argentina. "For Christ's sake, Pete," one officer said to him after tensions had eased, "what are you trying to do, start a war?" Five days later, Quesada completed his flight to Norfolk, Virginia, and became the first aviator to fly that route solo.[47]

A great deal had occurred while he was away. Europe was now embroiled in World War II, England was weathering Hitler's massive effort to bomb it into surrender from the air, and the air-arm chief, Major General Hap Arnold, was busy preparing the Air Corps for a war that many believed would surely engulf the United States. With Quesada's overseas experience in mind, Arnold had particular tasks for the young captain and ordered him to the War Department. His new jobs once again placed Quesada near the center of activity in the Army, and offered him a bird's-eye view of the Army and its Air Corps. With war looming ever closer for the United States, that kind of perspective was becoming an especially valuable asset.

Not surprisingly, the European conflict had created a flood-tide of growth in America's armed forces. At first all services shared equally in the build-up, but Roosevelt eventually decided to concentrate rearmament efforts on air power after Adolf Hitler had used his own air force to win appeasement at the Munich Peace Conference in 1938. "Hitler," the president said, "will not be impressed with anything but airplanes—and lots of them." Accordingly, in late 1938 the president ordered 20,000 planes built within a year and an annual production capacity of 24,000 planes by 1941—enormous numbers next to the air arm's existing force of 4,060 aircraft.[48]

Privately, Arnold wondered about the logistics of such tremendous expansion, but he assured Roosevelt that the Air Corps was up to it. Like Benny Foulois before him, Hap Arnold was a can-do officer, a true air pioneer with almost unbounded faith in the potential of strategic bombardment. Besides, from where he sat, Arnold was not about to allow personal doubts to jeopardize the Air Corps' biggest boost since the Great War. Years later he remembered the president's directive as the "Magna Carta of the Air Corps."[49]

Other officers did express reservations about the program. George Marshall was then the Deputy Chief of Staff, and he was slated to take the Army's reins when Chief of Staff Malin Craig retired. He feared that this forced expansion might further distort an already imbalanced force structure. His were legitimate concerns, for many Army branches were deplorably unready for war. As late as the fall of 1938, the Infantry had under 50,000 rifles out of an intended minimum of 227,000. The Artillery Corps had 141 of an authorized 1,500 75mm guns, and just one of 3,750 60mm mortars. The infant Armored Corps had a mere 300 of a planned 1,344 light and medium tanks. If he tried hard, Marshall could perhaps muster an army of five field divisions from these scanty assets. By comparison, across the ocean, Hitler commanded thirty-one armored and fifty-nine well-equipped infantry divisions. For Marshall, that disparity was more frightening than the air imbalance. "Of course we had to have an air force," he remembered. "But if we didn't have an army—and a ground army—we didn't have anything." As he figured it, sooner or later the United States might have to fight the Germans, and they had best be prepared for the ordeal.[50]

Still, Roosevelt pushed air-arm growth into an upward spiral that did not reach its apogee until 1944. In 1939, Congress authorized $2.6 billion to Army aviation, as much money as flyers had received in all the years since World War I. Arnold initiated research on four major airplane designs, doubled the air arm's aircraft inventory to 8,025 planes, and recruited hordes of cadets. As 1940 came, so many inductees flooded into the Air Corps that Arnold drafted civilian flying schools to instruct the trainees. The race for war was on.[51]

A whirl of activity swirled about Arnold's office as Quesada arrived in October. Along one hallway a procurement panel grappled with the immense buying spree; down another corridor technical advisors poured over countless engineering data, flow charts, and research reports from around the world. Other groups were spending seven days a week devising strategy, hoping against hope for time to implement their plans. Arnold sat above all the scurrying activity, in the back corner office, trying to coordinate an effort that so far was little more than controlled chaos. To Quesada, fresh from the relative quiet of South America, the scene must have made a powerful impression. He was no stranger to the corridors of power, but what a change it was from the tranquil days of the Depression, when the Army had little money and all the time in the world.[52]

Arnold was too busy to see Quesada when the captain first reported for duty. For four days, Quesada sat in Arnold's reception room, waiting for the chief to brief him on his new assignment. Many times Arnold rushed through the area, motioned for Quesada to stay put, and hurried off to a meeting, briefing, or planning session. Sooner or later, Quesada kept thinking, the Old Man would call for him.[53]

At 1900 hours on the fifth day—a Saturday—Arnold finally bellowed out from behind his desk. "Quesada, get in here!" It was hard to look crisp and fresh after so long a wait, but Quesada straightened his uniform, and in his best military form reported to the Chief of the Air Corps. "I have a job for you, Quesada," the general began. "You're my new liaison chief with all the embassies here in town. I don't think captain is sufficient rank, so we'll make you a major. Good luck, that will be all."[54]

The meeting did not last five minutes, but it was vintage Arnold—gruff, abrupt, and to the point. Arnold led by the sheer force of his personality and had little time for details or daily routine. He left the nuts and bolts of jobs to others, and as long as his lieutenants performed adequately he allowed them considerable leeway. On the other hand, if someone made a mistake, they were subject to Arnold's near-legendary temper. As Tooey Spaatz remembered, Arnold was "the closest thing to Dr. Jekyll and Mr. Hyde that I ever knew. As long as you did your job, he was Dr. Jekyll, but if you messed up or were incompetent, Mr. Hyde appeared."[55]

That brief encounter demonstrated something more than Arnold's leadership style, however. The president's ambitious expansion had turned the Air Corps on its head. Previously well-defined jobs changed rapidly as everybody and everything associated with the air arm hustled to meet Roosevelt's goals. Neither Arnold nor anybody else could predict the exact demands of any given position, and the Air Corps chief gave few instructions to Quesada because he himself did not know what the job would bring. In many ways, the post was Quesada's to define. As he left the War Department that night, the young officer was sure of only one thing. Fourteen years after his first flight with Tiny Harmon, he was now a major.

Quesada mapped out his responsibilities in the weeks that followed. In the interwar years, the foreign-liaison job had entailed little more than attending an endless array of diplomatic receptions and parties in the nation's capital. But after Germany invaded Poland and before America entered the war, the post gained status and responsibility. By 1940, the foreign-liaison office was coordinating most of the contacts between the Army Air Corps and governments around the world. When the United States abandoned its strict neutrality to supply the Allies with war goods, the scope of the office expanded again as it managed the transfer of American air assets to friendly belligerents.[56]

Quesada's first months in Washington passed in a frenzy of work. Congress had already passed the "Cash and Carry" legislation, which allowed Allied nations to buy U.S. war material with cash. England, struggling to maintain her centuries-old empire, deluged Quesada's little office with information requests and orders for everything from parachutes to airplane tires. He and his four assistants routinely spent fifteen-hour days routing requests for information to "the appropriate office, air field, or unit. When we received actual orders for goods, I went to Arnold. He would either sign off on it or, if it was of a particular nature, go get Marshall's permission. I was essentially an errand boy on a grand scale."[57]

Occasionally, Hap Arnold or George Marshall refused to approve Allied requests. The Air Corps needed material, too, and Arnold jealously guarded the air arm's prerogative vis-à-vis American defense manufacturers. Moreover, the Army was wary of releasing state-of-the-art technology to any nation, Allied or not. When the top brass nixed requisitions, Quesada had to deliver the bad news to British, Chinese, and later Russian attachés. With Hitler bearing down in Europe and Japan occupying Shanghai, Allied officers often did not understand what they saw as America's miserly allotment of war material. The United States was, after all, at peace. Their countries, on the other hand, were fighting for national survival.[58]

The pressure, conflict, and clamor to supply both the Allies and the American forces for war soon reached an unrelenting pace. After

France fell to Hitler, Great Britain wanted 14,000 planes of all types. At the same time, the Air Corps modified its own expansion program upward, to 21,470 tactical and training planes within the year. American industry was nowhere near able to fill both orders, and everyone knew that something must give. The German Luftwaffe was then bombing London in the Battle of Britain, and Roosevelt, determined to give preference to Britain's needs, pared the Air Corps request by 8,586 planes and directed manufacturers to prioritize British orders.[59]

The decision was a blow to Arnold and the American air arm. In Arnold's mind, it did much worse than set Air Corps efforts back six months; it also subordinated his hopes for a modern bomber fleet. The English had ordered pursuit planes to protect the skies over London, and the British buying practices decreased U.S. production of big bombers in favor of smaller aircraft, denying the Air Corps sufficient bombers until very late in the war. But Roosevelt's inclination to favor the British paid dividends for America, too. Although nobody realized it at the time, the momentary shift away from large-bomber production prepared U.S. industry for later manufacturing runs of P-38 and P-47 fighters, planes that became workhorses in the tactical air war in Europe.[60]

Nevertheless, Arnold disagreed with Roosevelt's decree, and he skirted defiance of his president by slowing its implementation by manipulating the maze of obscure procurement agencies through which material flowed. Quesada's office became part of this game of bureaucratic intrigue, placing him in a dicey spot. Periodically in late 1940 and early 1941, the American air-arm chief would appear before Quesada to see what, if anything, could stem the tide of U.S. air materiel flowing to Britain. Arnold was too shrewd to interfere openly with Roosevelt's wishes, but he knew that all sorts of small, mysterious obstacles could arise in the complicated procurement process.[61]

Quesada usually walked a thin line between presidential policy and Arnold's wishes in such instances. He halfheartedly delayed certain requisition forms, was slow to gather information for the British attaché, and added a few layers of red tape to the processing of Britain's purchases. He did a good job, as his immediate boss Colonel Robert Candee testified: "A splendid officer of fine character and delightful personality, is loyal, versatile, zealous, industrious, persistent, and impulsive." In the end, however, these efforts to slow the English orders did not amount to much. No one wished to resist the president's directive flagrantly, and the Royal Air Force received the lion's share of planes while the Air Corps waited out the Battle of Britain.[62]

Congress liberalized the rules of American aid to England with the passage of the Lend-Lease Act in March 1941, which on the surface seemed to exacerbate Arnold's difficulties. The British Treasury was then nearly bankrupt, and the new law sought to ease the financial burden of the island nation. In return for access to British military bases, Roosevelt agreed to "lend" war material to His Majesty's government and help transport it across the Atlantic. Although naval equipment constituted the bulk of Lend-Lease support, Secretary of War Henry Stimson directed the Air Corps to step up its efforts as well. In particular, Stimson ordered the air arm to devise an "air transportation system by which priority war material may be flown to Allied territory with the greatest expediency."[63]

The new task did not overjoy Hap Arnold, but he played the dutiful soldier and made hasty plans for a trip to England, where he would make his own observations of the European war and work to establish an air-ferrying route across the Atlantic. Since Quesada had dealt with the Royal Air Force for over a year, Arnold had the major accompany him to England. In early April, Quesada did the spadework for the tour, planning Arnold's itinerary, preparing issue books, and memorizing scores of facts for the discussions. On 9 April, the two left on a commercial Pan Am Clipper flight from New York, passing through Bermuda and Lisbon before reaching Bristol on 12 April, the day before Easter.[64]

England made a powerful impression on them. As they drove to London they passed one airfield after another, each cluttered with air and ground defenses. Many houses alongside the road had smashed windows and doors, some had no roofs, many were abandoned. In the city, the Americans were met by RAF Chief Air Marshal Charles Portal, a young savvy man of 47, and Air Vice Marshal John Slessor, director of the Air Ministry's planning branch. Arnold declared that he had come to England to "find out a practical way in which the Army Air Corps could help the British," and after a perfunctory glass of sherry, he and Quesada retired to a suite at the Dorchester Hotel.[65]

Their work began in earnest on Easter Sunday. Arnold spent the bet-

ter part of the next two weeks meeting with Portal and with RAF officers, British politicians, American representatives to British agencies,
Winston Churchill, and King George VI. Quesada usually accompanied
him to working sessions of policy and planning, but rarely attended the
ceremonial visits to high officials. Within a week, the Anglo-Americans
had established the Ferrying Command, the first official joint and combined operation of the war. To the end of the hostilities, it performed
yeoman service and became the postwar Air Force's largest command.[66]

The trip was Arnold's first experience of a nation at war, and when
not in meetings he took every chance to tour the countryside and watch
the workings of the war effort. On 15 April he and Quesada traveled to
the headquarters of Britain's Fighter Command, which had recently
fought back Hitler's efforts to cow Britain from the air. "Airdromes prepared for attack," Arnold wrote of the visit in his cryptic diary, "planes
all dispersed in positions sheltered by embankments. . . . Low Hangars
sunk almost to level of ground. Barbed wire everywhere. Infantry
guards. Armored cars. All men looked alert, eager, keen."[67]

That night after they returned to the Dorchester the Germans
bombed London. "The searchlights, the starlike shells bursting, the incessant cracking of the guns, always getting closer and louder," Arnold
wrote. "A fire here, another there. They seem to cover as much as a city
block. Closer and closer. Br-r-ump. Flames high in the sky—two, three
city blocks on fire. The noise recedes. The night becomes silent again,
but the fires burn on. The raid is over. I leave the window and go to
bed."[68] Hap Arnold and Pete Quesada had just encountered their first
bombing, not as attackers as perhaps they had expected, but as observers on the ground.

The next day dawned bright blue, and along the horizon barrage balloons hung from the sky. Smoke drifted from the ruins. There were
large holes in the streets, vacant spots where row houses had stood,
stores without fronts, glass strewn everywhere. Walking to the Air Ministry, Arnold was struck by "pathetic sights of people trying to gather
such of their belongings from wrecked homes." In the afternoon, he
and Quesada went to High Wycombe, home of the RAF Bomber Command. Watching planes return from a mission over Europe, Arnold took
heart, knowing that the destruction of London had been visited in turn
upon Hitler's domain.[69]

Actually, although bombing raids in the war's early stages were capable of much damage, neither British nor German strikes seriously curtailed the other's war effort nor undermined civilian morale. If anything, the English populace rallied to fight on more stoutly than ever after the Battle of Britain. In Germany and the Axis-occupied countries, RAF strikes were so inaccurate as to be wholly ineffective. A study in the summer of 1941 concluded that a mere one sixth of British bombers had placed their ordnance within five miles of their targets, a finding entirely consistent with reports from American observers deep inside the Third Reich. Not until much later in the war was there any general destruction in Berlin, and the Germans continued to buy and enjoy fruits, vegetables, and other peacetime commodities that had been unavailable to Londoners from almost the very outset of the hostilities. Indeed, with poor bombsights and bomber fleets that still measured in the meager hundreds, 1941 was still the Stone Age of bombing.[70]

But some airmen on both sides of the Atlantic persisted in a kind of self-delusion about the early achievements of bombing, elevating it to a principal weapon of war. Air Chief Marshal Arthur Harris soon came to lead Bomber Command, and a more devout convert to strategic bombing would have been hard to find in England. Arnold shared Harris's fire, writing toward the end of his trip to London that "war is an Air war today. The Air alone can bring Germany to its knees. . . . The Air can bring the war to Central Germany and break down morale." Now deeply impressed by the devastated scenes of bombardment, the American air chief hardened his belief in strategic air power. "We must plan new equipment out for 1943," he scribbled in his diary as his trip to England wound down, "pressure cabins, long-range bombers, larger bombers." For Arnold the need was always for bigger, faster, heavier bombers. Not even Hitler's failure to force England's surrender by air attack during the Battle of Britain weakened his faith. If Germany had only had the magnificent B-17 Flying Fortress instead of smaller two-engine bombers, he believed, His Majesty's government would surely have been no more. Arnold's conclusions were shared by most of the American air leadership at the time, including Quesada's old friends Tooey Spaatz and Ira Eaker.[71]

A few observers came to different conclusions. William Kepner, who later headed the Eighth Fighter Command, believed that "the Battle of Britain was won by the English fighters," not lost by the German bombers. Quesada agreed, writing his mother from England on 20 April that "the British Spitfires are marvelous planes all right, and have single-handedly defeated the Boche in the sky." Kepner and Quesada were mostly correct, for the Battle of Britain was in essence a struggle for air superiority, a fight to control the skies that had little to do with the relative strengths of fighters and bombers. But some aviation enthusiasts, committed to notions of independent air power, were blind to the subtle lessons of the battle.[72]

Not surprisingly, Arnold's beliefs set the tone for the Air Corps' own war planning when he and Quesada returned to Washington on 1 May. The Army and its air arm perpetually planned for war, of course, but in 1941 those preparations moved beyond the realm of academic abstraction and adopted an immediacy all their own. Already, secret American and British conferences had produced a report, known as ABC-1, which spelled out the general outline of a joint war against the Axis powers and advocated an increase in the production of aircraft by both nations. Now Arnold asked officers in the newly created Air War Planning Division to plan for further expansion in Air Corps growth and to delineate the contours of an air offensive aimed at Germany.

The AWPD group worked under the supervision of Tooey Spaatz, by then Arnold's chief of staff. Most of the planners were veteran instructors from the Air Corps Tactical School at Maxwell Field. Colonel Harold George headed the AWPD committee, and Lieutenant Colonel Kenneth Walker, Majors Haywood Hansell and Laurence Kuter, and Captain Hugh Knerr constituted the bulk of the committee's brain power. With the exception of Knerr, they were all ardent air-power partisans, sharing Arnold's mystical confidence in bombers.[73]

Not surprisingly, the hopes of America's air men since the days of Billy Mitchell guided their work. The panel recommended an early massing of bombardment units in England and a vigorous attack on the sources of German military power. The basic feature of their plan lay "in the application of air power for the breakdown of the industrial and economic structure of Germany." This involved "the selection of a system of objectives vital to the continued German war effort, and to the means of livelihood of the German people, and tenaciously concentrating all bombing toward the destruction of those objectives." Reflecting Haywood Hansell's work at the Tactical School on precision target selection, the panel identified the electric-power grid in Germany, the transportation network, and the oil-refining industry as critical targets. Unlike the British, the group did not envision midnight area raids, and bet instead on the prowess of B-17s to run the gauntlet of the German defenses in daylight.[74]

The planners subordinated all other air functions to the assault on Germany. Reconnaissance and pursuit activity were considered only peripherally important, and the committee judged the close air support of ground troops even less vital, listing that function near the bottom of all the contemplated Air Corps tasks. Even the build-up of air units reflected the dominance of bombardment doctrine. While Harold George's group estimated that their strategy required a total of ninety-eight bomber groups with nearly 7,000 aircraft—some of them with the then fanciful range of 8,000 miles—they mandated just twenty-six groups of fighters and fighter bombers. In other words, they conceived a force structure three times heavier in bombers than in fighters.[75]

Some Army leaders expressed reservations about both the planners and their blueprint. George Marshall had no trouble with Arnold, but viewed the air staff as a group of "immature" men who did not value the importance of impartial planning. "They were antique staff officers . . . because they were not trained at that kind of staff work and they were busy taking stands." Not surprisingly, Marshall believed the air scheme "placed too much faith in the probability of success solely through the employment of bombing." In his view, the Army had already paid too little attention to building a balanced force structure, and he feared that the massive air plan would bleed scarce resources away from the Infantry and Cavalry.[76]

But the flyers ably defended their plan with help from administration officials and a keen bit of compromise. Secretary of War Henry Stimson, who had ascribed Paris's fall the year before to "French deficiency in air power," helped to allay Marshall's concerns. The airmen themselves stepped yet closer to a deal in July when they presented a modified production schedule, which preserved the essential bombardment-first strategy while paring the increases in bomber building. Finally in September Marshall approved the basic plan outlined in

AWPD-1, and the document became the fundamental guide for America's war effort in the air.[77]

Although Pete Quesada did not take part in these war preparations, he was aware of the plan's central contours. Spaatz's group occupied a suite of rooms across the hall from Quesada's liaison office, and the major had known most committee members for years. In visits at the drinking fountain, lunch at the officers' mess, and casual conversations in the hall, Quesada learned of the strategy sessions, Marshall's criticisms, and the ensuing compromise plan.

Mostly, however, Quesada focused on the possibility of an operational command, a prospect that Arnold had dangled before him since their return from England. The Army's rapid mobilization in the summer of 1941 was producing a new air unit every week, forcing Arnold to look to deserving junior officers for squadron and group commands that usually went to more senior flyers. By July it was only a matter of time before Quesada, with more than a dozen years' good service, received a command. When an acute shortage of lieutenant colonels and colonels developed, Quesada's chance to lead became imminent.[78]

In late July Arnold gave Quesada command of the Thirty-third Fighter Group at Mitchell Field, Long Island. His orders sent Quesada to New York almost immediately, and the posting could not have made him happier. After all those years as a staff officer, flying aide, or executive assistant, he at last had command of an actual flying unit. Better still, the Thirty-third flew the P-40, an innovative fighter that had just replaced the P-36 as the Air Corps's best pursuit ship. Since his training days, Quesada had enjoyed the challenges of smaller planes more than the demands of large aircraft. After saying good-bye to his mother, with whom he had lived while in Washington, Quesada headed north, tracing exactly the route he had taken in 1934 at the outset of the air-mail mission. The journey reminded him of that whole fiasco, and as he arrived at Mitchell Field in early August, he hoped it would not be an omen of things to come.[79]

The Thirty-third's executive officer was William Momyer, and that, at least, was good news for Quesada. The two had known each other since 1933, when Momyer was ferrying Douglas MacArthur around and Quesada was flying for Trubee Davison. Like Quesada, Momyer

spent most of the 1930s as somebody's pilot, and the common background engendered a kind of fraternity between the two men. Much
more than that, though, Momyer was an intelligent and efficient officer,
destined to play a prominent role in World War II and beyond. With
that sort of executive officer, Quesada was sure to benefit from a capable
support staff.[80]

Their first duty was to familiarize the pilots with the P-40s. Only one
third of Quesada's group had already received the new planes, but in
the months ahead the entire unit would get its birds. The P-40 represented the air arm's biggest single technological leap in pursuit ships
since the introduction of the P-26 ten years before, and only a few in the
group, including Quesada, had ever flown the plane. Learning its characteristics would require thorough ground and aerial instruction, and
Quesada hoped to proceed with caution.[81]

But as summer turned to fall, operational commanders throughout
the air arm came under increasing pressure to ready their units. Relations with Japan were deteriorating rapidly, and most officers infused a
new sense of urgency into military preparedness. On 17 November the
War Department told Quesada to plan for deployment to Hawaii in the
middle of December, and to "complete the P-40 phase-in by 1 December." The order meant a tight schedule, one unimaginable in peacetime.
In late 1941, however, the nation was running short on time and everyone scrambled to meet the demands of war.[82]

The attack on Pearl Harbor plunged the United States into the fray.
The Japanese bombing placed high demands on military mobilization,
and Hap Arnold decided against sending an East Coast fighter unit to
the Pacific. To him, it made more sense to send the Thirteenth Pursuit
Group, already at March Field in California, to Honolulu. Also, the
German declaration of war against America on 11 December had
heightened concern about Nazi harassment off the Atlantic coast. The
Thirty-third was needed right in its own backyard, and on 21 December Arnold ordered Quesada's group to Philadelphia to serve as that
city's air defense force. There, Quesada's pilots would also help Coast
Artillery units, the Navy, and the Coast Guard protect the nation's Eastern seaboard.[83]

From the outset, the deployment to Philadelphia reflected the disarray of the war's early operations. Luftwaffe planes had as great a chance of reaching the moon as of flying all the way to American in 1941, but political and civilian pressure required a strong and combined defensive effort along the East Coast. Years later, Quesada recalled the endeavor in Philadelphia as "a little bit foolish. There we all were, thinking how strenuously we had to defend the United States, when in reality Hitler then could not have mounted an attack any better than Joe Blow in Thailand." This was a sentiment echoed by Quesada's successor in Philadelphia, who believed "We wasted an awful lot of effort on that—the air defense mission."[84]

The whole affair might have been comical had it not produced tragedy. By February the Coastal Artillery was zealously playing searchlights on any and every plane in the air, and Quesada feared for his inexperienced pilots in the new P-40s. He asked Brigadier General Sanderford Jarman, the local artillery commander, to change the searchlight protocol. When Jarman dismissed the Air Corps major and told him to do a "better job training" his men, Quesada cabled the air staff in Washington to intercede in the dispute. Before they could respond, however, disaster struck. On a dark night in early June two young pilots were approaching Philadelphia from an Atlantic patrol. Coastal spotlights blinded the small planes and disoriented the flyers, and just three miles from their landing field, the two collided and plunged to earth.[85]

The deaths infuriated Quesada. They were his first soldiers killed, and writing to the next of kin "was the hardest thing I ever did during the whole war." As a sad feature of the requirements of command, Quesada would become almost used to such duty by war's end, but in early 1942 it was hard to relay the senseless deaths of two youngsters to parents and wives. Three days after the accident and still full of anger, Quesada issued a written order banning the searchlights. No Germans could possibly be overhead and every plane, he directed, should be assumed to be friendly.[86]

The directive represented a serious encroachment on Jarman's command prerogatives and put Quesada at direct odds with the general. Incensed, Jarman sought to court-martial the brash major. News of the affair quickly reached the War Department, where George Marshall was busy with the work of world war and had little time for petty squabbles. In late June, the Chief of Staff sent his inspector-general to investigate the matter. The inspector concluded that Quesada had indeed acted in haste and without proper authority, but added that Jarman had been wrong, too, in his stubborn use of searchlights. In the end, the inspector recommended that the case go no further.

Marshall took the report under advisement and made up his own mind. He viewed the potential court-martial as an absurd distraction at a critical time, and rebuked both Quesada and Jarman. But more than any other senior Army leader, Marshall appreciated air power's potential and, from the days when Quesada was his pilot, knew the major as a bright, energetic officer. Moreover, Marshall understood that the war ahead would require the stamina of young officers. "Warfare today," he constantly reminded his own staff, "is not a game for the unimaginative plodder . . . It will take a great deal of vigor in order to lead the vast Army we are starting to build up."[87]

The Chief of Staff did not want to confine Quesada to the backwaters of command. He ordered the spotlights turned off, and quickly jumped Quesada through three ranks, making him a one-star general by the fall of 1942. After warning the new general to avoid provocative acts, he sent Quesada back to Mitchell Field to activate the First Air Defense Wing. In just months, according to the activation orders, Marshall planned to deploy the wing to North Africa, where a battle of major proportions was already brewing.[88]

Years later Quesada downplayed Marshall's support, seeing his jump to a brigadier general as a natural function of the Army's incredible growth. Indeed, in the preceding two years, air-arm expansion plans had grown from a 45-group program to a 115-group program. Subsequently it grew to a 224-group program, and finally to a 274-group program in September of 1942. To a great extent, Quesada believed that advancement to major commands was natural for "experienced officers who had at least a modicum of competence." But if some officers were quickly promoted at the beginning of the war, most were not. Quesada was among the select few, and in that summer of 1942 he went once again to Long Island—site of his only operational duty in fifteen years—to begin his wartime service in earnest.[89]

The short period after his return from Argentina had been a watershed in Quesada's career. As his mother pinned a silver star on his uniform for the first time, Quesada reflected on the irony of it all. For years, he had served general officers as aide and pilot. The duty had been difficult at times, and often demanding. As time wore on, he had tried increasingly to avoid the assignments. Still, many of the generals he had served were good officers, some were excellent, and a few were exceptional. Now a general himself, Quesada could not help but wonder about his own qualifications and preparation. How would he measure up?[90]

Yet another question begged an answer in the fall of 1942. The Army Air Force, as the air arm was now officially designated, was committing large bomber fleets to the war. Since the days of Billy Mitchell, air leaders had bet heavily on the efficacy of strategic bombardment theory. Some, including Hap Arnold, had wagered a great deal of personal and professional capital on the issue. Now these men had to justify spending billions of dollars, and the use of almost a third of the army's manpower on independent air power. To do so, they created a war plan that mirrored their beliefs and hopes, or as Pete Quesada recalled after the war, "they allowed their doctrine to become their strategy." In so doing, they reversed the traditional practice of developing doctrine from operational tests and actual war, and instead sought to fit the war into their own ideas of combat. How well would such an approach work in the vast terrain of World War II?[91]

Chapter Three

We All Learned a Hell of a Lot

THE MEDITERRANEAN. 26 JANUARY 1943. 0115 HOURS. The klaxon horn woke Pete Quesada from his first good rest since the convoy left the Staten Island piers twelve days earlier. He stumbled from his berth and staggered to the bridge, where the ship's captain informed him that a German submarine was off the port beam. As the ranking Army officer abroad the converted civilian liner USS *Ancon*, Quesada had come to know the captain well and immediately realized this was not another of the Navy's incessant drills. "What can I do?" Quesada asked. "Stay out of the way," was the hurried reply. Heeding the advice, Quesada stepped out onto the observation deck, slipped into a corner, and withdrew into his own thoughts.[1]

The continual challenges of creating a military organization had marked the month and a half since Quesada's First Air Defense Wing (ADW) had been activated. First, his 1,000-plus force had undergone daily drilling and continuous instruction in aircraft identification, radar operations, signal codes, and intelligence procedures. Then, on the voyage across the Atlantic, members of the wing attended lectures on enemy aircraft tactics and the difficulties of war in desert terrain. Throughout the six weeks, a particularly harsh winter, seasickness, and cramped space had all conspired to thwart the training. Despite these hardships, however, no U-boats or Axis planes had bothered the twenty-eight-ship flotilla. On 25 January the convoy passed into the Mediterranean Sea, and by the evening of the 26th the *Ancon* would arrive at Oran, Algeria. How ironic, Quesada thought, that the dreaded attack from beneath the waves should come less than twenty-four hours before the perilous journey's end.[2]

Muffled explosions snapped his attention back to the observation deck. A mile away an American destroyer shot depth charges into the dark sea. Again and again the sub-chaser hurled explosives at the enemy below. The men of the *Ancon* could see water spraying into the moonlight. At 0313 hours a massive air bubble burst from the sea, signaling the end of the submarine and, probably, all her crew. After what seemed like days, the *Ancon* battle-station bell fell silent. Only then did Quesada return to his cabin to toss and turn until the convoy sailed into Oran's harbor and safety some fifteen hours later.[3]

Early on 27 January Quesada left the ship and stepped into the war. Until then, his career had undoubtedly given him a balanced view of the Army Air Forces and a broad understanding of air-power precepts. But he had served just two of fifteen years in operational jobs, and this lack of regular experience had denied Quesada much practice at the subtle art of military leadership. Now with the hot desert sand and deep blue sea all around, he had to grasp both the peculiar demands of Allied coalition warfare and the difficulty of a combined air, sea, and land campaign. Looking back at the *Ancon*, he could not have known how his close brush with the submarine would foreshadow his duties in the Mediterranean, and ahead lay only the hard lessons of the arid Sahara.

But Pete Quesada would not learn alone in the sand dunes. American ground forces had been battling there since the previous November, and for the men of the New World this introduction to combat had been tumultuous at best. In fact, virtually no prewar strategist in any nation had seen the south coast of the Mediterranean as a likely place for a clash, despite its awesome history as a battleground between civilizations. Americans had always viewed continental Europe as the most probable battleground. Adolf Hitler's Germany had looked always to the west or east, to the nuisance of British capitalism or the threat of Russian Bolshevism. For its part, the Soviet Union had hoped to gain hegemony in Eastern Europe. England, in the tradition of hesitant belligerents, wanted merely to preserve the status quo. And across the world, Japan was fighting to gain control of natural and industrial resources in Asia.

As is often the case with fragile coalitions, however, there lay a loose cannon among the alliances formed for war. Italy, the weakest of the major warring nations, had seen in the gathering storm an opportunity to build an empire. Dreaming of global glory, Benito Mussolini annexed Ethiopia in 1936, spawning intermittent skirmishes with French and British forces fighting to retain their own colonies in Africa. When the European war broke out in 1939, Hitler joined the North African fray as a member of the Axis Pact. The Japanese attack on Pearl Harbor made the war truly global, and transformed the North African combat from a strange backwater war to an important contest for desert land routes that would bridge the Allied efforts in the western and eastern hemispheres. Thus began the seesaw battles between Erwin Rommel's famed Afrika Korps and Bernard Montgomery's Eighth Army, with struggles like Sidi Rezegh and El Alamein filling newspapers in the distant capitals of both sides.[4]

As in the ancient battles of the Roman Empire, the great expanse of Africa demanded more and more resources from those who wished to control the Sahara. On 8 November 1942 the Allies launched Operation TORCH, an invasion of Northwest Africa meant to sandwich the Axis forces between the TORCH troops in the West and Montgomery's Eighth Army then closing from the East. The hope was to squeeze Rommel's troops out of the continent, and under Lieutenant General Dwight "Ike" Eisenhower the plan went well at first. By late November the Allies were just twelve miles from Tunis, a critical port and a nucleus of enemy activity. In December, however, massive and experienced German reinforcements thwarted the drive, and the rainy season helped to stall the advance dead in its tracks. On Christmas Eve, Eisenhower abandoned plans to expunge Axis forces from Africa before winter. Instead, he tucked in for the season and waited for spring. The campaign could now be nothing but a long and arduous battle.[5]

The Tunisian standoff produced a crisis of confidence among the Allies. Montgomery was the most vocally critical of numerous British soldiers aghast at the poor showing of the American forces. Watching from his own triumphant march across the Libyan frontier, he declared that "The party in Tunisia is a complete dog's breakfast. . . . Ike knows nothing whatever about how to make war or to fight battles; he should be kept right away from all that business if we want to win this war." Eisenhower publicly protested such criticism, but to his closest friends the Supreme Commander wondered if the indictment was just. "I think the best way to describe our operations to date," he wrote one, "is that they have violated every recognized principle of war, are in conflict with all operational and logistical methods laid down in textbooks, and will be condemned in their entirety by all Leavenworth and War College classes for twenty-five years." Inter-Allied bickering was so intense by January that it was the first thing Quesada heard about upon reaching North Africa. "I was aware of the discord and rather distressed by it. It resulted in complete chaos in North Africa."[6]

The U.S. Army Air Forces were as responsible as any combat arm for the poor showing of American forces. The air arm's prewar stress on independent bombardment rendered its pilots poorly prepared for the desert. The fundamentals of strategic bombardment and the plans of AWPD-1 had assumed an enemy with a traditional economic infrastructure, but in the desert there was no industrial base, and the lines of communication were primitive. The enemy's civilian population lay a thousand miles to the north; bombing sand piles would not break their morale or will to resist. Even Hap Arnold acknowledged that "TORCH offered about as poor an air deal as could have been dreamed up. Practically every one of our own principles for the use of air power . . . had to be violated." He explained to Tooey Spaatz, now Eisenhower's air commander, that the basic problem was "The development of the war in just about the worst case scenario as far as our air plans are concerned." That was true enough, though the airmen should have prepared for the unexpected, because war is the last of all things to go according to plan.[7]

All this meant that close support of ground troops, not strategic bombardment, was to be the hallmark of air operations in North Africa. Predictably, the pilots were not initially up to the task. As early as December, radar difficulties and arguments over the proper relationship between air and ground units hampered the advance on Tunis. In early 1943, deficiencies in American air doctrine contributed mightily to Rommel's routing of U.S. soldiers in the battle at Kasserine Pass. As these problems mounted, Eisenhower griped about "our own air's fumbling and apparent inability to hit" German strongpoints. Arnold admitted as much, reporting to President Roosevelt that the "air participation in the North African campaign are [*sic*] still a rather difficult arrangement to work out." Following yet more reports of poor air support, Arnold promised a renewed effort to develop air-power applications to aid the desert soldiers.[8]

Despite these and other setbacks, the New Year brought restored hope. Eisenhower, buoyed by encouragement from George Marshall, determined to reorganize his troops, shake up his air forces, and launch a truly decisive assault. Like all campaigns, however, the coming battles had their own rhythm and would bring both tragedy and triumph to the Allies.

This was the situation when Quesada set sole to sand in Oran on 27 January 1943. Eisenhower's command rearrangements immediately affected his wing. The First Air Defense Wing had been scheduled to provide coastal and port defense across North Africa, but now headquarters higher in the chain of command commandeered Quesada's combat elements for the impending spring offensive. Three hours after disembarking, the wing consisted of a mere hundred administrative and support personnel. Adding insult to injury, the Oran port captain refused to yield important space on the congested harbor roads to noncombatants, and made Quesada's men walk two miles to waiting trucks.[9]

"With right face and forward march," one officer remembered, "we turned our backs on our 13-day voyage with regret and relief, and marched down the decks toward things to come." In full pack, they boarded their vehicles, traveled to the city's train station, waited four hours, entrained, and arrived at the desert village of Ste. Barbe du

Thékat at 1800 hours. Then they marched another five miles to their assigned bivouac area. "Thoroughly exhausted and hungry, sleep came easily that night without benefit of mess or tents," recorded the wing diarist.[10]

Things only worsen in the following weeks. In seven days the wing was in Casablanca to help defend that port from air attack. With no aircraft, however, they could do little more than sound the alarm whenever Axis raiders appeared on the horizon. Very few German planes ventured that deep over hostile territory, and Quesada quickly grew discouraged with his limited role. "I was kind of a misfit to be frank about it. I didn't have any substantial command, and they did not know what the hell to do with me or my men." Soon, he was joking to friends that he wished he "were back in Long Island as I understand the place is overrun with widows." After further thought, the bachelor general remained frustrated about the war but changed his mind about Long Island: "There is, of course, some local talent and I am working hard at my French hoping to be able to open negotiations with the natives."[11]

In truth, Quesada and his troops were caught in the Allied state of flux in Africa. The air arm was woefully ill-prepared to fight a desert war, and the disarray was evident everywhere. Africa's terrain and climate played havoc with equipment, especially at the airfields, where airplane tires blew from the heat and where pilots contended with short, sloping, and rough landing strips. These difficulties extracted a predictable toll, claiming more planes than actual combat losses in the first four months of 1943. On any given day, mechanical difficulties grounded half the aircraft. Even simple biology brought misery. Diarrhea developed at a disproportionate rate among the airmen, and for one group, the affliction "became so serious at one point that all activities, including flying, were severely curtailed." In such circumstances, the word "abort" surely took on a new meaning.[12]

Together, these problems represented more than the challenges of an army in early operations. Air planners, busy sketching high-tech strategy with big bombers, had failed to address the mundane and ageless campaign burdens of weather, terrain, and disease. Eisenhower himself believed that inattention to these stubborn but predictable problems had affected the scope of air activities, and to solve many of these difficulties he instituted sweeping changes in his air forces.

In February Eisenhower created the Mediterranean Air Command and made Air Marshal Sir Arthur Tedder its leader. Below this umbrella organization sat the Northwest African Air Forces (NAAF), commanded by Tooey Spaatz. Spaatz, in turn, split the NAAF into five subordinate commands: the Northwest African Strategic Air Force (NASAF), the Northwest African Tactical Air Force (NATAF), the Northwest African Coastal Air Force (NACAF), a training command, and a reconnaissance wing. By mixing U.S. and British forces, these commands set a radical precedent in Allied cooperation. It was a drastic move, but one that most senior leaders deemed necessary because of the manifold duties required of aircraft in the Sahara. Time alone would tell how well the revolution in command would work.[13]

Choosing leaders for the combined commands presented a sticky problem. In mid-March, Spaatz convened all his general officers in the Libyan outback to parcel out the assignments. There, nationalism engendered ugly competition for the best posts. Americans lobbied for the choice jobs based on their numerical superiority in men and equipment, while British officers countered that they had a considerable edge in wartime experience. At one point, Quesada challenged the Britons' reasoning, asking the English leaders if "the experience to which you refer is Dunkirk, Singapore, Norway, Crete, and Greece?" These were the major British setbacks in the war to date, and Quesada's comment infuriated the British. "Take it easy, Pete," Spaatz whispered for all to hear, "everything is all right." Quesada's impetuous and contentious personality could be assets to a combat leader, Spaatz knew, but the British were right: the younger Americans needed seasoning in war.[14]

Having failed to obtain a consensus among the officers, Spaatz made the command assignments himself. He gave the strategic forces to Major General James Doolittle, the tactical units to Air Vice Marshal Arthur "Maori" Coningham, the Coastal Air Force to Air Vice Marshal Hugh Lloyd, the training command to Major General John Cannon, and the reconnaissance wing to the president's son, Colonel Elliot Roosevelt. Each command, Spaatz decreed, would name a deputy commander from the nation opposite that of the commander to preserve a sense of equity among the forces.[15]

On 15 April Spaatz invited Lloyd, the new Coastal Air Force commander, to meet American generals for the express purpose of choosing a subordinate. Subsequent war events buried Hugh Lloyd's name under a pantheon of British Field Marshals and Air Marshals, but in the spring of 1943 he was perhaps the best-known British soldier in North Africa save Montgomery. He had been the commanding air officer on Malta when that island fortress shone as the Empire's only beacon in the dark early days of the war. On his return to London in late 1942, King George VI had knighted him, Churchill had praised him, and admiring countrymen had mobbed him. He then traveled to Washington, where Franklin Roosevelt found him "one of the more charming Londoners I have met," an impression shared by many War Department generals. In fact, Lloyd's congenial tour around the American capital contrasted starkly with the ill will displayed among the Allies on the battlefield.[16]

From America, Lloyd had made his way to Africa, arriving on nearly the same day as Quesada. "Shortly after my arrival in Algiers to start NACAF," Lloyd recalled, "General Spaatz asked me to dinner with a dozen or so generals to select one as my deputy. I indicated to Spaatz my liking for one of the older ones present. He had other ideas, and told me of the attributes of one of the younger, if not the youngest, one. He prevailed on me to choose that man." That man was Pete Quesada. Like others, Spaatz had seen in Lloyd a mature soldier, and had concluded that Quesada could learn from such a mentor. Indeed he would. Quesada's long association with Spaatz had just paid its first wartime dividend.[17]

The Coastal Air Force was an obscure yet critical command. Spaatz had assigned it a diverse list of duties, including air defense behind the active front, operation of the theater's air communication systems, and convoy defense and patrol over the Mediterranean. In short, Coastal was to help defend Allied logistics and interdict Axis supply lines. These were vitally important tasks in a battle where soldiers depended to an unprecedented degree on the sinews of war, and where everything—food, arms, ammunition—had to traverse at least a sea, often an ocean, and sometimes a continent before reaching them in the Sahara. To accomplish its diverse tasks, Coastal received an assortment of planes: three Royal Air Force fighter wings, two American fighter groups, Quesada's old air defense wing, a B-26 medium bomber squadron, four torpedo bomber squadrons, and an amphibious aircraft detachment. In all, Lloyd controlled some 400 aircraft and 5,000 men stretched along Africa's northwestern coastline.[18]

Quesada reported to Lloyd in Algiers on 27 April, thrilled to be part of the shooting war. "My new job is a break for me," he wrote friends, "it is certainly bigger and permits me to occasionally be in the thick of things." Resolving to make the most of his good luck, Quesada spent the first weeks dutifully inspecting the American units assigned to Coastal. Instead of making a good impression during this initial tour, however, Quesada often displayed an unbecoming bossiness and conceit. The ugly side of inexperience now showed in him, confirming for Lloyd why Tooey Spaatz had wanted the young American under the older man's guidance.[19]

Quesada had an especially nasty brush with the American Eighty-first Fighter Group. They were veterans of the Tunisian campaign, stationed at a Bône airfield, and they represented the single biggest U.S. unit in Lloyd's command. Quesada flew there for an inspection on 30 April. The inspection went well until Quesada suggested that the group commander, Colonel Kenneth Wade, relieve Major Alex Jamieson, one of the squadron commanders. "Why?" Wade asked. "He's phlegmatic," Quesada replied. Wade stood his ground. "Jamieson is the quiet type, all right, but he always gets the job done, inspires loyalty, and I am too short of qualified personnel to summarily fire someone in a critically important position." There the matter sat as Quesada whisked away in his P-38, silently stewing over Wade's rebuff.

Two weeks later, Quesada's operations officer, Lieutenant Colonel Phil Klein, literally flew out of the blue and into Bône with orders to replace Wade and relieve Jamieson. As the popular Wade bade the group good-bye, he wondered what had happened. Reporting back at Algiers, Quesada told Wade he had "failed to follow specific orders." That was a misstatement of Quesada's earlier advice regarding Jamieson, but colonels rarely won those arguments with generals, so Wade reluctantly stepped aside.[20]

Back at Bône, Jamieson rendered outstanding service before Klein could find a suitable replacement for him. In three short weeks, his squadron tracked and helped sink a U-Boat, successfully defended an attack on the Algiers port, and downed numerous German fighters. The performance was good enough to garner personal congratulations from Lloyd, and Quesada travelled with his boss to add his own praise.

By then, rank-and-file pilots had come to resent Quesada's overbearing disposition. Almost to a man they displayed a genuine aversion to the American general. "He flew in with that toothy grin which always seemed to be contrived and phony and took all the credit for himself," one officer recalled. "General Quesada was an egotistical S.O.B," added Lieutenant Richard Carter, "great on public relations but didn't give a damn about junior officers or enlisted men." One pilot was especially succinct with his judgment that day: "Quesada was an unmitigated ass." Together, these impressions were the just rewards for a raw general learning to lead men in harm's way.[21]

Alex Jamieson managed to save his job that spring, but Wade's relief remained on his permanent service record. Fifty years later, Wade still harbored bitterness about the whole affair: "I thought Quesada was opinionated, self-serving, played favorites, and was unduly biased against certain officers junior to him, particularly West Pointers like myself."[22]

Relations down the ranks were not Quesada's only problem in his early tenure at Coastal Air Force. Soon after arriving in Algiers he and Lloyd began quarreling over lower-echelon organization. Initially, Lloyd had planned to place a British commander with an American deputy at each combined unit, a scheme Quesada knew would deny his countrymen a chance to lead even the smallest of elements. After Lloyd refused to modify the plan, Quesada complained directly to Spaatz, a move the British general viewed as an unseemly breach in the chain of command. For his part, Tooey Spaatz loathed national parochialism and told both men he was "disappointed that [this] has arisen." After repeated failures to mediate the dispute, Spaatz ordered both men to his headquarters, curtly telling Quesada to "have a damn good reason if you cannot make it." In the end, Quesada's arguments for placing some Americans in command positions carried the day, but not without consequences. Following the incident, Lloyd wrote his wife that he "should have taken that older general to be my assistant." That would be difficult now, however.[23]

By early May the two men were barely on speaking terms. Fortunately, Coastal's forces were sprawled along the entire Northwest African coast and the command's efficient operation required a main headquarters near the Allies' administrative center and an advanced headquarters close to the front lines. As summer came to the desert, Lloyd and Quesada reached a working solution to their personal animosity. Lloyd would stay in Algiers to direct the main headquarters while Quesada would run Coastal's forward command post. For Quesada, the compromise proved fortuitous. Away from the office intrigue that always seemed to spell trouble for him, the young general could now focus on operations, and witness up close the details, skills, equipment, and personnel that drove twentieth-century warfare.[24]

On 6 May, shortly after establishing his first advance command post, Quesada traveled to the field of the Royal Air Force's 323 Group. That evening, during mess, the base's flight siren blared into the air. Rushing to a small communications hut, Quesada watched as a radar operator coolly set a deadly rendezvous between British Spitfires and German destroyers steaming for Tunis: "Red M, Hazard calling, Vector 275-two-seven-five for 110-one-one-zero miles, over." At 2015 hours the planes reported the ships in sight. They quickly sank one and damaged two. The remaining four vessels slipped through the air screen, but not before Allied naval forces were alerted to their presence. The Germans were blocked. None of them reached Tunis with their vital caches of fuel and ammunition for Rommel's men.[25]

That was but one in a series of strikes where Coastal planes helped intercept critical German supplies as the land campaign in Africa entered its final stages. Hitler's forces in Africa needed some 69,000 tons of material per month for the fight, but in April and May just 14,000 tons managed to break through the Allied blockade. Although Anglo-American naval forces were largely responsible for cutting enemy supply lines, Coastal's planes added an aerial dimension to the effort. Quesada took pride in this, his first notable combat duty since his arrival. "We began to think any ship in the pond was ours for the taking, and we took great care not to let a single god-dammed one through. If a ship got through, we failed."[26]

The mere trickle of support reaching the Germans finally compelled the Axis troops in Africa to cease formal resistance. By early May, Allied troops had surrounded the last of the enemy soldiers in the port of

Tunis, and on the tenth the Germans surrendered. In the end, shortages were so acute that some high-ranking Wehrmacht officers were able to escape capture only after finding a lone barrel of aviation fuel that had washed in from the sea.

With the fight in North Africa now over, the Allies prepared to chase the fleeing enemy across the Mediterranean. Eisenhower's strategists quickly laid plans for an invasion of the ancient island of Sicily, an operation that would stretch their shipping resources to the limit and raise critical questions of tactics and logistics. Air cover for the invasion fleet was a particularly thorny issue, since most aircraft based in North Africa lacked enough range to protect a navy off the Sicilian shores. After Washington and London denied Eisenhower's request for eight aircraft carriers to provide the all-important air cover, the Supreme Commander ordered his forces to capture the small island of Pantelleria and the tiny Pelagian atoll. Not much more than volcanic outcrops, their airfields would nevertheless put fighters well within range of southern Sicily, resolving the Allied air-base dilemma.[27]

In late May Eisenhower gave his air forces carte blanche to pummel the islands into submission before an expedition was to storm Pantelleria on 11 June. Airmen, eager to vindicate their theories of independent bombardment after the North African campaign, jumped at the chance to "bomb the hell out of them." Hap Arnold told Tooey Spaatz to "spare no quarters," and the NAAF commander designated the bulk of his planes for the task. In all, over 1,100 aircraft would fly 7,000-plus sorties and drop 6,200 tons of bombs on the small outcrops of land. If this new experiment in strategic bombardment, code-named CORKSCREW, failed, it surely would not be for lack of effort.[28]

At first glance, Pantelleria offered an ideal laboratory to test the limits of air power. This Italian Gibraltar boasted a wealth of natural and manufactured defenses, including a coastline of cliffs, over 100 large-bore guns, a good airstrip, an eighty-plane hangar carved deep into rock, repair facilities, an underground electric plant, and enough supplies for a protracted siege. Yet the little island was isolated and its 10,000 troops were of low quality. To a man, they suffered from poor morale because Rome and Berlin had repeatedly told them to expect no outside help if they were attacked. In fact, Germany had already evacuated all but seventy-eight of its soldiers from the islands. In sum, though the Pantelleria forces were equipped to mount a vigorous defense against air attack, their poor fighting spirit made them an unconvincing lot to prove or disprove the efficacy of bombing.[29]

Quesada, eager himself for a respite from important but routine patrol duty, grabbed the opportunity for "some real action against determined foes." As dawn broke on 31 May, he turned over the cold engine of a P-40 and lifted into the surly sky with the flyers of the 350th group. Assigned to escort B-17s, the fighter planes reached Pantelleria at 0715 hours. "There were uncounted numbers of friendly aircraft—P-40s, B-25s, B-26s, Fortresses, P-38s, and Spits [British Spitfires] in the area," one pilot recounted. "A-36s were dive bombing the coast defenses, the bombers were laying a pattern that made the Northeast section of the island appear like a volcano." Within minutes, the entire atoll was lost in smoke. "You could not even tell if you were over land or sea," Quesada remembered.[30]

The carnage from a concentrated air raid was truly appalling. As the pilots turned home they mulled over the destructive firepower of 600 planes aimed at so small a target. Most were sure the garrison would soon fall under such attack. Said one: "We relished the role of reducing Pantelleria to cinders and daily expected the white flag of surrender."[31]

Quesada flew three more missions over the embattled Italian island in the next days. In the catbird seat, he witnessed the most complete air assault the world had ever known. In the week before 11 June, American and British pilots mounted 4,973 sorties and dropped over eight million pounds of bombs on Pantelleria. Sometimes German FW-190s rose to defend the place, but their efforts were merely a nuisance to the hundreds of Allied planes in the sky. When on 6 June the Pantelleria commander informed Rome that he could not "hold out much longer in face of air attacks," NAAF leaders grew confident that "the island will give up without action by ground forces." Even Quesada now figured that there was "no way the Boche can continue to endure the stuff we throw at him day after day."[32]

Instead, the Axis forces dug deeper into the rock and survived. They twice refused Eisenhower's surrender offers, and on 11 June the Supreme Commander committed ground forces to Pantelleria. Assault troops sailed into the island's sole harbor at 0900 hours and prepared to disembark. At that point, the defenders at last hoisted a white flag over their airfield and quietly laid down their arms. At 1125 hours the Allied force waded ashore free from attack, the only casualty being a British infantryman bitten by a jackass—a male donkey! By nightfall, the entire place was in Allied hands. In effect, active resistance on Pantelleria ceased the moment the amphibious forces arrived.[33]

Next, Eisenhower prepared to take Lampedusa, the largest of the Pelagian Islands and the only one with a decent airstrip. Lampedusa had absorbed far less bombardment than Pantelleria, and with 4,300 troops, two tank platoons, four minefields, and thirty-three coastal guns, was just as capable of a fight. Instead, in one of the more incredible stories of the war, the troops there surrendered to a lone British flyer who had mistakenly landed on the island the day before the planned invasion.

RAF pilot Peter Cohen had gotten lost and set down on the small sliver of land. When enemy soldiers surrounded his bird he figured his war days were over. The Italian commander had other ideas, however. First he ordered Cohen's plane gassed up, and then he sent the wayward pilot back to the Allied lines with a surrender letter. In short order, the other Pelagian islets gave up, too, and Peter Cohen became known as the hero who single-handedly captured Lampedusa. In reality surrender, not capture, was the keynote of this remarkable tale.[34]

Operation CORKSCREW quickly became a mere footnote as the war rushed on toward Sicily, but it exercised a profound influence on future fighting. For air-power enthusiasts, it solidified strategic bombardment's place in modern war. In Washington, Hap Arnold rejoiced at CORKSCREW's outcome, and in Africa, Tooey Spaatz declared the old debate about bombardment dead. "The application of the air [forces] available to us can reduce to the point of surrender any first-class nation now in existence," Spaatz wrote a week after Pantelleria fell. For him, the only mistake in the operation had been to place "air as a secondary power to the ground forces and not giving them the top command when air success is first in importance." Another pilot summed up well the sentiments of his fellow airmen when he stated that "the islands surrendered to bombing before a landing could take place." Although ground officers had rarely shared the conviction of their cousins in the air, they too were inclined to support the consensus that strategic bombardment had been essential in CORKSCREW. After all, the easy conquest ensured adequate close air support for the invasion of Sicily, now scheduled for 10 July.[35]

But there was reason to temper the prevailing enthusiasm for bombardment. First, the bombings had not sapped enemy morale on the islands; that had already been low. Beyond that, Pantelleria's weak esprit de corps had made for sloppy defensive preparations, including poorly-camouflaged batteries and pillboxes, above-ground communication lines, and virtually no dug-in field fortifications. Yet, despite these advantages over a hapless enemy, the air attack had not destroyed the citadel. Less than 5 percent of the bombs had fallen within a hundred yards of their targets, few big guns had been destroyed, and even the occasional direct hit had failed to damage Pantelleria's underground hangars. Tooey Spaatz privately relayed these shortcomings to Arnold, telling him that the "material damage done to the defenses is not as great as might be expected, particularly to the emplaced batteries." Moreover, it remained an undeniable, if inconvenient, fact that Pantelleria had not surrendered until ground troops had appeared on the horizon. The Lampedusa garrison had conceded the battle before assault forces had approached its coast, of course, but their surrender to Cohen revealed that the defenders had been willing, indeed eager, to give up even before the air attacks began.[36]

In truth, troops on neither island would have mounted much of a defense regardless of the Allied air assault. An unbiased review of CORKSCREW, then, would have left unanswered the central question of bombardment theory: Can air power defeat a determined enemy? Even if the bombers had truly coerced the islands to surrender, rarely in a modern conflict can an army devote so much time and so many resources to capture so little. Years later and with the benefit of hindsight, Pete Quesada summed up the whole affair best when he said that "CORKSCREW was operational wasted effort." Yet in the summer of 1943, bomber barons took great heart and placed great stock in the experiment, and marched onward, their faith in independent air action restored.[37]

Once established on the conquered islands, the Allies resumed preparation for the siege of Sicily. Of military importance since Romans had used it as a stepping-stone to hegemony in the Mediterranean, Sicily assumed new significance in the age of airplanes. Eisenhower hoped to use the island as a huge launching pad, staging raids from its runways into the heart of the Third Reich. Accordingly, his plan, code-named HUSKY, aimed for a quick capture of airfields and control of the major ports of Palermo and Catania. The whole affair required a combined force that would have made Sicily's ancient god Hercules proud: over 1,200 vessels, 160,000 men, 600 tanks, and 14,000 vehicles. These resources represented the bulk of Allied assets at that time, and Eisenhower placed a high premium on their protection. The Strategic, Tactical, and Coastal Air Forces were to provide bombing, close support, and convoy cover respectively. In all, 4,000 planes would fill the skies to support and safeguard the amphibious armada.[38]

As higher commanders worked out broad policy, Lloyd and Quesada readied Coastal for its convoy-cover role. In Algiers, Lloyd concentrated on logistical requirements while Quesada focused on day-to-day operations from his new command post on Lampedusa. The sheer number of Allied warships needing protection strained Coastal's resources severely, and Lloyd managed to snare another RAF group and four additional torpedo squadrons for the task. Even so, Coastal pilots flew more operational hours in the run-up to HUSKY than at any other time while Quesada served in the Mediterranean. The busy schedule was in part the product of anticipation: Lloyd and Quesada knew that the growing fleet and supply convoys were tempting targets for Axis planes and submarines, and both men expected enemy attacks.[39]

They did not have to wait long. At 1525 hours on 27 June, Coastal radar screens sweeping off Cape Bon went bright first with dozens and then with hundreds of contacts. Quesada was called to the Lampedusa radar trailer, and quickly concluded that this was not just another German reconnaissance mission. This was a serious attempt to intercept convoy TEDWORTH, a forty-two-ship flotilla then in the Sicilian Straits. At 1535 hours, he dispatched planes of RAF 242 Group stationed at Bizerte and Tunis and continued to monitor the radar. Forty minutes later the first waves of German Junker-88s and British Spitfires clashed in the sky over TEDWORTH. Boldly flying into the attack formations, the Spits forced the Germans off their bombing runs. No ordnance found its mark on the ships below.[40]

While the British pilots filled the airwaves with cheers, another set of enemy aircraft appeared on the radar screens along Cape Bon. Quesada dispatched P-40s from the 52nd Fighter Group at Sousse, and wondered how many birds the Axis would throw at the convoy. This time, Focke-Wulf-109 fighter-bombers came in low and alone. Reacting to the new tactics, the P-40s challenged each run. For the second time in two hours, Allied flyers repulsed the attack with no loss to TEDWORTH. The Coastal Air Force was batting 1.000, but the game was not over.[41]

A third German surge gathered over the horizon as the sun dipped lower. Quesada now faced a dilemma. His planes were low on fuel and no other front-line fighters were within striking range of the vulnerable convoy. If he kept his defenders over the ships, many pilots might crash into the sea; if he sent them home, the ships would be alone. Scanning the dull green radarscopes, Quesada hesitated only a moment, then decided. The airborne pilots would defend the convoy until the last possible moment before returning in pairs, while the ragtag headquarters squadron on Lampedusa took off and sprinted to the scene. A few P-40s, some P-39s, Beaufighters, and Quesada's own P-38 then hurriedly rolled off the island tarmac, racing the third wave of German fighters to the convoy.

Attackers and defenders met over TEDWORTH, and the day's third major dogfight ensued. Two German bombs did some damage to ships this time, but when it was all over more than 220 Axis planes in three assaults had failed to harm any ship seriously. For their part, Coastal's pilots had shot down eight birds to just two P-39s lost. As dark settled over the blue sea, the Lampedusa-based planes went home satisfied with the day's work.[42]

The successful defense of convoy TEDWORTH compelled a shift in the Axis' Mediterranean strategy. German planes continued to harass Allied convoys, but never again did they seriously challenge the Allied fleet. From that moment, Axis strategists preferred to harness their air assets for special occasions, offering only token resistance to regular Allied shipping. The Anglo-Americans had won the battle of the Mediterranean. The observation of one Coastal pilot best told the story after TEDWORTH: "Whenever our patrols turned to pursuit, the Jerries always went home."[43]

June 27 also marked a personal watershed for Quesada. No amount of peacetime service could have prescribed a decision in those moments in the radar trailer. In those moments he had been noone's aide or attaché; he had been a war commander. Although the United States had entered the fight with a cadre of senior generals who had gained substantial experience in the last war, most junior leaders were too young to have seen command service in the Great War. Some, like Quesada, did not serve at all in 1917–1918. The performance of American tactical leadership in World War II depended on the aggregate outcome of these individual and isolated baptisms by fire. Tooey Spaatz understood this, and told Quesada the TEDWORTH defense "reflects great credit on your men and you personally. . . . I am very pleased with your progress." Clearly, one day did not make a leader, but Quesada had won a step to a higher tier in the Allied war effort. Starting on 30 June, messages between Spaatz, Arnold, and Ira Eaker, then commanding the Eighth Air Force in England, contained discussions of promotions for their young friend. For the moment, Pete Quesada had faced the burden of battle decision and he had won.[44]

Air attacks, however, were not the only way for the Axis to interdict Allied shipping. After TEDWORTH, Germany relied increasingly on submarines, sending no less than twenty-seven U-boats into the sea around Sicily. The Coastal Air Force reacted to this by intensifying its patrol activity, which reached a summertime peak in the two weeks before HUSKY. In that period, Coastal Beaufighters and B-26s tracked twenty-five U-boats, sighted seven, attacked five, and sank two.[45]

Lloyd's efforts to shield HUSKY shipping were a resounding success. From 5 to 10 July, his pilots flew 6,174 sorties and protected 1,068 ships. The Allies lost only six vessels. Three times in five days Quesada flew patrol missions with the flyers, and from the sky the fleets approaching Sicily were an awesome sight. The great capital ships HMS *Nelson* and HMS *Rodney*, the carrier HMS *Indomitable*, HMS *Howe* and HMS *King George V*, together with hundreds of cruisers, destroyers and troop ships, moved in unison toward the target beaches. Lessons learned in the TORCH operations had helped to create a complex communications and recognition system that coordinated the air, sea, and ground units on the approach. Ship foredecks were marked in white code letters, all convoys floated large barrage balloons on 2,000-

foot tethers, each vessel had an air-defense zone within which she could fire on any airplane, and intricate schedules dictated when and where one flight would replace another above the ships.[46]

On 9 July Quesada returned to Tunisia to monitor Coastal Air Force's air-sea rescue operations for 10 July, D-Day. At first only the sporadic comments of bored Beaufighter pilots interrupted the steady drone of empty airwaves. Then, just after midnight, the VHF crackled with an excited American voice. "New Box, New Box, New Box, from Hazard M, from Hazard M. Bearing for Kairouan base . . . left motor shot up and gravy very low. New Box . . . from Hazard M. If you read me, give me a call, New Box, over to you, over." One of the C-47 troop carriers, returning from an ambitious and botched airborne drop behind enemy lines, was in trouble.[47]

"Get that fix in—fast!" the radio controller yelled. Quickly, the signal crew fed weather information, altitude, and the radar bearings of Hazard M into a primitive computer that calculated aircraft positions. Armed with this readout, the deputy controller lunged at the plot table with parallel rules and a compass. Seconds later, he was talking to Hazard M. "Vector 275, 110 miles. 35 minutes at indicated air speed 130." A relieved pilot replied, "R-Roger, New Box, Roger. Hazard M, over and out."[48]

Other C-47s then jammed the radio for help. "New Box, this is Marty L . . . Alice K here . . . Victor Ack over to you . . . New Box, Donald Beer calling. Gravy very low, can't make Field K, need fix to Monastir." The distress calls, each representing a separate navigational problem, swiftly overwhelmed the little station's capacity. Diverting half the contacts to another control squadron aptly code-named Frantic, the two radar stations handled pleas from eighty-seven lost or crippled birds in the wee hours of HUSKY. In the end, all but four found safe haven at various airfields. Throughout, Quesada sat and watched as his control squadrons performed their jobs. At 0500 hours he stepped outside the little radar hut, lay down, and went to sleep under the brightening sky.[49]

An hour later an Anglo-American force hit the Sicilian beaches with few losses. Everywhere the Italian coastal divisions folded without much resistance. In fact, only the U.S. airborne operations blotted the invasion for the Allies. In that fiasco, high winds, smoke, and a complicated flight path made it hard for C-47 pilots to position their birds over the drop zones. As a result, many paratroopers fell miles from their assigned drop sites and sustained hundreds of needless casualties. Compounding the confusion, anxious gunners on both American and British ships shot down twenty-two C-47s full of their own men.

For their part, Army Air Force pilots had been woefully unprepared for the intricate night operation. To Brigadier General Matthew Ridgeway of the Eighty-second Airborne Division, HUSKY "demonstrated beyond any doubt that the Air Force . . . cannot at present put parachute units, even as large as a battalion, within effective attack distance of a chosen drop zone at night." Had not Quesada's radarmen helped many lost planes get home, the sorry affair could have been even worse.[50]

Within a week, however, Quesada cabled Spaatz that something could be learned from the airborne debacle. "Although the operation was ill conceived and ill planned," he wrote "it has served a useful learning purpose." Specifically, the effort to direct planes to safety "showed the value of our equipment, its operational setup, and the personnel operating the equipment . . . [I do not remember] a better example of Air-Ground personnel cooperation and Air-Ground communication. Every man knew his job and knew it well." The "African Incident," as Quesada referred to it in subsequent correspondence, planted in his mind fundamental precepts of combined-arms combat. From that point on, Quesada consistently recognized the importance of signal communications and radar in tactical operations. He had added yet another building block to his understanding of war.[51]

Members of the Strategic and Tactical Air Forces were also trying to learn from their efforts to aid the Allied troops now ashore in Sicily. Despite warnings from the African fighting, close air support in July and August was not much better than it had been in January and February. Pilots flew no missions on behalf of the Seventh Army during the critical first forty-eight hours after landing, and the U.S. II Corps received no air help for another two days.

As the campaign progressed, pilots were often slow to reach their targets or got lost altogether. In some instances, flyers undershot the bomb line and attacked friendly forces; in other cases they passed up large formations of enemy troops only to be shot at by Allied guns. In time, it became increasingly evident that American air and ground forces not only were failing to work in close cooperation but were in fact hurting each other on the battlefield. "It was absolutely true that the air helped the ground in Tunisia and Sicily far less than in the World War [World War I]," wrote a disgusted Lieutenant General Leslie McNair.[52]

These difficulties aside, the Allies' overwhelming superiority on the ground won a quick victory in Sicily. By late August, the last of the defenders had fled across the Straits of Messina to mainland Italy. The Anglo-Americans had accomplished in six weeks what took the Saracens thirty-one years and the Normans a quarter of a century. Still, had the German and Allied ground forces been more evenly balanced in Sicily, the Americans would have paid a heavy price for their sloppy close air support. In the future, they would have to pay more attention to combined training and operations if they hoped to be successful.

The strains of CORKSCREW and HUSKY had exhausted the Coastal Air Force by mid-July. For six weeks the command had deferred crucial maintenance on equipment and planes, crews had operated on limited sleep, and small luxuries like hot food had become a distant memory. Lloyd's men needed a rest, and after HUSKY had moved off the beaches and into Sicily proper, they got one. From 17 July to late August the Coastal Air Force returned to the relative routine of aerial patrols and coastal defense. With most of the Mediterranean now under Allied control, even these traditional chores slackened. The quiet was a welcome change, as one pilot recalled shortly after his group moved to Sicily in early August. "It was nice to be in Sicily and out of the damned desert. Local fruit and produce made our diet outstanding, and we could at last replenish our mechanical and human stamina." The slow weeks were a deserved break for the men of Coastal Air Force, and now, in August, Quesada had but one major task to accomplish in the Mediterranean: the invasion of Italy.[53]

Although the offensive against Italy, code-named AVALANCHE, was the chronological sequel to HUSKY, a great strategic chasm separated the two assaults. Operations in North Africa and in Sicily were designed to secure global supply lines through the Mediterranean, and the Allies had accomplished as much even before the Sicilian fighting ended. The decision to attack Italy, on the other hand, was an opportunistic and pragmatic judgment call born of politics and geography. It was already too late in the year to shift Allied landing craft to England for an assault on western France, and Russia's Joseph Stalin would not brook a long pause in the Anglo-American fight against the Axis powers. His own forces had shouldered the brunt of Hitler's juggernaut for two years, and if the Allies could not invade across the English Channel, he demanded action somewhere else. Thus Italy, just miles from where thousands of Allied soldiers now stood, beckoned. As August came to a close, Eisenhower settled on a plan that included a diversionary landing across the Straits of Messina by British troops on 3 September. Six days later, American forces would make the main landings at Salerno. As a corollary goal, Ike hoped that AVALANCHE would provoke Italy's surrender.

By this point in the war, the invasions of both North Africa and Sicily had defined clearer roles for air power in amphibious operations. Starting in mid-August, the Strategic Air Force smashed port facilities, marshaling yards, and transportation hubs to prevent an Axis build-up near the landing areas. Once troops were ashore, the Tactical Air Force planned to provide close support on the model of the Tunisian and Sicilian campaigns. Throughout the operation, the Coastal Air Force reenacted its role of convoy cover, this time for more than 600 ships in sixteen convoys. As with HUSKY, Lloyd received an assortment of additional planes for his tasks, bringing Coastal's operational strength to some 850 birds. The old troop transport USS *Ancon*, the ship that had brought Pete Quesada to Africa, was now a floating communications center and served as the control ship coordinating air-sea-ground operations. Viewed together, this whole setup also fit into the emerging pattern of the Allied way of war in 1943, reflecting the growing importance of communications in combined-arms operations.[54]

Despite the influx of aircraft and a growing base of experience, Lloyd and Quesada did not anticipate that protecting the convoys would be a cakewalk. Germany could still call on 1,500 operational planes within range of southern Italy, and Hitler might be more willing to risk them in mortal combat now that an invasion of mainland Europe hung in the balance. Indeed, on 17 and 18 August at least sixty German planes raided Bizerte, sinking a large infantry-landing craft and damaging three other vessels. On 27 August forty-four Junker-87s and -88s attacked Algiers. Then a German night raid over Palermo sank two Allied submarine chasers and caused heavy casualties. Though these forays yielded modest results against the backdrop of hundreds of Allied vessels massing for AVALANCHE, they were Germany's most vigorous sallies in months. To careful observers, the air activity meant that the Axis had good intelligence on AVALANCHE arrangements. This time a land invasion might well be met with prepared opposition.[55]

Italy certainly anticipated a strike into her heartland, and sued for peace just hours before the first landings took place on 3 September. For many people, the surrender removed the only compelling reason for AVALANCHE, but by then the vast invasion armada had been inexorably committed to the task. Still, Pete Quesada was pleased that the Italians had left the war. He had already described them as "filthy," "smelly," "degenerate," and "vile." During HUSKY he wrote to his mother that the "Wops are getting just about what is coming to them and I am very glad to be taking part in it." Now he elaborated further. "The Wops are out of the war and things look quite rosy. They are a funny race. They went into the war, rammed a knife in the back of the French and at the other end of the war they stab the Germans."[56]

Collectively, these remarks revealed a distinct change for a widely-traveled man of Spanish descent raised in the melting pot of America by an Irish Catholic mother. Helen Quesada noticed her son's hardening, and directed Pete's brother Buddy to remind him of Christian charity. Admirable as his mother's goals were, Pete Quesada's assessment of an adversary merely reflected the unsavory changes that war requires of men. In more ways than one, Pete Quesada was becoming a veteran.[57]

On 3 September Quesada flew above the first U.S. assault convoy as it slipped past the Oran port quays. With enemy airfields now so far from North Africa, no raiders appeared on that day or the next, but Quesada felt that the Luftwaffe would attack when the fleets got nearer to Salerno. As it happened, however, the Germans merely shadowed the ships and never seriously challenged the convoys. The British landings on 3 September jumped off without a hitch, and everything proceeded apace with the U.S. force headed to Salerno. On 7 September

Quesada hopped into a P-38 once more, and as the Italian coast appeared on the horizon the next day, all seemed ready for a successful American assault.[58]

But from there things went badly. German intelligence had indeed forecast the Allied plans, and the defenders greeted the attackers as they waded ashore on 9 September. "Welcome," blared loudspeakers arrayed along the beach, "come in and give up. We have you covered." For the American men of Lieutenant General Mark Clark's Fifth Army, it was a nightmare come to life. Crawling onto the Italian sand, they suffered heavy casualties from well-placed artillery, mortar, and machine-gun fire. A combination of bravery and death bought the Americans a tenuous foothold that first day, but the battle lay in the balance for another week. Then on 12 September the Germans threw fresh units into the fray. A critical situation became acute. Suddenly, the Anglo-Americans were nearer to a serious defeat than they would ever be again during the long war.[59]

The exposed beachhead put a high value on air support. Throughout the ordeal, Lloyd, in Algiers, and Quesada, who had boarded the auxiliary control ship HMS *Hilary* on 10 September, supplied beach cover for more than 200,000 troops, 100,000 tons of supplies, and 30,000 vehicles. At first the Germans managed to sink five ships and damage nine, but the Luftwaffe soon abandoned their night attacks in the face of increased U.S. air patrols.

For their part, the Strategic and Tactical Air Forces flew 6,000 sorties and dropped 3,500 tons of bombs on German shore emplacements, bringing the total AVALANCHE effort to 24,500 sorties. Although radar troubles, especially ground echoes from coastal hills, seriously hampered the success of individual missions, the sheer number of these sorties helped the ground troops wrestle the Germans off the beaches. Surgical drops by thousands of paratroopers on the nights of 13–14 and 14–15 September were a far cry from the incompetence of the HUSKY airborne operations, and the influx of fresh and well-equipped soldiers turned the battle for the Allies. On 16 September Mark Clark's forces began a slow but steady drive inland. Each yard traveled carried them farther from the ocean and defeat. The beachhead was soon secure, but it had been a close call.[60]

In reports back to Washington, Eisenhower was "convinced" that his

air forces had saved his ground troops from disaster. Even in the battle's dim early days, he had told Marshall that "our Air Force [and] the
fighting quality of our troops" would bring victory. Indeed, AVALANCHE
witnessed some of the best air-ground cooperation thus far in the war.
Bombers consistently cut road, rail, and bridge lines. Fighters provided
fire support without the plethora of botched incidents that marred earlier operations. Still far from perfect, the Allied pilots were nonetheless
much better now than they had been in North Africa and Sicily.[61]

Operation AVALANCHE also revealed a telltale pattern of aircraft employment. Though prewar doctrine had anticipated that light and
medium bombers (not fighters) would fly the bulk of close-support
missions, actual combat experience challenged this paradigm. In the
month of September, fighters conducted 63 percent of such operations;
light bombers 7 percent; medium bombers 20 percent; and heavy
bombers 10 percent. For the rest of the war, the use of aircraft for tactical work did not change significantly. Where planners had failed to
foresee the perils of modern war, battle leaders were innovating adequate solutions.[62]

The completion of the Salerno landings marked a vast reduction in
Coastal Air Force's varied duties in the Mediterranean. There were
very few enemy submarines to hunt, and no Axis supplies traveling the
seaways. Recognizing this, in mid-September Spaatz stripped one RAF
group, three American squadrons, one fighter-control squadron, two
radar platoons, and a signal air-warning battalion from Lloyd's command and sent them to the Strategic and Tactical Air Forces. Of Lloyd's
remaining units, one group recorded no combat missions after 15 September, and the only fatality in another was a flight accident. For Quesada, things had come full circle. His first assignments in North Africa
had required little work, and now he was idle again after the rush of
Pantelleria, Sicily, and Italy. As he recalled, by the fall of 1943 there
"wasn't a hell of a lot for the Coastal Air Force to do."[63]

It was fortuitous, then, when orders sent Quesada to England, the
springboard for the climactic western campaign of the war. As early as
June Tooey Spaatz and Major General Ira Eaker, the commanding general of the Eight Air Force in Britain, had pondered other jobs for Quesada. First they considered giving Quesada the Eighth's Fighter

Command, a substantial jump that might have meant another star for the young general. But when Hap Arnold selected Major General Hugh Kepner for that post, Eaker tried to get Quesada to England in another capacity. AVALANCHE planning put the whole issue on hold, but during an August tour of North Africa Eaker asked Quesada if he wanted a change of scenery. Pete Quesada jumped at the chance to go to England, telling Eaker he was "looking forward to the job that you said would be mine with great anticipation and enthusiasm." On the first day of September, a delighted Quesada wrote to his mother that "Ira Eaker was here not long ago and, I am glad to say, he has been soliciting for my assistance. Hence, I expect to be with him in about a month taking on the largest job of my career." Three weeks later, he finally received orders to report to Major General Lewis Brereton, who was then reforming the Ninth Air Force south of London. There Quesada would assume control of the Ninth Fighter Command.[64]

On 4 October, Brigadier General Gordon Saville took over as the deputy commander of the Coastal Air Force, and eight days later Pete Quesada left Africa for England. As he flew north from Algiers, he reflected on his service since leaving America. He had undergone tremendous personal development. Somewhere in the desert he had worked out his differences with Lloyd. In a letter playfully addressed "Dear Huff Puff," Quesada thanked the senior airman for his "excellent and thorough training." Years later, he recalled the importance of his time with Lloyd: "He had a great deal of experience, and I was anxious to have some of that experience rub off on me. If I did have any success thereafter, a great deal of it must be attributed to the fact I was able to mimic him." For his part, Lloyd now believed that "[my] previous concerns about my deputy were unfounded. He is, in fact, a splendid leader." Tooey Spaatz agreed, believing that Quesada had "handled a difficult assignment with firmness and tact."[65]

Quesada had also improved his dealings with subordinates. His twenty-one operational missions, and a growing reputation as a flying general, no doubt helped to forge bonds with the regular pilots. A more mature and balanced style of command that now recognized the attributes of underlings helped as well. "You would be most proud of the way our boys are holding their own against a skilled opponent," he had written one friend in July. "Our lads have eliminated all doubts that were left in the minds of the most skeptical. I have never been so proud of the Air Corps personnel." Even members of the Ninety-third Fighter Squadron, the unit whose leader, Alex Jamieson, Quesada had wanted to sack in May, sensed this shift in Quesada and modified their initial judgments. Lieutenant Paul Christy still believed Quesada was a "flying enigma," but allowed that he "could have a good side, too." Though this was only a qualified endorsement, it was a whole sight better than the earlier consensus among the rank and file.[66]

Quesada could now point to valuable operational experience that would serve him well in the future. From start to finish, the Mediterranean battles had been inordinately connected to logistical imperatives, and Quesada's Coastal Air Force played a silent yet crucial role in the battle of supply. Its diverse tasks and constantly expanding territory and area of responsibility required quick adaptation to altering circumstances and demanded a high degree of coordination with other combat arms. These basic requirements were all the more important in a command that included elements of the British, American, and French air forces. In sum, by the time Quesada left the Mediterranean, he had encountered many of the problems he would later face in Normandy, including the problems of amphibious warfare and the importance of effective signals communications.[67]

Many military leaders continued to view the Mediterranean effort as a diversion from the crucial invasion of France, yet the campaign had not been a waste. Quesada and others had learned much in the desert. For prewar bomber enthusiasts, the early fighting in North Africa had revealed the one-dimensional nature of bombardment theory and fostered a broader conception of air power needs. In Washington, no less a kingpin than Hap Arnold made a few grudging concessions away from his faith in bombers. In the summer of 1943, he sent an observer to the Mediterranean "to capitalize on the practical field experience . . . which may be at variance to more established theories of air warfare, and to codify these lessons and make them available to training missions in the United States."[68]

War Department Field Manual 100-20 (FM 100-20) was the result of this effort. Based largely on British practices developed in their march across the desert, this new directive embodied most of the lessons of the Mediterranean fighting, especially the importance of joint planning, liaison officers, and adequate communications. Above all else, it ac-knowledged the importance of modern combined-arms conflict. "Land power and air power are coequal and interdependent forces; neither is an auxiliary of the other."[69]

Many American pilots, conditioned by the struggle for air autonomy in the interwar years, saw in FM 100-20 only independence for the air force, with one future four-star general calling it the "emancipation proclamation of air power." But viewed within the context of its birth, FM 100-20 was not a plan to widen the gulf between pilots and sol-diers, but rather a tentative start toward better air-ground operations.

All was not right with the world, however. By the Air Force's own ad-mission, its new directive on close air support, FM 31-35, "Aviation in Support of Ground Forces," still failed to visualize the flexibility re-quired in tactical operations and remained "obsolete and wholly inade-quate." Still, FM 100-20 and, to a lesser extent, FM 31-35 were important first steps toward a working understanding of tactical air power.[70]

As Quesada himself later admitted, "We all learned a hell of a lot in the Mediterranean." How true that was. But as he landed at a field in southern England on 12 September, one thing occurred to him. "I knew very little about my new task, and I don't think anybody knew much about the job, actually."[71]

There was more learning ahead.

Chapter Four

All That I Can Do Is Far Short of That Which Is Required and Expected of Me

HIGH WYCOMBE, ENGLAND. 12 OCTOBER 1943. 1030 HOURS. Eighth Air Force commander Major General Ira Eaker promptly convened the meeting, and eleven generals found their places at the conference table. Eaker scanned their faces. Major General Lewis Brereton, commanding the Ninth Air Force, sat to his immediate left. On his right was Major General Hugh Knerr, the Eighth's chief administrative officer. Pete Quesada took a seat directly opposite his old friend Eaker; around the table were the other principal officers of both air forces.

Ira Eaker had known them all since before the war, when they were junior officers together in the tiny Air Corps. Now, less than two years after Pearl Harbor, these men would plan and execute the U.S. air component of the climactic campaign in the West, the invasion of France code-named Operation OVERLORD. War can compress the experience of time like no other human endeavor, but on this drab autumn day a simple fact remained: Not long ago these had been unimportant men, either pushing paper up and down the halls of bureaucracy or commanding small detachments on sleepy airfields. Now, each was responsible for thousands of lives and thousands of planes, and each had a thousand things to do before the Allied infantry stormed the ancient Norman coast.[1]

A great deal of planning had already occurred at higher levels of command. Franklin Roosevelt and Winston Churchill had tentatively approved the OVERLORD scheme some months before. They had settled on Field Marshal Bernard Montgomery as the ground forces leader and Air Chief Marshal Trafford Leigh-Mallory as the commander of the Allied Expeditionary Air Forces (AEAF). Soon they would select Dwight Eisenhower as overall Supreme Commander, in charge of all land, air, and sea forces arrayed for the assault. In London, the Royal Air Force had established the Second Tactical Air Force (TAF) to fulfill Commonwealth obligations over the invasion beaches. In Washington, Hap Arnold had decided against expanding the Eighth Air Force to an unwieldy size, and instead moved the headquarters squadron of the Ninth Air Force to England from the Middle East to prepare the close support for the American troops of OVERLORD.[2]

Despite this groundwork, considerable preparatory work remained undone, and Eaker did not waste a minute during the meeting. He focused his remarks on the task of building up the Ninth Air Force for its gigantic role in the invasion. Eaker had earlier pledged pieces of the Eighth Air Force to the Ninth, but that was just a start. Lewis Brereton had brought only a cadre of staff officers with him from Egypt the month before, and his command would receive the bulk of its 230,000 men and 4,000-plus planes directly from the United States through the spring of 1944. When Eaker finished speaking, he turned to Brereton for any comments the Ninth commander might add.[3]

In the Fall of 1943, Lewis Brereton was uniquely qualified for his task. As one of the air arm's most senior pilots, he had led an Aero Squadron in World War I, had held important overseas posts between the world wars, and had served as an instructor at Leavenworth when Quesada attended the Command and General Staff School in 1935. Since Pearl Harbor, he had headed the American Air Forces contingents in the Philippines, Java, and India. In June 1942 he assumed command of the Ninth Air Force in Cairo, where under British apprenticeship he became one of the United States' most experienced tactical airmen. Although legitimate doubts later developed about Brereton's capacity to lead an OVERLORD air force, in the autumn of 1943 he was a sensible choice. As Eaker wrote Arnold after the meeting at High Wycombe: "You could not have selected a better man for the Ninth Air Force."[4]

Brereton outlined his command's massive expansion schedule before calling on the Ninth's chief subordinate commanders. Major General Henry Miller of the IX Air Service Command talked of aircraft maintenance and airfield construction. Brigadier General Paul Williams sketched the plans of the IX Troop Carrier Command. Brigadier General Orville Anderson described the early preparations of the Ninth's complement of medium bombers. Collectively, these were the important details that comprised the nuts and bolts of war. How successfully these men addressed these minutiae before D-Day could well determine the outcome of battle on the beaches; they exercised a profound influence on the Normandy campaign without leading a single soldier to the front.[5]

Quesada spoke next. Commanding the IX Fighter Command and its two major subheadquarters, the IX and XIX Tactical Air Commands, Quesada would control all the fighter planes providing close air support for the American invaders on the ground. Having been in England for less than a week, he was still cramming the practice and theory of tactical air power as it then existed, so he merely summarized his first impressions and offered an "honest promise to do the best I can." Quesada's terse and forthright remarks must have pleased Eaker. When Eaker had first arrived in England more than a year earlier, he had told the British, "We won't do much talking until we do more fighting. When we leave, I hope you'll be glad we came." Like Eaker before him, Quesada was not quite sure how it would all turn out, but he was happy to be in Britain.[6]

After a break for lunch, the generals clarified the roles of each air force in the Allied organization. For the time being, at least, the Eighth Air Force would continue its year-long bombing offensive against occupied Europe while the Ninth readied tactical-air-support plans. "The Ninth will be tactical," Eaker declared, "and the Eighth strategic. I'll remain in charge of both until the time comes to shift the Ninth over to Air Chief Marshal Leigh-Mallory and the AEAF." Eaker realized that some temporary conflicts in authority might arise between himself and

Leigh-Mallory, but he was "sure they could be kept straight." Such faith is necessary at the outset of critical ventures. As time passed, however, everyone came to realize that optimism alone was no cure for the deeply-rooted doctrinal disputes and personal animosities that were endemic throughout the Allied leadership.[7]

Eaker adjourned the meeting at 1430 hours, rallying his charges for the task ahead. "With 40,000 men arriving a month, a big organizational job must be done in a short time." It was a huge expansion program, and if all went according to plan, the Ninth Air Force would be the most numerous air force in the world by D-Day, even bigger than the famous Eighth.[8]

With that, an obscure yet important conclave of World War II ended. History's enduring fascination with high strategic leadership on the one hand, and its attention to the innate drama of the battlefield on the other hand, has pushed these planning conferences from memory. Yet these assemblies were the critical crossroads of command in World War II. Operation OVERLORD spawned a huge bureaucracy laced with innumerable headquarters and countless planning divisions. Somehow the grand schemes of Eisenhower and Montgomery had to filter through the organizational maze to realization at the front lines. In the months ahead, Eaker's generals were to fuse the efforts of ordinary American pilots into the big picture. How well such welding held together under the strain of battle might determine the result of the invasion. If for Allied foot soldiers the far shore would be laced with mines, for Pete Quesada and others lack of time, resources, and experience were equally dangerous obstacles that lay in wait much closer to home.

Returning to his own headquarters at Middle Wallop, Quesada pondered the Herculean effort that OVERLORD would require of his men. The planned growth of his IX Fighter Command staggered his mind. A small group of less than a dozen men in October 1943, by D-Day it would be a force of over 35,000 airmen and nearly 1,600 planes. In that time, the command was slated to add five fighter wings, nineteen fighter groups, one tactical reconnaissance group, three night fighter squadrons, two signal construction battalions, five signal air warning battalions, one signal aviation company, four communications squadrons, five fighter control squadrons, eight airdrome squadrons,

Quesada's close relationships with ground officers was a hallmark of
his service and contributed to an effective close air support system
during the war. On 21 June 1944 Quesada holding pointer and the
VII Corps commander, Major General Joe Collins, briefed air leaders
on the air/ground assault aimed at Cherbourg. (From left, Major
General Hoyt Vandenberg, Lieutenant General Tooey Spaatz, Major
General Jimmy Doolittle, Quesada, and Collins.) *Courtesy Dwight D.
Eisenhower Library.*

Just weeks later, on the Fourth of July, Quesada took Dwight Eisenhower on a tour
behind enemy lines with very little escort and no parachutes. *Courtesy Dwight D. Eisenhower Library.*

In October, he dined with the three ground generals whom he worked with most closely. (From left, Quesada, Collins, First Army Commander Lieutenant General Courtney Hodges, and Lieutenant General Omar Bradley.) *Courtesy Dwight D. Eisenhower Library.*

That same month, in a subtle yet important recognition of his contributions to the ground war, Quesada was the only air general to be invited by Eisenhower into a picture of thirteen U.S. Army commanders in Europe. (From left, First Row: Lieutenant Generals George Patton and Omar Bradley, General Dwight Eisenhower, and Lieutenant Generals Courtney Hodges and William Simpson. Second Row: Major Generals William Kean, Charles Corlett, Joe Collins, Leonard Gerow, and Quesada. Third Row: Major General Leven Allen and Brigadier Generals Charles Hart and Truman Thorson.) Note Quesada's "50 Mission" crush hat, an adaptation of the Army uniform popular among airmen. *Courtesy Dwight D. Eisenhower Library.*

Pete Quesada's flying career spanned the golden age of flight, from the World War I "Jenny" to modern jumbo jets. Flying in the early days was both hazardous and haphazard, and Quesada survived six crashes from 1924 to 1938. All the while, he developed a reputation as a great pilot. One of Quesada's earliest crashes occurred while he was still a flying cadet in Texas, when he lost control of his taxiing craft and ran into his commander's plane. Later, he graduated to crashing while in actual flight. *Courtesy Dwight D. Eisenhower Library.*

Quesada's impatience and active command style sometimes brought trouble. On 1 August 1944, at the height of the Allied breakout from Normandy, Quesada conducted a personal reconnaissance of the front. Traveling with Colonel Dyke Meyers, the two men whipped past numerous U.S. posts until they were within a mile of German infantry positions and right next to German tanks. "Say, that tank there doesn't look like it's been knocked out yet," Quesada mused to Meyers at one point. Just then the German tank fired its cannon and machine guns at the two-star jeep, and Quesada and Meyers dove into the brush, somehow managing to escape. The jeep was later recovered, and here Meyers and Quesada inspect it. *Courtesy Kate Davis Quesada.*

In the weeks before the COBRA bombardment on 25 July 1944, German units had skill-fully camouflaged their men and equipment from air strikes. The Allied breakout in late July and early August forced them from their protective cover, presenting rich targets for American and British fighter bombers. Although many soldiers escaped capture to fight another day, most of their equipment did not. Here, fighter bombers from the 367th Fighter Group strike retreating German columns near Roncey on 29 July, leaving substantial destruction on the ground. *Courtesy Dwight D. Eisenhower Library.*

In total, the tactical air forces destroyed thousands of German vehicles and killed count-less German soldiers in the summer of 1944. *Courtesy Dwight D. Eisenhower Library.*

Before World War II, air power enthusiasts believed the technology of flight would overcome any obstacle and revolutionize warfare. They were partly correct, though military aviation was still limited by age-old logistical and environmental hardships during the war. In Normandy, temporary airstrips of light-gauge wire mesh and tar paper increased the maintenance demands on aircraft, and hindered the performance of the tactical air forces. *Courtesy Dwight D. Eisenhower Library.*

In the Battle of the Bulge the same winter weather that hampered Washington at Valley Forge and bedeviled Napoleon before Moscow hurt the efficiency of fighter bombers. *Courtesy Dwight D. Eisenhower Library.*

In the race across France, the need to refuel and re-arm planes quickly sometimes led to expensive mistakes. *Courtesy Dwight D. Eisenhower Library.*

Effective close air support in World War II was dependent on good signal and communication systems. On D-Day, a massive communications center at Uxbridge tracked thousands of airplanes over the invasion beaches. *Courtesy Library of Congress.*

Once the Allies were on the Continent, the IX Tactical Air Command maintained ten thousand miles of wire connecting Quesada's command post to infantry and armored units, and each move by headquarters required a monumental rerouting of wire. *Courtesy Dwight D. Eisenhower Library.*

Despite such technological efficiency, however, men on the ground and in the air sometimes relied on simple means to communicate. In large bombardments, they often used crude ground panels of canvas to mark the front lines, as in this picture taken at the outset of Operation QUEEN in November 1994. *Courtesy Library of Congress.*

two signal battalions, five detached signal companies, eleven military police companies, and eighteen station-complement squadrons.[9]

Beyond mere growth, a whole way of fighting had to be developed. Airmen in North Africa, Sicily, and now Italy were learning important lessons in the tactical support of ground troops, but these new notions now had to be absorbed by new pilots fresh from the States and then adopted for the particular demands of France. The task was daunting. "All that I can do," Quesada confided to a friend after the High Wycombe meeting, "is far short of that which is required and expected of me."[10]

This sense of urgency combined poorly with Quesada's inexperience and brought out the worst in him. In early staff meetings officers found him "tough, adamant, and implacable." In November he suspended all recreational activities at his bases until the men improved their aircraft-recognition test scores, even though they had performed better than most other commands. On Christmas Day, steamed over what he thought were high abort rates on takeoffs, he declared that an "investigation will be conducted after each and every scratched mission, and whether the individual be a line chief, or a mechanic, or the goddamned base commander, if the situation warrants, I'll court-martial the bastard."[11]

All of this ranting and raving left its mark on Quesada's men. According to one officer, "Many people developed a distinct fear of Quesada's temper, many people were afraid of him, physically afraid of him." Although service under Lloyd had moderated Quesada's stormy personality, he could still be overly brusque. It was little wonder that in time, through letters to wives, mothers, and sweethearts back home, men of the IX Fighter Command came to describe Quesada as "the terrible-tempered Mr. Big."[12]

Still, there was a logic to Quesada's unforgiving attitude. He could ill afford incompetence with so little time before OVERLORD. One officer remembered that in November and December Middle Wallop became a "no man's land for older lieutenant colonels and colonels. If you did not measure up, and General Quesada didn't give you much time, you were simply gone." Quesada would have agreed with that assessment, for he told his subordinate commanders to expect their men to "be perfect at all times. You must be prepared to weed out the incapable and the inefficient . . . and you must do so with courage and conviction, setting aside personal feelings, sympathy, and friendship." In a command responsible for close air support, he particularly disliked airmen who were wedded to the primacy of independent bombardment. "I had little patience for those who turned out quite parochial regarding air–ground matters. I tried at first to move them around a bit, but eventually I sent the bad ones home. It usually meant the end of their careers."[13]

If this treatment seemed harsh to those Quesada sent packing, he was at least fair to the members of his command. "He called a spade a spade, I'll tell you that," Colonel Blair Garland, his chief signal officer, remembered. "More than that, he called it a shovel, and you'd better get the hell out of the way when he got going on something. At staff meetings he was forceful and sometimes impatient, though if you were forthright and honest and competent, you got along fine. If you were those things, you always got along fine."[14]

While Quesada worked out these relationships with his Middle Wallop staff, his first fighter groups began arriving from America. On 2 November the initial group disembarked at Liverpool, and in the next three months Quesada welcomed fifteen more groups to England. Unlike the ground forces slated for OVERLORD, these pilots were swiftly pressed into actual service. Eighth Air Force bombers had proved far more vulnerable to the German defenses than the prewar theorists had ever imagined, and the big planes desperately needed the aerial protection of Quesada's new long-range P-51 Mustangs.

The 354th, led by a charismatic twenty-seven-year-old lieutenant colonel named Ken Martin, was the earliest group in England with the new planes. Arriving in the first week of November, Martin had just six short weeks to ready his 1,000-man, seventy-five-plane command for operations. On 13 December he and his pilots flew from their Boxted airfield on the first of many escort hops with B-17s, and by January the group was an old hand at the air war in Europe.[15]

What operational routine there was in the IX Fighter Command emerged first with them. Most missions started predictably enough. Flyers woke as early as 0300 hours and headed to the mess for a quick breakfast. While ground crews readied the planes, Martin and the intelligence, weather, and operations officers explained the day's job to the pilots in a briefing room filled with charts and wall maps. Ninety min-utes after waking, the group pilots throttled up and climbed into the sky. Then anything could and often did happen.[16]

January 18th was like that. That morning, Squadron Leader Major Jim Howard led forty-nine fighters on an escort mission to Oscher-sleben. After taking intense flak over the target, bomber and fighter pi-lots alike hoped for an easy return. A maelstrom of Messerschmitts ambushed the formations over Belgium, however, and Howard found himself alone near the forward box of B-17s. Thirty Luftwaffe planes pounced on the Fortresses. Howard chopped his throttle, dropped his flaps, and slashed in like a man possessed. For him, the decision to fight against such long odds was simple. "I seen my duty and I done it."

Bomber pilots saw it differently. "It looked like one American against the entire Luftwaffe," recalled one. "He was over us, across the forma-tion and around it. For sheer determination and guts it was the greatest exhibition I have ever seen." Howard shot down five planes that day, and the quiet, lanky thirty-year old with a slow smile won the Congres-sional Medal of Honor.[17]

Not all days were so good. On 11 February Colonel Martin led the group on a difficult escort to Frankfurt. German flyers rose in droves to defend the city. Martin engaged in a high-stakes game of chicken with an ME-410. Neither man relented, and their planes collided with a fatal impact faster than the speed of sound. Instantly, the heart and soul of the group was gone. It was a bittersweet moment the next day when Quesada promoted Jim Howard and gave him command of the group. "It is not possible," wrote one officer later in the month, "to put into words how greatly the loss of Col. Martin is felt." For Howard and oth-ers in the 354th, the war had become very real. The exhilaration of great success and the pain of immense loss were now a part of their own history. They were the war's new veterans, knowing already the face of battle that awaited the OVERLORD troops.[18]

Aided by the fighter escorts, the big-bomber campaign finally began to dent the German war machine after years of trying. In one five-day span in mid-February bombers dropped almost 10,000 tons of ordnance on Luftwaffe factories, an effort equal to the Eighth Air Force's entire first-year total. For a week, American, British, and German fighters swirled about the bomber fleets in some of the war's greatest air battles. Collectively, these dogfights cost the Luftwaffe more planes than it lost during the entire summer following the invasion. Quesada's planes sortied over 700 times in support of the raids, and afterward Eighth Air Force leaders thanked him for "the magnificent support your fighters rendered." In the excitement of it all, Quesada boasted to his mother, "We seem to have the Huns on the run. He has taken quite a beating the past week or two."[19]

Yet Big Week, as it was dubbed, was a classic example of the merits and limits of strategic bombardment. The raids no doubt denied the Germans hundreds of aircraft that were later missed over Normandy. But the operation also cost the Allies over 250 planes and 2,600 casualties. Worse, Nazi factories continued to produce new fighter planes at an increasing pace even after February 1944. As the U.S. Air Force official history later admitted, the planners had "failed to take into account the phenomenal recuperative powers of the aircraft industry." More than that, by the end of February, IX Fighter Command's groups had done nothing but escort heavy bombers, and remained "woefully unprepared to assist in the invasion." As with the operations against Pantelleria, the vexing questions of strategic bombardment persisted after all was said and done: Did such limited achievements justify the vast expenditure of scarce resources? Was there a better way?[20]

Already, joint air–ground exercises for OVERLORD had revealed the consequences of diverting so much fighter strength to the bombardment campaign. The infantry divisions slated for the invasion had been war-gaming along the southern English coast since early January. Operation DUCK, the first of these maneuvers, was a rehearsal for Major General Charlie Gerhardt's Twenty-ninth Division. As landing craft churned toward shore on 30 December, Gerhardt searched the sky for the fighter planes that the air leaders had promised for the exercise. The birds never showed. DUCK lasted four more days, and not once did a sizeable complement of tactical aircraft arrive to practice close-support techniques with liaison parties and attack battalions. Each day, planes were siphoned off by urgent Eighth Air Force escort requests. Gerhardt hated it, and Quesada did not like it much, but neither could do much about it as long as higher authorities placed greater stress on the bombardment campaign than on OVERLORD rehearsals.[21]

Operation KNOCKOUT, a small-scale rehearsal in mid-January de-signed to train soldiers for quick movement on the Continent, was not much better. Operation FOX, an ambitious amphibious exercise con-ducted on 10 and 11 March at Slapton Sands, was the worst. Military police had evacuated a vast portion of southern England, and over 18,000 ground troops, 1,700 vehicles, and 740 aircraft were supposed to participate in this "invasion." Instead, escort missions or poor weather at airfields prevented most of the planes from participating in the exer-cise. Air force ground-liaison parties landed on the beach with inopera-ble radios, and as a result the one squadron of planes that did get into the air had shaky communications with naval and ground batteries. Now, just ninety days from D-Day, there had yet to be a realistic test of American air support in England.[22]

This failure produced sharp criticisms from ground officers. At one meeting, Quesada's operations officer, Colonel Ray Stecker, told Gener-al Gerhardt's staff that "the Ninth Air Force regretted as much as any-one the lost opportunity of actually deploying with the ground forces. As you all realize, the present employment of our combat units is far di-vorced from the employment of those fighters in the support of a ground army." That may have been true, but it did little to blunt in-fantry concerns. Charlie Gerhardt had participated in many prewar ma-neuvers where the Air Corps had exhibited at most an indifferent enthusiasm for anything other than independent bombing, and he now saw these OVERLORD exercises in the same light. He told Lewis Brere-ton that his airmen were using the war only to "bring about an indepen-dent air force," and that pilots were "little interested in the support of ground forces." The airmen denied it, but even a member of Brereton's staff admitted that his boss "treated the role of support as a cancer the air forces had to deal with." For Pete Quesada, the bickering revealed how prewar struggles sometimes colored the conduct of World War II. "A lot of these people were still fighting the battles of the 1930s, and it hurt our efforts in the execution of the war. Of that there is absolutely no doubt."[23]

In an effort to build stronger links with ground commanders, Quesa-da invited Gerhardt to spend a night at Middle Wallop in February. There, they enjoyed a game of squash, dinner, a movie, and good con-versation. When Gerhardt left the next morning, he thanked his host for the "most interesting talk I have yet had with a pilot on the subject of air support." Quesada, in turn, hoped Gerhardt would "stop by again some time soon and take advantage of the open door that we have for you and your chaps." Gerhardt's little visit produced no sea change in the interservice tension that by then permeated both ground and air commands, but at least it was a tentative start toward better relations among the soldiers and pilots who were to reach Normandy first.[24]

It was a different story further up the chain of command. The competing demands of bomber escort and infantry support produced an ugly fracas among the senior Allied leadership. On a personal level, most ground complaints targeted Brereton and the AEAF Commander, Trafford Leigh-Mallory. Nearly everyone harbored doubts about Leigh-Mallory. A veteran of the Battle of Britain, his austere, reserved manner matched badly with the self-confidence of most other commanders. Bomber Command's Air Chief Marshal Arthur Harris and the Eighth Air Force generals regarded him as a lightweight. The British Second Tactical Air Force commander, Air Marshal Arthur "Maori" Coningham, felt much the same way, and Montgomery lent more weight to the appraisal. Eisenhower, for his part, was only half joking when he described his air forces as led by "some guy named Mallory."[25]

As for Brereton, Major General Leonard Gerow of the U.S. V Corps added to Gerhardt's protests and alerted the First Army commander, Lieutenant General Omar Bradley. Bradley was sympathetic to these grievances, for by then he had developed his own reservations about Lewis Brereton and the Ninth Air Force. Although Bradley had traveled to Brereton's headquarters several times to confer on joint plans, Brereton rarely went to First Army, preferring instead to send a junior aide. From this, Bradley soon concluded that Brereton was insincere, lazy, and uncooperative. For Bradley's money, the Ninth commander "did not realize [the] full use that could be made of air effort in assistance to ground operations . . . [and made] no effort to work out the problems of air–ground cooperation." When these complaints reached the Supreme Command, Dwight Eisenhower added his own doubts. "I have never been able to rid myself of a slight uneasiness about Brereton," he once confided to George Marshall.[26]

These misgivings were hard to dismiss when even other air officers felt similar qualms. At the IX Fighter Command, Blair Garland figured that Brereton "should never have been put in charge." Quesada himself admitted that Brereton was in over his head, but from his unique perspective he was glad to serve under him anyway; Brereton's meager interest in close air support meant more command prerogatives for Quesada. "Lewy cared more for his troop carriers and medium bombers, so he gave me all the freedom in the world to do my thing." Indeed, Quesada's headquarters essentially wrote the U.S. tactical-air-support plan for OVERLORD, and by D-Day the ground generals took to calling the Ninth "Quesada's air force." Whatever others said about Lewis Brereton, Pete Quesada knew there were advantages to serving under him.[27]

But that did not change the big picture, and skepticism about certain generals bred a crisis in March. "As we always anticipated, the Air features of our plan have been difficult to get completely in line," a concerned Eisenhower wrote to George Marshall on 3 March. Since before the New Year, Eisenhower had struggled with the details of an integrated Allied air organization, and now he could endure no more. On 22 March he told Marshall that "the air problem has been one requiring a great deal of patience and negotiations. Unless the matter is settled at once I will request relief from this command."[28]

To help assuage his qualms about the AEAF commander, Eisenhower then assembled his trusted air advisors from the North African campaign. Sir Arthur Tedder, his chief air assistant in the desert, came to England as the Deputy Supreme Commander. Tooey Spaatz became the head of all U.S. air forces in England. Jimmy Doolittle became the Eighth Air Force commander, displacing Ira Eaker, who then went to Italy to replace Spaatz.

Although well intentioned, these moves only escalated the personality problems that existed between some of the highest-ranking officers, and spun a grand web of intrigue. Leigh-Mallory, Brereton, and "Maori" Coningham viewed Tedder and Spaatz as interlopers. The growing tangle of air headquarters eventually worried Bernard Montgomery so much that he had Air Vice Marshal Harry Broadhurst assigned as Coningham's fighter boss. Coningham could hardly refuse Broadhurst, who had won both Montgomery's and Coningham's respect with an excellent tour in the desert, but he was annoyed by outsiders meddling in his command. In the end, this soap-opera story produced a hopscotch chain of command, and fueled internecine fights well into the Battle of France. "It was a lousy organization," Spaatz later admitted. "From an organizational point of view, it was just lousy."[29]

Personality conflicts certainly contributed to this messy setup, but there was something else fueling the turmoil. In many ways, the problem was not so much who commanded the airplanes but what air power could and should do in the invasion. Bomber barons like Spaatz, Harris, and Doolittle believed that the strategic air offensive represented the best way for heavy bombers to aid OVERLORD. "Diverting our best weapons from the military function for which they have been equipped and trained," declared Arthur Harris, "to tasks which they cannot effectively carry out would be the greatest disservice." In contrast, tactical airmen like Leigh-Mallory steadfastly advocated a more tactical role for the heavies as D-Day drew near. "I intend to help the Army all I can," he stated, "because that is what I am convinced the Air Forces should now do." More than anything else, it was Leigh-Mallory's steadfast endorsement of tactical aviation that unsettled the bombardment enthusiasts, and the personality conflicts of March merely masked these doctrinal disputes.[30]

Finally, late that month, Eisenhower fashioned an accord between the strategic and tactical airmen that freed fighters to train with ground forces and required bombers to contribute mightily to the invasion preparations. Under the guidance of Eisenhower's deputy commander, Air Marshal Sir Arthur Tedder, the Allied bombers began blasting rail and road centers, coastal batteries, and airfields within 130 miles of Caen in an effort to isolate or interdict the battle area. In April and May the U.S. Eighth Air Force devoted more than twice the sorties and nearly two and a half times the ordnance to these tactical targets as to traditional strategic operations. Predictably, Tooey Spaatz did not like it. "In my mind, I thought we were wasting a lot of effort. We could have probably ended the war quicker by continuing to bomb the targets in Germany." Valid or not, his complaint ignored a fact which had escaped most air enthusiasts. World War II was blurring the neat prewar differences between strategic and tactical air power, and the distinction would only grow muddier on the French shore.[31]

The difficulties within the Allied air command as late as mid-March would have stunned the Germans preparing the Norman defenses. Indeed, that the Anglo-Americans, after years of war, had not yet worked out the broad outline of air employment or the specific air organization for an invasion just two months away would have surprised any thoughtful observer. Perhaps worse still, the new agreement among airmen proved precarious at best. Quarrels over air employment lingered on into the summer. The whole affair was a sad commentary on the polarized nature of Anglo-American air power.

Despite all this, those most directly responsible for the air support of ground troops were at last able to prepare for their task. Pete Quesada looked forward to BEAVER, the first joint exercise to be held under the new arrangements. Conducted during the last two days of March, it was meant to approximate the conditions of actual war. Most naval and air support and some ground fire was live. Perpetual communications problems and bad weather once again foiled effective air operations, however. Air–ground communications were so bad that afterwards one officer suggested using pigeons in the future. Ground requests for air support took almost three hours just to reach AEAF headquarters at Uxbridge. But that was probably just as well, because ground forces had incorrectly marked the pretend front lines. Any live air support could have killed friendly infantry.[32]

Still, none of these deficiencies had anything to do with the lack of planes for the exercise, and Quesada used BEAVER to forge stronger ties with ground commanders. To Omar Bradley, he pledged to drill his pilots in artillery spotting, a World War I function of aviation and something that the ardent strategic air enthusiasts would never have offered in 1944. He invited every general participating in the invasion to his headquarters for consultations, and at least one found the visit enlightening. Invasion preparations did not revolve around the IX Fighter Command, of course, and many officers found no time in their busy schedules to travel to Middle Wallop. To these men Quesada responded with good cheer. "Even the birds were walking that day," he wrote one general when bad weather cancelled a visit. For those accustomed to air–ground relations marked by tension, Quesada's natural enthusiasm and cooperative spirit were a welcome respite. Slowly, the young general was making a name for himself.[33]

As March drew to a close, Quesada hosted a fighter wing inspection by Eisenhower, Leigh-Mallory, Spaatz, Brereton, and Coningham. As the generals deplaned from Eisenhower's C-47, Quesada trotted past the wing officers and over to Sergeant Roy Hrivnak, the second-ranking master sergeant in the Army Air Forces and an old friend. "They jigged around with all kinds of back-slapping and greetings, and only then did Quesada return to the greeting party busy with the Supreme Commander," remembered one junior pilot. "We were duly impressed with the high regard that a senior officer so clearly demonstrated for a highly skilled and vital asset."[34]

Also impressed was Eisenhower, himself an expert at the occasional conversation with enlisted ranks. Earlier the Supreme Commander had outlined to George Marshall the qualifications he wanted in tactical airmen, explaining that air support was "[a technique] not widely understood and it takes men of some vision and broad understanding to do the job right." He now figured he had found one such man. "I was," Eisenhower wrote the Chief of Staff the day after the inspection, "very much impressed by General Quesada." Recalling his old flying aide, Marshall may not have been surprised. For all the interservice bickering surrounding him, March was a good month for Pete Quesada.[35]

March 1944 was also an important demarcation for the IX Fighter Command. Almost five months had passed since Quesada's first fighter group had reported for duty, and nearly four months ago his planes first crossed the skies of Europe. Now, in April, the IX Fighter Command reached its full complement of fighter groups: thirteen P-47 groups, two P-51 groups, and three P-38 groups. Most of these units had undergone initial training. The high accident rates of December were now reduced to within reasonable limits. Pilots had acquired a working proficiency in flight, and the few veteran groups had reached great levels of experience.[36]

Equally important was Quesada's assembly of a core group of capable subordinates. Brigadier General Alvin Kincaid, like Quesada a bachelor and a non-West Pointer, had replaced Colonel John Whitley as chief of staff. Neither brilliant nor charismatic, Kincaid had a keen eye for administration that relieved Quesada of the bureaucratic demands of generalship. The IX Fighter's new operations officer, Colonel Lorry Tindal, had witnessed German tactical air operations as a War Department observer before Pearl Harbor, and his sharp insights were instrumental in developing air-support procedures. Colonel Ray Stecker, a West Point football hero, became one of the few Academy graduates in Quesada's inner circle. A transplant from the old Ninth Air Force in Africa, Stecker had desert experience in close support, which made him Quesada's ideal representative at the AEAF Combined Operations Center in Uxbridge. Together, Kincaid, Tindal, and Stecker liberated Quesada from the confines of Middle Wallop and allowed him the freedom to practice his own brand of leadership. "I would be a flop," he once wrote a stateside officer, "if I remained at headquarters at all times. I need continuous circulation to all my units."[37]

The IX Fighter Command had collected a competent cadre of wing and group commanders, too. Brigadier General O. P. Weyland was another non-Academy officer. A top graduate of the Air Corps Tactical School, he arrived in England with his 84th Fighter Wing on 29 January 1944. It took Quesada just five days to concur in the judgment of wing officers that Weyland was "an exceptionally gifted leader." On 4 February he gave him command of the XIX TAC. Although a mild rivalry grew between Quesada and Weyland when the XIX TAC became operational in France, in the spring before D-Day these two men enjoyed a supportive and efficient partnership.[38]

Four group commanders filled out Quesada's complement of outstanding subordinates. Gilbert Meyer and Dyke Meyer were not related by blood, but they came to share a strong friendship with Pete Quesada. Fighter pilots to their core, both had logged countless hours in the air and earned reputations as hard and charismatic leaders. They were Quesada's kind of people, and he relied on them to check planning theories against operational reality. Colonel James Ferguson had been a squadron commander for Ira Eaker before the war. He brought his P-47 group to Europe in February 1944, and on D-Day he was one of two American air controllers at Uxbridge. Quesada liked "Fergy," and so did others; he eventually rose to four-star rank. Lastly, Jim Howard's stock had grown steadily in Quesada's mind since he won the Medal of Honor. In April, Quesada ordered the P-51 leader to join the Fighter Command planning staff. Although operational experience was at a premium before D-Day, Quesada could not allow one group to monopolize Howard's wisdom.[39]

All together, these men reflected Quesada's determination to "weed out the incapable and the inefficient." Gone were the career officers not up to the rigors of modern war. Gone were the men of limited imagination. Gone were the advocates of interservice partisanship. Gone were those who postponed making decisions. In their places stood officers in the mold of Pete Quesada: youthful, creative, energetic, decisive, and sometimes brash and rude. For Quesada, the ideal officer was a "fellow who knows what a fighter and fighter-bomber can and cannot do . . . who has some consideration for the lads that do the flying . . . [and] possess an intellectual honesty and character sufficiently strong to pursue honest and well-founded convictions in the face of great adversity and immense stress." By April, he felt sure that he had successfully assembled just such underlings. "Though war is a helluva thing," he told his old boss Trubee Davison, "some of our lads who are now group commanders or squadron commanders are the finest type of manhood that the world has produced."[40]

Quesada grew with his staff that spring. He became less abrupt, less severe, and developed a keen eye for leadership. He learned that the "more I see of the war the more I realize there is a difference between men." He had become more even-handed. "General Quesada was always patient with my eruptions and suggestions and still managed to put down my impertinences without ruining my fire and enthusiasm," remembered Colonel Morton Magoffin of the 362nd Group. After a rough start, Quesada had now impressed his men as a "smart, colorful, and dynamic personality—an experienced airman and not just a political appointee." As one declared flatly, "I loved the guy, and it could not have been a more fortunate thing for me when I went to serve in the IX Fighter Command." Although Quesada may not have recognized his own ripened leadership style, others did. On 28 April, George Marshall approved his promotion to Major General.[41]

With a freer hand to aid in invasion preparations, with a full complement of fighter groups, with a solid cast of supporting characters, and with a mature view of leadership, Pete Quesada turned toward the invasion and D-Day. In early April his flyers began a systematic attack on the transportation network of western France. Isolating the Normandy area would not be easy. Northwest Europe had the world's densest railroad and road network in 1944, and nothing but its near-total destruction could limit Hitler's ability to move war material about the front. Total destruction was not feasible, however, and in reality the only hope for effective interdiction lay in destroying spans across the Seine and Loire rivers, which sliced Normandy off from the rest of France. But striking the critical bridges might well reveal the planned landing site, so air forces prefaced these attacks with missions against marshaling yards, rolling stock, and locomotives. Only when the invasion was much nearer could pilots aim for the critical river crossings and risk revealing the point of invasion.[42]

IX Fighter Command pilots mounted their first major interdiction strikes on 8 April. Over a hundred P-47s attacked railroad repair shops in Belgium, and the area was still smoking when fifty-six P-51s returned two days later. On the ninth a P-47 group stopped troop and freight-train movements in northern France and inflicted damage on several road junctions. Ten days later, fifty fighters attacked Malines and Namur, and P-47s dive-bombed Mantes-Gassicourt, between the Loire and Seine rivers, on 20 April. In the most spectacular attack of all, over a hundred P-51s and P-47s seriously damaged railway installations near Namur on 23 April. In all, Quesada's planes attacked twenty-two targets in the last two weeks of the month. For the first time, dive-bombing missions had outnumbered escort sorties for Quesada's flyers. On 16 April a pleased Quesada wrote that his pilots were "having a wonderful time over here and we are doing a lot to insure a speedy end to this war. The weather couldn't be better and there is little for me to complain about."[43]

Actually, there was. The French rail and road networks proved resistant to Allied air attacks. Germans forced French laborers to repair marshaling yards and tracks almost as fast as aircraft bombed them, and the Third Reich experienced no insuperable difficulties in supply movement. An Allied intelligence report estimated that Hitler still had three times the rail capacity needed for military traffic, four times the required number of cars, eight times the required locomotives, and ten times the required servicing facilities. By late April it was clear that while most of the individual missions had fulfilled their operational goals, the overall effect on Europe's transportation system was not yet posing serious problems for Germany.[44]

To combat this, Quesada sought to make fighter tactics more lethal. Traditionally, the Air Corps had considered fighters to be either high-altitude escorts or air-to-air interceptors, but dive-bombing missions required different equipment and tactics from those employed in these conventional roles. The three aircraft types in Quesada's command reflected this lack of foresight by the war planners. The newest of them, the P-51 Mustang, had great range and speed, but it suffered from excessive oil loss, poor visibility, and a liquid-cooled engine vulnerable to ground fire. The P-47 Thunderbolts, destined to become the mainstay of Quesada's force, were hampered by limited range and poor visibility, and as late as December 1943 most of them carried no bomb racks or bomb sights. The two-engine P-38 Lightning was more resilient to flak and its pilots could see well, but the plane was designed for hot, dry climates and its engines often failed in the damp air of northern Europe.[45]

Beyond needed equipment modifications, dive-bombing required a major attitudinal change among pilots. Weaned on the spectacular aerial battles of the Great War and the propaganda of the bomber offensive, fighter pilots were slow to appreciate the value of close-support operations. One flyer aptly summarized the rank-and-file perception of the new task when he said in April, "I don't believe in all this dive-bombing shit, it ain't natural." Yet this was precisely the chore Quesada's men had to perform on the far shore. If Quesada did not tackle such problems in the spring, they would haunt him into the long summer days. "So many of those fighter boys came into the war intoxicated with the glory of aerial dog-fights or the fame of big bombers," he recalled. "My assignment was somewhere in between, and we needed to devise a way to teach a new way of air warfare."[46]

In search of advice, he wrote to Major General Joe Cannon, the best qualified U.S. tactical airman in Italy. "My job is very much like the one you are now performing in that I work side by side with the Army. I am wondering if you have any literature that your headquarters has prepared on this subject of supporting the ground forces? It would be most helpful." Cannon had very little written material, but suggested Quesada send selected officers to Italy to observe his tactical operations. In the following sixty days, no less than 227 officers of the IX Fighter Command traveled to Italy to absorb air-power lessons. In addition, Joe Cannon sent his own pilots to England to help staff the air-support schools there. In the spring of 1944 over two hundred of the Ninth's fighter pilots attended these improvised service courses, afterward returning to their units to teach fellow flyers. As one officer described it, "Our job required new ways of doing things, so it was back to school for hundreds of us."[47]

Quesada also insisted that his group commanders "do something to get the pilots to take to bombing." On the last day of April Quesada assigned two groups to a Southampton gunnery range to literally invent better dive-bombing techniques. "We've got to teach these kids to fly on the deck and to arm the bombs," he explained to a friend at the air forces' proving ground in Florida. "We've got to figure out the best angles of dive, type of bombs, and release tables if we want to make any impression on this war."[48]

He was right, but it was a little late to be starting from scratch. Nevertheless, the 365th and 405th Thunderbolt groups reported to Southampton for a two-week experiment. Each dawn they took to the sky, attacking the same pretend targets from varying heights, speeds, and angles. Beyond the actual method of attack, flyers also experimented with different types of bombs, including fragmentation and napalm shells. They developed an electrical bomb release, an innovation that brought about numerous modifications in fighter aircraft. Although none of their findings were definitive, and prescribed tactics later changed, flyers absorbed important lessons in the primitive art of close air support. When the fortnight in Southampton ended, officers of both groups fanned out through the Fighter Command, passing along their newly acquired insights.[49]

In early May, armed with these new procedures, Quesada directed his pilots to attack moving locomotives, believing them to be the least replaceable cog in western Europe's transportation system. On 9 May, the 367th Group conducted a fighter sweep across France, destroying four steam engines. Quesada committed two other groups to the hunt the next day, and within the week the command killed nine more locomotives. On 20 May Leigh-Mallory at AEAF ordered other commands on similar missions. The next day 1,263 planes swept over France and Germany looking for thin streams of black smoke, the telltale sign of a moving train. On 25 May over 1,000 planes repeated the exercise, and Quesada's birds continued the practice until forty-eight hours before

D-Day. In the two weeks before the invasion, these CHATTANOOGA CHOO-CHOO missions claimed 475 locomotives and cut rail lines in 150 different places. One squadron destroyed thirteen locomotives in a single day. Although these strikes did not paralyze the French rail network, the cumulative losses meant reduced transportation for Germans on the eve of a new battle front in Europe.[50]

Quesada also hoped the improvements in technique and equipment would garner for his pilots a role in the important planned strikes against Seine and Loire river bridges. When, in early May, senior leaders finally authorized attacks along the Loire, Quesada lobbied for a chance to demonstrate his groups' training. At first, his offer to assist medium and heavy bombers only produced snickers at AEAF headquarters, where many planners still adhered to the "bigger is better" ideology of the bomber age. Planners had allotted 1,200 tons of explosives for each steel span, and a fighter plane's two-ton payload seemed inadequate for the job. But with almost insubordinate pleading, Quesada finally won permission for a few missions.[51]

On 7 May he ordered the 365th to attack bridges at Vernon and Mantes-Gassicourt. At dawn two squadrons lifted from their tarmac fields. Once near the target, each Thunderbolt dropped down to the river, below the height of the bridge. They aimed their two 1,000-pound bombs into the embankments before zooming upward. The squadrons achieved terrific results on the Vernon bridge, where just eight planes with sixteen bombs—a mere eight tons—cut the span in half. The encased concrete of the Mantes structure was more tenacious and only sustained heavy damage, but senior AEAF airmen in England judged the mission a resounding, and for them surprising, success. Quesada sent a group out the next day, and on 10 May Leigh-Mallory sanctioned the IX Fighter campaign against bridges on an ongoing basis. "We've convinced the Old Man," Quesada jubilantly told his staff.[52]

The target list expanded again on 24 May when Leigh-Mallory lifted the ban against Seine River bridges. In conjunction with B-26s from IX Bomber Command, Quesada's fighters targeted bridges at Rouen, Juvisy, Conflans, Pointe-de-l'Arche, and Mantes-Gassicourt. Planes of the British Second Tactical Air Force and the Eighth Air Force joined the raids in large numbers. From 27 May to D-Day, IX

Fighter Command planes sortied 1,181 times against thirteen river bridges and dropped 854 tons of ordnance. They managed to knock out twelve of the spans.[53]

Air strikes against bridges were the interdiction campaign's one great success. Though German tenacity in rebuilding roads, marshaling yards, and aircraft factories had thwarted other Allied efforts to isolate Normandy, replacing river crossings was not so easy for them. Workers rebuilt one trestle in Rouen seven times, for example, only for the Americans to return to smash it again on eight separate occasions.[54]

By D-Day, not a single railroad bridge crossed the Seine and virtually all roadways above the river had sustained serious damage. Leigh-Mallory extolled his pilots for their "concentrated, determined, and highly skilled" raids. Brereton told Quesada that his flyers had "proved by far the most efficacious in knocking out these difficult and well-defended targets." Even Tooey Spaatz admitted that the attacks had "opened the door for the invasion." After the war, the Luftwaffe's Reichsmarshall Hermann Goering believed these attacks hurt Germany's defense of Normandy more than any other single factor.[55]

Although the strikes revealed important limits of tactical air power, notably the rigidity of concrete and the inefficiency of certain fragmentation bombs and fuses, the fighter planes won newfound respect as bombers. Quesada's planes were carving a fresh niche for themselves, it seemed, which pleased the IX Fighter commander. "It is indeed gratifying to deliver these powerful and punishing blows day in and day out to those damn Germans," he wrote his mother on 10 May.[56]

As he penned this note, he must have known how little time his command had in the relative safety of the British Isles. D-Day was now less than a month away, and though the operational flurry of April and May may have obscured the arduous and secret invasion planning at Middle Wallop, it had not diminished the importance of such work. For weeks, IX TAC staffers had toiled away behind guarded doors, sketching the movement of air liaison parties into marshaling areas, preparing supply schedules, and mapping out far-shore command posts and airfields. In line with directives from Tedder and Leigh-Mallory, these planners earmarked five of Quesada's P-47 groups for high beach cover on invasion day, two P-38 groups for convoy cover, six P-47 and P-38 groups for scheduled attacks on beach batteries, and five groups as a command reserve.[57]

In one of the few mistakes in the OVERLORD design, no one at Middle Wallop or AEAF Headquarters fashioned an adequate plan to cope with unanticipated demands. Despite thousands of aircraft, AEAF planners at Uxbridge allocated just forty-seven group sorties for urgent-request missions. One memo aptly summed up the conventional wisdom: "The majority of close-support aviation will be employed on planned operations." As a result, the procedure for emergency operations remained as cumbersome for the invasion as it had been for maneuvers earlier that spring. Infantry pleas for help would have to travel from assault battalions to fighter-direction control ships to headquarters ships to Uxbridge, and back to the air force units in the task force. Staffers estimated the delay between requests and action at ninety minutes to three hours for fighters, and at least two hours for light bombers. Thus, one of the central lessons of the springtime maneuvers was not incorporated into the OVERLORD setup.[58]

In other respects the planners did learn from the past. By 1944, most officers familiar with emerging tactical precepts recognized that signals communications were fundamental to effective air support of ground troops. "We all knew we were going to live and die by communications," was how Quesada put it. But until then, efficient contact between pilots and ground officers in the heat of battle had eluded the Americans. In 1942 and 1943 the close air support of ground troops had relied almost exclusively on a crude system of ground markers that were time-consuming to display, vulnerable to weather and battle smoke, and easily compromised by enemy troops. In the spring of 1944, therefore, Middle Wallop staffers spent considerable time before and after D-Day searching for the right combination of wires, receivers, transmitters, and antennae to do the job. The end result was perhaps IX Fighter Command's most important contribution to tactical air power in all of World War II.[59]

It was Quesada's great and good fortune to have Colonel Blair Garland as his signal officer. Before coming to IX TAC, Garland had been the chief communications officer in the Eighth Air Force, and had been instrumental in developing H2S, H2X and OBOE radar bombing techniques. In the summer of 1943 he had taken charge of all U.S. Air

Forces signal planning for the Normandy invasion, and when a personnel shuffle displaced him as the Eighth's ranking communications expert he called Quesada and asked for a job. Aside from his own experience, Garland brought to Middle Wallop others who had worked on OVERLORD preparations, including a civilian radar expert from the Massachusetts Institute of Technology and two AT&T telephone experts. Amazing as it was, with one chance phone call, Quesada had "inherited the very people who'd been planning the invasion for over a year." Though the competence of his staff was in many cases a reflection of Quesada's own demands for the best, sometimes—as now with Garland—he was simply lucky.[60]

Quesada admired Garland's technical genius and the two men worked well together. Quesada held Garland in "great esteem, both as a friend and as a well-qualified professional soldier." For his part, Garland felt that "Quesada was very interested in communications. Spaatz and Eaker, all they wanted to do was fly airplanes and drop bombs. Quesada realized you had to have a few messages with the ground. He recognized without communications, fighter aircraft could not operate."[61]

Garland's signals plan for OVERLORD certainly underscored that point. He placed five Signal Aircraft Warning Battalions along the southern coast of England, six Fighter Control Squadrons at airfields, and four Tactical Communications Squadrons into assault ships to direct OVERLORD air traffic. Air Support Parties with ground and air radios would accompany the first assault waves onto the beach. If that equipment failed to reach shore, Garland had established a visual communications systems of large red, orange, and yellow ground panels which would tell pilots to start, resume, or cease fire. By D plus 2, Garland would have over 400 men and an airstrip in Normandy. In order to connect these dispersed forces, Garland created fifty-three radio and telephone channels sprawled across southern England.[62]

Microwave Early Warning (MEW) Radar was the most innovative cog in the plan. Radar was the biggest technological advance of the war save nuclear fission, but until 1944 it had been a defensive and passive weapon. Then a Massachusetts Institute of Technology research team developed MEW radar, which used shorter frequencies that could identify individual aircraft with unprecedented precision. Because it was tremendously complicated and bulky, MEW equipment defied mass production, and less than a dozen sets existed by the spring of 1944. The War Department sent one of them to southern England, where the Royal Air Force's Coastal Command used it to locate distressed Allied aircraft over the Bay of Biscay and bring them home. It was, however, capable of so much more.

Garland, who had learned about MEW from one of the MIT scientists on his staff, dragged Quesada to see this new radar. Intrigued by its potential to place pilots over targets as well as to direct lost planes home, Quesada swapped two of his conventional radars for the MEW. Garland then dismantled it and packed it on eight trucks for the journey across the Channel. Against all odds, the IX Fighter Command finagled shipping space for the equipment just ten days before the invasion, and the MEW set was in Normandy soon after D-Day. It took a while for the men there to learn to use the equipment properly, but in the end it was hard to overstate its importance. "We just absolutely lived off that radar," Quesada recalled.[63]

Garland's signals plan was not perfect, but it represented a sophisticated solution to a problem that had generally eluded American forces. His scheme was so advanced that it embarrassed the First U.S. Army's signals net for OVERLORD. Two weeks before D-Day, a communications officer from that command arrived at Middle Wallop for last-minute planning. He was the officially designated Pigeon Officer, and he wanted to discuss the routing and care of birds. "The Pigeon Officer was a very serious man," one Middle Wallop staffer recounted, "but the Signal Section could hardly keep a straight face when they talked to him."[64]

Quesada had reason to feel good about his command, then, when he traveled to Bernard Montgomery's headquarters for a major OVERLORD briefing on 15 May. A gray sky spilled an endless drizzle across the greening land as Quesada's driver bumped over the roads toward London. Hugging his overcoat closer against the damp cold, Quesada reached St. Paul's School at 0915 hours and crowded into an auditorium with the other Allied leaders. Everyone was there. Prime Minister Churchill, Field Marshal Jan Christiaan Smuts, Eisenhower, Montgomery, Tedder, Admiral Bertram Ramsey, Leigh-Mallory, Sir Alan Brooke, and the other British chiefs of staff all took wooden chairs in the front row. Bradley, Generals Miles Dempsey, Courtney Hodges,

William Simpson, Henry Crerar, George Patton, the British, Canadian, and U.S. corps and division commanders, and air and naval task force commanders sat behind them, huddled together on hard wooden benches. They all rose when King George arrived, but beyond that there "was a singular lack of ceremony . . . [in the] dark and uninspiring lecture room . . . There were no cheers, no applause." The generals had other things on their minds.[65]

At 1000 hours Montgomery sealed the doors and commenced the conference. His high-pitched voice resounding with confidence, he outlined the invasion plan against an immense wall map and floor model of Normandy. On D-Day, over 2,000 ships of every description and size would spirit five divisions across the Channel to what would become five legendary beaches. At dawn, the American First Army would besiege Omaha and Utah Beaches while the British Second Army stormed Gold, Juno, and Sword. In each landing, select combat brigades would hit the sands first, swiftly followed by combat engineers and vital supporting forces like Blair Garland's Air Support Parties and the Royal Air Force's Advance Liaison Squadrons. The overall goal was to secure a firm beachhead by the first night and then move rapidly into the interior. All in all, the briefing was a vintage Montgomery perfor-mance, buttressed by a magnificent plan. The Twenty-first Army Group Commander was to the point, in firm grasp of all details, and supremely self-assured. To at least one attendee, "it was a curious experience to see so great and vital a secret, written so large and revealed to so large a company." In closing, Montgomery invited his major subordinates to fill out the particulars of the army, naval, and air roles.[66]

Leigh-Mallory detailed the air plan. After 1 June, not only would he control the British Second and the U.S. Ninth Air Forces, but he would also have temporary command of all strategic air power in England. His plan matched Montgomery's in scope. In the early hours of D-Day, over 1,900 British and American bombers would blanket the invasion beaches with 10,800 tons of ordnance. After returning to their bases to reload and refuel, the heavies would then carry out missions against bridges and towns like Caen, Carentan, and Villerville. Pathfinder air-craft equipped with H2X radar would lead the bombers if poor weather obscured the targets. Among other things, the heavy use of bomber planes for OVERLORD underscored the large tactical demands made of strategic air forces in the European campaign. "With God's help," Leigh-Mallory finished, "this great operation will be brought to a successful conclusion."[67]

Brereton delegated the Ninth briefing to Quesada, who knew better the plans for tactical airplanes in OVERLORD. Barely forty years old, and a brand new major general, Quesada took the stage in front of the august group. He began with the IX Troop Transport Command. Just after midnight on D-Day, over 1,000 C-47s would drop the 101st and Eighty-second Airborne Divisions behind the two American beaches in a daring attempt to create havoc among the German defenses and secure strategic transportation points. As dawn approached, IX Bomber Command's mediums would target specific coastal batteries and strong points near Utah Beach. After outlining the duties of these other commands, Quesada turned to his Ninth Fighter Command. All the while he spoke in short, abrupt sentences, a believer in his and the broader Allied plan. Explaining Ninth Air Force intentions through the weeks after D-Day, he swept a pointer across the map of France, grinned, and said, "We will move like that throughout our progress over the continent of Europe." A British general in attendance remembered that the wry comment raised the only laugh of the somber day.[68]

"Pete," VII Corps commander Major General J. Lawton Collins asked, "how are you going to keep the German Air Force from preventing our landing?" Lightning Joe Collins was the best corps commander of the war and had come to appreciate enemy air power as a divisional commander in the South Pacific, battling Japanese Zeros. "General," Quesada replied "there is not going to be any German Air Force there." Hushed snickers drifted up to the rafters. "Ahhh, young man, how can you be so sure?" asked Winston Churchill. "Mr. Prime Minster, because we won't let them be there. I am sure of it. There will be no German Air Force over the Normandy invasion area." Although it was a brash statement, Quesada was probably right. For D-Day, the Allies could call on almost 13,000 aircraft against a total of 3,222 Luftwaffe birds. For a long while, Churchill took the measure of the young general. At last he spoke. "You are very confident," he managed. "At least that is a great asset." With no other questions, Quesada sat down, no longer sure whether the briefing at St. Paul's was the great opportunity Brereton had said it would be.[69]

The St. Paul's generals rose when the Prime Minister spoke near the end of the day. "Let us not expect all to go according to plan," he warned. "Flexibility of mind will be one of the decisive factors." Risks would have to be taken. He exorted the men to "remember that this is an invasion, not the creation of a fortified beachhead." When the meeting closed at 1700 hours, all of the generals, from Eisenhower to junior men like Quesada, would do well to remember the Prime Minister's admonitions. In Normandy, flexibility and boldness would be required in large supply, and sometimes the Allies would muster too little of both.[70]

Quesada drove back to Middle Wallop that evening. For weeks now, planes had attacked Loire and Seine River bridges, hunted rolling stock on French rail and roadways, hit selected beach defenses, and practiced close support at proving grounds in southern England. The invasion was near, and with each day, the Allied destiny passed more and more from the high generals to the battle commanders, to the group and regimental officers, to squadron and company-grade ground officers, and finally to individual pilots and infantry grunts. Pete Quesada went to bed early that night, skipping an officers' dance. As he lay there, he must have wondered how well the carefully-laid plans would work. How accurate were his planning assumptions? How ready were his own pilots? How ready was he?[71]

After the high assembly at St. Paul's, activity throughout England intensified with preparations for the imminent attack. Vast supply dumps along peaceful country lanes filled up with ammunition, mines, engineering stores, barbed wire, and planks. Over the last days of May and the first days of June, massive columns of men and vehicles streamed south, where vast coastal areas had been sealed off to all but local residents. Into the American assembly areas came 130,000 men, tens of thousands of wheeled and tracked vehicles, and 3,500 artillery pieces. Sherman tanks, jeeps, and Dodge trucks crowded rural fields to the horizon. Within their secret tented domains, soldiers received ammunition, life jackets, and seasickness pills. The flood of food, fruit, and cigarettes thrust upon them made one man feel "as if we were being fattened like Christmas turkeys." Some were homesick, some excited, and a few eager to escape the terrifying adventure in front of them. Most wanted only to end the months of training and begin "this thing upon which all their thoughts had been focused for so long."[72]

Quesada's Air Support Parties, engineering regiments, signal construction battalions, and supply companies spilled into one of these marshaling areas. As is always the case with colossal human enterprise, last-minute troubles bedeviled attempts to put matters into final order. In spite of obsessive efforts to waterproof their vehicles, Quesada's men never did master the technique and sailed for France conscious of the possibility of stalling under fire, stuck in the surf with a flooded engine. And although his men tried in vain to remedy a critical shortage of ordnance and materiel, on D-Day Quesada had just 10,129 bombs against a planned inventory of 63,100, and only 9,000 of 20,000 jettison-fuel tanks.

An air-raid drill on 30 May underscored the fragile level of readiness. In the excitement, one man shot off his carbine by accident because he did not know how it worked. Quesada busted him to the lowest enlisted rank. Clearly, airmen were not doughboys. To a man, they all hoped no unforeseen difficulty awaited them on the far shore.[73]

Unfortunately for them, in western France the Germans were busy brewing difficulty. Throughout the spring Hitler had shored up his "Atlantic Wall" defenses after years of neglect. Total combat strength under Generalfeldmarschall Gerd von Rundstedt had increased from forty-six to fifty-eight divisions organized into six armies. Unknown to the Allies, there were two veteran attack divisions and a crack Panzer division in Normandy. The German Navy had planted sixteen huge mine fields in the narrow English Channel. Along the coast itself, laborers sprinted to bury mines and place hedgehogs, tetrahedra, Belgian gates, and simple stakes slanted seaward in order to wreck landing craft. Fortified resistance nests and concrete batteries went into beach bluffs. Inland, the defenders had blanketed likely parachute-drop zones with deadly antipersonnel stakes.

Although most of the defenses were of the simple field variety, von Rundstedt was making "Fortress Europe" less a mere propaganda slogan with each passing day. The frenzied pace reflected a growing realization in Germany that only victory in the west could now save the Third Reich. In the year preceding the Normandy invasion, Hitler had endured severe setbacks in the East against the Russians and had lost over a million men. "If they attack in the West," Hitler declared, "that attack will decide the war." The defeat of OVERLORD was so important that the Führer even sent Generalfeldmarschall Erwin Rommel, the famed Desert Fox, to take control of immediate defense readiness.[74]

For all their efforts, however, there remained serious chinks in the German armor on the eve of D-Day. Most of their troops were of dubious quality, particularly in the static coastal divisions. The average age in one was thirty-six, and another was composed almost entirely of men with stomach disorders. Most importantly, von Rundstedt and Rommel had placed German resources in limbo by disagreeing over defense strategy. Von Rundstedt saw no hope of preventing a landing, and wanted to throw the Allies back into the sea by mobile counterattack using large manpower reserves, whereas Rommel believed that Allied air superiority would prohibit the mobility required for von Rundstedt's scheme, and aspired to deny rather than repel the invasion by placing nearly all the defenders right at the sand's edge. Neither argument had won clear approval from Hitler, and the result was a makeshift settlement which served neither strategy well. Compounding matters was the success of a grand Allied plot, FORTITUDE, which feigned an invasion of the Pas de Calais. As a result, the best and brightest of the German order of battle was assigned near Calais, well to the north of the Norman beaches.[75]

Still, Allied soldiers, sailors, and airmen had sound reason to fret as they contemplated the invasion. Amphibious assault is the most difficult and dangerous of all military operations. Weather, tide, timing, and men must be in precise harmony. Armies, navies, and air forces must be in perfect order. Defenders have a huge advantage over attackers.

To make matters worse for Quesada, he received a memo from John Cannon in Italy on 2 June. The lessons of the Italian campaign were clear to Cannon. "Air power alone cannot defeat a highly organized and disciplined Army, even when that Army is virtually without air support of its own," he began. "It cannot by itself force a withdrawal by drying up the flow of command supplies . . . it cannot absolutely isolate the battle field from enemy supply or reinforcement. It cannot absolutely guarantee the immunity either of our forward formation or back areas." All in all, it was a gloomy account, and Cannon reserved scant praise for air power, merely writing that air strikes "can turn an orderly retreat into a rout."[76]

Cannon's words were a far cry from the wild claims made by strategic-air enthusiasts, and carried more sophistication and subtlety than history usually grants air leaders in war. Although the evaluation caused Quesada even more worry in the last days of preparation, at least he now knew the hard lessons of the Italian campaign. If he grasped more of tactical air power's limits than its accomplishments, that was half the battle in the spring of 1944.

On the evening before the invasion, Quesada briefed his group commanders for the last time. In an easy banter which belied his own state of nerves, he addressed the small assemblage about D-Day. He defined the contours of the ground invasion, the Allied order of battle, and the efforts of other air force commands. He then concentrated on the thirty specific tasks assigned to Middle Wallop. The vast majority of the duties were planned to the smallest detail, and if on the appointed day all went well there would be little for Quesada and his commanders to do save follow the detailed script. By June of 1944, however, most men in the room knew that war had a way of skirting intended schemes.[77]

For the group commanders, the briefing inspired confidence. "I had never heard such a pep talk before or since," remembered one fifty years later. "I have never had nor met a commander with such charisma. By the time he finished talking I wanted to forgo the dinner and rush back to my base and start the invasion."[78]

Pete Quesada went to bed on the eve of D-Day filled with some apprehension and a good deal of hope; hope that the interdiction campaign had been successful enough, hope that improved fighter-bomber tactics would pay dividends in France, hope that the lack of air–ground exercises would not impair the battle, hope that the MEW radar would live up to its billing, hope that the fragile alliance between bomber and fighter enthusiasts would hold in the face of hard fighting, and hope that the Germans would be taken sufficiently by surprise.

Throughout England, around America, in Canada, Australia, New Zealand, and indeed in most of Europe, people waited and hoped. To a young girl hiding in occupied Amsterdam it was "no exaggeration to say that all Amsterdam, all Holland, yes the whole west coast of Europe, right down to Spain, talks of the invasion day and night, debates about it, and makes bets on it and—hopes." As dusk settled on 5 June, the world, and Anne Frank, waited.[79]

Chapter Five

The Fighter Bomber Boys Are Doing More to Make This Campaign a Success Than Anyone Ever Anticipated

---

UTAH BEACH, NORMANDY. 8 JUNE 1944. 0945 HOURS. Pete Quesada slammed his plane onto the one dirt strip behind Utah Beach, nearly cutting to pieces an engineer still clearing brush from the field. Commandeering a jeep, he met hurriedly with Blair Garland, who had arrived in France on D-Day. Then he rushed to the VII Corps command post to confer with John Collins and Omar Bradley before meeting with representatives from his own support personnel who were crowded onto the beachhead.

A lot had happened in three days. On the sixth of June, Canadian, British, and U.S. forces had crawled onto five beaches along the Normandy coast in Operation OVERLORD. For the most part, the invasion's first day had been successful, although at Omaha Beach, poor weather, stout German resistance, and the inherent difficulties of amphibious assault had pushed the Americans to the brink of defeat. On 7 June only extraordinary heroism on the ground and swift action in the air had saved the situation. Aided by thirteen close-air-support missions, battalion-sized assault teams had pushed slowly inland. Thirty-six hours after the initial landings, the Americans had established a foothold on Omaha Beach, and all along the coast the Allies were finally ashore.

But then the invaders had failed to advance as planned. Just behind the beaches a thin German defensive crust held, creating a logistical bottleneck for the Anglo-Americans. Shipping and beach space were so limited that it was difficult for even the most critical American air support personnel to reach their appointed places on the soil of Normandy. A precious few men from forward directing posts managed to squeeze onto the shore that first day, but their equipment had been lost in the heavy surf and the battle had blocked them from moving inland. When two of Quesada's radar units at last disembarked into the battle on D plus 1, they found that all the choice high ground remained in enemy hands.[1]

There were other problems as well. Hewing airfields out of the Norman *bocage* was difficult if not impossible as long as the beach was taking German sniper fire. By the night of 7 June, aviation engineers had managed to cut only one makeshift landing strip of 2,000 feet from the pastureland behind Utah Beach. It would be another two days before a single respectable runway existed in the American zone.[2]

By then, the Germans had recovered from their initial surprise and were rushing reinforcements into northwestern France from as close as Brest and as far away as Poland. Within days, Erwin Rommel would be confident enough to report that "a quick enemy breakthrough to Paris is now hardly a possibility. We've got lots of stuff coming up." On the Allied side, First Army Commander Omar Bradley foresaw the colossal battle that would be Normandy and declared "this war will be won or lost on the beaches." For everyone, the next fortnight would pass in a whirl of activity as attackers and defenders alike struggled to contain the inexorable momentum of war.[3]

It was to this purpose that Quesada had flown to France on 8 June. To him it seemed that everyone in his command had problems. The aviation engineers found it hard to work with hoe and shovel in one hand and gun and grenade in the other. For two days, Master Sergeant Charles Lane's platoon had calmly surveyed a potential airstrip while Germans fired a four-inch field artillery piece less than a hundred yards away. "We walked the center line of a mile-long runway," Lane recalled. "We figured those Germans would be interested in bigger things than us." For a while he was right. The defenders ignored the construction until heavy graders arrived, then they destroyed the equipment and killed thirteen men. Not trained as riflemen, Lane's group and other engineers soon grew frustrated with their lot. "Who do they think we are, the bloody infantry?" complained one to nobody in particular. The delays and deaths eventually abated as engineers learned the value of deep foxholes, but in the meantime the all-important airfield construction was far behind schedule.[4]

Members of the 70th Fighter Wing, from which Quesada would draw the nucleus of his command post, experienced similar obstacles on the way to war. Like many, they had sweated through the invasion delays aboard landing craft since the first of June. The beachmaster finally ordered them ashore at 1600 hours on D plus 1. Wading in from five feet of water, they beheld a vivid portrait of modern combat. "The beach is a scene of intense activity and confusion; bodies are everywhere strewn about haphazardly," one officer recorded. All around there were "bits of clothing, destroyed vehicles and equipment. As we continue walking up the beach, a bulldozer digs a ditch to serve as a common grave for the dead, Americans and Germans."[5]

Sniper fire beleaguered 70th-Wing personnel as they passed through Colleville and St. Laurent on their way to Cricqueville. When darkness came their destination was still in German hands, so military police halted the 220-man procession. For two days, they bivouacked where they stopped, unable to move against stubborn defenses. As the situation stagnated, Quesada grew as worried as he would ever be in the war. "I knew if we did not bring some order to the situation soon, get some airfields up and communications going, our [air] efforts would be disabled."[6]

At last the situation improved. Pushing hard, Quesada's men reached a small crossroads just short of Cricqueville called Au Gay late on 9 June. Within twenty-fours hours they had precious land-line communications with ground units, and Blair Garland had jury-rigged a wireless signal apparatus. Slowly, the disorder of war of was starting to swing in Quesada's favor.[7]

The throng of complications delayed but did not cripple Quesada's command. Although by 10 June his MEW radar was not yet ashore, he had two conventional radars on the beach. His signals plan was not fully implemented, but he now had direct communication with First Army headquarters, with the two corps already in the battle, and with Eisenhower's headquarters in England. Three of his forward directing posts were still on the water, but two were ashore in Normandy. Many of his support personnel remained mired in a traffic jam stretching back to British ports, but he had in France 449 headquarters troops at Au Gay and Grandcamp, and some 1,600 engineers, ground crew and signals troops sprinkled throughout the beachhead. Airfield construction was behind schedule, but the engineers finally had momentum, and two decent strips would soon be operational. There was still considerable confusion on the ground, but Allied airplanes based in England continued to assert their near-total domination of the skies.[8]

To be sure, there was still reason for pessimism, but there was also justification for hope that men were now besting the chaos of war. So at 1530 hours on 10 June, Pete Quesada wired London a simple message: "Headquarters IX Tactical Air Command established on the continent."[9]

The critical battle of Carentan was already in full swing. After the difficult landings on Omaha Beach, the Allies needed to link the two U.S. beaches and block German reinforcements rushing to the area. The land between Utah and Omaha Beaches was dominated by a thirty-mile flood plain stretching inland to Carentan. Earlier, the Germans had flooded this region with water to stall the attackers, and on 9 June Bernard Montgomery had decided to avoid a costly fight in the swamps and concentrate on the capture of Carentan. If successful, the operation could envelop the Germans in the coastal lowlands and bridge the two American beachheads.

On the ground, the task of tying the beachheads together fell to the 101st Airborne Division. While the 101st had only the light equipment common to airborne troops, well-equipped elements of both the German Sixth Parachute Regiment and the 17th SS Panzer Grenadier Division were already marching toward Carentan. If Montgomery hoped to link Utah and Omaha Beaches with this attack, the Americans would need air power to compensate for their lack of artillery and to intercept the Germans massing along the front. The Carentan battle, then, would place a premium on air support.[10]

As early as dawn on 9 June the first request for air support crackled over the Ninth Air Force radio net. It was a gloomy morning and bad weather canceled the mission. But by 0900 hours the sky looked better, and air controllers in ships offshore approved a strike against four concrete gun emplacements blocking the airborne forces. In England, a group of Quesada's planes roared from their runway. Crossing the coast of France, they quickly passed the bright cerise panels marking American positions and aimed their 500-pound bombs. Erratic weather conditions stymied another request that evening—this one a personal appeal by corps commander J. Lawton Collins—but late in the day fighter-bombers managed to strike two German command posts.[11]

Planes were busy behind enemy lines as well. Mustang pilots ranging thirty to fifty miles beyond the battle spied *Kampfgruppe* Heinz, a two-division battle group scheduled to lead a German counterthrust at the American beaches. Sweeping down, six planes hit the first of a dozen trains before three antiaircraft artillery pieces swung into action. With little ammunition and fuel left, the pilots escaped from the area and radioed their discovery to Middle Wallop. They left behind a smashed train and a thousand stranded Germans.[12]

Quesada quickly sized up *Kampfgruppe* Heinz as a serious threat to the U.S. position, and directed other Mustangs to the area. Before the day was out, additional planes struck at two trains, destroying one but completely missing the other. Aided by medium bombers from the IX Bomber Command, however, the attacks did manage to cut both sets of railroad tracks, stopping all train movement in the area for twelve hours. That was enough to prompt Quesada to boast that he was "quite proud of our ability to cut railroad tracks and destroy bridges with a minimum number of sorties. That makes a helluva mess."[13]

On the German side, these raids delayed all movement. Three Wehrmacht staff officers had spent the day trying to reach the battle, only to find travel in a single automobile nearly impossible. As one of them explained, their journey "was a nightmare of ditching the car, running for cover, being machine-gunned, resuming the journey and having these same events repeated every few miles. Any vehicle attempting the trip must have at least three on board, one to drive and two to act as forward and aft aircraft spotters."[14]

Erwin Rommel agreed. "I was at the front yesterday and am going again to-day," he wrote his wife on 10 June, "the enemy's air superiority has a very grave effect on our movements. There's simply no answer to it. It's quite likely to start at other places soon." The famed Desert Fox could not have been more correct.[15]

The next day's sky was blue, and the Allied flyers answered every petition for help. Over seventy planes in three waves supported a ground advance into the outskirts of Carentan early in the morning. Later, Lightnings of the 373rd Group strafed motor transports unloading ammunition, and another two groups cut nine rail lines between the advancing *Kampfgruppe* Heinz and the front. By nightfall, the Americans on the ground had advanced considerably closer to Carentan and were poised to charge the town center on the eleventh.[16]

As would keep happening for the rest of the war, weather then interrupted the momentum of attack. June 11 was neither a windy nor a rainy day, and to the uninitiated it seemed good enough for war planes. Experienced airmen knew better. The cloud ceiling was simply much too low for dive bombing. "It is depressing to think I have ... more than 11,000 aircraft and I cannot make full use of them," AEAF commander Leigh-Mallory complained in his diary. "I confess to experiencing a certain sense of frustration."[17]

The low clouds compelled air controllers to refuse all requests for air support near Carentan. Five times J. Lawton Collins asked for help, and five times air controllers or Quesada told him no. Collins became angry, arguing that there was no heavy rain or fog to preclude air operations. His ire only grew when the first combat companies of *Kampfgruppe* Heinz finally limped into Carentan late in the day. Clearly, given the preinvasion squabbles between air and ground officers, it would take a while before the Allied battle leaders worked well together on the far shore.[18]

Fortunately, the weather improved slightly on 12 June, the fourth day of the attack. In a midmorning strike over two hundred planes wrecked trucks, killed horses, and mangled an entire German company. Beyond the immediate battle area, Lieutenant Wilford Crutchfield winged his Thunderbolt through low clouds and found a motor convoy and train moving gingerly toward Carentan. After relaying his find to controllers, he hit the deck and came in shooting. He destroyed seven troop trucks before other pilots zoomed overhead and wrecked forty-one trucks, seven locomotives, and fifteen flatcars loaded with vehicles.[19]

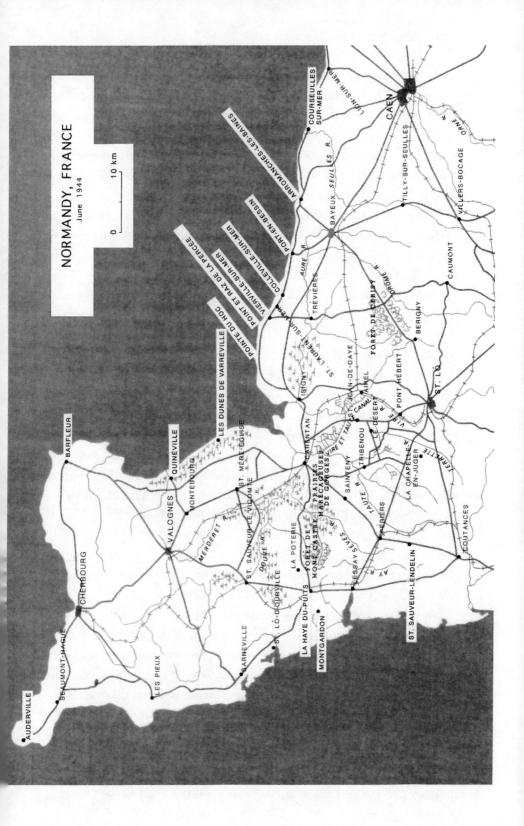

NORMANDY, FRANCE
June 1944

0   10 km

Further inland, Captain Robert Stephens led the 354th Group on a banner day. Striking hard at an airfield near Le Mans, the Pioneer Mustang Group destroyed fifty railways cars, several flak towers, and a radio station. In the raid an American pilot sustained several hits in one of the few serious dogfights above Normandy in June. Nearly lifeless, he slumped over his controls and his Mustang banked violently. He managed to bail out but his chute failed to open.[20]

Remarkably, Germans continued crawling into the Carentan line on 12 June. But denied effective rail and road transport by incessant air raids, the troops of *Kampfgruppe* Heinz were tired, hungry, and disorganized. "After four attacks by the fighter-bomber in three days of slow advance, we finally ran out of ways to wind through the maze of broken tracks," recounted *Feldwebel* (Staff Sergeant) Karl Laun. On bicycles, horses, or foot, the journey had become more dangerous and time consuming. Originally slated to take positions at the front on 9 June, the leading elements of *Kampfgruppe* Heinz did not arrive until two days later. The bulk of surviving reserves did not reach action until 17 June. In the tough fighting of Normandy, a week was a long time to wait for reinforcements to fill the ranks.[21]

Without effective reserve support, the Germans finally evacuated Carentan on the afternoon of the twelfth. Air power had ruined the place and played a decisive role. According to the German army commander, Gerd von Rundstedt, the town fell because of "unbearable" Allied air superiority, which rendered "daylight movement impossible" and caused a severe "lack of ammunition." Indeed, from the outset, Ninth Air Force planes had made up for the paratroopers' lack of artillery and impeded German efforts to mass a counterattack.[22]

No doubt prewar theorists would have opposed this substitution of planes for cannon as a waste of resources. But as one corps commander put it, "Fighter-bomber support is extremely important until such time as field artillery with sufficient ammunition is in position." Clearly, for the soldiers of the Normandy campaign, theory was one thing and practice was quite another. More often than not, the exigencies of battle— not principles—dictated their actions.[23]

The assault on Carentan challenged other preinvasion assumptions as well. Before D-Day, Quesada and most planners believed that interdiction efforts would dominate early air operations in France. Close-air-support missions, they thought, would develop only after the Allies had a firm beachhead some thirty miles deep and there existed sufficient distance between defenders and attackers to conduct safe operations. Instead, U.S. ground units asked for close air support 184 times in the week following the invasion. In the British zone, where the bulk of German defenses had stopped the English before Caen, support sorties were even more common. Without a doubt, German tenacity and Allied difficulties in getting artillery ashore had combined to put a high value on the mobile firepower of aircraft. If they did not know it before the invasion, battle leaders learned fast that close support was an early and important component of the air war. As Pete Quesada told his group commanders, "The fighter-bomber boys are doing more to make this campaign a success than anyone ever anticipated."[24]

Of course, interdiction remained a vital air force task. With the exception of British Bomber Command, every Allied air force spent considerable effort in the early weeks of OVERLORD intercepting defenders hurrying to the battle zone. The race to build up forces was critical for both sides, and leaders all around understood that the outcome rested not so much on battle heroics as on simple logistics. In the month after 6 June, the Germans would attempt to transfer some twenty-three divisions to Normandy, which would bring their battle total to nearly thirty divisions. The Anglo-Americans would have nowhere near the equivalent. If the Germans succeeded, the fighting, already difficult, could only get worse for the Allies.[25]

To avoid that potential disaster, from 2 to 17 June Jimmy Doolittle's Eighth Air Force flew just two strategic missions and dedicated virtually its entire effort to tactical interdiction. On 15 June, over a thousand B-17 Flying Forts ruined seven key Loire River rail bridges. The next day Doolittle's fighters wreaked havoc on eight trains chugging toward Normandy, destroying nine locomotives and hundreds of cars with a loss of just three P-38s. In eight days, the Eighth, conceived and developed as a strategic air force, flew no less than 5,900 bomber sorties and dropped over 14,000 tons of bombs in direct support of land operations. In total, they struck at fifty-eight marshaling yards, thirty-eight bridges, twenty-two trains, and nine convoys. Although bomber pilots were not trained in the intricacies of tactical work, and they were more easily hampered by poor weather than Quesada's flyers, the sheer weight of these attacks produced good results. According to Germany's armaments Minister Albert Speer, the strikes were catastrophic.[26]

Medium bombers of the IX Bomber Command and the British Second Air Force also attacked marshaling yards and bridges. At the Foligny rail station, an American B-25 raid caught two idling troop trains and cut tracks in forty places. The damage there and at thirty other yards was notable, though the Germans patched the lines expertly and their troops were usually delayed only a short time. Strikes against isolated bridges were more effective. Thirteen times, IX Bomber mediums blasted rail and road spans. Marauder and Mitchell pilots wrecked crossings at Laval, Pontaubault, Coutances, Chartres, and Beaugency. Like the Flying Fortresses, these two-engine bombers experienced little opposition from the Luftwaffe, and the IX Bomber Command lost just twelve planes to combat in the entire month of June.[27]

From the German perspective, the combined interdiction efforts by the Allied air forces produced swift and horrific results. The 266th Division left Brittany for Normandy on 10 June but, denied rail transport and the use of major roads, the soldiers advanced less then ten miles a day; they did not reach the front until the twenty-fifth. The journey of the 353rd Division was longer still. They left Brittany on 14 June and finally marched into Normandy on the month's last day, advancing at a pace slower than that of a typical American Civil War march some eighty years earlier.

German reinforcements traveling from southern France had still greater trouble. The 271st, 272nd, 276th, and 277th were all crack attack divisions and Hitler had pinned high hopes on their combined ability to check the invasion. But despite generous motorized complements, their trek north took, on average, a full month. Along the way they contended with French sabotage, blown bridges, and fighter-bomber raids. The 276th was repeatedly strafed at crossroads, towns, and clearings. Elements of the 272nd tried passage by train on four separate occasions before air strikes convinced them to walk the last 180 miles at night. In a journey that became all too typical for the Germans they crept through the darkness, past destroyed rail lines and ruined communications outposts. Increasingly, the few vehicles they did use were makeshift wood-burning trucks, so critical had their supply situation become.[28]

The fate of the Panzer Lehr Division was the most demoralizing for the Germans. A reinforced Panzer unit, it had been specifically organized to repel the invasion. Two thirds of its personnel were veterans, and it had more tanks, armored half-tracks, trucks, and motor transport than any other German division. Its commander, Fritz Bayerlein, was a soldier's soldier who had served with distinction in Africa and Russia. The Panzer Lehr Division was stationed in the center of France, ready to meet the invasion anywhere it occurred, and the Germans' best chance to repel the Anglo-Americans rested on its shoulders.

Higher commands had ordered the division to the beach as soon as the Allies waded ashore. From the start, it was dogged by saboteurs and ceaseless air attack. British and American fighter-bombers came day after day, sweeping down with fury and leaving death. Bayerlein himself was twice the target of direct strikes. When it finally did reach the front, the division was shattered. The journey had cost it 130 trucks, a half-dozen tanks, eighty-four half-tracks, and casualties too numerous to count. Above all, the Panzer Lehr Division had suffered incalculable frustration and delay.[29]

Everywhere the story was the same. The daily struggle to avoid air attack, the lack of food, and the strain of clandestine night marches along deserted country lanes all took their toll on the Germans. At first rushing into Normandy, reinforcements from every quadrant soon trotted, then walked, then crawled to the battle zone. Many grew frustrated with their own lack of air support. "Yah, for eleven days I saw seven Luftwaffe and seven thousand Thunderbolts," one prisoner complained bitterly. Yet he and thousands of others were compelled to carry forward across what von Rundstedt termed a "traffic desert." Soon, Wehrmacht soldiers would have a new name for Allied fighter planes: *Achtung Jabos*—literally, "attention bombers," but roughly translated as "most terrible weapon."[30]

For some the strain simply became too much. Adolf Eisenreich was a new officer and just nineteen years old. After enduring strafing attacks near Dinan, Dol, Avranches, and Granville on four consecutive days, he turned his Luger on himself. Those that did survive to reach the battle were almost always too tired and demoralized to take immediate positions in the line.[31]

As the Germans struggled to cope with the incessant strikes by Allied heavy and medium bombers, Quesada's fighters continued their support for American ground troops at the front. In the days after the Carentan battle, the Ninth Air Force mounted numerous close-support missions as J. Lawton Collins' VII Corps swung west to sever the Cotentin Peninsula and isolate the port city of Cherbourg. Quesada's P-47s flew five missions on 13 June and medium bombers from the IX Bomber Command joined the fighters for ten missions on the fourteenth, one of which saved the First Division from an imminent counterattack. Weather on the fifteenth was poor, and flyers roared from their English bases only three times in support of the doughboys. The sun came back the next day, however, and the tactical air war reached a new high as seven of Quesada's Thunderbolt and Mustang groups flew eleven missions.[32]

Despite that effort, on the night of 16 June J. Lawton Collins complained to Omar Bradley that one of his regiments had been delayed by strong enemy air action. Bradley in turn complained to Quesada, who investigated the incident and discovered that two ME-109s had indeed harassed the regiment in question. He was amazed, however, to learn that two planes constituted a "strong enemy air action." Apparently, American ground troops had grown spoiled by their unprecedented air superiority.

In fact, given the Anglo-American difficulties on the ground, it was hard to imagine a successful OVERLORD without the Allies' air strength—a point Quesada now determined to drive home. He ordered reconnaissance photographs taken of both the Allied beachhead, crammed with equipment and men in broad daylight, and the German rear, devoid of any movement save three horses. "Air superiority does not mean immunity from harassing attacks, General," Quesada told Bradley as sternly as he dared when he showed him the pictures, "it means relative freedom of movement." The Army commander did not say a word. Instead, he hurried off to Collins, who took both Quesada and Bradley to the regimental commander. There, Bradley stole Quesada's lecture. "You cannot expect to never be under air attack, Colonel," announced the Army Commander. "This is a war, for God's sake."[33]

On 17 June the infantry and supporting air elements launched their

final push to cut Cherbourg off from the rest of France. At 0830 hours
the 363rd Group scrambled to strike German troop concentrations outside Carteret, a coastal town at the far edge of the Cotentin Peninsula.
Later that morning forty-eight Lightnings joined the attack, though a
lack of appropriate marking panels on the ground forced controllers to
cancel three additional strikes. That problem was cleared up in the afternoon, and nearly two hundred fighter pilots staged five more missions. With each attacking wave, pilots did material damage to German
gun emplacements, command posts, and troop and tank concentrations.
By nightfall the Americans were just miles from cutting the Cotentin
peninsula in two and sealing Cherbourg's fate.[34]

June 18th would be a big day. As the sun came up, eight fighter-
bomber groups based in southern England launched 384 planes toward
France. Forty-five P-38s from the 367th Group streaked across the clear
sky of Normandy near La Rouche and dive-bombed a bridge and power
station. Turning home, they strafed anything that moved, turning the
French village into a smoking ruin. Captain Joe Rettig even claimed the
destruction of an enemy vegetable cart before ground fire crashed his
plane.[35]

While Rettig shot at potatoes and carrots, Harold Holt's 366th Group
headed for Périers. Screaming along at 1,500 feet, the sixteen-plane
flight spotted vehicles along a wooded lane. "Red leader going down,"
Holt radioed. His ship banked suddenly toward the vehicles and settled
into a smooth dive. He fired his guns, the incendiary slugs sparkling
like diamonds all over the trucks. More flyers followed, and soon there
was only a burning mass of metal along the quiet country lane. With
bombs still under his wings, Holt searched for another target. Thirty
minutes later he set fire to a power station and returned to England.[36]

Clear skies and plenty of targets made for a good day all around. The
405th Group managed to ruin a column of armed vehicles. Pilots of the
370th Group cut rail lines in thirty-eight places, destroying forty-five
freight, ammunition, and fuel cars. The 371st Group bested that record
in a fighter sweep near Valognes, where they killed 800 to 1,000 men
and wrecked ninety-eight motor vehicles. By the end of the day Collins'
VII Corps had at last traversed the Cotentin Peninsula and isolated
Cherbourg from the rest of the Third Reich. Now the Allies had a con-

tinuous front from Caen through the peninsula, with Cherbourg behind them and Paris beckoning in the distance. A new phase of the war was about to begin.[37]

By then Quesada's flyers had tallied over 13,000 sorties in support of the invading troops. In addition to their growing close-support mission, they had cut rail tracks at 170 locations, destroyed thirty-eight bridges and tunnels, seventeen supply and ammunition dumps, and fifty-three marshaling yards. Taken together, the fighter sweeps, beach patrols, dive-bombing, and close-support operations had set a dizzying pace.[38]

Amid all the action, pilots learned the basic tactics of what would be their work for the next year. They learned to skim the treetops at slow speed to better spot camouflaged Germans. They learned that the Germans often used houses or chateaux for gun emplacements and usually placed antitank weapons just around road curves or intersections. From mistakes that cost lives, they learned to respect German 20mm flak guns on half-tracks. They learned to use 100-pound bombs, which did not cause craters, for soft targets like troop concentrations. They learned to value the blast effect of 500-pounders for hard targets like tanks and armored vehicles. They learned that 1000-pounders were best for general interdiction work. Members of the 367th Group even learned to carry two 2000-pounders on the twin-engine P-38s, nearly equaling the payload of bombers.

Beyond these tactical lessons, pilots came to appreciate the growing number of advance landing fields in Normandy. Constructed from light-gauge wire mesh and heavy tarpaper, there were five such runways in Normandy by mid-month; each one allowed as many as three fighter groups to refuel and rearm between missions without returning to England. Before groups moved to France, this "roulement" system worked wonders, in effect increasing the operational strength of Quesada's command by one third. In the weeks after D-Day, these fields dispensed over thirty thousand gallons of fuel, a hundred thousand rounds of ammunition, and hundreds of bombs.[39]

Quesada's staff learned important things, too. To accommodate better the infantry's high demands for fighter bombers, Colonel Gil Meyers, a former All-American football player at West Point and a key Quesada subordinate, devised armed reconnaissance missions. Consisting of flights of four to sixteen planes, these missions roamed the

French countryside without portfolio, searching for the random train or armored column. Under ideal conditions it was a poor use of resources, and placed unanticipated wear on the fragile runways in France. But Quesada approved the strategy anyway, telling one officer, "We must make concessions every day to this war if we want to win. The unimaginative and doctrinaire chap is lost in this war." Omar Bradley certainly agreed, calling armed reconnaissance missions "one of the outstanding developments of the tactical air force supporting our armies."[40]

Perhaps most important of all, the fighter-bomber flyers learned to hold in high regard their mission of close air support. Weaned on the glory of big bombers and dogfights, they came to the war without any basic enthusiasm for their tactical tasks. But witnessing their own handiwork against the Germans day after day had been a strong medicine for disappointment, and they now embraced their assignment. "The boys hitherto had considered their airplanes high-altitude fighter planes and were somewhat skeptical about its [sic] abilities as a fighter-bomber," explained one group executive officer, "though they soon began to like the work close to the ground, where they were aware of the speed and destructive force of the planes."[41]

All these developments made Quesada happy. In the middle of June he told a former commander of his that "Our lads are doing a splendid job," an assessment Omar Bradley would certainly have endorsed. On 20 June, the Army Commander asked Quesada to thank the pilots for "the fine work they have been doing and of the close cooperation they have given the ground troops. Their ability to disrupt the enemy's communications, supply and movement of troops has been a vital factor in our rapid progress in expanding our beachhead. I realize that their work may not catch the headlines any more than does the work of some of our foot soldiers, but I am sure that I express the feelings of every ground-force commander from squad leaders to myself as Army Commander when I extend my congratulations on their very fine work."[42]

Throughout these first weeks in France, Quesada had directed his air war from two bases, one at Middle Wallop in England and one at Grandcamp in Normandy. The constant commuting took a toll on him, and he complained to his brother that sometimes he felt he was "nothing more than a messenger boy." This back-and-forth travel abated at about midmonth, however, when the IX TAC established a full command post on the Continent adjacent to First Army Headquarters. It was a true field headquarters, an austere place alternately dusty or muddy and always dirty. At first Quesada lived in a tent; later he moved into a dingy trailer. In either place, his bed was never far from his communication and operation huts. The mess, where a vase of flowers was daily placed on a white linen tablecloth, was the only island of civilization in the whole compound.[43]

The efficiency of tactical aviation depended on close air–ground cooperation, and from their first moments in France Quesada and First Army commander Omar Bradley worked to forge an alliance. Bradley was a sturdy, prudent, and shrewd Missourian. His father died when he was fourteen, and young Omar worked in a railway workshop until he won an appointment to West Point. He graduated with Dwight Eisenhower, and served in the U.S. Army for thirty-two years before seeing his first action as a corps commander in Tunisia. Like Quesada and so many other generals of the war, he was a Marshall man, having impressed the future chief of staff in the mid-1930s at Fort Benning. Bradley lacked George Patton's imagination and flamboyance and Eisenhower's charm and grace, but he was thoroughly loyal and completely dependable. A soldier's soldier, he lived an austere field existence and tolerated diverse temperaments down the ranks. That he fought his wars strictly by the book was both his virtue and his vice.

At fifty, Bradley was ten years older than Quesada and on the surface little seemed to suggest that the youthful, rambunctious air general would serve well with the staid, cautious army commander. But the two had a common zeal to win the war and to ignore the bitter history of air–ground animosity. They set up their command posts adjacent to each other, and their sleeping vans were never more than thirty feet apart. As Quesada recalled, "The only thing that separated us was a hedgerow, that so a single bomb could not kill both of us."[44]

Bradley and Quesada also shared a dislike of Lewis Brereton. The Ninth Air Force commander had by then established his own advance command post in a magnificent three-story chateau two miles from the First Army/IX TAC compound, a development that prompted Bradley's aide Chester Hansen to remark derisively that "Fighting a war is more than finding a nice place to live." Quesada had long been ambivalent about serving under Brereton, and now Bradley reaffirmed his own judgment that Brereton was "difficult to do business with" and "not sincere nor energetic nor cooperative like Quesada. He did not seem interested in air–ground team, was a purist in air effort. Difficult for him to realize full use that could be made of air in assisting ground operations."[45]

For these reasons and more, Quesada and Bradley developed an extraordinary working relationship. As no other human endeavor could do, the crucible of combat command forged a quick and easy friendship between the two men.[46] "I liked him right off," remembered Quesada. "Brad did not tell me how to run the air war, and I did not interfere with the alignment of divisions along his front. We spent an awfully [sic] lot of time together in Normandy, and we never once had a substantial disagreement."[47]

For his part, Bradley appreciated Quesada's enthusiasm and can-do attitude. "Nothing conventional about Quesada," wrote Bradley's aide after the two generals spent 17 June touring the battle zone. "When he talks power, he means everything but the kitchen sink." Three weeks into the Normandy fighting, the consensus at First Army was that "Quesada was a fine unpretentious field soldier and has done more than anyone else to bring air and ground closer together in this operation."

Like themselves, their respective staffs at IX TAC and First Army interacted continuously and created an efficient system of tactical operations. Each night at 2000 hours, air and ground staffers gathered in a tent to plan the next day's action. Colonel Robert McClenahan, Quesada's intelligence chief, commenced the meeting with a brief summary and overview of the battle. The First Army meteorologist then forecast the weather, followed by reports from Bradley's intelligence and operations representatives. Twenty minutes into the conference, the ground officers presented requests for air support. Colonel Lorry Tindal, IX TAC operations officer, then allotted groups to each mission deemed appropriate, carefully setting aside required reserves for escort duty with heavy and medium bombers.

The entire plan was then given to Quesada and Bradley for approval. Confident in the competence of subordinates, they seldom made adjustments. Clerks pounded the plan into operations orders, which were sent out to the appropriate groups and the combined Allied air force nerve center at Uxbridge. At Uxbridge, Trafford Leigh-Mallory rarely invoked the veto power he had over all tactical air operations. He understood well the need for a decentralized command in the war and granted Quesada and his British counterpart, Harry Broadhurst, unusual latitude. The whole process was usually over by midnight. On clear mornings, Thunderbolts, Mustangs, and Lightnings were in the air just hours later.[48]

Yet, despite the general efficiency and goodwill at First Army/IX TAC Headquarters, there was persistent tension about the air war elsewhere in the Allied camp. Leigh-Mallory's rejection of Montgomery's plan to capture Caen with an airborne operation reignited this bickering. Montgomery was incensed, and his relationships with other air barons then further deteriorated. He exploded when the commander of the British Second Tactical Air Force, Arthur "Maori" Coningham, withheld important close-air-support missions at midmonth in deference to Allied interdiction efforts behind the German front. Writing to Chief of the Imperial Staff Sir Alan Brooke, Montgomery declared that "[My] main anxiety these days is the possibility that we should not get the full value from our great air power because of jealousies and friction among the air barons. The real 'nigger in the woodpile' is Mary [sic, for 'Maori'] Coningham; I know him well and he is a bad man, not genuine and terribly jealous. There is constant friction between him and L-M [Leigh-Mallory]. L-M does not know much about it but he is a very genuine chap and will do anything he can to help win the war. . . . Mary [Coningham] spends his time in trying to get L-M to trip-up. . . . We manage all right so far. But several hours a day are wasted in argument with the opposing camps, and in ensuring that the air jealousies do not lose us the battle."[49]

It was a harsh triad, but even Leigh-Mallory found truth in Montgomery's complaints. In the privacy of his diary, he confessed that both Coningham and Eisenhower's deputy, Air Chief Marshal Sir Arthur Tedder, were indeed "double dealing" in their allocation of air assets. The result, in his view, was to sometimes "deny the Army what it wanted in the field."[50]

Frustrating news from the front only exacerbated these air–ground animosities. Excepting J. Lawton Collins' slow but steady march across the Cotentin Peninsula, there was little in the early going of OVERLORD to foster optimism among the Allies. British forces had been rebuffed at Villages-Bocage. Caen, with its crucial road net, was still in German hands even though Montgomery had planned to capture it on the invasion's first day. In the American sector, troops remained far short of intermediate objectives like St. Lô and Coutances. Everywhere, the invaders had paid in blood for each yard gained, and casualty rates in some Allied divisions exceeded 50 percent. There were already 26,000 dead or wounded soldiers in the ten U.S. divisions that had seen substantial action. Soon certain units would be in utter disarray, prostrate from losses or low morale. Already there was quiet talk of stalemate.[51]

This latent crisis made the swift capture of Cherbourg all the more important. Collins' VII Corps had isolated Cherbourg on 18 June, and now the Americans commenced their campaign to grab the Allies' first major port on the continent. The planning had begun in earnest at First Army headquarters near Grandcamp on 17 June. At their nightly meeting, Omar Bradley lobbied Quesada for an unprecedented air attack to blast a path into the fortress city. For twenty minutes Quesada mulled over the maps, charts, and reconnaissance photos; then he announced his support for the scheme. He told Bradley that the contemplated show was too ambitious for his command alone, however, and that he would go to England the next morning and sell it to his superiors in the air forces. With luck, they could launch the attack within forty-eight hours. A buoyed Bradley adjourned the meeting, and the two generals enjoyed a late dinner together. Toward midnight, Bradley's aide, Major Chester Hansen, happily reported that "Quesada and General [Bradley] agree perfectly on use of air power for Cherbourg."[52]

Quesada clambered aboard his P-38 and winged to England early on the eighteenth. At Hillingdon House he briefed the Allied air commanders on the plan. His maps showed the terrain before Cherbourg divided into grids with surveyor-like precision. The ground troops wanted each section saturated with bombs. The proposal would require nearly 2,000 planes. Only the action at Cassino in Italy earlier that spring had been a bigger air-ground show. Nervous lest his colleagues balk at such a large operation, Quesada moved quickly through his presentation. Then he awaited the judgment of others.[53]

The conferees broke into alliances that had become, by then, all too common. Arthur Harris of Bomber Command and Jimmy Doolittle of

Eighth Air Force weighed in against the plan, doubting the wisdom of using precious bombers for anything save strategic missions deep behind enemy lines. Just as predictably, Trafford Leigh-Mallory and the tactical air force commanders, Lewis Brereton and "Maori" Coningham, argued for the attack. Brereton, in particular, spoke persistently of the effort "to blast all the way into Cherbourg." These factions haggled back and forth until Tooey Spaatz threw his support behind the plan. Because he was the senior U.S. airman in Europe, Spaatz's approval carried the day and guaranteed that some 1,200 of Doolittle's heavy bombers would participate in the raid. As the meeting adjourned Quesada's face cracked into his signature smile. "That settles that," he said to Harris with whispered bravado.[54]

Armed with the endorsement, Quesada raced back to Grandcamp late in the day. There he, Bradley, and VII Corps Commander J. Lawton Collins quickly readied operational orders for the following morning. Though it was a swiftly prepared offensive, it was neither reckless nor imprudent. Indeed, the plan was a logistical extension of the air-ground fighting since D-Day. For ten days, the tactical air team had successfully intercepted German reinforcements and had helped the infantry plow through the rich Norman countryside. Now that they were fighting an offensive campaign with a firm foothold on the Continent, it was only natural that American aircraft would participate in the move on Cherbourg.

Weather, the only element that could kill the air effort, reared its ugly head on 19 June. A terrific storm slammed into the Normandy coast and compelled Bradley's troops to slog forward under a gray sky empty of planes. The Ninth and Seventy-ninth Divisions made good headway nonetheless, advancing about a mile on their left flank and more than eight miles on the extreme right. But the wind on that day and the next wrecked the Allies' artificial harbors along the invasion beaches, and an already tenuous supply situation became acute. The swift capture of Cherbourg and its valuable port facilities had suddenly become all the more critical to the Allies.

The principal air and ground commanders conferred again on 21 June to address this urgent situation and to accommodate new ground positions. While staff generals met in London and reviewed the use of heavy bombers, Quesada and J. Lawton Collins convened a hasty field conference near Ste. Mère Église. The forty-eight-year-old Collins was an independent, aggressive, and astute commander. More important for Quesada, Collins was by his own admission "a tremendous believer in doing everything we could in the combined arms." As a division commander facing the Japanese during the Guadalcanal campaign, Collins had learned that effective fighting required "a coordinated attack and that means infantry, artillery, air, and engineers." Like Quesada, he owed his military thinking more to interwar developments than to World War I experience, and like Quesada he was energetic and comfortable with the nuts and bolts of planning.[55]

Spreading his maps across fallen trees, Collins asked Quesada for an "air pulverization" across some twenty miles of front. With his troops now closer to Cherbourg, his goal was no longer a direct preparation for ground advance but a general assault on the enemy's morale and communications. Accordingly, he wished to change the composition of the proposed air armada, wanting more fighters and fewer bombers. These changes made sense to Quesada, and without hesitation he reached for a field telephone and wangled some British Spitfires from Harry Broadhurst. Then he scratched the greater portion of Doolittle's heavy bombers from the show.[56]

Marking smoke and bomb lines were the only sticking points with Collins. Quesada wanted easily-seen yellow smoke to mark targets for his pilots, but Collins felt that standard-issue white smoke was sufficient and would spare the trouble of collecting yellow canisters on short notice. They agreed to use both.

Placing the bomb line was more problematic. With the less-accurate heavies no longer involved, Collins wanted the front marked as close to his troops as possible, hoping to exploit quickly any break in the German lines. Quesada concurred in theory, but as a matter of practice he urged a security zone. Colonel Harold Holt of the 366th Group, who was at the meeting, agreed with Quesada. Stressing imperfect bomb-release mechanisms and human error, he told Collins that a buffer of at least a few hundred yards was required to minimize friendly fire. "Joe, you had better listen to these men," Quesada said. "They've been doing it successfully for many weeks." Collins did listen, and with that the sole remaining issue for the attack was settled.[57]

Quesada conferred with Louis Brereton and Bradley one last time when he returned to Grandcamp at 1400 hours. He then huddled with his own staff while Brereton flew back to Uxbridge and Hillingdon House to relay the updated plan. Time was of the essence. That night the staffs of a dozen air commands on both sides of the Channel hustled to produce the detailed orders that were the sinews of complex combat. The final plan was approved in the predawn hours of 22 June, and General Richard Nugent flew it to the Continent in the morning darkness. In the end, it called for ten squadrons of British Spitfires and twelve groups of Quesada's fighters to strafe enemy positions in the hour before the ground attack. Once the attackers took off, eleven groups of medium bombers would support the advance with raids on pinpoint targets, much like a rolling artillery barrage. In all, over 1,500 aircraft would attempt to crack through Cherbourg's defenses and demoralize her ground troops. Though the attack had been planned with dispatch, revised due to weather, and hurriedly set up, most participants were optimistic as 22 June dawned.

From start to finish, these preparations revealed important changes in the execution of the tactical air war. The quick conference before the operation would have amazed any officer who had observed close air support in North Africa or Sicily. There, the Allies were not only operationally incapable of such large efforts but also lacked the requisite staff expertise to stage them. Now, just weeks after the Normandy invasion, tactical aviation was common enough to render close air support almost routine if not perfect.

Moreover, in contrast to other air–ground efforts, the local commanders had bickered little while planning the Cherbourg assault. Despite history's constant attention to air–ground disagreements among the Allies in western France, some tactical commanders on the far shore reached an accommodation that seemed surreal against the backdrop of the prewar and preinvasion squabbles. Cast together, and facing an enemy more dangerous and immediate than doctrinal disputes, these men forged compromise, agreement, trust, and even genuine friendship. Bradley, for example, once told Hap Arnold that "this man Quesada is a jewel," and later wrote that Quesada was "unlike most airmen who viewed ground support as a bothersome diversion to war in the sky. Quesada approached it as a vast new frontier waiting to be explored." Indeed, at the crossroads of command between the most senior generals and the men who did the dying, people like Bradley, Collins and Quesada found a common ground. Therein lay the significance of the early Normandy campaign for air–ground relations. The friendships these men developed paid dividends in the future. Later, when the campaign stalled on the German frontier, when there was little optimism among officers, when frustrations among men ran high, these commanders would need to call upon this reservoir of good will.[58]

June 22 was a beautiful day. Collins, Quesada, and Nugent drove to the front near Valognes, a mere half-mile from the German positions, to watch the attack. The VII Corps troops were already there, waiting in foxholes that were perhaps a little deeper than usual. At 1240 hours more than a hundred British Spitfires screamed overhead, sweeping first this way, then that way, riddling the front with bullets and bombs. Smoke rose from the ground. German shrieks wafted through the fleeting silence that sometimes punctuates the roar of war. As the Royal Air Force left, the American generals hunched further behind their hedgerow, peering through slits of brush. American planes would be above them soon.[59]

Back at Christchurch in the south of England, Colonel Chuck Young had just led forty-eight Lightnings of the 367th Fighter Group into the air. Joining 509 other IX TAC planes over the Channel, they stormed over Cherbourg at 1300 hours. The Spitfire attack had both obscured the area and alerted the defenders, who were now throwing up an unprecedented barrage of flak. For an hour the pilots flew into the dust, smoke, and chaos of war. Although they were aiming for six defensive clusters scattered over twenty-five miles, the confusion and gunfire forced a haphazard approach. Pilots merely formed up over the front and attacked any target of opportunity.[60]

Lieutenant Edward Michelson realized immediately that he and his fellow flyers were ducks in a shooting gallery. "The ground fire was so intense it seemed the only safe place to be was below treetop level." Every farm, crossroads, and tree grove was alive with German gunners. Pilots traveling 300 miles an hour strained to orient themselves as black billows rose from the ground. Some got lost. One flight fired on friendly forces.

"We were on the deck in a ravine when all hell broke loose," Captain Jake Reed recalled. Caught in a deadly crossfire of flak, two planes immediately in front of him burst into flames and crashed to the earth. Within minutes, pilots Deuron Robertson, John Morgan, John Langston, Frank Golden, and Donald Stevens were dead. Reed managed to survive, dropping his bombs on a flak battery and gun position. But losing his friends was demoralizing. When he left the skies over Cherbourg, he felt the raid had been "pretty futile."

For the 367th Fighter Group the plight did not end with the turn for home. Lieutenant Vernon Wedul had run full bore into a tree, clogging his P-38 engine intakes with twigs and leaves. He navigated the English Channel on first one propeller and then the other to stave off a meltdown. Just when it appeared that he would make it home, both his engines burst into flames and he crashed into the sea. Coastal naval patrols were slow to reach him, and his entire flight watched him drown in the cold sea.

The skies over Cherbourg and Wedul's death spooked the survivors when they arrived back at Christchurch. That night, the living sat as if dead, quietly trying to comprehend the day. "The milk run to Cherbourg was an unqualified disaster for the 367th Fighter Group," one remembered. In sixty minutes over Cherbourg, Quesada's command had lost twenty-seven aircraft. Allied pilots were not used to this kind of fighting. The air war, which they had dominated for weeks, had just tightened up. To make matters worse, the flyers had missed their intended victims all along the front, though they had cut German communication links and had shot enough ammunition to preoccupy the defenders for crucial minutes.[61]

At precisely 1400 hours, ground troops just a fifth-mile off the bomb line rushed across the choppy Cotentin terrain, taking sixty-five shaken prisoners in a 1000-yard sprint. As the infantry continued this forward rush, 400 medium bombers staggered over the battle. Not accustomed to close support operations, these pilots experienced even more difficulty than their fighter cousins. By now clouds had rolled in from the sea, forcing the use of blind-bombing techniques. Disaster ensued. Twice the mediums attacked the American Ninth Division, making that division doggedly air-shy for the rest of the war. But it could have been worse. Forward components of the Seventy-ninth had overrun their own bomb line and were in territory vulnerable to yet more friendly fire. Fortunately, no flyers found them in the haze.[62]

When reports of the tragedy reached Collins, he was glad Quesada and Nugent were there "to observe this incident firsthand, as we flattened ourselves against our hedgerow while several successive flights roared by." Closer to the fighting, division commanders were less concerned with pilot errors and more interested in the actual results of the attack. But even there the medium bombers fell short of Allied hopes for them. As the Fourth Division commander sadly relayed, "The medium bombing did not destroy the permanent fortifications."[63]

The whole performance added to a growing disdain for medium bombers among the ground forces. By both conception and capacity, the B-25 and B-26 were caught between the strategic and tactical missions of the air force. Requested for missions every day by both tactical and strategic air leaders, the medium bombers needed at least forty-eight hours' notice for any operation. As a result, with the single exception of interdiction, they did no mission well. Commanders at all levels complained of lengthy liaison procedures, and General George Patton bluntly declared that it took "too damn long to get medium bombers when needed." Bradley concurred, believing the mediums left "much to be desired in close-support operations." For that, he blamed both misconceptions among ground officers and a "hesitancy on the part of air forces to employ bombers in close-support operations for fear of violating the sacredness of their air doctrine."[64]

Even pilots disliked medium bombers and their orphaned status in the war. Flyers had nicknamed the B-26 Marauder the "Murderer" after some pilots had died in training accidents. Later, they took to calling it the Flying Prostitute because with its hefty fuselage and slight wings it lacked any visible means of support. "The Marauder is a wonderful invention," one pilot recorded, "but it will never take the place of the airplane." Whatever the cause of medium-bomber impotence, the net effect among ground leaders was to rely increasingly on fighters for the close work required in combined-arms operations. This would prove to be both a windfall and a headache for Pete Quesada.[65]

With less then stellar air operations, the VII Corps had overrun only a small fraction of the battle by nightfall on 22 June. American infantry managed a few penetrations of limited depth along the city perimeter, but there was no clear breakthrough anywhere. In most areas the Germans clung to their dug-in positions with skill, tenacity, and fear. Still, the Allies did take important high ground in the outskirts town of Chèvres. Though the U.S. penetrations did not constitute a clear victory, the tough German perimeter had been pierced. There was hope for the next day.

Poor weather on 23 June reduced air support over Cherbourg to just three small missions. Nonetheless, effective artillery fire and aggressive leadership at regiment and battalion levels produced good gains. The fighting was tough and at close quarters. In many places men fixed bayonets. When dusk came the VII Corps was well within the city limits, just two miles from the harbor at some points.

Good weather returned the following day. In midmorning Thunderbolts struck strongpoints along the main harbor road, tearing up concrete, tumbling buildings, and bringing terror to the populace. Not wanting to jeopardize the momentum they had worked so hard to get going, leading American ground elements bypassed some defensive strongpoints, including a German concentration at La Mère à Canard, a commanding hill that had been a popular picnic ground before the war. In the early afternoon, the Germans began shelling the Americans from this fortified height, threatening the drive into the city center. At 1500 hours an American battalion commander requested an air raid on the hill. A fire-support officer questioned whether artillery would be better suited to the task, but at 1615 hours Bradley himself asked Quesada for the strike.[66]

Quesada acquiesced and hurriedly called twenty-seven-year-old Colonel Gilbert Meyers. Meyers had just moved his group to the Continent and was not expecting any operational duty for several days. Now all that changed. Swiftly summoning his pilots, Meyers explained that "This mission is hot. General Bradley requested it himself. It's a strongpoint that's raking our troops from the rear." At 2027 hours group deputy commander Lieutenant Colonel Frank Perago led twenty-four Thunderbolts down the dirt runway, kicking up huge clouds of dust. In minutes the Battle of Cherbourg lay before them. "American lines were clearly visible—intricate trench systems jammed with soldiers who seemed to just be waiting," remembered one flyer. "The roads back from the front were clogged with vehicles . . . a big artillery duel was in progress . . . there was lots of light flak coming up. . . . The city was enveloped in smoke."[67]

Perago and his wing man, Lieutenant Joe "Noodles" Nolan, were first to dive-bomb the target. They fell to 800 feet and dropped their 1000-pounders into the thick black smoke. A tremendous red explosion licked up at the planes, and German 88mm shells chased the two fighters from the scene. Behind Perago and Nolan more planes swung from the sky and attacked. When the last bird cleared the area, American doughboys climbed from their trenches.

No Germans challenged them. While the infantry filtered into the shattered enemy fortifications, Perago's pilots returned to their base. Their first operation from a French field was a success. When Quesada recounted the mission to an officer he had served with earlier in the war, he wrote, "We are so far ahead of what we were doing in Africa that the whole thing is pathetic. We have a setup beyond your imagination."[68]

Throughout the city it was the same. Effective infantry-artillery-air strikes mauled the defenders. In underground tunnels, Germans by the thousands huddled beneath the bombardment. Support personnel and combat troops alike crowded together, depressed by their isolation and disheartened by days amid the stink of generator motors and their own dank sweat. On a wall map, the garrison commander, Generalleutnant Karl-Wilhelm von Schieblen, marked the remorseless progress of the American advance. Even tiny German victories reflected the inevitable destiny of the battle. Lieutenant John Wheeler of the 405th Fighter Group had been shot down the first day of the attack; after two days his captors stopped pressing him for information. "We will probably be your prisoners tomorrow," they explained.[69]

On 25 June the only defenses left were isolated, yet tenacious, pockets of determined Nazis. Collins' troops advanced neighborhood by neighborhood, street by street, and sometimes house by house in the kind of combat all men fear. Spread pellmell across the urban landscape, Germans and Americans fought to the bitter end. There was no longer any coherent front, which made air support missions difficult if not impossible. Little by little the defenders surrendered their arms. On 26 June von Schieblen was captured, and most organized resistance ceased the next day. The city was clear of enemy soldiers by the twenty-ninth, although by then the Germans had thoroughly destroyed the harbor facilities.

In a strategic sense, the campaign to capture Cherbourg was a hollow victory without the use of the port. The harbor would not handle any Allied supplies for months, and it was well into autumn before it reached its peacetime capacity. Yet Cherbourg was the first major tactical success on the Western Front at a time when the Allies were advancing much more slowly than anticipated. Armies sometimes need such morale builders, and Cherbourg gave the Anglo-Americans a reason to be optimistic.[70]

Air power's role in the victory was hard to judge. Against a determined foe in well-fortified positions, 1,822 sorties and nearly 500 tons of bombs were not enough to cow Cherbourg's defenders into submission. In the end, the city surrendered not from fear of air strikes but from the force of ground action. Bradley understood this and reflected that even with relentless pounding from the air, tactical aviation could at best only neutralize a fortress city. As with wars in past centuries, "the doughboy was going to have to move in at high cost. Air could not do it alone."[71]

Since the early spring, Quesada's men had been preparing to provide the best air support possible, but in the Cherbourg assault they had learned that there was no substitute for the hard classroom of the battlefield. Although tactical aviation in Normandy was at times breathtakingly effective, particularly in interdicting the battlefield, it was not perfect. In Normandy, airplanes were not able to destroy well-fortified positions with impunity; area air attacks on towns could be wasteful of scarce resources; friendly fire could poison the relationship between pilots and soldiers; and there remained no good mechanism to shift planes already in the air in response to urgent pleas for air support or to avert friendly fire.

Nonetheless, these were indeed the critical days in the development of tactical aviation. War can compress time, accelerate learning, and engrave lessons like no other human endeavor. The first weeks in Normandy did what two decades between the wars could not. In a fortnight, the basic patterns of tactical aviation emerged. Amid the mud and blood a system was born—crude perhaps; flawed certainly; impotent sometimes. But still a system, a scheme around which to operate, a structure on which to drape the many components of tactical air power.

Besides, Quesada now had some of his groups stationed on the continent. He had nearly 18,000 airmen in France. His pilots had flown nearly 25,000 sorties in over 800 missions, and they had compiled an impressive tally of destruction: 203 Luftwaffe planes; 24 bridges; 506 railroad engines and cars; and nearly 1,300 motor transports.[72]

So on average Quesada was pleased with the balance sheet. "We are now in France and going strong," he wrote to his brother on 28 June. "The Hun is a pushover in the air. Our tail is up and his is down and we are beating up everything in sight. I have a fine bunch of boys whose enthusiasm is boundless. . . . There are a lot of dead Germans but not enough." That same night he escorted a pretty International News Service photographer to Bradley's mess for dinner. It was his first date since May. All in all, at both the IX TAC and First Army compounds, there was much more optimism than pessimism that evening.[73]

The very next day, near the sleepy English town of Mudeford, pilots from the 405th prepared for a routine armed-reconnaissance mission. As they climbed into the air by twos, one pilot lost power and crashed into a row of houses with eight machine guns blazing and two bombs ramming into the earth. Within moments the plane's belly tank erupted, sending a huge fireball into the air, which dragged another plane to the ground. Firefighters and civilians rushed to the scene. Lieutenants Art Williams, Chuck Mohrle, and John Drummand tried to keep the crowd from the unexploded bombs. They failed. One exploded, killing Williams and fourteen townspeople. It was a depressing day and a powerful reminder that war is a tragic business. For the Americans in France, the next month would bring still more evidence of war's cruelty.[74]

Chapter Six

Remember That Our Work Is Really Just Starting

IX TAC COMMAND POST, NORMANDY. 2 JULY 1944. 1110 HOURS. Quesada's new operations officer, Colonel Gil Meyer, was on the phone with Ninth Air Force Main Headquarters outside London. Reconnaissance reports had just identified German trains and trucks moving along the front near St. Lô, and the Americans were trying to scramble fighter-bombers. "Weather is impossible over bases here," the controller in London told Meyer, "we need to have the routes attacked by groups based in France." But the skies over the Continent were no better, and despite an enticing target the Americans would have to wait until the heavens cleared. The weather never did change. Sometime in the late afternoon Meyer came to the unhappy conclusion that nature had won, and he aborted efforts to strike the convoy.[1]

That evening, across the lines, part of the German Third Parachute Division slipped into defensive positions east of St. Lô. Theirs had been a harrowing journey to the front. For two weeks they had moved forward, mostly under the cover of darkness, and each dawn it seemed the *Jabos* found them before they could camouflage their equipment. Impatient with such progress, on 1 July higher authorities ordered them to reach the front the next evening at whatever cost. Marching in daylight, the ranks advanced gingerly for thirty-six hours, heads cocked to the sky and eyes fixed on the horizon.

The poor weather saved them; the high whine of small attack planes never pierced the air above them. Reaching their destination on 2 July, they drew on the tough lessons of Normandy and hurriedly dug foxholes and slit trenches, draped camouflage netting over their vehicles, and stuffed their field guns into thick shrubbery. When they had finished, even the most experienced fighter pilot could have easily overlooked the strongpoint.[2]

Poor weather or not, Pete Quesada wanted the Germans who had slipped through his interdiction screen. On the morning of the third he sent the 474th Group on an armed reconnaissance of the area. Colonel Clinton Wasem and thirty-five other P-38 pilots left southeast England and reached France a little after 1030 hours. Scouring the area at first 5,000, then 3,000, then 1,000 feet, they found nothing. Below them the Third Parachute Division watched the Lightnings crisscross the sky, safe in the cover of the lush Norman countryside. Near 1100 hours, one flyer glimpsed what looked like a huddle of trucks. Lunging toward the earth like hungry animals, the pilots flamed two vehicles, one of which was already inoperable, and set a course for home.

Quesada was not satisfied with such meager results. He ordered a duplicate mission later in the day, and once again the 474th loaded up and flew over to France. For ninety minutes the flyers scanned the earth below, finding even less this time. Renowned for crack eyesight, the fighter pilots failed to spot the expertly camouflaged defenders. With twilight approaching, the flyers turned away, disappointed and low on fuel. An entire fighter-bomber group had spent an entire day searching for a small assembly of Germans. But they killed none, and destroyed only one working truck.[3]

The return trip to England compounded their woe. One flyer developed engine trouble and was forced to set a course for a Continental airstrip. On the ground, Richard Turner was checking his own plane for the next morning when he heard the distinct sound of a P-38 in the landing pattern. "Surprised that one of our own fighters was so low over the beachhead this late in the day, I rushed outside the engineering office to check what was happening." Running to the mobile truck tower, he alerted antiaircraft positions to hold their fire. But one jumpy gunner shot at the plane anyway, and others quickly joined the salvo.

The pilot reacted immediately, stowing his landing gear and maneuvering his ship at full power. "He made a heroic effort, managing to fly the length of the runway unhit," Turner remembered. Just as the pilot neared the shelter of the dark night, however, his right engine flamed and he plunged to a fiery death. Turner stood in the middle of the runway for a long while, silent and horrified, staring at the burning metal and flesh. "Finally, I slowly returned to my squadron area with heavy heart." All in all, concluded the diarist for the 474th Group, it had been "a most depressing day."[4]

From start to finish, the effort to strike at the Third Parachute Division foreshadowed a new and more difficult phase of the campaign for Quesada's pilots. After completing mop-up operations in the Cotentin Peninsula in late June, the Americans had turned south toward St. Lô and Coutances. There, after weeks of struggle, many Germans had finally reached their places along the front. Though tired and disorganized, they were still remarkably willing to fight. Compounding their threat to the Allies, poor weather and ideal defensive terrain would now collude to help the defenders. While the attack on Cherbourg marked the high tide of early U.S. operations on the Continent, this new phase brought only delay and frustration. When Quesada realized that a change in the war was afoot, he cautioned his group commanders to "remember that our work is really just starting." He probably meant it as a reminder to himself as much as to anyone else.[5]

As is often the case in war, many soldiers were slow to understand this ebb-tide phase in the campaign. "When we hit the enemy this time we will hit him with such power that we can keep going and cause him a major disaster," a confident Bradley had written Eisenhower on the eve of an early July assault. This optimism, shared by most battle leaders, even bred an atmosphere permitting mild shenanigans. Following a 4 July planning conference at First Army headquarters, for example, Eisenhower and Quesada crammed into the cockpit of a P-51 for a tour over the battlefield. Without parachutes, they took off just before noon with three other planes and headed out to the German lines. For half an hour they ranged as much as fifty miles beyond friendly ground forces. Finally, Quesada "started getting anxious about the fact I had the Supreme Commander stuffed behind me in a single-engine airplane with no parachute over enemy territory." Although Eisenhower was having a great time—repeatedly asking how fast they were flying and requesting that the young general quicken the pace—Quesada turned back to the Allied lines.[6]

Bradley and a bevy of war correspondents met them, which was bad news for both men. Brereton had previously cautioned Quesada to stick to the ground, where he was worth more in a swivel chair than in a cockpit, and Eisenhower had no doubt that George Marshall "would give me hell if he found out" about the flight. For those reasons, Bradley thought the two looked "like sheepish schoolboys caught in the watermelon patch" as they climbed from the cockpit. Both Eisenhower and Quesada were indeed reprimanded, though in his own defense the Supreme Commander claimed that the trip "was pure business, (1) to see the country and (2) [as] a gesture to our pursuit pilots who are doing yeoman work in attempting to find and plaster targets." Still, Eisenhower never again took such risks, and Quesada was careful not to court such danger again.[7]

In any event the war quickly grabbed everyone's attention again. On 3 July Collins' VII Corps, Major General Troy Middleton's VIII Corps, and Major General Pete Corlett's XIX Corps had begun an attack south toward Coutances and St. Lô. Anticipating a brisk advance, Omar Bradley projected that his forces would capture the important town of St. Lô by the tenth.[8]

As was by then routine, the daily air-ground conferees at First Army/IX TAC headquarters had requested strikes on moving columns, troop concentrations, and gun batteries. On the first day Colonel Chuck Young and pilots from the 367th winged past Middleton's men, dive-bombing railroad tracks, trains, and assembly areas. Just to the east, another fighter group flamed a German company convoy, ruining nine lorries full of ammunition and killing all the drivers. At the same time, medium bombers of the IX Bomber Command struck bridges over the Seine and Loire rivers, further complicating German efforts to reinforce the battle zone. The next day was much the same, as over 150

Lightnings and Thunderbolts destroyed an entire train column near Chartres.[9]

Together, these missions were entirely consistent with the pattern of interdiction so well practiced and established in June. It came as a surprise to some, then, that the ground forces moved nary a yard in the first days of July. All along the front, from Middleton's VIII Corps in the west to Gerow's V Corps beside the British, the Americans were stuck. On 6 July Bradley wrote to Eisenhower that he was "disappointed at the slow rate of our progress but everyone concerned informs me that we are running against very carefully prepared positions and are walking into some pretty good troops." Struggling to get the attack moving, Collins asked Quesada for an unusual mass fighter bombardment very close to the battle lines. Both men knew that their interdiction efforts were succeeding by any standard measure, and they hoped that new tactics could break the impasse.[10]

Accordingly, at 0600 hours on 6 July two fighter groups raced up and down the thirty-mile front, literally pacing in the sky, seeking targets of opportunity. But the defenders were well hidden, and barring conspicuous movement would remain so. Finally at 1530 the flyers caught a break when a limited skirmish between the U.S. Fourth Division and the Second Panzer Division revealed some Germans. Sweeping low and bombing level, two squadrons ravaged the area with 1,000-pound bombs. The defenders scurried into slit trenches and survived the attack with few casualties. A strafing raid fifteen minutes later produced better results, "benumbing" the Germans and, in fact, aborting a planned counteroffensive by the Panzers.[11]

Later that same day and farther to the east, the commander of the Twenty-ninth Division requested an air strike at enemy guns a mere 300 yards from his own men. For three days his troops had tussled with stubborn German defenses before St. Lô, and he was now concerned lest his advance become completely stalled. So, early on the 7th, Thunderbolt pilots from the 370th lifted from their base in England and headed for the German positions. Armed with 250-pound fragmentation bombs fused for minimum crater damage, they zoomed past the colored panels of the U.S. 115th Regiment and dropped their ordnance.[12]

Contrary to popular belief, this and similar missions did not represent pinpoint targeting. Moving nearly 300 miles per hour and so close to U.S. soldiers, flyers could do little save locate friendlies and drop bombs at timed intervals after crossing the front. They aimed at nothing, and exact accuracy was a matter of pure providence. To be effective, 250-pound bombs required hits within 100 yards of machine-gun nests or foxholes, 500-pounders needed to be only within 225 yards, and 1,000-pound bombs could inflict serious damage to moderately prepared defenses as far as 400 yards from the point of explosion. On 7 July, none of the bombs fell close enough to make a difference, and men of the Twenty-ninth moved forward against undamaged enemy positions. The result was predictable: fifty yards forward, fifty yards back, and nineteen casualties.[13]

The next day was not much better. As the sun rose above the horizon, fighter-bombers struck in support of the 83rd Division just to the west of the 29th. Carrying 500-pounders, they knocked out two of five German batteries, although defenders up and down the line suffered few actual casualties. One Wehrmacht soldier claimed that his foxhole had offered "complete immunity" from the raid, and another reported that in concrete shelters or slit trenches he felt "completely safe from all forms of attacks," even highly accurate air strikes. American rifle companies did manage a 200-yard advance by nightfall, but again the cost was high: twenty-seven ground casualties, two planes, and a pilot. The day's only bright spot came farther to the west, where fighter bombers helped stop a counterthrust by a resurgent Panzer Lehr Division.[14]

By 8 July the lack of advance on the battlefield worried American commanders. On the Allied side, supply problems and battle fatigue explained some of the difficulty. The wrecked condition of the port of Cherbourg had seriously upset Allied logistics, and casualty rates as high as 150 percent in some U.S. units had bred fear of endemic battle fatigue. With the story essentially the same in the British camp to the east, a simple conclusion slowly became inescapable to the Allied leaders. A month of hard fighting had simply exhausted the soldiers.[15]

On the German side, phenomenal resiliency under these same battle pressures and near-ideal defensive terrain also helped explain the Americans' troubles. Throughout the war, the Germans were undoubtedly the world's best soldiers, outperforming their adversaries on every battlefield. Their divisions were leaner than their British or American counterparts, and man for man they inflicted more casualties then they incurred.

Now, in western France in July, Germans used the region's unique hedgerows to buttress this basic fighting superiority. The product of a millennium of farming, the hedgerows of Normandy were earth dikes about four feet high, covered with tangled hedges, bushes, and small trees. Together they boxed in fields and orchards of varying sizes and shapes, few larger than a football field and many much smaller. Designed in peace to reduce topsoil erosion, in war they became earthworks into which the defenders cut foxholes, trenches, and machine-gun nests. Known in local French as the *bocage*, the land was ideal for static defense when fortified with determination; each little field became a battlefield in itself, conquered only by slow and costly company, platoon, and squad action. The British had contended with the *bocage* since the first days of OVERLORD, and now the Americans were learning firsthand how well the Germans had used the land to their advantage.[16]

Moreover, the Germans had by then codified and assimilated the tough lessons of Normandy. By avoiding main roads, by marching in strict discipline during darkness, by expert use of foxholes and slit trenches, and by nightly changes in front-line positions, the Germans had been able to reduce the effect of Allied air strikes on them. No doubt many divisions had suffered substantial losses and delays in reaching the front, but by early July most of those who had survived the trip had completed their journey. More and more, the defenders were now shrewdly burrowed into their fighting positions. For the Allies, the great need—and opportunity—to intercept battle reinforcements waned day by day. As late spring passed into high summer, it was becoming clear that another mode of air war was required if aviation was to continue its contribution to the ground campaign.[17]

For Quesada and others associated with the air war this became their new charge: to find a better way to help the infantry. Already there had been grumblings in the past days about air support. One division commander felt that he had received "little assistance from the air forces" in his plodding advance, and incidents of friendly fire were finally receiving more attention. Although there had been twenty cases of friendly fire in June, the U.S. advances during that month had mitigated any misgivings about it among air and ground elements. But as the American pace stalled, every accident—whether it was a plane firing at friendly ground troops or antiaircraft batteries shooting at friendly planes—was now cast in relief.[18]

The strongest criticisms came from ground and air officers at lower levels, where the urgency of life and death were closest at hand. The 112th Regiment endured four attacks by the Army Air Forces in Normandy, costing thirty lives and over 100 casualties. Not surprisingly, its members developed little affection for pilots. "All we could do was hide and pray" whenever air support thundered overhead, Private Robert Lewis dryly recalled. When pilots did drop their bombs short, the sheer terror of an air strike added to the infantry's anger. Sergeant William Nelson believed that nothing was worse than an air attack. "It makes you feel very helpless. It's like a huge sewing machine coming at you, and you can't get away from it." Clifford Cunningham was even more descriptive. During one raid, he "had a baseball in my rear, I was so scared." In time, some units became so wary of friendly fire that they took to declining air support altogether.[19]

But mistakes were made on the ground, too. Allied antiaircraft artillery was responsible for nearly as much damage to Quesada's command as the Luftwaffe and German flak combined. The 67th Tactical Reconnaissance Group lost one pilot and four aircraft to friendly ack-ack. Another group lost two pilots to naval guns offshore. On 10 July a Lieutenant Carpenter of the 354th was attacked by friendly gunners near Carmolain. The battery men ignored his recognition flare, and with guns blazing he slammed into the ground doing 450 miles an hour. When the smoke cleared all that was left was a crater fifteen feet deep and forty feet across. "When this war is over," vowed Carpenter's wing man, "I will attend every one of those sonsobitches' courts-martials."[20]

Attitudes in the lower ranks did not go unheeded at higher levels, but the generals sought a broader perspective that balanced the advantages of air power against problems like friendly fire. Eisenhower believed that while both air and ground forces had committed mistakes, "these errors have been of such a limited extent as compared to the overall picture." Hoping to kill the perception of poor air support among the troops, he was "particularly anxious that any such occurrences do not discourage ground forces from calling upon the air for maximum assistance." Bradley shared Eisenhower's outlook, and rebuffed suggestions that the bomb line be placed twenty miles beyond the ground forces.[21]

Though Quesada understood the measured response of the ground leaders, each incident of friendly fire caused him distress. "An examination of these accidents reveals contributory negligence on the part of ourselves as well as the ground units," he wrote his command. "To avoid discord and lack of confidence between the forces ... the error on our part must be avoided at all cost." Quesada understood that friendly fire had not yet become an endemic problem, that it had not yet measurably affected the ground war, and that most soldiers still shared the view of Captain Malcolm Marshall of the 112th Regiment, who complained of being strafed and bombed but who admitted that "in total, air did a good job." Rather, Quesada was concerned lest the perception of lousy air support poison the fine relationship that he and Bradley had worked diligently to build out of a long history of distrust between soldiers and pilots.[22]

That even loyal Air Forces men began to question the efficiency of the tactical air war underscored Quesada's worry. Brigadier General O. P. Weyland, his own fighter groups still under Quesada's operational control but soon to establish his command post in France, urged Lewis Brereton to review the performance of tactical air operations. In one recent forty-eight-hour period, he told Brereton on 5 July, fighter pilots had failed to find fifteen of eighteen close-support targets. The next day Weyland declared that fully 80 percent of all requested missions were falling short of expectations, faulting in part IX TAC's lack of liaison with rear echelons in the air forces. Although his calculations and criticisms were exaggerated, Weyland had in fact given voice to a fundamental truth: the Germans were getting harder for the airmen to find.[23]

At first the Allies responded to this new challenge in a typically American fashion: they ignored the cautionary lessons of the Cherbourg assault, and simply poured more men, more bombs, and more planes into their operations. On the night of 7–8 July, nearly a thousand English heavy bombers and U.S. medium bombers plastered Caen in an effort to blast a path into the city for the British Second Army, which had lain immobilized before the town for thirty days. The bombardment was less than accurate, however, and the defenders weathered the storm well in their fortified positions. It took the British two days of bloody fighting against the indomitable Twelfth Panzer Division just to clear the city center of resistance. Even then, the defenders still held critical high ground in Caen and could mark every Allied move. To thoughtful observers, the air strike had been a worthless backdrop to the street fighting; it did not help the British much and did not cost the Germans much in men or materials. In the end, only the city itself paid the full price for the operation—the place was in ruins. Thirty-eight civilians died in one cellar, fifty were killed in a single street, and the beautiful old Norman town called Caen was no more.[24]

Despite the ineffectual aid of the big bombers, the growing ground standoff created an inexorable pressure to use every available resource close to the battle, including the heavies. On 9 July Quesada and his operations officer, Gil Meyers, laid plans for a large-scale support bombardment in the U.S. zone for early the following day. By aiming six groups of fighter and medium bombers at a 2,250-by-800-yard rectangle astride the Périers–Carentan road, they hoped to pierce the stubborn German defenses and spill elements of Collins' VII Corps into the enemy rear. After consulting with group leaders and ground commanders, Quesada set the bomb line and parceled out targets to each group. Early the next morning the ground forces would guide the planes to their marks, using white smoke for the medium bombers and red for the fighter-bombers.[25]

The mission got off to a bad start. At 0820 hours a plane from the 405th Fighter Group crashed on takeoff, damaging a new airstrip and upsetting the initial time-over-target schedules. Twenty minutes later, poor weather in England grounded the medium bombers scheduled to participate. Without the bigger planes, Quesada postponed the whole morning show and hoped for clearer skies in the afternoon. But the clouds stayed.

Trying to salvage something of the day, Quesada released his groups for other operations at 1215. In mid-afternoon weather had improved enough in England for the mediums to take off, but by then the fighter planes were busy with other missions. Although planners then made a hasty attempt to launch the operation the following evening, the ground forces were no longer properly arrayed for a combined-arms assault, and friendly troops were nearly bombed. The entire plan had been a response to a fleeting opportunity, and that was now gone.[26]

Weather seemed to have beaten the flyers once again. Time and again since D-Day overcast skies had shackled the efforts of airmen, and the problem promised to get worse with the onset of the rainy season in France. From 20 June to 25 July, overcast skies curtailed air activity fully half the time, and among commanders the cloud cover was becoming a favorite subject for complaint. Eisenhower called the weather "abominable," Montgomery labeled it "the very devil," and Bradley told staffers he had "never seen such lousy weather."[27]

Quesada agreed. His intelligence staff later estimated that poor weather reduced the IX TAC's effort by 40 percent in July and grounded fully a quarter of the American air resources in Europe over the campaign's entire duration. "The weather here has been just beyond your imagination," Quesada wrote friends that summer, "which is a real kick in the teeth for us and a great boost for the Germans."[28]

As real as the problem was, Allied gripes about the weather were unjust. Popular belief to the contrary, the rainfall in northwestern France in the summer of 1944 was entirely consistent with the region's long-term weather history. Poor flying days averaged one in three during the campaign; but this was right in line with Normandy's climate pattern over the previous twenty years. The Allied grievances, then, were not so much the response to an unusual French summer but rather natural annoyance at the Anglo-American failure to anticipate an entirely predictable climate.[29]

This lack of foresight was most striking among the air planners, because pilots were especially dependent on good weather. Before the war, weather was rarely, if ever, mentioned in Air Corps training texts, and after Pearl Harbor air strategists continued to adopt a casual attitude toward climate. This indifference had bothered Eisenhower enough to cable Marshall and Arnold a mere month before D-Day, reminding them to allow for ghastly weather in their projections for the European campaign. Arnold promptly relayed Eisenhower's concerns to Tooey Spaatz back in London, but the U.S. air command in Europe would remain curiously confident in the ability of GEE, OBOE and H2X radar to overcome the constraints of clouds, despite battle experiences to the contrary.[30]

This nonchalance was a symptom of the air arm's faith in its capacity to overcome any obstacle with technological innovation. Pilots' can-do attitude had helped revolutionize air power between the world wars, to be sure, but now in Normandy it sometimes worked against them. Try as they might for the rest of the war, men like Quesada would never completely beat the weather. Like the barren desert of Africa or the broken terrain of Normandy, there was nothing anyone could do about the storm clouds that seemed to roll in daily from the sea.

Because, despite, or regardless of the weather, Omar Bradley sensed the campaign slipping from his grasp. "By 10 July we faced a real danger of a World War I-type stalemate in Normandy," he recalled. "Montgomery's forces had taken the northern outskirts of Caen, but the city was not by any means in his control. . . . My own breakout had failed. Despite enormous casualties and loss of equipment, the Germans were slavishly following Hitler's orders to hold every yard of ground." Characteristically, Eisenhower tried to buck up his subordinate, telling Bradley, "I will understand that you are having tough going, both from the ground and from the enemy. However, I am perfectly certain that you are on the right track." He might have been right, but the silence from the stagnant front had a way of muffling optimism, even if it came from the Supreme Commander.[31]

Bradley's pessimism was shared down the ranks. The slow progress was especially discouraging to everyday soldiers accustomed to advances of a mile or more in return for a day of hard campaigning. "We were stuck," remembered Corporal Bill Preston. "Something dreadful seemed to have happened in terms of the overall plan. . . . The whole theory of mobility that we had been taught, of our racing across the battlefield, seemed to have gone up in smoke." Throughout the Anglo-American army, the troops began settling into a disturbing routine of war: dawn stand-to; breakfast of coffee or soup; infantry patrolling or tank deployments; dinner; return to the same positions as night fell. From the dawn of time, this almost comfortable way of war has been a sure sign of stalemate. It was now a new and different war, and the Americans did not like it much.[32]

Pete Quesada counted himself among the frustrated. He had chafed at the recent criticisms of his air war, and a 13 July battlefield tour by two Soviet air generals underscored his troubles. The Russians were young like Quesada, and distinguished by their baggy trousers, tight tunics, knee boots, and peaked hats. Recent Red Army breakthroughs in Prussia and Latvia had given them a considerable swagger, and at lunch with Bradley and Quesada they joked of signposts on the Eastern Front that marked the miles to Caen. As the Soviets traveled to the U.S. front lines, the sight of them prompted excited comments among everyday GIs. "My God," exclaimed one, "have the Russians broken through at St. Lô?" Everyone laughed, although Bradley and Quesada seethed at the remark.[33]

Unable to change the lay of the land, helpless in the face of poor weather, less and less effective against a cleverly hidden foe, and faced with simmering complaints of friendly fire, in mid-July Quesada turned to deficiencies over which he might hope to exercise more control. He threw himself into an effort to improve air–ground communications, a task that just might reduce accidental killings and help locate and strike enemy strongpoints. Under the preinvasion signals plan, each request for air support had been routed from the requesting ground unit to rear signals junctions, to the tactical air command, and finally to a fighter group for action. It was a tedious system that had worked tolerably well for the set-piece advances early in OVERLORD operations. But the bulky setup had become a hindrance now that the front had congealed. At best, planes appeared over distressed troops sixty minutes after a plea for help, which was usually too late to render effective assistance. The commander of the veteran First Division ranked these delays high on his grievance list in July, and Charlie Gerhardt of the Twenty-ninth Division sometimes did not bother to log requests at all because of the "insupportable" signals system. If the Allies ever entered a fluid war of movement, their communications net would be woefully inadequate.[34]

One day Quesada asked Bradley if they could place common radio sets in the cockpits of tanks and planes so as to allow the actual men fighting the war to talk to each other. Back in Africa as a corps commander, Omar Bradley had complained bitterly about laborious air–ground communications, and he immediately warmed to Quesada's thinking. "I don't see any reason why we can't try."[35]

Bradley promptly ordered two Sherman tanks to Quesada's signals post for the experiment. When the First Army ordnance officer got the directive to dispatch two tanks to IX TAC, however, he assumed it was a mistake and instead sent them to the Ninth Division. Officers there knew nothing about any tanks and refused them. Eventually, the Shermans found their way to Quesada's compound, but again some staffer hurried to turn them away. "Get the hell out of here! This is the Air Corps. What the devil would we be wanting with tanks?" After considerable delay, the Shermans were at last delivered for testing. The radios worked, and in an instant a whole new world of close support seemed possible.[36]

Once the basic hardware was in place, ground and air officers moved to refine what later became the basis for armored-column-cover missions. Quesada recognized that "air and ground speak a different language, and what a tank driver might see as a good landmark might be something virtually invisible in the air." As a remedy, he placed a pilot in each of the radio-equipped tanks, displacing the armorer in the crowded space. "This way," Quesada explained to Bradley, "the direction from the ground will be in language the fighter boy in the air can understand." To ensure that fighter-bomber planes would always be near a specially-equipped tank, Quesada next instituted regular one-hour flights of four planes over each armored column.[37]

In retrospect, placing compatible radios in tanks and planes was so simple, so sensible, so obvious a solution. That it had not been done before spoke volumes about the friction between air and ground men. "You have to remember the jealousy," Blair Garland explained after the war. "These were two separate and distinct organizations—the Air Corps and the Army." For most airmen, any attempt to tighten communications between front-line pilots and soldiers carried with it the ominous potential for ground commanders to control airplanes. But for Quesada, the clear experience of battle demanded such a setup. "Although Quesada could have passed for a prototype of the hot pilot with his shiny green trousers, broad easy smile, and crumpled but jaunty hat," Bradley recalled, "he was a brilliant, hard, and daring air-support commander on the ground. He had come into the war as a young and imaginative man unencumbered by the prejudices and theories of so many of his seniors on the employment of tactical air. To Quesada the fighter was a little-known weapon with vast unexplored potentialities in support of ground troops. He conceived it his duty to learn what they were."[38]

Learn Quesada did, in the heat and stalled campaign of mid-July. Beyond voice communications, he worked to connect his MEW radar to blind-bombing efforts. The MEW had been one of the campaign's early disappointments. Since D-Day, radar personnel had battled both the common problems of transit to the far shore and the singular challenges that befall new endeavors. The 555th Signal Air Warning Battalion, the unit in charge of the radar, had lost most of its original equipment on the journey across the English Channel, and—by their commander's own admission—when they received more supplies they "were not fully cognizant of their new mission." By 15 July the vaunted equipment had guided a grand total of five planes to targets. It had performed yeoman service as a flight-control station around crowded Continental airfields, but Blair Garland's vision of a revolutionary offensive weapon had remained a mere prophecy.[39]

Part of the problem lay in the attitudes of flyers. Weaned on the myths of seat-of-the-pants flight, the young, eager, and confident fighter-bomber boys were reluctant to use the new technology despite its tremendous capacity. Flights controlled by science simply did not fit the heroic parameters set by an earlier generation of airmen. No radar technician on the ground had ever told Eddie Rickenbacker when to drop his bombs or fire his guns. Technology, however grand, must fit the disposition of the people who are to use it, and Quesada spent the rest of the war building his pilots' confidence in a variety of newfangled gadgets.

The MEW also had inherent deficiencies as a blind-bombing tool. Although it could locate airborne fighters with unprecedented accuracy, the MEW alone could not correlate each plane's position to the ground with enough precision for bombing. Medium and heavy bombers had overcome this problem with airborne radar and the Norden bombsight, but fighters had neither the space nor the payload capacity for such solutions. Even if they did, the smaller ordnance that fighters carried demanded more accuracy than that afforded by the OBOE, GEE, or H2X radar systems in the bigger planes.[40] The tactical-air men required something new and different if they hoped to use radar to advantage in bad weather.

Blair Garland, Quesada's signals officer, spent considerable time searching for a solution within the limits imposed by fighter-plane size.

In the tradition of technophiles, his chief aide, Lieutenant Colonel Bill Cowart, had earlier scavenged a Signal Corps Radio 584 (SCR 584) from a nearby artillery unit and a Norden bombsight from a crashed B-17, just in case "they would ever be useful." The SCR-584 was a special radar designed to direct antiaircraft fire and was America's most accurate close-range radar. The Norden bombsight was a crude yet effective computer that tracked the variables of wind, speed, and altitude for bombardiers; it was perhaps the strategic air war's greatest asset. On 15 July, Garland and Cowart combined this foraged equipment, fashioning their own makeshift system to direct even the smallest airplane through the thickest soup.[41]

First, Cowart wired the SCR-584 to the MEW, combining the pinpoint accuracy of the 584 with the great range of the MEW. Then, right beside the MEW oscilloscopes, he built an ingenious map table that used detailed area charts and the Norden bombsight to approximate the more exact system used by bombardiers in heavier aircraft. In theory a pilot flying a route prescribed by the radar would radio his wind, airspeed, and altitude to the radar center, where a "bombardier" would feed the information into the Norden computer. Moving the bombsight over the map as the plane flew over the terrain, the radar operator would release the bombs by radio once the aircraft was over the target. The pilot did nothing but fly the plane. The ground controllers did the rest. It was a creative setup, one which used "the bombsight upside down and backwards to bomb from target to plane, not plane to target." If it worked, Garland believed, the airmen "could bomb with ceilings as low as 100 feet, provided we could land and take off from the airfields."[42]

This jury-rigged system had its first battle test on 16 July. Aviators of the 404th Fighter Group were surprised at the summons to quarters at 0900 hours. The day had dawned cool, gray, and windy, and most pilots had earlier settled back to sleep knowing there would be no air action that morning. Now, gathered in their briefing tent, they wondered what the hubbub was about. They rose when Colonel Carroll McColpin entered and called the meeting to order. As group and wing intelligence officers explained the special raid, ground crews busily installed Cowart's remote bomb releases into the Thunderbolt cockpits. By 1025 hours the briefing was over, though the equipment modifications took another ninety minutes. At 1220 hours, sixteen P-47s led by Captain John Marshall lifted from the new field near La Chapelle, France, and turned toward the stubborn front.[43]

Back at the radar station, Bill Cowart took control of the warplanes as they climbed into the sky, directing them to German positions along a conspicuous ridge just east of St. Lô. Humming along through the murky gray sky, John Marshall could see neither land below nor sun above. With the exception of his wing man's, the planes he knew to be all around him were little more than faint outlines against an ashen canvas. Cowart's voice and his own flight instruments were all Marshall had.

Like the pilots who had believed the overcast would cancel air operations, Wehrmacht soldiers guarding St. Lô atop its commanding height were surprised at the high pitched whine of small planes. Puzzlement turned to terror as the sound changed and told the defenders the planes had dived to the earth. Confused, they scrambled for cover.

Above, the attackers sweated out their rapid loss of altitude, hurtling through the air toward ground they could not see. They prayed for Cowart to drop their bombs so they could lift their ships upward. For both the radar controllers and the pilots, this new procedure demanded patience, confidence, and trust in equal measures. Finally, when the birds were 700 feet above the earth, Cowart released thirty-two 500-pounders. Relieved, the Thunderbolt pilots jerked their planes skyward.[44]

The results were discouraging. Just one bomb caused any appreciable damage to a German position. Five fell on a secondary roadway, which at least inflicted collateral damage. The rest dropped into a farmer's field, where, according to the proprietor, they killed nine cows, two horses, sixteen chickens, and a dog—but no Germans. Predictably, the strike failed to jump-start the ground advance. The American soldiers remained stuck against an implacable front.[45]

Undeterred, Quesada directed more radar operations for 17 July. An electrical glitch ruined the mission of the 366th Group, but a strike at a Seine River bridge in Rouen scored better. Flying blind, a squadron of Thunderbolts carrying 1,000-pound bombs reached that ancient town at about 0955 hours. Moments later, ground controllers released ten tons of explosives from the planes' bellies. Five of them registered direct hits and rendered two of four automobile lanes impassable.[46]

Quesada's keen interest in these tests brought him to his MEW station, code-named Sweepstakes, on the eighteenth. With Garland by his side, he observed yet another blind-bombing mission. Again the operation was a disappointment, this time ruined by a myriad of mechanical, electrical, and navigational problems.

As Quesada left the radar hut, mediums from IX Bomber Command reported a missed rendezvous with their fighter escort. He quickly stepped back into the little room. "What can we use for escort so that the mediums will not have to scrub their mission?" he asked. The Thunderbolts from the failed radar operation were still airborne with plenty of fuel. But they "had not been briefed on the escort job," a controller reminded Quesada, "and don't even know the rendezvous point." That reality would have killed Quesada's idea a month earlier, but now the SCR 584/MEW apparatus allowed the controllers to brief and to redirect the planes in midair. The fighters did indeed join up with the mediums for a successful interdiction mission. In the end, the day had not been a complete loss for the radarmen.[47]

Such flexibility was an important, if unintended, product of the novel radar setup. The sweep, scope, and speed of aviation in World War II demanded a revolutionary and almost reflexive ability to change plans. In Africa, Sicily, and Italy, Army-style command-and-control systems had proved too cumbersome in an air war where forces routinely deployed at the rate of five miles a minute. With the adoption of SCR 584-equipped missions, Quesada now had the technical ability to shift planes already in the air. That capability would pay large dividends in the future.

For this and other reasons, Quesada did not easily grow frustrated as Garland's extemporized radar system faltered in early trials. On the contrary, Quesada truly enjoyed the complex challenges presented by the air war, and, more than most generals, strove to grasp the workings of the new technology. He habitually toured his signals installations, often showing up in a zippered jacket with no rank showing. "Lord help any guard or any people on the location who failed to challenge or ask for ID," recalled Lieutenant James Tilford, one of the bright young men of the Signal Corps. Always a stickler for appearance, Quesada once busted a controller for wearing loafers on duty. Still, many radarman believed Quesada was "the only general officer who knew what was going on. His likely question was 'Who sited the radar, and why so much ground return?' As a result, he acquired an up-front knowledge of radar, which was black magic to most high-ranking officers."[48]

Lacking Signal Corps training or expertise, Quesada nonetheless grasped the pace and progress of technical developments; he recognized trial and error as part of the process. Garland believed that "Quesada was one of the very, very few commanders that had any idea about communications. He backed me on everything I ever wanted to do." If Quesada was disappointed in early efforts to integrate the SCR-584 and MEW, he knew there was sufficient promise of better things to come. Indeed, the technology and administration of the system was sound. Fighter-bomber pilots needed more time to work out the kinks.[49]

Besides, other developments assuaged any impatience Quesada may have felt about the radar tests. While Garland was tinkering toward precision bombing, others at IX TAC had been working to improve the ordnance of close air support. Until the summer of 1944 the tactical air forces had used essentially the same explosives as the strategic air forces, despite very different objectives and tactics. Reflecting again the meager forethought given to close air support before the war, the planners had believed that simple adjustments to bomb weight, fuse length, and fragmentation characteristics could meet the unique needs of both industrial bombardment far behind the front and precision air strikes on the battlefield. Experience in the tough hedgerows of Normandy now strongly suggested otherwise, and in July Quesada's ordnance department introduced new explosives more suited to the task at hand.

In the third week of that month these technicians began adding airborne rockets to the IX TAC arsenal. The British Second Tactical Air Force had used rockets with varying success since before D-Day, so when a U.S. Navy rocket displayed great promise in the Pacific, Quesada rushed to get it for his own men. By the sixteenth of July, the same day as the first MEW experiments, pilots and planes of the 406th Group were ready to try the new weapons. With the rockets, the versatile P-47 Thunderbolt was now the most heavily-armed fighter in any theater of war. In addition to the two five-inch-by-four-foot missiles under each wing, the planes carried two 500-pound bombs and 6,400 rounds of 50mm ammunition.[50]

The next day Colonel Anthony Grossetta guided his pilots from their base in Ashland, England, to marshaling yards near Nevers in Quesada's first mission to use rockets. They were in luck. Over fifty locomotives, an increasingly scarce resource for the Germans, were sitting idle, probably waiting on repairs to tracks to the north. Screaming down to 150 feet, Grossetta and his flight launched forty-eight rockets at the prize target. Thirty-eight found their mark on twenty-five engines, an amazing percentage. German railroad workers had not a clue how it happened. "One could see a bomb falling and therefore had some small chance of avoiding it," one shaken survivor explained. "But rockets appeared out of the blue." Jubilant, Grossetta turned into the westering sun and headed home.[51]

Quesada shared Grossetta's elation when he learned of the score. In a rare move, he wired Hap Arnold directly with the good news. The Air Chief in turn reported to Marshall and Secretary of War Henry Stimson that the rockets' first European trials had produced "excellent to remarkable" results.[52]

Of course, back in Normandy there were a few technical problems and mild disagreements over the best use of the new weapon. Some, like XIX TAC commander O. P. Weyland, believed that conventional bombs could blast marshaling yards as well as rockets, and wanted to save the missiles for rich tank and armored targets. He was right, but target doctrine for new weapons usually lags behind their introduction in battle, and rockets were no different; they were employed indiscriminately for the remainder of the summer campaign. For his part, Pete Quesada did not at first grasp the unique strength of missiles, only that they worked. "The rocket is here to stay," he declared to Assistant Secretary of War for Air Robert Lovett.[53]

The introduction of jellied gasoline, or napalm, into tactical air power's arsenal was much the same. Experimenters at IX TAC had fiddled with ways to drop and explode napalm as early as March, but the fuel burned too quickly and Quesada dropped the idea. Then in June reports from the Pacific told of startling success with flame-throwers against well-fortified Japanese positions. Despite Lewis Brereton's belief that "further attention to the use of incendiary gas tanks was unnecessary," Quesada renewed his efforts to develop fire bombs. He wangled a supply of thickened fuel from Bradley's First Army depots and directed the 370th Fighter Group to conduct operational trials. It suggested something of the bureaucratic nature of the army, even in wartime, that Air Forces research teams in America had been developing napalm since early in 1944, but Quesada, an operational commander who might benefit most from the weapon, did not learn of these tests until well after he had made his own.[54]

His napalm bombs were ready on 16 July. Disaster struck when one of the tanks exploded while ground crews at Andover, England were strapping it underneath a Lightning. The fire killed two men and literally melted the plane to a clump, scrubbing the operation for that day. So the first FIREBALL mission did not take place until the seventeenth. But at least now the pilots knew the destructive force they carried with them as Colonel Howard Nichols led his P-38s to a reputed German command post near Coutances.[55]

Flying 300 miles per hour at low altitude, Nichols barely spotted the heavy woods that marked his target. When his squadron was a mile from the trees, the pilots formed up tight and descended to 1,000 feet. They dropped their cargo directly over the German buildings. The earth was scorched with heat and flame. Smoke curled 2,000 feet into the air. Within minutes, nothing but stumps remained of the small forest. Turning for England, Nichols was exuberant and recommended further napalm attacks on any wooded areas, motor convoys, trains, personnel, gun emplacements and supply dumps. Back at Coutances, the fire did less damage than the Americans had hoped, but still managed to produce a level of fear theretofore unknown. Although supply problems would severely limit the use of napalm in the tactical air war until late autumn, Quesada told Lovett that this first attack, like the experiments with radar and rockets, "provides endless possibilities."[56]

Possibilities, however, were not enough to enable the planes to blast a path into St. Lô for the ground forces. Limited by weather, frustrated by a well-hidden foe, and still working out the bugs in combined air-ground operations, pilots did not dramatically help American troops capture the town. Since the fall of Cherbourg, the Allied assault on St. Lô had destroyed three regiments and an entire division. Casualties in certain rifle companies ran as high as 80 percent, and months would pass before their commanders considered some units again fit for combat.

Mercifully, the Germans finally evacuated the town on the eighteenth. The campaign had embodied some of the grimmest and bloodiest fighting the Americans would endure in Europe. "Brad," Major General Pete Corlett of the XIX Corps told Omar Bradley afterward, "I cannot ask these boys for more. They need rest or they will break." To make matters worse, ammunition shortages had shrunk stockpiles to new lows: the Allies now had enough ordnance for just four days of heavy fighting.[57]

More and more, the Anglo-Americans sensed the deadlock that seemed to have gripped their beachhead. Disappointment, frustration, and tiredness all sapped patience from the men as they crawled, bellied, and pushed their way slowly into the interior of France. In England, the usually unflappable Eisenhower "smoldered" at the battle's pace, lashing out at Montgomery and suggesting that the British had not made a "determined effort to prevent a stalemate. . . . We have not yet attempted a major full-dress attack on the left flank supported by everything we could bring to bear." Montgomery bristled at such talk, telling Chief of the British Imperial Staff Sir Alan Brooke that Eisenhower's "ignorance as to how to run a war is absolute and complete."[58]

Excepting the harmonious Bradley-Quesada team, Allied command strains and continuing battle difficulties badly undermined already fragile air–ground relations. In England, British Bomber Command's Arthur Harris and Eighth Air Force commander Jimmy Doolittle fumed each time higher authorities diverted heavies from raids deep into Germany to tactical missions close to the front. Montgomery's stock with flyers deteriorated so much that he and "Maori" Coningham of the British Second Tactical Air Force nearly came to blows, Coningham still angered by Montgomery's failure to adequately acknowledge his, Coningham's, air support in the North African campaign. To Montgomery's staff, Coningham was a "prima donna," a sentiment Coningham's staff no doubt harbored about Montgomery in return. If not for the efforts of Coningham's subordinate, Harry Broadhurst, the English tactical air team would have been nonexistent in July.[59]

As always, these tensions stemmed in part from personality conflict but they also reflected disagreement over air power's place in the battle. By July, commanders in every service branch had adopted an abiding faith in the revolutionary nature of aviation. Bomber barons, of course, had always believed that strategic raids would bring victory without costly ground fighting, and now Allied ground generals, consistently willing to expend resources instead of men, began looking to tactical strikes as a substitute for hard campaigning. From very different perspectives, then, battle leaders of every ilk had come to conclusions that differed in their particulars but shared a common denominator. For all of them, air power had become some sort of panacea for all the bleeding and dying at the front.

Already there was evidence of the ground forces' growing addiction to air support. Eisenhower had reacted to the slowing advance by first declaring that "we should strive in every possible way to make maximum use of our air," and then insisting that his generals "make the maximum demands for any air assistance that can possibly be useful." With this tone set by the high command, corps and division leaders began logging almost indiscriminate requests for air support.[60]

Overwhelmed by these pleas, Lewis Brereton was soon forced to institute tougher standards for future operations—a move which meant that more requests would be denied. Predictably, Army officers grew disgusted when air-support officers scratched missions. "We feel that we are competent to judge proper air and artillery targets," the Fourth Division commander complained, "and it is rather annoying to have staff officers in higher headquarters tell us that requests for air should not have been made." Still, Brereton stood firmly behind the new guidelines, although as the shortage in artillery shells grew so too did calls for air support.[61]

Few men proved able to look past this bickering and grasp that there were limits to the use of air power in World War II. Only a handful even hinted at understanding this. Eisenhower's English deputy Sir Arthur Tedder was one of them, believing that "the limitations of air support on the battlefield were not sufficiently understood." Pete Quesada was another, now doubting that even the big air strike during the Cherbourg attack had killed more than ten Germans. "Of course, our Army loved to see it before they went in," he recalled, "but it made me more skeptical about whether we should be using the air force as a USO show. I believed in attacking specific, identifiable targets that could be destroyed by aircraft."[62]

The problem was that there were fewer and fewer of those targets in July. The Germans had expertly deployed their forces throughout the haphazard Norman maze of copses and woods, reducing the effects of Allied air strikes by as much as 75 percent in some cases. Slowly, a disquieting conclusion became ever more apparent: despite the vast resources the Allies had sunk into their air forces, flyers were unable to inflict sufficient damage upon German positions to offer the attackers on the ground an easy passage anywhere. "The Germans were experienced, and the hedgerow country in Normandy gave them a series of natural defenses," Quesada stated. "The ground fighting was very tough and at times brutal."[63]

Lacking a codified doctrine of close air support, the Anglo-Americans pushed on, using air power in ways that were sometimes shrewd but often dubious. Montgomery's failure to blast past Caen earlier in July bred a yet bigger air strike to accomplish the same thing later in the month. Contemplating a 17 July assault with Lieutenant General Richard O'Connor's three armored divisions against the dominating ridges south of Caen and into the good open tank country beyond, Montgomery asked Eisenhower to "issue orders that the whole weight of the air power [sic] is to be available on that day to support my land battle." Eisenhower complied and, ever the cheerleader, overlooked concerns among his air staff to assure Montgomery that "All senior airmen are in full accord because this operation will be a brilliant stroke which will knock loose our present shackles. Every plane will be ready for such a purpose."[64]

Unknown to the Allies, the Germans had prepared the strongest defensive line yet in Normandy to counter this operation, now codenamed GOODWOOD. Under the direction of a new commander, General Heinrich Eberbach, the defenders had constructed five lines of tanks and antitank guns directly across from the British. Moreover, German intelligence had uncovered the basic contours of GOODWOOD. Thus on 18 July, when thousands of planes spearheaded a charge by 2,650 British tanks, the Germans were hunkered down, waiting.[65]

Between 0530 and 0830 hours, English and American heavy and medium bombers blasted the earth with abandon. Bomber Command came first, dropping the first thousands of tons of ordnance onto German positions along the Orne River. "It was a perfect opal summer morning," remembered one witness. The planes "looked just like a swarm of bees homing upon their hives. . . . One appreciated the great bravery of those pilots and crews as they flew straight into the most ghastly-looking flak. Every now and then an aircraft would burst into flames." Thick clouds of smoke and dust obscured targets for a second wave of medium bombers at 0700 hours, and many aircraft returned to bases without dropping their ordnance. The floating debris cleared by 0800 hours, however, and Eighth Air Force B-17s released nearly 90,000 bombs over the critical Bourguebus Ridge.[66]

On the ground below, German battery guns were wrecked or twisted, armored cars were hurled into the air, tanks were buried by earth and rubble, and men were deafened or blasted into fragments. All together, over 4,500 Allied planes had carpeted the place with nearly 7,000 tons of general explosive and fragmentation bombs. As they peered from their trenches, British soldiers felt that surely everything and everyone in the target zone had been obliterated.[67]

Hoping to rectify the mistakes of earlier bombardments, when soldiers had waited too long after the bombing to advance, O'Connor's men now emerged from foxholes as soon as the rain of destruction stopped. Shortly after H-Hour, an English scout car euphorically reported that it was well on the way to the Eleventh Armored Division's objectives and could see no evidence of opposition. Learning this, Montgomery sent an exuberant signal to London: "The weight of air power used was very great and decisive. Second Army has three armored divisions now operating in the open country to the south and S.E. of Caen." The report was premature, for from that point on things went badly for the British.[68]

Time and again, soldiers of World War II survived what appeared to be overwhelming concentrations of explosives only to emerge fighting with skill and determination. So it was now with the men of the Panzer Group West. At the outskirts village of Cagny, a battery of 88mm antiaircraft guns delayed O'Connor's spearhead division, knocking out sixteen tanks. Armored thrusts elsewhere met similar German resolve. By midafternoon, the three British divisions were either held up tight against the important heights on the far side of the city, checked in side skirmishes at isolated crossroads, or still having trouble getting going. To make matters worse, the Eleventh Armored's sole forward air controller had been knocked out, eliminating close air support for much of the advance.

The critical moment had arrived, and O'Connor requested another bombardment to knock out the stubborn 88mms and surviving German artillery. His plea was denied; there was simply not enough daylight left to mount another heavy mission. By nightfall, the men of the British Empire gazed dumbfounded, their objectives still in German hands. As the light faded in the warm air, Corporal Peter Roach took stock of GOODWOOD over a cold tin of rice pudding. It had been a bad day, and all he remembered were his hands, "gory with dried blood and brains." The offensive continued for two days, though the first hours had robbed the attackers of their heart and hope.[69]

In truth, the British and Canadians seized most of Caen in the bitter urban brawl that followed. But the Germans held firm atop the high ground south of the city, and even managed to strengthen their positions during the hours of darkness. There was no breakthrough into the Falaise plain, and the meager Allied gains had come at high cost. The battle had consumed nearly 6,000 casualties and over 400 tanks—more than a third of the British armor in Normandy.[70]

Operation GOODWOOD failed for many reasons. On the German side, the defenders saw the attack coming and burrowed deep into the earth to wait out the bombing. The delay between the aerial onslaught and the ground advance, although shorter than in previous bombings, still afforded the Germans valuable time to collect themselves. On the British side, a disjointed armor-infantry plan hurt O'Connor's forces once the battle commenced. Without the flexible air–ground communications that the Americans were just then developing, there was no effective and ongoing air support to meet the battle's exigencies.

Allied overconfidence in air power doomed GOODWOOD more surely than any other single factor, however. By mid-July, every soldier in every rank had witnessed the calamity of an air strike, some had seen it many times, and all were consistently amazed and mesmerized by aviation's destructive force. Heartened by GOODWOOD's call for a massive bombardment, ground soldiers no doubt expected little opposition and adopted a casual approach to their own advance. But when the German resistance held, these attackers were easily overcome by the unexpected strength of the defenders. For the Allies, too much of a good thing had become bad.

Although no one yet fully grasped the depth, scope, or complexity of the air-support problem, the consistent failure of bigger and bigger air strikes to blast past the enemy had at last begun to impress some Allied commanders. After GOODWOOD, Eisenhower remarked that 7,000 tons of bombs had yielded an advance of just seven miles. Bewildered, he asked his staff the critical question. "Can we afford a thousand tons of bombs per mile?"[71]

Apparently they could, for even while GOODWOOD faltered, the Americans to the west were conceiving a scheme of their own that paid homage to the seductive promise of air power. As early as 12 July Omar Bradley had pitched a new plan predicated on a four-thousand-ton bombardment in a very small sector of the front west of St. Lô. "It is just a slugger's match now and it is too slow a process," he told his four corps commanders and Pete Quesada during a conference. Bradley hoped that the air strike would allow two armored and three infantry divisions to spill into the enemy rear, power toward Coutances and perhaps even capture Avranches, nearly thirty miles behind the German lines. At its core, the plan aimed to break the thin but strong defensive crust along the St. Lô-Périers road. The Americans could then plunge headlong into the high prairie of central France, where good roads and open fields favored Allied mobility, and leave forever the tough *bocage*. "The whole thing depends on certain assumptions," Bradley concluded. "Move boldly and be ready to take stiff losses if necessary."[72]

The others expressed immediate accord with the plan. The only real question was the weight of the bombs. Bigger bombs would inflict more damage, but would also expose American troops to more danger and leave larger craters. "The number of times we have actually bombed our people has been very small," Collins declared. "I've said more than once I'm willing to take that risk." The fear of scattering huge craters about the battle proved the bigger fear, however, and the generals decided to use small 100-pound bombs. That settled, Bradley adjourned the meeting, saying "this thing must be bold. We must have this."[73]

That night, the Army commander underscored again the importance of the attack. "I've been wanting to do this since we landed. When we pull it off, I want it to be the biggest show in the world. We want to smash right on through." Toward midnight, he happened upon an apt code name for the operation. "We had a total of twenty-one divisions on our beachhead. It was like a coiled snake with that many divisions ready to break through one narrow hole that it looked to me like COBRA was the best description I could give it." When Bradley finally went to bed, all he had to do was wait for St. Lô to fall and for his soldiers to reach the Périers-St. Lô road, COBRA's demarkation point.[74]

On 19 July, the day after Americans captured St. Lô, Bradley and Quesada flew to Trafford Leigh-Mallory's command post outside London to sell the senior air commanders on the plan. Views from the air had always helped Bradley conceptualize the war, and heading toward London stiffened his resolve for COBRA. From 3,500 feet, the Allied forces looked very cramped indeed in their small part of France. Airstrips were crowded together, one nearly running into another. Bradley's aide Chester Hansen wrote of a similar flight: "You could see all our real estate in one glance. Cherbourg, Cap de Hague, both beaches, the front lines." The Allied zone was no more than an extended waterfront, and even the simplest of troop movements were now troublesome. The invaders needed to do something, fast.[75]

Leigh-Mallory's headquarters was an old and neglected mansion in Stanmore that befitted his lean, austere personality. It was, Hansen reported, a "horrible old house trimmed with Victorian monstrosities and painted a dreadful OD color." He remained unimpressed when someone told him that an ancient monarch had died in the place. "I wish they had embalmed the house with the queen."[76]

A pantheon of Allied air generals convened to listen to Bradley and Quesada. There was Leigh-Mallory, staid and trimly dressed. There was Tedder, small, wiry, and intellectual. There was Quesada's old friend Spaatz. There was Brereton, still uncertain of his place in the war. There was the jovial but deeply resentful Coningham. Boyish, ingratiating Hoyt Vandenberg, Leigh-Mallory's deputy, rounded out the major brass. In a corner, off to the side, sat a civilian, Solly Zuckerman, a meek and mysterious man who nonetheless provided the bulk of the scientific rationale for strategic bombing in the war. A zoologist by training, he wore a rumpled tweed suit and looked as though "he should be the chemistry professor in a small college." To a man, they had all come to hear what Bradley had termed the day before a "radical plan to break the stalemate."[77]

Bradley expected a hard sell on the heels of GOODWOOD, and he wasted no time once the meeting started. "I ran swiftly through our plans for COBRA, emphasizing our choice of the Périers road as a ground marker that might guide the heavy bombers to their target."[78] Pausing for effect, he then boldly requested 1,500 heavy bombers to saturate a two-by-eight-kilometer rectangle astride the road. In all, he hoped to drop 72,000 tons of bombs in a single hour on a small piece of Norman countryside.[79]

Leigh-Mallory heartily supported the plan in principle, seeing it as an unrivaled chance to test the effect of saturation bombing in a tactical role. Still, important issues took hours to thrash out. No one knew much about saturation bombing. The strategic air forces of both nations had trained for another kind of air war, and tactical commands lacked the heavy bombers to even contemplate such attacks under normal circumstances. Perplexing problems included ordnance loadings, fuses for the bombs, overcast bombing techniques, and coordination among the different air forces.

The size of the safety zone evoked considerable discussion. The Eighth Air Force representative at Stanmore advocated a 3,000-yard withdrawal from current positions, giving the bombers a margin of almost two miles. Even that space, he warned, did not guarantee a strike free of friendly fire. Bradley and Quesada frowned at the suggestion, knowing that the corps commanders in France would be loath to give back ground so hard won. Besides, they understood that the troops would have to exploit any bombardment quickly. Bradley offered an 800-yard fallback, and the planners compromised at 1,250 yards.[80]

The approach that the heavy bombers would make to the strike zone was not so easily decided. To minimize the danger of friendly fire, Bradley and Quesada urged a route parallel to the St. Lô–Périers road. If the bombers did not fly over his troops, Bradley reasoned, their pilots could not accidentally bomb soldiers. The bomber barons at Stanmore agreed in theory, but objected to the parallel flight on other grounds. Fifteen hundred heavy bombers simply could not be shoved through a chute two kilometers wide in sixty minutes. Only a route perpendicular to the road could accommodate the strike in anything like an hour.[81]

Besides, there were other bonuses to a perpendicular flight path. Flying at right angles to the front would expose bombers to less German ack-ack, and if the weather should compel blind bombing, the earth's magnetic field would play less havoc with radar calculations on north–south routes than on east–west paths. For all these reasons, Vandenberg "pointed out that the Eighth would desire to bomb perpendicular to the front." Others, notably Leigh-Mallory, adamantly supported Bradley's recommendation: "No, it would be done parallel." After some discussion, the generals left the critical issue hanging in the air. Perhaps they were conscious of the coming twilight, and knew that Bradley and Quesada needed to return to France before dark.[82]

Despite that piece of unfinished business, the conference had gone exceedingly well for the men from France. The bomber boys had been unusually cooperative, not voicing their customary doubts about the wisdom of using strategic bombers in close support of ground troops. As the meeting adjourned, Leigh-Mallory promised 2,246 heavy, medium, and fighter-bombers, more than even Bradley requested. "When we left," the Army commander recalled, "I carried air's commitment for a far heavier blitz than I had dared dream of." Arriving in France as night came, Bradley and Quesada passed the good news on to Collins, who could hardly believe he would have so many bombers for the strike. Lost in the hurry to adjoin the Stanmore meeting, and buried in that night's optimism, was the unresolved confusion over bomber approach paths. No one imagined that the lack of consensus could mean tragedy.[83]

Operation COBRA was scheduled for 21 July. Orders went out to air and ground forces headquarters. Infantry troops readied for the appointed day. Soldiers hated to give up hard-won ground, and some units like the Thirtieth Division hedged on the 1,250-yard withdrawal, crawling back just 800 yards "at the last practicable moment." Over at IX TAC, 700 of Quesada's fighter-bombers would start the operation, followed by 1,586 heavy bombers. The big planes would come in three fifteen-minute waves, with five minutes between surges. They would come in tight box formations of twelve planes at 18,000 feet, dropping their sticks in unison. When they finished, the medium bombers of IX Bomber Command would fill the sky, attacking targets in the German rear. If the assault failed, it would not be for lack of effort.[84]

High hopes pervaded the U.S. camp. The tough and realistic J. Lawton Collins dared to dream that his soldiers would meet little resistance after the cataclysmic bombing, and exhorted them to "vigorously push the attack across the highway to insure annihilation of any remaining enemy." When one correspondent who learned of the secret plans asked General Omar Bradley when he expected to reach Avranches, that normally judicious commander replied, "In 48 hours." By nightfall on the twentieth, all was in place for the greatest, if not the most novel, use of air power in support of ground troops that the war had yet seen.[85]

Not surprisingly, and befitting the history of Normandy, rain and wind and cloud postponed the attack. July 21 dawned "a miserable gray morning with heavy rain that has turned the engineer roads into quagmires and soaked down the fields," Hansen lamented. In France for a briefing on the attack, Eisenhower scowled at the sky. "How damnable that we should have 7,500 ships ready to fight and we can't get a single one into the air because of weather."[86]

The following days were not much better. With the sky still solid gray on the twenty-third, Bradley resorted to a rare use of profanity. "Goddamnit. I'm going to hate to court-martial the chaplain if we have very much more weather like this."[87]

American anxieties were justified. By late July there were 1,450,000 Allied troops ashore, and they were gobbling 26,000 tons of stores a day. Logistically, Eisenhower's temporary supply setup would soon cease to sustain this huge force. Tactically, the vast crowds of soldiers threatened to choke the Allied battle plan. In the British sector, manpower problems already imperiled the Empire's fundamental ability to carry the fight forward, and within weeks Montgomery would, under the greatest secrecy, break up an existing infantry division to feed troops into other units.[88]

For Quesada, the condition of airfields and planes in France constituted a crisis. Hardly designed for prolonged use, the wire-mesh-and-tarpaper runways were falling apart. Every storm found aviation engineers draining small lakes from runways, and patching the wire mesh was becoming a full-time chore. The choking dust, abundant mud, and bumpy tracks exacted a heavy toll on planes. The wings of Mustangs and Thunderbolts buckled under the combined strain of heavy bombs and bumpy strips. The 368th Group suffered twenty-four engine failures in July, twenty-three of them the result of high oil consumption caused by dust. Ground crews cannibalized older birds to keep others in the air, and Quesada reduced the standard squadron complement from sixteen planes to twelve to stave off an emergency.

But in so doing he sliced by one-quarter the effective strength of the IX TAC and, worst of all, it was only a temporary solution. Everywhere, it seemed, there was reason to worry.[89]

Yet in Quesada's command there was also cause for cautious optimism. His flyers had learned important tricks in two months of fighting on the far shore. They now knew the relative merits of dive, glide, and level bombing. Although hitting the Germans had become increasingly difficult, they now knew when the enemy traveled and where he hid. Although kinks persisted in the use of napalm and rockets, they now had them in their arsenals. Although blind-bombing techniques still worked imperfectly, the bomber pilots now had MEW and SCR 584 at their disposal. Beyond all this, Quesada now had most of his eighteen groups in France, eliminating vast amounts of time, energy, and fuel spent on commuting to and from the war. Despite the frustrations of July, for Quesada and those associated with the tactical air war it had been a productive month. Every essential feature of tactical air war, virtually nonexistent a short year earlier, now existed.

Besides, across the lines the Germans faced a greater plight than the Allies. Though they had measurably increased their paper strength, the actual ranks of the German fighting divisions were anemic. For two months the attackers had exacted a terrible toll on the defenders, and even veterans of the Eastern Front had tired of hurling themselves again and again against the vast steamroller of Allied resources. "Our casualties are so high that the fighting power of our divisions is rapidly diminishing," Rommel had reported to Hitler on 15 July. "Replacements from home are few in number and, with the difficult transportation situation, take weeks to reach the front. . . . The fighting force is fighting everywhere heroically, but the unequal combat is coming to an end. It is [in] my opinion necessary to draw the appropriate conclusions from the situation."[90]

Perhaps worse for the Germans, their high command on the Western Front was now in disarray. Von Rundstedt had lost the Führer's confidence and had been replaced by Field Marshal Gunther von Kluge on 1 July. On the seventeenth, an Allied fighter sweep attacked Rommel's staff car and critically injured the famed Desert Fox, sending him home and forcing additional duties on the newly arrived von Kluge. At that critical moment, von Kluge was implicated in the attempt to assassinate

Hitler on 20 July. The Führer, growing increasingly paranoid, never fully trusted his generals in the West after that date. Sapped of fighting strength and hampered by command problems, the German war machine could not hold the Allied juggernaut much longer.

When the weather finally cleared enough to try to launch COBRA on the twenty-fourth, the Americans were ready. "My high hopes and best wishes ride with you in your attack today," the Supreme Commander wrote to Bradley. "Speaking as the responsible American rather than the Allied commander, I assure you that the eyes of our whole country will be following your progress."[91]

Eisenhower's hopes were not misplaced. What happened next was no less than a revolution in warfare.

Chapter Seven

Our Most Recent Effort
Seems to Have Fallen Short

THE NORMAN COUNTRYSIDE SOUTHWEST OF PONT HÉBERT, 24 JULY 1944. 0915 HOURS. A slew of generals gathered at a small stone farmhouse with yellow brick trim to watch Operation COBRA commence. The once-quaint place bore every indication of a hasty abandonment: furniture thrown about, curtains ripped from windows, spoiled food in the pantry. An artillery shell had slashed a gaping hole in one corner of the roof, and barn swallows and rodents had made homes in the rafters and rubble. One by one, Generals Bradley, Brereton, Quesada, Courtney Hodges, William Simpson, Ralph Royce, and Matthew Ridgeway filed into the tiny living room. Beyond the back door a small army of aides milled about, nervous at so much brass in one room so close to the front. "Something was bound to happen," Hansen wrote later. "We moved around, sighting any number of slit trenches and fox holes that we could occupy."[1]

Forced jokes showed the tension they all felt. Bradley, especially, had wagered heavily on COBRA. For him, COBRA had "vast importance. . . . If it succeeded, I was certain it would give everybody a much-needed shot in the arm . . . if it failed, it could develop into much more than another military setback. It could mean defeat." Toward 1100 hours, all the generals crowded around the windows, scanned the still overcast sky, and awaited the air strikes.[2]

Less than two miles away, assault regiments of the Fourth, Ninth and Thirtieth Divisions withdrew from their forward positions, falling back 1,200 yards. In England, more than a thousand heavy bombers filled the sky, struggling to form up and navigate the Channel in thick clouds. At a dozen French fields, hundreds of Quesada's fighter pilots marked their watches and lifted into the air, having their own difficulties massing into the huge armadas that Operation COBRA required. "The extremely low visibility added the hazard of head-on collision to our other headaches," Colonel Harry Holt recalled. His group narrowly sidestepped two such crashes, but elsewhere the delicate task of forming up in midair cost five fighters and four flyers.[3]

On both sides of the English Channel the clouds threatened to play havoc with COBRA's complex and precise timing. Leigh-Mallory, in whose hands the air strike rested, first canceled, then confirmed, then again canceled the bombardment. By then, most of the bombers were over the English Channel and all of Quesada's planes were airborne. Only a few heavies and half of the fighters received the order to turn back; the rest flew onward unawares. News of the postponement reached all the infantry units, however, and they swiftly moved from protective cover to retake their morning positions closer to the Germans. As the sun reached its zenith, Americans in the air and on the ground moved toward a terrible destiny. For Leigh-Mallory, as with most men of World War II, hesitation would cost lives.[4]

Bradley's group was surprised when first four, then eight Thunderbolts streaked across the horizon shortly after 1200 hours. The sky was soon full of the P-47s. From the little stone house, the generals could see the planes sight their targets and peel off in long glides to the earth. "Suddenly four cut loose and followed by four more turned in our direction," Hansen recalled. "We scurried, one flight sliced off to the left of us, the other came straight for us and let their bombs go. We hit the ground as they went off, felt the ground shake and knew they were in our lines." Within minutes, the pilots flamed an American ammunition truck, killing the men aboard it and sending a huge fireball high into the sky.[5]

The heavy bombers, whose potential for destruction was much greater than that of the small fighters, arrived thirty minutes later. Under strict orders to abort if clouds remained heavy, most of the heavies in the first two waves circled and returned harmlessly to England; perhaps just thirty planes dropped their sticks. But back over the Channel, the third and final bomb division dipped from 18,000 to 16,000 feet to duck beneath the cloud cover. Just minutes from the target area, bombardiers worked furiously to recalculate the altitude change into their Norden bombsight computers. Some made mistakes. Although most of the 317 aircraft dropped bombs within the strike zone, many missed their mark by as much as 2,000 yards.[6]

At the stone house, the generals watched with growing horror. "Soon the heavies came in, we heard them long before seeing them," Hansen remembered. "Suddenly when the next flight came over there was a sharp deadly screaming whistle. I had heard it before in Tunisia when we were bombed near El Guettar."[7]

The generals had heard it before, too. According to Hodges's aide-de-camp, Major Bill Sylvan, "there was a wild scramble for cover, but few reached farther then the rear of the house before the bombs hit, crunch, wham, thud, some 500 yards to the southwest of us." As angry black spirals of dirt boiled up from the ground, they all knew something had gone terribly wrong.[8]

Not that anyone had to tell that to soldiers along the front. The scene at the Fourth Division command post was a mixture of chaos and terror. As one staffer related, "in a second we all were diving into water-filled slit trenches. Between the whoosh and the wham all two dozen had burrowed into the mud of a few holes. The noise was terrific, went on and on. We tried to wiggle lower among each other's arms and legs."[9]

At least they survived, which was more than some in the Thirtieth Division could claim. Moving forward on open ground, they fell easy prey to errant bombs. Shrapnel killed first one, then three, then eight soldiers. In the Ninth Division zone, swift-thinking Germans used the Allied friendly fire to spring a local skirmish, cutting down one of the finest and best-liked regimental commanders of the war, Colonel Paddy

Flint of the 39th. Although the rain of bombs no doubt demolished some German defenses, it also claimed 156 casualties in the U.S. sector, twenty-five of them fatalities.[10]

"How the hell did that happen?" Omar Bradley demanded of Quesada after the planes had left the sky. Quesada had not a clue, and placed a quick telephone call to AEAF headquarters and Leigh-Mallory. Bradley was particularly aggrieved because the bombers had flown directly over the American troops, not alongside the front as he had expected. "Bradley, Quesada, and I were greatly upset," J. Lawton Collins recalled, "when we learned that the heavy bombers had approached the target area from the north, perpendicular to the Périers–St. Lô road, instead of flying parallel to the road, as Bradley understood had been agreed at the July 19 conference with the Allied Air Commanders." When Quesada reached Leigh-Mallory on the phone, Bradley protested vigorously about the bombing path. The AEAF Commander was likewise surprised at the bomber route and promised an investigation.[11]

At Stanmore, Leigh-Mallory discovered that the perpendicular course was no mistake. Eighth Air Force planners had determined that that was the only way to stuff their planes over the target within Bradley's tight time frame. When Leigh-Mallory called Bradley back with this information, the Army Commander grew still more angry. He had left the 19 July planning session at Stanmore "with the distinct understanding in my own mind that the bombing would be made parallel" to the front. So had Quesada, who refused to believe the first reports of perpendicular paths until eleven witnesses verified it.[12]

But now all that was neither here nor there, and Leigh-Mallory needed to know only whether Bradley intended to try COBRA again the next day. "I had to make a quick decision over the phone whether to accept" the Air Forces plan, Bradley recounted. Convinced that the bombing had tipped the Germans off, he believed that time was of the essence. "And, of course, I needed them [the heavies] so badly I decided to—right over the phone there—to go ahead with it their way." Now properly and fully informed of the air plan, Bradley explicitly accepted the risks of COBRA and waited for the next day. But he continued to stew over the incident. Later, he would accuse the AEAF of "a shocking breach of good faith. . . . Had I known of Air's intent to chance the perpendicular approach, I would not have consented to the plan."[13]

Bradley's amazement was no doubt sincere, as was the surprise of others. Indeed, in some respects the short bombings were the product of honest misunderstanding. As Quesada put it, "The human truth is that people heard what they wanted to hear" at the planning sessions for COBRA.[14]

Rapid technological change in general and radar techniques in particular also help explain the short bombings of 24 July. Like Quesada's command, the Eighth Air Force had spent much effort developing its radar to beat the ruinous effect of poor weather. By the summer of 1944 the American strategic forces had adopted two British radar systems, OBOE and H2X, as their own, and had incorporated them into distinct bomber units called Pathfinders. Because COBRA's special targets required uncommon accuracy from a huge number of bombers, the operation had obliged the Eighth Air Force to use the more numerous H2X Pathfinder squadrons on the mission. That choice in turn compelled the planners to choose a course perpendicular to the front. The H2X's range errors (bombs forward or behind the target) were small, but its deflection errors (bombs to the left or right of targets) could be substantial. For COBRA, then, a blind bombing run parallel to the front would, contrary to Bradley's understanding, actually have increased the likelihood of friendly fire. As a result, Eighth Air Force planners chose to play to the relative strength of H2X and plotted a perpendicular approach to safeguard the ground troops.[15]

During World War II, only a handful of experts around the globe understood these exceedingly new and arcane issues in the air war. Even Quesada, who grasped the parameters of scientific war better than most commanders, did not fully fathom its intricacies. The simple fact was that in 1944 military aviation was in fundamental transition, relying at once on machine guns developed a generation earlier and on radar, then at the cutting edge of human understanding. And without an articulated doctrine of tactical bombardment, there was no framework within which to disseminate these new developments and integrate them into established procedures. So it was that Bradley, Quesada, and others complained of weather and misunderstanding while they waited for 25 July, the first nice day in a week.

Across the lines, the redoubtable Fritz Bayerlein, commander of the once proud Panzer Lehr Division, also endeavored to decode the Allied bombing of 24 July. While Bradley and others had feared that the aborted attack would tip the Germans off, Bayerlein had in fact drawn very different conclusions. He felt that the bombing was "simply a matter of a strong, but still only a partial attack, which will possibly lead to the main attack . . . [with the] intention of reaching the St. Lô–Coutances highway." Accordingly, to increase his tactical advantage, Bayerlein moved more defenders nearer the southern edge of the road late on the twenty-fourth.[16]

Early the next morning Bayerlein once again misread Allied intentions when reports trickled in that U.S. infantry were retreating from their positions. He now supposed that the Americans had gotten cold feet and had called off the whole attack. Then the field telephones in his farmhouse at Canisy began to ring incessantly, reporting "bombing attacks by endless waves of aircraft." Operation COBRA had at last sprung from its coils.[17]

Colonel Harold Holt's 366th Group led the American planes into the strike zone at precisely 0938 hours. Trying to avoid more accidents, the ground forces had retreated even further than on the previous day. "As we approached the target area we had to gasp to ourselves," Holt recalled. Below them, hundreds of U.S. tanks and armored vehicles idled bumper to bumper, ready to jump forward on signal. Across the lines there was no movement, no visible strength. The Germans were well dug in and camouflaged.

Holt's Thunderbolts rolled into their dive. "Stretched before us was a veritable battlefield. . . . Exploding shells, colored smoke pots billowing red clouds to outline our bombing area, and panels providing a well-defined troop line." In four minutes they were done. They left their corner of the battle zone completely covered by smoke and dust. Returning to their base, the flyers "gazed at the string of bombers stretching as far as we could see."[18]

Bradley, Quesada, Hodges, and Collins watched from the stone house as wave after wave of fighters pummeled the leading edge of the German defenses. Eight groups totaling some 350 planes darted across the sky at exact three-minute intervals, Holt's at H minus 85 minutes, the last at H minus 64. There were so many planes that the pilots had to alternate bomb runs between the eastern and western sectors of the front to avoid traffic congestion. They carried anything from 500-

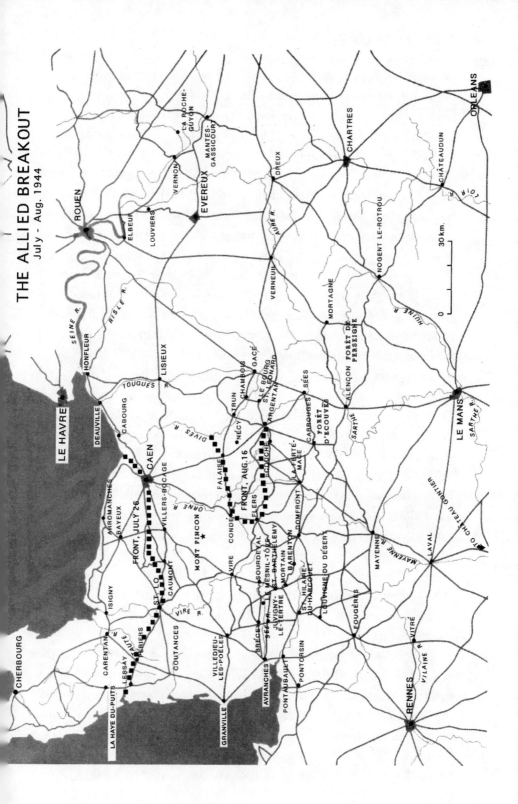

THE ALLIED BREAKOUT
July - Aug. 1944

pounders to fragmentaries to incendiary bombs. They dropped everything. If the heavies were merely hoping to hit the general area, these fighters aimed at definite positions. "My fighter-bombers came in with specific targets, a specific area, we did not try to carpet bomb, and it worked," Quesada remembered.[19]

In fact, it worked beautifully. The Ninth Division commander sent word to Bradley of the "perfect support" of fighter bombers. "The dive bombers were perfect," Hansen echoed, "hitting their targets with incredible accuracy in wave after wave with none falling behind our lines." When the last of the fighter pilots retreated from the sky, one flyer reported that "there was a pall of smoke over the entire area. It was about eight-tenths smoke up to 2,000 feet, funneling out toward the North and beyond Carentan, where it stretched 8 to 10 miles wide, about 12 to 15 miles from the target." Among the ground generals in the little stone farmhouse, Quesada stood tall.[20]

For a brief moment, the sky was eerily empty. Then shortly after 1000 hours a flotilla of B-17s and B-24s cast a shadow over the land. Their deep, guttural thunder filled the air. Coming in three waves as they had the day before, they found their target partially obscured by smoke and already pockmarked with bomb craters.

The first wave of planes dropped their bombs. "First few flights of Forts came over," Hansen recorded, "dropped their sticks on the forward elements of the enemy and the bombs cascaded down, spewing earth skyward, erupting with a thunderclap that never seemed to subside as wave after wave picked up the terrible tympani of the movement." The sight of the sky, again filled with heavy bombers on a close-support mission, made a myth of the neat distinction between tactical and strategic operations that theorists had postulated before the war.[21]

The explosions were tremendous. At the little stone house with the yellow brick trim, vibrations broke what few windows remained after a month of fighting. Miles from the front, in rear reserve areas, men of the Fourth Division likened the attack to an earthquake. Five miles back, near St.-Jean-de-Haye, some First Division troops "sat spellbound in a farmhouse and watched a peculiar little statue on a pedestal hop and turn at each bomb blast, then suddenly crash to the floor."[22]

Everyone on the American side could only guess at the German experience. When the explosives started to rain down, Bayerlein remembered, "every living person immediately went for whatever cover he could find, and stayed there." The ground bubbled and boiled, tossing tons of dirt into the air. The destruction knocked out half of Bayerlein's prized 88mm guns. To the German commander, hunched at his post outside Canisy, the planes just kept coming, "like a conveyor belt, seemingly without end." When the first wave mercifully abated, his entire communications net was ruined. By 1100 hours, Bayerlein, the principal German commander in the immediate area of attack, could contact no one and no one could contact him. He was nearly incapable of orchestrating a defense.[23]

Desperate, Bayerlein mounted a motorcycle and set out for his regimental command posts. To him the earth resembled a "*Mondlandschaft*," a moonscape, all craters and death. Everywhere, "the shock effect on the troops was indescribable. Several men went mad, and rushed dementedly around in the open until they were cut down by splinters." Bayerlein discovered the 902d Regimental command post completely demolished and deserted; soldiers there had already concluded that their only hope lay in "running to the American side." At the 901st Regiment, he found a colonel sitting alone in a cellar beneath an old stone tower, mumbling that his entire front line had been devastated.[24]

Then the second wave of bombers slammed explosives into the ground. Through slits in the medieval tower, Bayerlein watched helplessly as great bomb carpets unrolled in giant rectangles.

Throughout his division, Bayerlein estimated that the air assault's first two waves permanently reduced his effective force by one fifth. Most of the casualties occurred along the leading edge of his defenses, and he now cursed himself for having moved troops there the night before. Worse still, he figured that "at least 70% of the personnel were temporarily out of action, either dead, wounded, crazed, or dazed." Captured Germans could babble only incoherently and many spoke of the "hell of La Chapelle," a key crossroads in the center of the bombing.[25]

By 1200 hours, Bayerlein could see nothing in any direction, so thick was the smoke, dust, and murk. The ground literally smoldered. Now, between the second and third bomb waves, he noticed for the first time that there was also heavy artillery fire. The Americans would jump off soon, he thought, and he had nothing with which to fight.[26]

The Germans caught a break when the third and final wave of Allied heavies made their run. The small target zone was by then draped in smoke, and a breeze had drifted the floating debris north, over American troops. Some of the Flying Fortresses, high in the sky and entirely detached from the action below, took aim at the smoke line and the friendly forces. Still others had trouble with bombsights or with liaison with other planes. One entire formation bombed short on a false cue from a lead plane. Within twenty minutes, forty-two heavy bombers had dropped explosives on their own troops.[27]

On the ground, the results—and reactions—were predictable. "As we watched, there crept into our consciousness a realization that windrows of exploding bombs were easing back towards us, flight by flight, instead of gradually forward, as the plan called for," wrote the intrepid war correspondent Ernie Pyle, who was with front-line troops. "An indescribable kind of panic comes over you at such times. We stood tensed in muscle and frozen in intellect."[28]

Others ran like hell. In the 120th Regiment men dove into foxholes. "The ground was shaken and rocked as if by a great earthquake," said Lieutenant Colonel George Tuttle. "The concussion, even underground, felt as if someone was beating you with a club." Another officer remembered that "The earth trembled and shook. Whole hedgerows disappeared and entire platoons were struck. Huge geysers of earth erupted and subsided leaving gaping craters."[29]

When Lieutenant Sidney Eichen popped his head from the ground, he thought, "Goddamit, they're coming for us again. My outfit was decimated, our anti-tank guns blown apart. I saw one of our truck drivers, Jesse Ivy, lying split down the middle. Captain Bell was buried in a crater with only his head visible. He suffocated before we could get him out."[30]

In the VII Corps center—the heart of the planned attack—explosives hit every assault company of the Fourth Division. The bombing wiped out an entire battalion command group in the Ninth Division. The Thirtieth Division suffered more casualties than on any other day of the war. All around, maimed men lay screaming for aid. Some, maddened by the attack, were forcibly carried to the rear. Throughout the corps, casualties from the short bombings totaled 111 killed and 490 wounded.[31]

One of those killed was Lieutenant General Leslie McNair. The former commander of the U.S. Army Ground Forces, McNair was in Europe to replace Patton at the head of a phantom group in the FORTITUDE plan, which had deceived the Germans about the invasion site. Despite warnings from both Eisenhower and Bradley about unnecessary risk, McNair had sneaked his way up to the front lines as an observer. Shortly before 1200 hours, a direct hit obliterated his slit trench, throwing him sixty-five feet. His body was unrecognizable save for the three stars on his tattered uniform.[32]

J. Lawton Collins was appalled when he learned of the tragedy. "He was right up in the very front line where he really didn't belong." Others agreed and worried the incident might increase air–ground tensions. In Washington, Arnold reacted with characteristic zest: "The goddamn fool, what was he doing there?"[33]

But whatever his own culpability, McNair's death cast a pall of sadness over those who knew him. To preserve FORTITUDE, he was buried in secrecy on 26 July. Besides the Army quartermaster and chaplain, only Generals Bradley, Hodges, Patton, Quesada, Royce, Kean, and McNair's two aides were present. He was the highest-ranking American officer to die in combat in World War II.[34]

Back on the COBRA lines, the short bombings had left the generals in shock and disbelief. Animosity toward the flyboys boiled to the surface. "We're good soldiers, Courtney, but there's absolutely no excuse, no excuse at all. I wish I could show some of those boys, decorated with everything a man can be decorated with, some of our clearing stations," Major General Leland Hobbs of 30th Division complained to Hodges. Hobbs' deputy, William Harrison, won a Distinguished Service Medal for dragging men from their shock and paralysis that day, and he echoed his boss's anger in a bitter letter home. "When you hear of all the great glamour of our flying friends, just remember that not all that glitters is gold."[35]

At Bradley's farmhouse, Quesada struggled to understand the disaster. "The St. Lô road was never the visible landmark you thought it was," he recalled. "No one thought that the dust would rise and drift."

For a long while, Bradley merely sat still in a corner, shaking his head. "Christ, not again!" he muttered.[36]

Actually, by Eighth Air Force standards, the strikes of 25 July were good. Compared to the low level of accuracy usually attained in the strategic air war, all three bomb divisions covered their targets well. In a little over an hour, a total of 1,495 heavy bombers had attacked their primary targets with 4,406 tons of high explosive and fragmentation bombs. Given the size and pace of the operation, it was ludicrous to think that accidental bombings would not occur, especially since the new bombing methods involved many thousands of fallible airmen and an enormous quantity of complicated equipment. In fact, the percentage of errant bombs in this operation was well below Eighth Air Force averages for the war. As Spaatz tried to explain it, the problem lay elsewhere; the ground forces had simply attempted to "place too heavy of an attack in too short of time."[37]

To any careful and disinterested observer that July day, the lesson was simple. Strategic air forces were poorly suited for delicate tactical work, and the commanders ought to have anticipated problems when the war demanded the participation of heavy bombers in the ground fighting. Yet everywhere confusion, anger, and desperation reigned supreme. Among the American leaders there was a real and legitimate fear that the short bombings might have ruined the momentum of the attack.

At 1300 hours, as medium bombers struck targets three miles behind the front in the last of COBRA's initial blows, American ground troops warily advanced from their positions. They were startled by dogged German resistance. Somehow, incredibly, unbelievably, Bayerlein had managed to mount a makeshift defense with his tattered forces. Although the bombing inflicted tremendous damage to the German command and control systems, surprisingly few rank-and-file soldiers had been killed by the massive strike. Fanatical young Nazis of the Fifth Parachute Division, who were stationed west of the Panzer Lehr Division and who had escaped most of the bombing, shifted into some of Bayerlein's positions. On the St. Lô–Périers highway itself, Germans engaged the American 120th Regiment in a bitter fight for the road. One of its companies lost three successive commanders in forty minutes. Finally, only the aggressive reconnaissance of Lieutenant Ernest Aas's tank company propelled the Americans across the open ground.[38]

Although Quesada's fighters returned twice to work over the flanks of the battle area and medium bombers continued to harass the German rear, at the point of ground combat the Americans found the Germans "doing business at the same old stand with the same old merchandise—dug-in tanks and infantry." There was no doubt of the massive destruction in the enemy zone, yet their practice of digging deep earthworks, their extraordinary recuperative qualities, and their knack for small-unit fighting helped the Germans stop any American plunge through the lines. "Neither the bombing nor the artillery preparation prevented a great many of the German front-line infantrymen from continuing to fight the same dogged hedgerow-to-hedgerow defense that they had carried on since the invasion," wrote the VII Corps diarist. Across the lines, at German Seventh Army headquarters, staffers even became optimistic on the evening of the twenty-fifth, speaking of creating a "solid barrier" along the front and still awaiting "the enemy's actual large-scale attack."[39]

As had so often been the case in the *bocage*, a promising start had bogged down. By nightfall, the Americans had advanced an average of only 1,000 yards. In many places, progress was even more meager. Despite the world's heaviest air strike aimed at an already beleaguered foe, the central lesson of COBRA was clear as the sun slipped from the horizon on 25 July. Massive air strikes alone could not puncture the tough, albeit fatigued German line.

That night, COBRA's failure bred more soul-searching among the generals. "We talked of the lesson to be learned from it. Apparently heavy bombers cannot be used in tactical support," Hansen reported. "This day, a day to remember for more than one reason, did not bring the breakthrough for which we all hoped," added Hodges' aide Bill Sylvan. "Two successive days of bombing of our troops took the ginger out of several of the front-line elements, and as was to have been expected, all surprise element from the attack itself."[40]

Eisenhower, who had traveled to France late in the day, told Bradley that he "did not believe in tactical use of heavies. I look upon heavies as an instrument for strategic attack on rear installations. I don't believe they can be used in support of ground troops. That's a job for artillery. I gave them a green light on this show but this is the last one." Three days later the Supreme Commander reiterated his sentiments in a letter to George Marshall: "Under no circumstances will I allow the heavies to again perform close air support. I let the air boys talk me into it this time, but it will be the last."[41]

Quesada did not go that far, but he agreed that the strike had failed. "Though you will read of our show in the papers before you get this, our most recent effort seems to have fallen short," he wrote Colonel William Momyer at the Air Forces proving grounds in Florida.[42]

Nearer the front and with a keen feel for the battle, General J. Lawton Collins drew different conclusions. "Perhaps expecting too much from the massive bombing, and shocked by their own unexpected casualties," he later explained, "divisions were discouraged that they had not been able to break through the main German defenses." Still, he sensed the Germans cracking, felt they could no longer man a continuous shield along the front, and believed they could be outflanked, bypassed. Where in most sectors progress had been limited to a hundred yards, in one place Collins' forces managed to advance half a mile. "It was not a breakout, but it was something," remembered one captain in the 120th Regiment. "Noting a lack of coordination in the German reaction, particularly their failure to launch prompt counterattacks," Collins concluded, "I sensed that their communications and command structure had been damaged more than our troops realized."[43]

He was right. The Panzer Lehr Division was on its deathbed. It had begun the day with only 2,200 effectives and forty-five tanks, and now its ranks were depleted further. That night, Bayerlein brought his last reserves into the line, managing to scrounge ten more tanks from workshops and to restore wire communications to lower units. Yet his only contact with higher headquarters was still by runner, and replacements from the Fifth and 275th Divisions were slow to reach critical weak spots. In all, fifteen well-rested and equipped American divisions faced only eleven seriously weakened German divisions.

When an officer from Field Marshal Hans Gunther von Kluge's headquarters arrived to order the St. Lô road held at all costs, Bayerlein lashed back: "Out in front everyone is holding out. Everyone. My grenadiers and my engineers and my tank crews—they're all holding their ground. Not a single man is leaving his post. They are lying silent in their foxholes for they are dead. You may report to the Field Marshal that the Panzer Lehr Division is annihilated." Bayerlein exaggerated, but only slightly. If the Americans promptly pressed their advantage, he would be a prophet. If they dallied, he might yet fashion another miracle defense.[44]

Collins was convinced that now was not the time to retreat to plan another headlong strike elsewhere in the line, giving the Germans valuable days to recover. Now was the time to press the attack with all deliberate speed. In a bold gamble worthy of his moniker "Lightning Joe," he determined to throw his armored reserve into the fray. On the morning of the twenty-sixth, the First Division, with a combat command of tanks, and the entire Second Armored Division would bypass the infantry units and try to puncture the German crust.

When Ninth Air Force staffers learned of Collins' intentions, they immediately designed an air-support scheme. From 0120 to 0535 hours a flurry of telephone calls set up initial air strikes. As tanks moved from their bivouacs at 0700 hours, 216 medium bombers plastered the Marigny area and five fighter groups strafed St. Gilles. The attacks shelled Bayerlein out of yet another headquarters, and it seemed to him that the "The whole thing just began all over again . . . there was not a second . . . when the air was not filled with thundering fighters." Bomb craters and the few remaining German strongpoints slowed Collins's initial advance, but in midafternoon the leading tanks were scheduled to pick up column cover from Quesada's planes, and the combination of tanks and planes promised great things.[45]

"All right, gentlemen—your attention please," Harold Holt began his early-afternoon briefing for the 366th Group. The group had flown sorties against St. Gilles in the morning, and now readied to support the tanks. Some of the Shermans were commanded by hard-charging Brigadier General Maurice Rose, Quesada's classmate at Leavenworth eight years earlier. "Your mission today is Column Cover with Combat Commands A and B of the Second Armored Division," Holt told his pilots. "Assist them in any way you can." A briefing for column cover was that simple. Taking off in squadron elements, the Thunderbolts staggered their planes so that a flight of four would be over the lead tanks at all times.[46]

"Hello, Booty, this is Slipshod leader," Holt called to the tanks as he took his place above the Shermans. "Have you any targets for us?" The tankers did—a shrewdly placed 88mm gun on the road to St. Gilles was blocking their path. "Booty" directed Holt to a position directly over the battery so that "Dropping our eggs on the located gun was easy." The highway now clear, the tanks rolled on to meet the next German roadblock.[47]

As Holt's group turned for home, errant flak hit the ship of Captain Jack Engman, one of the best-liked and, at twenty-six, one of the oldest members of the group. Once he reached American lines he bailed out, but his chute never opened. "We could actually see his body bounce several feet into the air when it hit the ground," Lieutenant Quentin Aanenson bleakly recalled. The next day, Engman's buddies found and buried his body.[48]

As that drama played out, pilots from the 405th and 368th Groups ranged over other tank columns. To the west, P-47s led by Major Randall Hendricks spotted three German armored vehicles advancing toward American lines. Diving, Hendricks saw soldiers lunge for a ditch and wave a white flag. Reporting the unusual surrender to nearby tanks, he then circled his prize every few minutes, waiting for U.S. soldiers to take them into custody.[49]

Forty minutes later and a mile further to the west, Captain Joseph McLaughlin and his flight of four Thunderbolts spied an American tank group that had stopped dead. Approaching, they could see Shermans stretching for miles to the rear. "We flew up to the head of the column," McLaughlin recalled, "and found two big German tanks just around the bend in the road." One by one, the four planes swooped down and flamed the huge Tigers. They left both tanks burning, one spewing shells like a "July fourth pinwheel." As the pilots turned for home, American bulldozers moved toward the flaming hulks to clear a path for the smaller American tanks.[50]

By midafternoon U.S. forces finally began shaking free of resistance. Rose's Combat Command A passed through St. Gilles at about 1530 hours, his tanks silhouetted against a huge inferno that had been the village. "The whole west side of the town was blazing fiercely from the successful work of the dive-bombers," remembered one officer.[51]

Toward evening, armored columns reached Marigny and the cross-roads at Canisy, Bayerlein's headquarters just a day ago. As some tanks rolled forward they came up against an 88mm gun that appeared from the air to be destroyed but that was very much in working order. It blew up the leading American tank, killing the crew and the forward air controller, Captain John O'Shea. The one surviving pilot with the column called for assistance. "We've already bombed that gun," a pilot replied to the hurried voice from the tank. "Goddammit, I'm telling you it just blasted a tank and killed John O'Shea!" With that, planes returned to Canisy and destroyed the battery.

Without armored-column cover communications, such a request would have consumed at least an hour and probably longer. By then it would have been too dark to mount any operation and the tanks would have been stuck for the night. As it was, the Shermans had been delayed just twenty minutes. Exhilarated, Rose drove his tankers on well past midnight, declaring that "he had an objective to take, that the whole operation depended on it, and that he was going to continue and take it despite the darkness and whatever the cost in men and tanks." Since noon, the cost had not been great.[52]

The day heartened Quesada and his pilots. "The war has been tough today," Quentin Aanenson wrote his sweetheart that night, "but our efforts have brought some good results. It gives me a good feeling to watch the infantry move up after we have bombed some Germans out up ahead. . . . History is being made." Quesada would have endorsed Aanenson's assessment. In a cable to his command he gushed, "There is no use expressing my appreciation for what you have all done these past three days because the results I feel are a just reward. A real breakthrough has been accomplished and by gosh! by gum! you have all done more than your share. I just cannot express my gratitude in words and just say simple thanks to every man and officer. . . . You have all done a grand job."[53]

Decent weather held on 27 July, and the Americans, conditioned to meager gains over weeks of tough combat, slowly realized that they were on the verge of accomplishing a rout. Bradley ordered the VIII and XIX Corps, the units that bordered VII Corps, into the attack to exploit the widening breach. The few Germans who were still standing firm soon found themselves holding isolated ground. Such positions were untenable, as Sergeant Hans Stober and his company of *Panzer-grenadiers* learned. Stober had been directed to hold a key crossroads for twenty-four hours, "But we found that American units in company strength had bypassed us. There was no choice but to order us to withdraw." In some places, the American columns advanced another five miles by night—a veritable light-year compared to advances that for weeks had been measured in mere yards.[54]

That evening, the Panzer Lehr Division died. At 1700 hours a messenger rushed into Bayerlein's command post and reported that U.S. tanks were within 300 yards. Fighter-bomber attacks ceased as the armor moved closer, convincing Bayerlein of the remarkably "close cooperation between air and ground forces" in the American camp. He and his small staff then hid in a derelict house as the Shermans rumbled up and riddled the place with .50-caliber bullets. As the tanks roared on ahead, fighters stayed overhead, circling like buzzards until dark. Bayerlein was finally able to crawl from the house and through underbrush until he found a German radio station. Calling his Seventh Army, he reported that of his division nothing remained: its armor was completely destroyed, its combat personnel killed, wounded, captured or scattered; its headquarter records, papers, and equipment were lost. Bayerlein had escaped with nothing but the clothes on his back. Even those were in sad shape—and he had been one of the lucky ones.[55]

July 28 brought profound relief for those who had struggled and worried over the Allied situation in Normandy. With no organized resistance before them, the Americans embarked on what J. Lawton Collins described as "some of the wildest melees of the war." It seemed that the Germans were in retreat everywhere as American columns sprinted ahead another five to seven miles. "To say that personnel of the First Army Headquarters is riding high tonight is putting it mildly," Bradley crowed to Eisenhower that evening. "Things on our front look really good. I told Middleton [of VIII Corps] to continue tomorrow morning toward Avranches and go as far as resistance will permit. As you can see we are feeling pretty cocky."[56]

The momentum of attack only grew in the last days of July. On the extreme right of the U.S. lines, VIII Corps broke free on the 29th and plunged down the Normandy Peninsula, while Collins and Corlett pressed onward in the middle and the left. With a playfulness impossible just days before, Middleton bet Hodges a bottle of brandy that Vire would fall inside of forty-eight hours.[57]

For the men of the American armies in Europe, they had embarked on the war's great high tide. Behind them lay their baptism by fire, their test of endurance, their trial in courage. Before them lay the promised land of the Continental campaign: the wide-open rolling terrain of the French highlands. Late on 31 July, the Fourth Armored Division's Major General Raymond Barton issued orders that any of the American commanders could have issued: "The Division is encountering only scattered resistance, some small-arms fire, but few defended positions. We face a defeated enemy, an enemy terribly low in morale, terribly confused. I want you to throw all caution to the wind. When enemy resistance is encountered, bypass it; if it is too troublesome, leave a force to contain it and move on. *Get on.*" The break through had become a break out.[58]

All the while, fighter-bombers picked off fleeing defenders. On the 29th, rocket-equipped P-47s of the 405th Group discovered a huge German convoy escaping the battle zone near Roncey. Learning of the treasure back at IX TAC, Quesada smelled blood and swiftly diverted all but one group to the area. Soon a near-continuous stream of dive-bombers was ambushing the hapless defenders.[59]

Desperate to recoup their losses in any way they could from the killing fields, Wehrmacht officers fluent in English took to the radio to impersonate Allied air controllers. The deception worked for an hour before one alert pilot discerned "something guttural about the voice" and asked an impostor to sing "Mairzy Doats." Then the attacks continued.[60]

"In comparison to Rommel's retreat in Africa," one veteran deputy group commander reported the next morning, "yesterday's withdrawal was completely disorganized. Rommel controlled his retreat and moved his vehicles rapidly through open country. But yesterday, the trucks were almost packed bumper to bumper, slowed up or completely jammed at the many crossroads which our bombs have torn up." It was a fighter-bomber's paradise, and in the midst of the fracas a ground general gushed over the radio, "Go to it. Get one for me." All together, the flyers left 204 trucks, sixty-six tanks, eleven guns, and innumerable horse-dawn vehicles in flames.[61]

Pilots wrecked another 500 vehicles elsewhere that day, leaving a truly astounding path of destruction on the roads of Normandy. Traveling by jeep, even J. Lawton Collins was amazed at the pall of waste. Reaching Roncey the day after the massive free-for-all, he discovered that the town square was "blocked by well over a hundred German motor vehicles that had been caught by our fighter-bombers and burned to a crisp." There was a "similar group of vehicles amounting to a hundred or more" beyond the village, and dead bodies filled the air with a putrid stench. To advance, First Army engineers literally bulldozed the corpses from their path.[62]

The entire war would see few better days for the American tactical air forces, and again Pete Quesada overflowed with pride. "You have taken this German army and torn it to pieces," he told one group. "The Hun has no means of transport left. . . . This work on the Peninsula may well be the greatest victory an American Army has had in any war." He could be forgiven for exaggerating. In the last week of July, his IX TAC flew over 9,000 close-support sorties, and claimed destruction of 384 tanks, more than 2200 motor transports, nearly a hundred artillery guns, and truly countless numbers of horse-drawn vehicles. Although later investigation reduced these numbers by perhaps one fourth, for the Germans the effect was devastating. On top of all this, Quesada now had seventeen fighter groups on the Continent supporting nineteen American divisions, a size of force not usually afforded a junior two-star general. "I have a terrific striking power at my beck and call and I use it freely," he wrote to his sister on 3 August, "and as a result I have created an unbearable position on the part of the German. I don't think I will be very popular in Germany before this war is over. At least, such is my aim."[63]

In an absurd counterpoint to IX TAC's great success in Normandy, certain air barons back in England began to question the value of air cover for armored columns. Deputy AEAF Commander Major General Hoyt Vandenberg felt that artillery, not planes, should handle targets so close to the front lines. In a memo to Brereton on the twenty-ninth, he criticized Quesada for a "malemployment" of air assets. "Too much of the force available to the commander, IX TAC, was being employed within an area of 30–40 miles in advance of the army's front line."[64]

The complaint revealed an astonishing ignorance of the battle. Throughout World War II—on both sides of the front—swift advances often separated leading spearheads from their own artillery, placing a premium on other forms of fire support. As the U.S. Third Armored Division commander explained it after COBRA, "In an operation of this kind where divisions are operating in numerous armored columns, artillery support is seldom immediately available and, therefore, column cover is depended on to bridge this gap." Omar Bradley went even further, believing that fighter planes destroyed field batteries better than artillery could, and Germans like Fritz Bayerlein would have no doubt agreed. Busy with the battle at hand, Quesada never learned of Vandenberg's protests, though he certainly would have denounced any challenge to armored-column-cover missions. Soon, however, he would have other, more profound reasons to clash with Vandenberg.[65]

Whatever Vandenberg's criticisms, COBRA's success bred a curious consensus about air power among ground generals. Although most of them had protested the disastrous short bombings on 24 and 25 July, many of the same leaders now praised the air show. The commander of the Thirty-Fifth Infantry Division, which did not endure COBRA's friendly fire, figured that the operation "was probably one of the most effective missions accomplished by the heavies at any time." J. Lawton Collins, whose men did suffer from Eighth Air Force mistakes, maintained that "There can be no question that the bombing was a decisive factor in the initial success of the breakthrough." If not for the big planes, he believed, "our losses would have been infinitely greater and our successes would perhaps have never materialized."[66]

Similar endorsements echoed up the chain of command. Bradley felt that air power was "critical to our success at St. Lô. Without it, we would not have broken out of the beachhead like we did." On 2 August Dwight Eisenhower, who just six days earlier had vowed never again to employ heavy bombers near the battlefield, told Jimmy Doolittle that the short bombings "must under no circumstances lead us to believe in the impossibility of supporting ground troops, under proper circumstances, by elements of Strategic Air Forces."[67]

What a difference a week of good warring made in the minds of men! Weaned on "bigger is better" assumptions and amazed by air power's truly awesome explosive might, even the best of the American generals mentally blurred the differences between the massive bombardment on 24 and 25 July and the armored-column cover on the 26th and beyond. For them, it had become impossible to take note of individual failures in an operation marked by overwhelming success. Looking back, the participants did not separate or distinguish the daily events of late July, and failed to recall that no substantial advances had occurred on COBRA's first day. By nightfall on that day, no officer on the line had recognized anything like a breakthrough. Tough fighting persisted well into the following day, and spirits at First Army and elsewhere remained quite low.

In reality, U.S. forces did not shake free from the German front until the afternoon of 26 July, when Collins' sound tactical initiative and Quesada's armored-column cover propelled the Allies out of their beachhead stalemate. Time and again before COBRA, the Anglo-Americans had employed over-muscled air strikes to little avail. In COBRA, the air-tank team, much more than the initial massive bombardment, was the key to success. A careful analysis of the summer campaign would have produced these conclusions, but the sheer pace of the advance discouraged any analytical look at air power. Even tactical airmen like Quesada, happy to assist the ground war, did not strive for a more subtle understanding of COBRA.

In some ways, then, COBRA was more than a breakthrough. It helped to legitimize a mythical notion of air power that profoundly influenced close air support policy for the rest of the war. The muscle of air power and the use of strategic forces in tactical operations became icons of the conflict. In the future, whenever the ground advance stalled, soldiers looked upward, hoping to see the defenders blasted with ever-heavier bomber attacks. In triumph, the real significance of COBRA was lost.

The great war journalist Ernie Pyle witnessed COBRA. "I have a hunch," he wrote a month after the great bombing, "that July 25 of the year 1944 will be one of the great historical pinnacles of this war. It was the day we began a mighty surge out of our confined Normandy spaces, the day we stopped calling our area the beachhead and knew we were fighting a war across the whole expanse of France." Pyle's hunch was correct, but people would sometimes remember COBRA for the wrong reasons.[68]

Chapter Eight

My Fondness for Buck Rogers Devices Is Beginning to Pay Off

IX TAC COMMAND POST. LES OBEAUX, FRANCE. 29 JULY 1944. 1830 HOURS. Pete Quesada and J. Lawton Collins studied the battle reports. Early that morning, Thunderbolt pilots had strafed some rifle companies in the Thirtieth Division, momentarily upsetting their spectacular advance. In the early afternoon, a similar incident had occurred in the First Division sector. There, Sergeant Leroy Stewart had been with a small group of trucks when four Thunderbolts blasted in "very low to our left and started looking us over." After three passes, one P-47 had broken formation and made a strafing run, hitting one truck and killing four men. Reading of these incidents, Quesada and Collins were of one mind. They both feared that an increase in friendly fire might taint the success of COBRA, and they wondered about how to contain the accidents.[1]

It would not be an easy task. Days of barreling down crowded highways, country lanes, and village streets had seriously snarled the American forces. In their exhilaration, some combat teams had strayed across unit boundaries. Out in front, armored columns from three different divisions were now competing for the same roadway, creating massive traffic jams. The confusion on the ground made it difficult for pilots to keep track of front-line positions and to know which troops were American and which were German; the strikes at U.S. soldiers had been the result. As Collins so aptly put it, if the Allies were not careful, they could all end up in "one hell of a mess."[2]

The two generals need not have worried. To be sure, U.S. troops were now spread higgledy-piggledy over hundreds of square miles. Often, ground leaders had no clear idea where their men were, and air-force command posts had even less information. But armored-column cover, with its direct communications between tankers and pilots, mitigated friendly-fire accidents at times when they were otherwise most likely to occur. More than this, the air-tank battle team helped push the Allied advance deep into northern France and beyond. Much more than the initial attempt to punch through the German lines with a huge bombardment, it was this armored-column cover, and the signals system which supported it, that made Operation COBRA a resounding success and a revolution in warfare. As Quesada later reported to his mother, "My fondness for Buck Rogers devices is beginning to pay off."[3]

On the battlefield, those closest to the fighting recognized the importance of armored-column cover and came to view friendly fire as a necessary cost for their great advance. "We could never have made it without the air support," declared Leroy Stewart. One armored division commander believed the column-cover flights "endeared the fighter-bomber to the hearts of our tankers forever. Many veteran tankers now refer to the P-47 as the best and only effective AT [anti-tank] weapon."[4]

Even Omar Bradley concurred, temporarily forgetting the praise he and other leaders had recently bestowed on the big bombers of COBRA. To him, the last week of July marked "the beginning of the most effective sustained close support in history." Reporting to George Marshall on 31 July, Bradley wrote that "The cooperation between the advancing columns and the fighters and fighter bombers of the Ninth Tactical Air Command has been of a very superior nature." For this, the Army Commander credited Quesada: "I simply can't imagine any other Air Officer that would have given us as much—certainly no more—help than Pete. He was willing to try anything."[5]

Despite this praise, Quesada still sought to minimize incidents of friendly fire. On 1 August he and Blair Garland reconnoitered the front lines to get a better sense of the ground battle. When they reached IX TAC's forward air control station at 1015, Quesada asked the radarmen for the latest information on the fighting. The duty controller had barely begun outlining the battle as of 0900 when Quesada exploded. "Goddamnit, when I left my headquarters that was the situation. What is it now?"[6]

The controller could not tell him. Furious, Quesada grabbed Garland and pushed onward to the wing commander's van, where he asked Brigadier General Jim McCauley for a situation report. "Well, at nine—" Quesada's face boiled red with rage. "Goddamnit, I bet my headquarters knows more about this than you do!" Storming past McCauley and into the van, Quesada grabbed the phone and demanded his own command post. Startled and nervous, the operator instead connected him to the quartermaster. Quesada slammed the phone down and glared at Garland. "Nothing works in this goddam command, nothing! It's the worst communications system I ever saw."

Now on a mission, Quesada was determined to find answers. Leaving Garland, he picked up another colonel, Gilbert Meyers, and headed toward the Twenty-ninth Infantry Division, which was fighting near Tessy-sur-Vire. There he announced to the division commander, Major General Charlie Gerhardt, that he was driving ahead to Villebaudon, where the Second Armored Division was leading the American advance. "Mighty fine," Gerhardt wryly replied, and offered Quesada a guide. "Hell, no. I'm used to moving among the enemy. I'm an airman. I can find my own way."[7]

After cruising past a regimental command post, Quesada and Meyers were now just a mile from the Allied spearhead. Negotiating a tight turn along the narrow country lane, they ran headlong into a Tiger tank that had worked in from the flanks. "Say, that German tank there does not look like it's been knocked out," Quesada mused.

Just then an armor-piercing shell from the tank slammed into their jeep. The shell passed directly beneath Quesada's seat, dropped the rear axle, and collapsed the wreck to the ground. Plunging into the surrounding hedges, Quesada and Meyers crawled until they were clear of the tank's machine-gun fire. On all fours, Quesada could not help but smile, remembering how he and Bradley had laughed just weeks earlier when they learned that a German general had slithered similarly to make his escape from Cherbourg.[8]

Finally reaching an American outpost, they hurried back to IX TAC headquarters. Blair Garland, who had packed his bags and was waiting to be fired, greeted them. "Garland, I've been thinking," an obviously relieved Quesada declared. "You must be the best goddamned signal man in the army." That was Quesada's way of apology, though neither he nor Meyer uttered a word about their adventure to anyone.

Charlie Gerhardt, however, did. When his forces came upon a mangled two-star jeep the next day, the old infantryman saw a chance for fun at the expense of the brash airman. He slapped a giant bow around the burned-out hulk and sent it to Quesada. "It is our practice to take care of our visitors," the accompanying note read, "but unfortunately in this case the enemy has us on the run trying to keep up with him." Quesada shot his own letter back, thanking Gerhardt for his "kind hospitality" and trusting that "[I] may soon have the opportunity to repay your kindness."[9]

All kidding aside, it had been a narrow escape and Quesada knew it. He described his adventure to a friend in Boston as "a close one and I don't know to this day how I got back. Between getting through the German lines and then getting through our own lines, it is a mystery. I hope someday to solve it."[10]

Beyond that, the incident highlighted just how confused the American advance had become by 1 August. Bradley's single army now controlled an immense array of corps and divisions along a quickly widening front, and he was already straining to control and direct the vast forces. From an administrative standpoint, Bradley needed help badly.

To get it, he activated another army headquarters in France, the Third, and created an Army Group to command both the First and Third Armies. Lieutenant General George Patton assumed command of the Third Army and promptly moved to the far right flank of the Allied lines. At the same time, Lieutenant General Courtney Hodges took control of the First Army from Bradley, who then moved up to lead the new American Twelfth Army Group. All these changes had been contemplated for some time, but as long as the Allies remained bottled up near the Normandy shores there was little room and less reason to establish additional battlefield headquarters. Now there was more than enough of both.[11]

These changes required corresponding shifts in the air-force infrastructure. As long as the First Army was the only U.S. army on the Continent, Quesada's IX TAC had been the sole headquarters running the close-support show. O. P. Weyland's XIX TAC had remained in England, and his groups had passed to Quesada's operational control as they moved to France. With the activation of the Third Army, however, Weyland established a command post in Normandy, regained authority over some fighter-bomber groups, and began providing close support for Patton's men. After 1 August, Quesada no longer controlled every U.S. fighter plane based in France, and he was no longer the only airman setting the pattern and tempo of tactical aviation above the American lines.

Perhaps a bigger blow to Quesada was the end of his fruitful and fulfilling daily collaboration with Bradley. Courtney Hodges now commanded the First Army. Quiet and handsome, Hodges was a refined Southerner from an earlier age. A generation older than Quesada, he was in the same West Point class as Patton until he flunked math; he then enlisted, winning a commission in 1909. He had participated in General John Pershing's Mexican expedition in 1916, and had been a regimental commander in France during the Great War, earning a Distinguished Service Cross. Between the World Wars, Hodges had preceded Bradley as Commandant at Fort Benning and had been the Army's Chief of Infantry, a prestigious job. He had brought the Third Army to England in early 1944, had given it to Patton, and since D-Day had been the commander-designate of the First Army.

Although he was well regarded by most, especially Eisenhower, Hodges was a man of limited imagination who disdained "the uncertain business" of "tricky maneuver" and thought it "safer, sounder, and in the end quicker to keep smashing ahead." Bradley believed him "one of the most skilled craftsmen under my entire command," but hastened to add that Hodges was "essentially a military tactician . . . a spare, soft-voiced Georgian without temper, drama, or visible emotion." In short, he was the opposite of Quesada in many ways. Still, Hodges and Quesada fashioned a good working relationship in the coming months, though theirs would never have the warmth of the Bradley-Quesada alliance.

Those two men would forever share a bond forged in the tough early days of Normandy.[12]

In addition to these changes, the Ninth Air Force got a new commander in early August. Lewis Brereton had never enjoyed the esteem of the ground leaders, and he did not help his standing among them when he told a press conference on 27 July that the short bombings of COBRA had been the infantry's fault. When Bradley heard of Brereton's remarks, he renewed his charge that Brereton was "a marginally competent airman who was not as interested in the war as he was in living in the biggest French chateau."[13]

That indictment was mostly correct. Brereton was a lax leader, and since the spring Quesada and Major General Samuel Anderson of the IX Bomber Command had exercised almost total control over the Ninth's fighter and medium bombers. As a result, in mid-July Eisenhower determined to remove Brereton from the everyday war and give him command of the Allied Airborne Army, an organization that would not see action for months. Although this was technically a promotion, even Brereton's friends agreed that he had been essentially "kicked upstairs." They could feel only pity for him.[14]

Quesada hoped to be the man to replace Brereton. As a senior subordinate in the Ninth Air Force and its best tactical commander, Quesada figured that the job was his unless Eisenhower asked for John Cannon, then commanding the Twelfth Air Force in Italy. Instead, on 5 August, Major General Hoyt Vandenberg arrived from London to assume this command. Tooey Spaatz, on whose judgment Hap Arnold and Dwight Eisenhower most heavily relied in air force matters, had secretly assured Vandenberg that the job was his when Brereton's position had became precarious—probably as early as late June and at least by 16 July. No one else knew of the arrangement for weeks and Quesada, it seemed, was among the last to learn of it. The IX TAC commander had never been seriously considered for the post, and the snub deeply hurt him.[15]

Like other air generals just under the most senior pilots, Hoyt Vandenberg was young, dashing, and a little arrogant. He had finished in the bottom 10 percent of the West Point class of 1923, but a reputation as a crack pilot had kept his career on track before Pearl Harbor. After that, he quickly ascended the ranks from major, serving as Eisenhower's air advisor in 1942, leading a military delegation to Moscow, and acting as Jimmy Doolittle's chief of staff during the North African campaign. The nephew of Michigan's prominent senator Arthur Vandenberg, Hoyt moved easily in high society and got along famously with superiors: he had attended the Quebec, Cairo, and Teheran Conferences as an aide to Hap Arnold. Like Quesada's, his uniforms were impeccable, and he always wore his cap at the rakish angle popular among airmen. A youthful forty-six, he was but four years older than Quesada and just twelve days senior to him on the general-officer rolls.[16]

Since January, Vandenberg had been the AEAF deputy commander under Trafford Leigh-Mallory, a job that afforded him an ample acquaintance with the tactical air war in France. Yet as a desk general he had been to the Continent just three times since D-Day, and he had spent a disturbing amount of time on office intrigue within the AEAF. He had always been near the strategic-versus-tactical air-power debates, and on occasion he had even conspired with Spaatz and Doolittle to get the Eighth Air Force out of tactical operations requested by his own boss at AEAF, Trafford Leigh-Mallory. Clearly understanding where influence resided in the European theater, he cultivated a good relationship with Spaatz, and thus corraled the Ninth Air Force job even though he had never commanded as much as a squadron in battle.[17]

Vandenberg's appointment irked Quesada, both because he wanted the command himself and because he believed Vandenberg had won it through unseemly machinations. Colonel Richard Hughes, the Ninth Air Force intelligence officer, declared that "there is no doubt whatsoever that Pete Quesada had confidently expected to be given command of the 9th Air Force and was bitterly disappointed" when he did not get it. Vandenberg was aware of Quesada's feelings, and for the rest of the war he kept his contact with Quesada to a minimum. One officer even theorized that Vandenberg was afraid of his new subordinate. That was doubtful, but Vandenberg did harbor insecurities about his command ability relative to Quesada's, and he gave Quesada wide latitude to act as his own boss.[18]

Pete Quesada was not the only one in France surprised by Vandenberg's promotion. Omar Bradley pronounced the new leader of the Ninth Air Force a good deal better than Brereton, but believed that he

had merely "inherited the footwork that Quesada had done in developing air-ground techniques." Although Bradley found Vandenberg pleasant and cooperative, he knew that Vandenberg was "not known as a
smart man" and that he "suffered by comparison to General Pete Q,
who is the doughboy's champion and the doughboy's idea of a very
great airman."[19]

Even some of Vandenberg's own staffers questioned the appointment. Vandenberg's chief of staff suspected his grasp of tactical matters.
Hughes, who rated Quesada a genius, thought Vandenberg was a "sub-
normal type, intellectually," though he marveled at Vandenberg's "almost animal-like instinct for self-preservation." Whatever the full and
complete reasons for Vandenberg's new posting, Quesada was stuck
with him until the war's end and beyond. It was destined to be a difficult association for both men.[20]

For Quesada there was, however, a silver lining in the changing organization for war. Bradley now exercised more control than ever over Allied operations, and Quesada continued to enjoy his unlimited
confidence. Such access helped Quesada remain a "first among equals"
as the number of tactical air commanders grew with the activation of
additional ground armies. In the months ahead, he often traded on his
greater experience and his friendship with Bradley to influence the tactical air war. But if such tactics won many arguments for Quesada, they
also earned him enemies who came to see in him an unpleasant arrogance and vanity.

All that, of course, was neither here nor there in early August 1944.
Regardless of any touchy issues in the Ninth Air Force, the war was
proceeding marvelously well for the Allies. On the far left flank, the
British had finally captured all of Caen. On the extreme right, Patton's
men had swung into the sparsely defended Brittany Peninsula after
spilling through the narrow passages around Avranches. Between them
stood the soldiers of the First Army, acting for the moment as the hinge
in the middle of the Allied line. Arrayed some ten to twenty miles south
of St. Lô on a front from Mortain to Vire, Hodges' men protected Patton's exposed flank while applying steady pressure on the crumbling
German defenses. No longer racing through the countryside, the soldiers of the First Army were finally offered a small respite, and Hodges
used the time wisely to regroup his badly fragmented order of battle.

The First Army's recess was IX TAC's godsend. The air war's supporting structure required constant physical maintenance in World War II, and a week of furious operations had left Quesada's airstrips, bases, and planes in serious disarray. The older airfields were literally disintegrating; those established just before COBRA were still without the most rudimentary amenities. Open tents, dusty runways, hot afternoons, cold rations, and eighteen-hour days were the order of the day for all ground crews. At most new bases, one officer related, mastery of the deft "technique of gently extending one's buttocks over a narrow slit trench" was as crucial a skill as replacing a propeller on a Thunderbolt. Not surprisingly, the number of mission aborts due to mechanical failure reached a wartime high on 2 August. To redress these difficulties, on 3 August Quesada began standing down two groups a day for maintenance. In four days, aircraft serviceability had climbed back to normal rates and one pilot happily reported that "tents in the modern manner with foxholes leading off the foyer and regular latrines were once again the thing."[21]

The Germans used the short breather to good advantage as well. By hook and by crook, they achieved a remarkable reorganization and mustered sizeable local strength across from First Army. To do so, von Kluge and Seventh Army's General Paul Hausser shifted units among corps and armies, dismantling some divisions, replenishing others, and siphoning in fresh troops from throughout the Reich. Luftwaffe leader Hermann Goering sent ground-crew personnel to the front, Admiral Karl Doenitz donated a large group of Navy youngsters, and propaganda chief Joseph Goebbels even mobilized entertainers, who until then had been exempt from military service. In laudable fashion and under great constraints, veterans swiftly trained these recruits in rudimentary skills and placed them along quiet sectors of the front. Then von Kluge concentrated many of his remaining tanks in the five armored divisions of XLVII Corps. Commanded by General Freiherr von Funck, this corps included the fanatical First and Second SS Panzer Divisions and represented the strongest concentration of tanks the Germans had had on the Western Front in some time. On 5 August, von Kluge shrewdly placed it near Mortain, right at the U.S. First Army-Third Army seam.

Von Kluge believed that victory was improbable but hoped that the tanks might yet buy precious time for an orderly withdrawal from Normandy. Hitler, however, now looked greedily at the revived armored corps and demanded that it be used to launch an aggressive punch between the U.S. armies. "We must strike like lightning," he declared, as if he still had the grand armies of 1940–41. "When we reach the sea the American spearheads will be cut off." Seeing in the attack a masterstroke capable of erasing two months of disaster, Hitler even promised renewed large-scale Luftwaffe operations. Von Kluge thought Hitler's vision was a fantasy, but he dutifully complied and ordered von Funck's tanks into the breach.[22]

Nineteen miles and a world away, Bradley knew the First Army's center, manned by Collins' veteran but tired VII Corps, was vulnerable. With Patton gleefully charging through Brittany as nobody else could, Bradley was determined to embark on no wild forays elsewhere until he had secured the Avranches-Mortain sector. "We can't risk a loose hinge," he explained to his staff. More than anything, he feared just the sort of plan Hitler now harbored—a German counterthrust from Mortain to Avranches, which would cut Patton's twelve divisions off from their supplies with disastrous consequences. But Bradley's forces were spread so thin across the lengthening front that he could do little materially to beef up the Mortain defenses. As darkness came on 6 August, he and Collins did the next best thing. They replaced the exhausted First Division, patrolling just outside Mortain, with the rested Thirtieth Division. Just as the divisions were switching positions, the Germans attacked.[23]

"On 6 August we were relieved at Mortain by the Thirtieth Division," remembered Sergeant Leroy Stewart. "We walked back a ways and got on trucks. I had just gotten on when I saw some planes coming in low and from the front. At first they looked like our P-51, but the swastika on the side said ME-109."[24]

With immense surprise and growing terror, Stewart and those around him realized that the Germans had somehow cobbled together a combined-arms attack. Throwing themselves into hedges and shallow foxholes, soldiers from both divisions scurried to organize some kind of holding line. They failed. By midnight, the Germans had overrun Mortain and were well on their way to key points just miles from Avranches.

For the first time in months, the Germans held a tactical advantage in the West. Steeped in the legend of the *Blitzkrieg*, Panzer drivers rode high in their tanks. The Luftwaffe was in the sky again, harassing American supply points behind the front. A crashed fighter-bomber blocked the First SS Panzer Division's advance, but that was the only real problem. On the U.S. side, Collins believed that if the Tiger tanks did somehow manage to get through and sever the U.S. supply lines, it would be a "disaster of the first order."[25]

Then the sun came up. By some strength of will, scattered American units still held critical heights that were now behind the German lines. One battalion successfully defended Hill 317 overlooking Mortain, and in the growing daylight the men there could observe virtually the entire German advance. Before breakfast and with adroit deftness, General J. Lawton Collins built a makeshift plan around these outposts and laid preparations for the Second Armored Division to counter-jab into the growing German flanks.

Quesada ordered his planes to support the American tank strikes. At 0830 hours Captain Joe McLachan led his flight of Thunderbolts up from a wire-mesh runway and banked steeply for Mortain. Without prearranged targets, his birds merely tuned into the close-support radio channel for instructions when they arrived over the Second Armored Division, now pushing along the edge of the German salient. Below, Lieutenant Joe "Noodles" Nolan, who had left McLachan's squadron two days before to begin his stint as a forward air controller, was frantically calling pilots from the cramped cockpit of a tank. McLachan was astounded to recognize Nolan's voice. "Here we come, Noodles, where are they?" Nolan steered the flyers to a pair of self-propelled 88mm guns. After a dry run the fighter pilots turned around and came in strafing, destroying both batteries. The action added to the twenty-eight tanks, ten half-tracks, and several 88mms the IX TAC knocked out that day. Together, the loss was nearly 20 percent of the entire German strength aimed at Avranches.[26]

Further behind the lines, British Typhoons prowled to intercept Luftwaffe aircraft. Already German planes had damaged service roads and attacked armored columns in the VIII Corps sector, and now hundreds of Luftwaffe planes were heading for the battle from air bases in northern France and on the Chartres plateau. Very few reached it. Aided by IX Bomber mediums, the Typhoons harassed, held, and blocked them with terrible consequences for the Germans. "The air situation in the forenoon of 7 August stopped the whole counterattack against Avranches," one Wehrmacht general bitterly reported. "Not even one of the announced 300 German fighters appeared. Afterwards the Air Force declared that the fighters had started but had either been contained by the enemy air force at their airports or during the approach flight to the operations area."[27]

The German general had overstated matters, for some planes did fight through and some Panzer elements did continue their advance. But his disappointment was consistent with the larger truth of the day. The Luftwaffe's influence on the battle waned steadily throughout 7 August, and by nightfall just one of the five Panzer Divisions committed the previous evening was making progress. In the darkness, against the fear of Allied air superiority, the Germans were reduced to old hopes. "Bad weather is what we need now, then everything will work out alright," one operations officer muttered. The Germans had fought 7 August to a draw, but in so doing they had lost the initiative.[28]

Not that the fight was over. In the next days Hitler's men threw all available reserves into the fray. Hanging tenaciously to their initial gains, the Germans also worked hard to mop up the Americans behind their front lines. In a spirited defense, the single U.S. battalion on Hill 317 suffered 300 casualties as wave after wave of Panzers failed to overrun the place. "We ran into everything the Germans could throw at us," one soldier remembered, "machine-gun fire, mortar and artillery shelling, even [rockets] came over. The resistance was terrific."[29]

In the air, fighter-bomber strikes bordering on the scientific aided the isolated Americans. Lieutenant Walter Ozment dropped a 100-pound bomb into the open hatch of a leading Tiger tank west of Mortain, stopping the following column cold on a narrow sunken road. Colonel Howard Nichols' squadron of Lightnings skipped bombs right into von Kluge's command post. One pilot braved a barrage of flak to deliver blood plasma to medical corpsmen operating behind the lines. As evening came on 9 August, German guns were once more pounding "Noodles" Nolan's tanks, and he again called for help. This time Captain Tommy Montang led his Thunderbolt flight to the deck, strafing the battery positions until Nolan reported no further trouble.[30]

On 8 and 9 August, the IX TAC flew 998 sorties in the Mortain sector, destroying seventy-six tanks and nearly a thousand motor transports. Very few of the missions were prearranged. Most were the product of the instant exigencies of battle and were directed by the likes of "Noodles" Nolan. Perhaps better than most, Nolan came to appreciate the direct and intangible benefits of armored-column cover. Although he preferred flying, service in a tank offered him a new perspective of the war. "Now I know what it's like down there," he said after he returned to flying in September. "If they ask me to strafe right in front of them and if they ask me to get a gun I'll know what it means. That goes for the Tanks and the Infantry and the others up front. They're full of guts and loaded with spirit."[31]

For those soldiers who did the actual bleeding, armored-column cover was about much more than superior communications. For tank commanders and for pilots it became a shared experience in lives that were otherwise starkly dissimilar. With their respective air and ground superiors often at odds over doctrine and strategy, this tie was an important link between the servicemen. As a result, at the most basic command levels—squadrons and groups in the air, company and battalions on the ground—officers from different arms often had better relations than their generals. Indeed, sometimes the rank and file succeeded in cooperating in spite of their leaders.

Although American generals were less aware of the intangible advantages of column cover, they nonetheless recognized the value of the close air support given at Mortain. An officer at Eisenhower's headquarters reflected opinions there when he wrote that the "defeat of this counterattack was largely the work of the Air Forces." Bradley's view was less sweeping, yet still afforded the pilots their due: "Air, I believe, slowed that attack a week." J. Lawton Collins was typically undramatic but concise in his judgment, stating that "Fighter-bombers, as usual, were highly effective." On the other side, the German Seventh Army also attributed their defeat to the fighter-bombers. After the war, Collins rated the Mortain battle "one of the outstanding small-unit actions of World War II." It was also the best single close-support operation in Europe by Quesada's fighter-bombers.[32]

Air strikes, brave stands by small groups of soldiers, and a swift armored response all combined to contain the Mortain threat by 10 August. But Hitler, nearly delusional and justifiably paranoid after an assassination attempt on 20 July, refused his generals' advice to withdraw and continued to pound against a solid American wall. As he poured ever more of his precious and dwindling resources into the cauldron, the Allies began to see a golden opportunity. With Bernard Montgomery's armies pressing down from the north and Patton's men marching at will from the south and west, the German battle position was growing more untenable by the day. If Patton turned north and the English drove hard, they could catch Hitler's men in a giant pincer, bagging thousands and perhaps hundreds of thousands of prisoners.

Montgomery, still the ranking Allied ground commander in France, was first to see the chance to surround the Germans. "The enemy attack at Mortain was just what we wanted," he wrote to the British Army Chief of Staff on 8 August, adding that the "pilots all had a great day" and that he was "aiming at closing in behind the Germans." Two days later, Bradley embraced the concept of a giant envelopment. "The German is either crazy or he doesn't know what is going on," he remarked to Chester Hansen. "Surely the professional soldier most know the jig is up." Unfortunately for Germany, its professional soldiers were not running their war. Hitler was.[33]

After agreeing on the general objective, Montgomery and Bradley ordered their forces on a collision course toward Falaise and Argentan, well behind the German tanks near Mortain. Patton turned 180 degrees from what was now a fruitless drive into Brittany, plunging in a wide arc through Mayenne and Alençon and on to Argentan to link up with the Canadian First Army pushing south toward Falaise.

To aid the Canadians, Montgomery launched a COBRA-like air strike called TOTALIZE. As in earlier operations, many of the Eighth Air Force Flying Fortresses bombed wildly, killing more Allied troops than they did on COBRA's first day. "How the hell could they fail to read a map on a clear day like this?" raged Corporal Dick Raymond of the Canadian Third Division. "A lot of our guns opened up on the Fortresses. When they hit one, everybody cheered."[34]

Still, the Allies made good initial headway, and most soldiers remained optimistic. Bradley warmed ever more to the thought of many prisoners and decisive victory. He told Secretary of the Treasury Henry Morgenthau, who was visiting his headquarters, that "this is an opportunity that comes to a commander not more than once a century. We are about to destroy an entire German army." Hitler had placed his men in a giant trap, it seemed, and now the Allies were about to snap it shut.[35]

On 12 August Vandenberg convened his first general staff conference at Ninth Air Force headquarters to coordinate tactical air operations in the American zone. He directed Quesada's IX TAC to strike enemy forces inside the developing pocket, keeping in close touch with British Spitfires operating in the same area. On the far left flank, Weyland's XIX TAC was to support Patton's bold enveloping drive. Consistent with the battle's fluid nature, Vandenberg authorized Quesada and Weyland to bypass him and call on each other directly for aid and support, "in case of immediate need."[36]

By the time the Third Army swung wide to the south toward Alençon, Weyland had already profited greatly from Quesada's experience. In the ten days since his XIX Tactical Air Command had moved to France, Weyland had embraced most of Quesada's major innovations in the close-air-support war. In fact, he had toured IX TAC installations so often that some on Quesada's staff had grown irritated. In short order, Weyland's command had a joint operations center with Third Army, its own MEW radar, and forward air controllers riding with Patton's tank drivers. Beyond adopting Quesada's systems, Weyland and Patton patterned their relationship after the Bradley-Quesada partnership. Each respected the judgment of the other. "We had a basic understanding," Weyland recalled, "that he would run the ground and I would run the air."[37]

For his part, Patton had carefully watched Quesada's service to First Army since D-Day and had supreme confidence in his own close air support. In typical Patton fashion, he wanted to concentrate his entire manpower on the dash forward and did not want to divert troops for flank security along the Loire River. Accordingly, he asked Weyland to secure his left line from the air. Weyland did, and for three weeks in August his fighter-bombers patrolled the river incessantly. So thoroughly did these pilots harass the few Germans that did try to enfilade Patton's army that one German commander insisted on surrendering to Weyland. In the high tide of that summer, the air support for Patton's mad dash justifiably became a legend.[38]

Quesada's planes performed less flashy tasks above the interior fighting in the middle of the Allied line, but there they ruined greater numbers of German tanks, trucks, carts, horses, and soldiers. On 13 August a forward air controller directed Colonel Chuck Young's 367th Group to a large German convoy. Attacking the rich target for nearly two hours, Young's flyers destroyed forty-five tanks. Elsewhere, IX TAC planes ruined 106 armored vehicles and 570 motor transports against a cost of eleven American planes, Quesada's single largest loss of the summer. Including the tallies of XIX TAC and the IX Bomber Command, the Ninth Air Force claimed 1,245 military vehicles of all descriptions destroyed that Sunday. Although subsequent ground surveys reduced that number by 287, by any measure it had been a good day.[39]

The Allies were nearly as productive on 14 August. Patton's army and Montgomery's men were now closing the German escape route from Normandy, and an increasingly desperate Wehrmacht retreat presented lavish targets for Allied airmen. In Quesada's sector, a flight of P-47s led by Captain Roy Bowlin thwarted a German attempt to outflank an American tank column and break to safety near Rennes. "There's a gun on the left giving the middle of our column a little bit of hell," an air controller had radioed Bowlin. When Bowlin saw the Tiger tank and three half-tracks pummeling the American flank, he immediately dove to the deck. "My bombs hit the Tiger and he blazed up." After destroying the three half-tracks, Bowlin and his flyers turned to strafe more vehicles half a mile distant. They ruined ten of them before exhausting their ammunition. "You'll have to watch them, particularly toward your rear," Bowlin warned the tankers as he left the area. But by then, the surviving Panzers were beating a hasty retreat.[40]

Late in the day a rare foray by the Luftwaffe sought to relieve the German defenders from the incessant air attacks. Just east of Flers, sixteen ME-109s and FW-190s surprised a single squadron from the 405th Group led by Captain Willingham. Unaccustomed to dogfighting and handicapped by the poor aerial-combat characteristics of the P-47s, the American pilots suffered in the early going. Four Thunderbolts quickly crashed to the ground, killing three flyers. Outnumbered two to one, Willingham's group nonetheless evened the score and scratched four of the Luftwaffe ships before breaking for home.[41]

A mile to the east, the 367th Group logged a better performance in their own tangle with an assortment of German aircraft. In that fray Captain Bill Blumer, until recently a farm boy in North Dakota, man-

The tactical air forces performed many tasks in the weeks surrounding OVERLORD. Before the invasion, they cut road and rail lines connecting Normandy with the rest of Europe, isolating the battlefield from German reinforcements. *Courtesy Dwight D. Eisenhower Library.*

Pictured here is a railroad bridge in Rouen, France, destroyed by the Ninth Air Force in the weeks before D-Day. *Courtesy National Archives.*

As D-Day neared, they took thousands of intelligence photographs to aid in the ground preparations. *Courtesy Dwight D. Eisenhower Library.*

On D-Day, they protected the vast Allied convoys from German attack. *Courtesy Dwight D. Eisenhower Library.*

Consistent with the Air Force's ambivalence toward close air support, Pete Quesada had enigmatic relationships with other air officers. One contemporary remembered Quesada as one of General Hap Arnold's "fair-haired boys," though Arnold was a vocal advocate of an air arm heavy in strategic bombers and did not believe close support operations were in the Air Force's best interests. Four days after D-Day, Quesada welcomed Arnold to Normandy. *Courtesy Dwight D. Eisenhower Library.*

March 1944. Pre-invasion inspection of Quesada's airfields in England. Quesada is on the left in profile. Trafford Liegh-Mallory is on Quesada's left. Eisenhower is in the center of the picture with part of his face obscured by airman. Louis Brereton, Quesada's immediate boss, is on the far right with the patch on his shoulder. *Courtesy Dwight D. Eisenhower Library.*

Quesada (at right in helmet) at his charismatic best—talking to members of one of his fighter groups. *Courtesy Dwight D. Eisenhower Library.*

Summer 1944. In the race across France, Quesada's planes often used airfields that just days before were used by the Luftwaffe. Here a P-38 sits alongside a burned out German plane. *Courtesy Dwight D. Eisenhower Library.*

A plane destroying an ammunition truck on the ground. The picture was taken in daylight, but the explosion was so bright, it reversed the exposures on film. *Courtesy Dwight D. Eisenhower Library.*

Quesada's greatest innovation in the air war was armored Column Cover, where planes and tanks worked in close cooperation to ferret out stubborn German resistance. Here an American P-47 flies over a procession of U.S. tanks in the summer of 1944. *Courtesy National Archives.*

The aerial destruction to the Port of Cherbourg was so great that the Allies could not use its facilities for months after the city's surrender. *Courtesy National Archives.*

The Fall of 1944 saw the Allies stalled along the German border after a spectacular advance across France. The Siegfried Line, portions of which are seen here, proved a formidable barrier for both ground and air forces. *Courtesy Dwight D. Eisenhower Library.*

Quesada with Brigadier General O.P. Weyland, the XIX Tactical Air Commander and Patton's air boss. *Courtesy Dwight D. Eisenhower Library.*

Fall 1944. Quesada with Brigadier General Richard Nugent, the XXIX Tactical Air Commander. *Courtesy Dwight D. Eisenhower Library.*

aged to down five planes in fifteen minutes to become an ace. All together, twenty-seven Luftwaffe and seven IX TAC planes tumbled to earth in five separate engagements that afternoon. Emasculated as it was by the summer of 1944, the German Air Force could hardly afford such losses on a daily basis.[42]

The dogfights of 14 August were but a small diversion to the American pilots. Before long, they returned to the task at hand: destroying German ground forces. There the Ninth Air Force did a masterful job. By day's end, fighter and medium bombers had ruined additional hundreds of German vehicles, bringing the Ninth's two-day total to sixty-three tanks, seventy-five armored vehicles, ten half-tracks, 1,081 motor transports, thirty-three trucks, twenty-nine artillery pieces, sixteen flank guns, seven staff cars, eight horse-drawn vehicles, nine railroad and freight cars, and eight ammunition depots. The total cost was twenty-four American planes and the lives of seventeen pilots. Claims were similarly staggering in the British Second Air Force sector. In terms of destruction, 13 and 14 August 1944 were for the Allies the best two days of the tactical air war in Europe.[43]

Engagements on the ground mirrored the wild encounters in the air. By midmonth Bradley once again hardly knew where his spearhead forces were, so swiftly had Patton's tanks hooked around the Germans. Reports first placed Patton's Third Army in Argentan, just fifteen miles from the Canadians closing from the north near Falaise. Later communiqués indicated that only a reconnaissance team had penetrated the town; more reports hopelessly muddied the picture. For Bradley, the confusion prompted fears of a head-on collision between the Third Army and Montgomery's men, a concern heightened by Patton's wild disposition to plunge ahead at whatever cost. "We now have elements in Argentan," he had reported, only half in jest, "Shall we continue and drive the British into the sea?"[44]

To avert possible catastrophe, Bradley halted the American march without consulting Montgomery and after only brief conversations with Eisenhower. "To have driven pell-mell into Montgomery's line of advance could easily have resulted in a disastrous error," he later explained, adding, "I much preferred a solid shoulder at Argentan to the possibility of a broken neck at Falaise."[45]

It was a controversial decision. Patton was miffed. O. P. Weyland could not believe it. "Oh, hell no," he begged Bradley, "why don't you just let us keep going? There's nothing of any consequence to stop us." J. Lawton Collins, whose corps now butted against Patton's Third Army, was also directed to halt. "I got orders from First Army to stop, and I pleaded with General Bradley; I said, 'Well, there isn't anything out in front of us at all, and we can go and maybe close this pocket.'" But Bradley remained firm; the potential for tragedy among the Allies hardened his resolve. As a result, a fifteen-mile gap from Falaise to Argentan remained open to the Germans for days longer. The passage allowed nearly 100,000 enemy soldiers and irreplaceable staff expertise to sneak away across the Seine River to fight another day.[46]

Ever since Hannibal cornered 80,000 Romans under Varro with tactical perfection in 216 B.C., military men have dreamed of decisive battle. Hindenburg and Ludendorff accomplished it in August 1914 when they captured Samsonov's army; Rokossovsky did it when he enveloped Paulus' force near Stalingrad in February 1943. Sadly, the Western Allies fell short of the mark in August 1944.

History has harshly censured Bradley for his caution, suggesting that better coordination with Eisenhower's and Montgomery's forces could have yanked the noose tight about the German neck without endangering friendly forces. That may well be so, but air operations in the days after Bradley's order underscored the real potential for friendly-troop clashes. Tactical air action was as sensitive to army boundaries as ground combat, and the situation in the sky, like that on the ground, had reached an uncontrollable crescendo by the middle of the month. Two to three thousand Allied sorties of every kind filled the tight air space above the imperiled Germans each day, and though the differences between U.S. and British close-support systems were slight, they were important enough to jeopardize Allied lives.

In fact, reports of friendly fire had already reached Bradley's headquarters. On 16 August Canadian troops who had marked their location with red smoke were bombed by IX TAC Thunderbolts, because red denoted enemy targets in the American scheme. With no direct communication between U.S. fighters and Dominion forces, more aircraft would undoubtedly have destroyed the Canadians had not poor weather intervened to ground Quesada's pilots. The next day, P-38s blasted an American combat command of the VII Corps, forcing a U.S. retreat and allowing Germans to reoccupy important defensive ground. "With that one, the Luftwaffe couldn't have done a better job had it tried," recalled one witness. On 18 August, the British Fifty-first Highland Division reported forty separate incidents of accidental air attacks, costing fifty-one casualties and wrecking twenty-five vehicles. Just to the left of them, Allied air strikes destroyed half the petrol reserved for a Polish unit fighting alongside Montgomery's forces.[47]

On 17 August Leigh-Mallory abolished the bomb line around the battle zone, effectively ending Allied air strikes inside the German pocket. Most tactical air leaders, itching to destroy ever more of the hapless Germans, decried the order. Quesada, in particular, continued to request raids into the forbidden zone and was, according to one officer, "furious when told he couldn't fly over the area anymore."[48]

But Leigh-Mallory's edict was a good one. There was very little in the way of German men and equipment remaining inside the pocket to destroy. Most who would escape the pocket already had, and the soldiers left behind were a sorry lot. Their food was either foul or gone, they had not rested for a week, and they had little of that most important of all fighting qualities, hope. As one Allied intelligence summary based on POW interrogations stated: "At the beginning, the enemy fought stubbornly but as they came to realize that they were virtually surrounded and in fact were told later by their Officers that bombing was cutting off their supplies, their fighting spirit fell rapidly."[49]

Besides, although many German soldiers had escaped the Allied trap, only a small portion of German machinery had eluded destruction. Not one of the Twenty-first Panzer Division's 127 tanks and forty assault guns survived the campaign. In all, seven Panzer divisions managed to spirit just twenty-four tanks and sixty artillery pieces across the Seine River to safety. Their losses numbered some 10,000 dead and 50,000 captured; 200 tanks, 300 cannons, 700 artillery pieces, 2,000 wagons, 5,000 vehicles, and 1,800 horses.[50]

On both sides of the line, soldiers credited Allied air power with this wholesale destruction. "You have bombed and strafed all the roads, causing complete congestion and heavy traffic jams," one prisoner told American interrogators. "You have also destroyed most of our gasoline and oil dumps, so there is no future in continuing the fight." Another German agreed in a letter to his wife. "It doesn't look very good. The most difficult thing has been and remains the enemy air force . . . it is there at dawn, all day, at night, dominating the roads."[51]

Allied leaders echoed these conclusions as they became aware of the horrific annihilation inside the Falaise Pocket. "I should doubt if ever before in the history of this war have air forces had such opportunities or taken such advantage of them," Montgomery cabled London. "The whole area is covered with burning tanks and MT [motor transport]. . . . I should say that any German formations or units that escape eastward over the Seine will be quite unfit to fight for months to come." Even after the war, Dwight Eisenhower had little difficulty recalling the fight: "The battlefield at Falaise was unquestionably one of the greatest 'killing grounds' of the war. I encountered scenes which could be described only by Dante. It was literally possible to walk for hundreds of yards at a time stepping on nothing but dead and decaying flesh."[52]

When the Allies finally flattened the Falaise Pocket on 20 August, a pall of decay and putrefaction drifted above the battlefield. Burnt-out vehicles blocked roads for miles around. In the hot summer sun, dead cattle and bloated German bodies crawled with maggots. In the most-bombed areas, fragments of bodies festooned the trees. Everywhere, there was very little dignity in death.

So, despite the inconclusive bag of prisoners, these were heady days for the Anglo-Americans. After Falaise, they pushed on into northern France. The first Americans forged the Seine River on 19 August, and Paris fell six days later. In Operation DRAGOON, the Allies invaded southern France from the Mediterranean Sea, rolling up what few Germans still held that part of the country. In an effort to stem this swelling tide, Hitler replaced von Kluge with the energetic Field Marshal Walther Model, but still the German flight continued.

Here, finally, was the wide-open and mobile war for which the American military machine was designed. The First Army drove to the German frontier with startling success. They passed the Soissons escarpment on the last day of August, entered Sedan on 7 September, Liège on the ninth, and liberated Luxembourg on the tenth. The next day they entered Germany, and when they freed Maastricht on 14 September they penetrated the outer defenses of the great Siegfried Line near Aachen. Three weeks after the Allies occupied Paris, Hodges' men were in five different countries.

Third Army's march was equally breathtaking. Patton's thrusting divisions crossed the Somme-Marne defensive line before Germans could occupy it, forded the Meuse at Commercy and St. Mihiel on 31 August, and had a solid foothold south of Metz by 10 September. The very next day, Patton linked up with Allied forces from the DRAGOON landings, and on 15 September his army occupied Nancy.

The air forces matched this progress. Aided by good weather, both the IX and XIX TACs continued their hail of destruction. Between 24 and 28 August, a single Thunderbolt group patrolling near Soissons destroyed some 400 vehicles. On 3 September, Colonel Ray Stecker reported a delicious traffic jam of German trucks, armored half-tracks, staff cars, and wagons near Mons. The Luftwaffe was nowhere in sight, and Stecker's pilots wrecked 294 trucks before two other groups finished what was left of the smoking convoys. Over a two-day period, airmen flew 1,053 sorties in the area, claiming nearly 1,200 vehicles destroyed.[53]

Everything from simple machine guns, to napalm, to rockets accounted for these kills. Due to a design fault in Tiger tanks, bullets from 50mm cannon fire entered their air vents and ricocheted throughout the crew spaces, killing everyone inside. "Strange as it may seem," Quesada explained to Assistant Secretary of War for Air Robert Lovett, "we are destroying German tanks by the use of machine-gun fire, which is something like 'man bites dog.'"[54]

Although only half as big as it was in July, Quesada's command flew more sorties, dropped more bombs, destroyed more German vehicles, and downed more Luftwaffe planes in August than in any other month in its history. The IX TAC's August box score was surreal to anyone who recalled the tiny Air Corps of the Depression years: 8,712 sorties, 21, 237 tons of bombs dropped, 634 enemy tanks destroyed, and twenty-six aerial victories. Radar-controlled flights, which Quesada and Garland had worked so hard to perfect, at last were playing the role scripted for them. Now connected to Quesada's groups by 10,000 miles of telephone wire, the combined MEW/SCR-584 radar center directed over 500 missions in August, up from thirty-eight in July. Although the weather in August was no better than in the previous month, clouds grounded fighters on only three days—as opposed to the eleven days that pilots had been forced out of the air in July.[55]

In fact, keeping up with the ground advance was the only real problem the air forces had in late summer. Confined to coastal fields since late June or early July, fighter groups now moved to new bases so as to stay within range of the front lines. Quesada moved his IX TAC command post five times in six weeks. Most fighter groups relocated three times; one moved five times. Often, they were moved 100 miles or less, but some moves covered as much as 200 miles. Even at that, certain groups were forced to adopt the old roulement system to reach their stations above the advancing columns.

Although they had been designed for mobility, this continual migration drained important time and energy from the fighter groups. Each transfer entailed 173 distinct steps, and as one commander remarked, "Moves involving 2000 men and sixty-seven tons of ground equipment are not small tasks." The chore especially strained the IX Engineer Command. Leapfrogging their resources from one location to another, these aviation engineers constructed sixty air bases in August and September, duplicating the near miracles performed by their brethren in nearly every theater of the war.[56]

The extra work failed to sap the high spirits of the airmen, however. One pilot recalled that "France suddenly became a beautiful country, reminiscent of each of the 48 states." Men of the Forty-eighth Group, based near Paris for a time after the City of Light was once again free, had a glorious few weeks. "Paris . . . women . . . sidewalk cafés, champagne and more women reigned supreme." Quesada's staff even managed to beef up their already ample mess. Liberating from a German officers' club wine, liquor, carpet, and a grand piano, Quesada enjoyed live music and "as good of food and drink as you could find in New York at any price." In more than an operational sense, August was truly a good month for the Americans.[57]

Optimism pervaded the Allied camp. In Washington and London, representatives to the Combined Chiefs of Staff bet on when the war would end. None picked a date beyond Christmas. On 15 August Leigh-Mallory discontinued his daily war diary, believing the war in Western Europe all but over. A few days later, Eisenhower suspended most air-interdiction efforts in southern Germany, hoping to preserve bridges, railroads, and marshaling yards for his own imminent use. At Ninth Air Force headquarters, staffers initiated plans to use German *autobahns* as airstrips within weeks.[58]

Quesada shared this faith in a swift end to the war against Germany. He wrote his brother Buddy, a Naval officer in the Pacific who wanted a posting in Europe, not to bother coming, for "the war will probably peter out here soon." To his old boss Trubee Davison, Quesada wrote, "We have had a very good two weeks and are taking quite a bit of France. . . . The Air Forces have literally blasted the way in front of the Ground Forces and I do feel that the Ground Forces appreciate our efforts and admit freely that they have never had air support on a scale upon which it is now offered." Quesada even contemplated returning to the States, writing his mother that "when I get home I am really going to have a blow-out. I am going to spend $1000 a day and I don't want any squawking from you."[59]

Soon, however, the great advance outdistanced even the Allies' ability to keep abreast of the surging columns. In September, fuel, food, and ammunition shortages became acute throughout the Anglo-American armies. At the IX TAC, Quesada's communications infrastructure bogged down. His FM radio faltered, despite a new relay station in Paris, atop the Eiffel Tower. Each day, the IX TAC communications center took in over 500 teletype, 200 radio, and over 5,000 telephone signals. The system was simply overburdened; secret messages were actually transmitted in the clear for lack of adequate staffing. The war was going well enough so that these glitches did not grab men's attention. But as the warm sun left the sky and the drab, muddy days of autumn set in, the Allies would come to recognize that their high summer was over.[60]

Chapter Nine

We Have Slowed Down Here and Nothing We Try Seems to Help

VERVIERS, BELGIUM. 23 NOVEMBER 1944. EVENING. Pete Quesada and Courtney Hodges were sitting in the parlor of Quesada's headquarters. From
one corner of the room a fire glimmered, and orderlies came and went
as the two generals visited over their meal. Around them were the ap-
pointments common to people of means—a big-game trophy hung
above the fireplace, mahogany adorned the walls, Persian rugs decorated the floor, the dining table dated from the eighteenth century, and the
china was over a hundred years old. Indeed, the peacetime owners of
this large chateau were members of Europe's landed aristocracy and
were reputedly one of the richest families in all of Belgium. As the two
men finished eating and sank into overstuffed armchairs, they, too
looked like members of Europe's affluent class, comfortable with old
money and ready to enjoy a leisurely conversation over a glass of port.[1]

Yet they spoke in tense and hurried tones. Just seven days earlier, on
16 November, Hodges and Quesada had hatched QUEEN, an operation
designed to break the German line near Cologne. Employing over
2,800 Allied planes and dropping over 10,000 pounds of bombs on

Jülich, Düren, and Eschweiler, QUEEN was bigger than COBRA; hopes had run high that it would spawn a dash across the Rhine and into Germany. Like COBRA, QUEEN was born of increasing frustration with the lack of progress along a resilient defensive line, was repeatedly delayed by poor weather, and relied on the muscle of big bombers to power the infantry through the German strongpoints.[2]

Unlike COBRA, however, no breakout had followed QUEEN's bombardment. Advances measured less than three miles even after seven days of intense campaigning. Far short of the Rhine, the assault had not even breached the smaller Roer (or Rur) River near Düren. Already, Bradley and Eisenhower had professed their disappointment with the air attack, and on the day Hodges and Quesada had dinner in Verviers, the IX TAC reported that "The initial impetus of the attack, and the benefit of the air bombardment, is now absorbed in the general effort." In other words, QUEEN had failed.[3]

Hodges and Quesada searched for answers to the apparent failure after dinner. The Army Commander was particularly agitated. "He went on and on about how we might lose the war," Quesada remembered. "As I listened to him, I noticed a kind of panic, that a kind of operational paralysis was setting [in] in him." Indeed, although the slow campaign of autumn would baffle many officers, Courtney Hodges would handle the frustration worse than most. Eventually, by the middle of December, he was in a virtual state of nervous collapse.[4]

"We could have used a bigger air effort," Hodges told Quesada that night. "The weather," he lamented, "cut out a lot of scheduled fighter-bomber support." Poor weather certainly had hindered the air effort, but Quesada believed that QUEEN had failed for other reasons. For him, the offensive had fallen short of expectations because "Ground forces failed to follow up the air attack by an immediate, full-scale assault."[5]

Both men were wrong. Although additional aerial ordnance might have marginally aided the ground attack, more explosives fell in the first hour of QUEEN than were unleashed during the entire Meuse-Argonne offensive in the First World War—and the construction of defensive positions in both the Queen and Meuse-Argonne battles were essentially similar. In war, armed forces must balance the expenditure of resources against any possible gain, and 10,000 tons of bombs in return for a three-mile advance would have struck no thoughtful observer as a sound trade-off. Quesada's notion that the ground forces did not aggressively follow the bomber effort was likewise mistaken. In fact, elements of the 104th Infantry and Third Armored Divisions reached the forward German batteries sooner in QUEEN than did the U.S. soldiers in COBRA.[6]

That even Pete Quesada, by November 1944 America's foremost expert on tactical aviation, misread the lessons of QUEEN was a good indication of the lack of sound analytical thought which marked the close air support of U.S. forces in World War II. Lacking a clear and articulated doctrine of tactical air power, not only were the Americans forced to devise makeshift plans and procedures for air support, they also lacked an analytical framework within which to evaluate the success of their tactical efforts after the event. Ironically, while the leaders' single-minded devotion to strategic precepts militated against a full understanding of the results of the war's bomber offensives, an underdeveloped doctrine of tactical air power likewise worked against the clear and sound practice of close air support.

Operation QUEEN did not stand alone as an example of the two-edged sword of tactical air power in the autumn of 1944. From September to December, those charged with the close air support of ground forces experimented with many tactics to help them crash into the heart of Germany. None seemed to work, and as the days turned to weeks and then months with no appreciable advance, the pressure grew to find a solution. On 1 December, Pete Quesada reviewed his own command's efforts in the battle of tactics. "We have slowed down here," he told William Momyer at the Air Forces's proving grounds in Florida, "and nothing we try seems to help." He could not have known it then, but his spirits would fall further with the great German offensive in the Ardennes, now just sixteen days away.

Just months before, the Allies were still flush with their summer victories. Paris had fallen on 25 August, and from then until 11 September the Anglo-Americans swept through another two hundred miles of the countryside of northern France, Belgium, and Luxembourg. By mid-September, four armies—the First Canadian, Second British, First U.S., and Third U.S.—sat astride the German border from Antwerp to Nancy. The Luftwaffe had not been an effective fighting force all summer, and the Wehrmacht appeared to have been totally destroyed in the West. With the Soviet Union in the final stages of its own offensive from the East, many Allied strategists believed that the Third Reich was doomed soon to fall.[7]

Military leaders created a gambling pool to predict the war's end; only George Marshall expected the war to last into 1945. Brooke, Eisenhower, Montgomery, Bradley, Hodges, and Patton all chose dates in late 1944. Plans for the proposed invasion of Japan were revised in light of the new situation in Europe, and many units in France, including the IX TAC, found themselves slated for Pacific duty. In the entire Allied High Command, only one person seemed truly sobered by the task ahead. Winston Churchill, who had spent a lifetime warning against the might and menace of a rearmed Germany, actually believed that the war would last well into 1946. Roosevelt chided the Prime Minister for his pessimism, but Churchill never did alter his assessment. "We are yet at the lion's gate," he told the president, "and the ghosts of Barbarossa and Bismarck, the legacy of Versailles, and the pathology of the Prussian spirit will drive the German on and on."[8]

Prussian pathology or not, there were in fact military clues to suggest that the glory of the summer campaign was over. By September, Allied logistics were strained to the breaking point. Swift advances have always placed heavy demands on supply, and in France the lack of ports and the distance between the front and rear depots exacerbated the problem. As a stopgap solution, logisticians inaugurated the "Red Ball Express." Closing roads from Normandy to northeastern France to all but military traffic, trucks moved nonstop across France to deliver vital war material. But still shortages persisted. Fuel levels fell so low early in the month that Eisenhower directed heavy bombers to ferry gasoline to Patton's armored divisions racing toward Metz. Artillery commanders rationed their ammunition at 15 percent of anticipated need. Despite such effort, Patton's tanks ran out of gas short of Germany anyway, and entire artillery battalions went into corps reserves for want of shells.[9]

At the human level, too, shortage snafus were evident. Cold rations became the order of the day even in tactical headquarters, winter issues of clothing were slow to reach the front, heavy boots were exceedingly rare, and trench foot became a dangerous problem. As hot food, warm days, and high morale grew scarce, tempers flared. For one veteran of the 104th Infantry Division, the cumulative misery of physical exhaustion, cold infected feet, inadequate clothing, and poor food proved too much to bear. Like many, he vented his frustration at supply officers. "After the war is over," he told a buddy before he went absent without leave, "I am going to go to every single one of those G-4 [logistics and supply] bastards' war crimes trials."[10]

In addition to the problems of Allied supply, by early autumn the German Army had crafted a tolerably strong defensive position in the wooded plains and valleys of Belgium and Luxembourg. Whereas only the fragments of three German armies existed along the front in July, the Wehrmacht now had six armies matched against the Allies' four, with total manpower roughly equaling that of the Anglo-Americans. More important than simple numbers, though, the Germans now occupied exceptionally strong positions on the Siegfried Line. Consisting of strategic defensive outposts in the interwar years, the Siegfried Line became known as the West Wall for its almost impregnable sets of pillboxes, antitank barriers, bunkers, observation posts, and communications trenches.[11]

While soldiers on the Allied side of the line became ever more frustrated with supply problems, on the German side loyal soldiers like *Oberleutnant* (First Lieutenant) Heinrich Schultz felt as though they now had their best opportunity to turn the war's tide since 6 June. "We thought that finally the nightmare of the summer was over," he told British interrogators after he was captured, "and maybe we might still save the Fatherland."[12]

To an uncanny degree, the American tactical air war mirrored the logistical and tactical predicament of the land campaign. Like his ground counterparts, Pete Quesada was slow to recognize the end of the quick advances. As late as 23 September, his letters to friends home reflected a man making ready for the end of the war. "The Hun is now taking a hell of a beating, and I don't see how much more he can take," he wrote to a staffer from his days in North Africa. "I don't think we will be fighting at Christmas." But Quesada, like others, learned that the Allied supply problems were more than a nuisance and the Siegfried Line was no mere German propaganda invention.[13]

The same gas, ordnance, food, and clothing shortages that plagued the ground forces dogged the airmen. Quesada commanded nine fight-er-bomber groups in September 1944 and none of them had adequate fuel or bomb supplies. Five groups reported shortages severe enough to force them to stand down on eleven separate days. The 365th Group ran completely out of aviation octane four times in the month, and Que-sada relegated the 404th to reconnaissance duty after it had used up its pile of fragmentation bombs.[14]

Blair Garland and Quesada were especially disheartened by the re-strictions on supplies after working so hard to overcome the hindrance of weather on close-support operations. "We're able to handle all kinds of crappy weather, but we are powerless to influence this whole supply mess," Garland said at the 5 October IX TAC staff meeting. Indeed, whereas overcast skies reduced the IX TAC's effectiveness by 25 per-cent in July, logistical deficiencies cost Quesada's command nearly a third of its striking power from late September to mid-October. Prewar Air Corps plans assumed that air power would revolutionize combat and reorder the battlefield. But the same supply limits that Charle-magne faced trying to reach Constantinople and Napoleon coped with near Moscow were now dogging the U.S. air effort.[15]

In the battle for Aachen in September, Allied ground and air forces realized that supply difficulties and the strength of the Siegfried Line meant deadlock. Of geostrategic importance since the early days of Christendom, the sentinel city of Aachen offered access to an open plain stretching to the Rhine. Its prewar population of 165,710 made it the first major city the Allies faced on the German border, and it was the key to the second-most-fortified position along the West Wall. As it did to Charlemagne—who made Aachen the capital of his Carolingian Empire—the Aachen Gap represented to the Americans the gateway to the German Reich. Its roads stretched in all directions, and it was the primary communications center between Antwerp and the Ardennes. It would come as no tactical surprise to Hitler, then, when VII and XIX Corps targeted the ancient forts around its perimeter in September. Al-ready, the German High Command was preparing to send the crack First SS Panzer Corps to the city.[16]

On 12 September, Courtney Hodges directed J. Lawton Collins's VII Corps to strike toward the city from the southeast. Employing the First and Ninth Infantry as well as the Third Armored Divisions, Collins began his attack the next day. Concentrating on a series of small villages in front of Aachen, U.S. forces came face to face with the harsh reality of the West Wall. From 13 to 18 September, the 39th Regiment suffered 20 percent casualties in its advance toward Rötgen, and the 60th Regiment lost its commanding officer, executive officer, and three-quarters of its company commanders taking the little town of Monschau. Tanks fared no better. Both mobile combat commands of the armored division came to abrupt halts at the outer reaches of the Siegfried Line; their 75mm guns were no match for its cannon, placed behind nearly seven feet of reinforced concrete. For a week, Collins pounded the fortresses around Aachen in a set-piece battle, and all he had to show for it was an advance through thick forest of three to five miles—and rifle-company casualties of over 35 percent.[17]

On 19 September, J. Lawton Collins asked Courtney Hodges for an increase in his air support to breach the perimeter around Aachen. Most of IX TAC's planes had been escorting Ninth Air Force medium bombers on strikes against Rhine River bridges for ten days, and at their nightly conference Hodges lobbied Quesada to return the fighters to their close-air-support role. Quesada won Vandenberg's permission for the shift, and beginning on 21 September five fighter groups assisted in the VII Corps assault. When Collins received word of the air support, he envisioned a return to the great days of summer and laid plans for a tank and armored-column-cover spearhead to the east of Aachen. Quesada, too, was pleased to engage once again in close air support. "Let's recreate the close cooperation we have enjoyed with the VII Corps," he told his staff on 20 September.[18]

The IX TAC Commander assigned the 366th and 368th Groups, by then Quesada's favorite groups, to armored-column cover and directed the 48th, 50th, and 367th Groups to bomb pillboxes and bunkers selected by the ground forces. Colonel Harold Holt of the 366th Group was an old hand at armored-column cover, and contacted the Third Armored Division commander to coordinate operations. "He and I laid plans to strike toward Stolberg," Holt remembered, "in an attempt to encircle Aachen."[19]

Early on the twenty-second Holt began rotating flights of six Thunderbolts over tank columns in anticipation of a lightning blow at the city. But the script failed to develop as it had in late July. Myriad enemy strongpoints on each flank of the tanks hindered their advance, and unlike the COBRA breakout these emplacements were bunkers built of solid concrete, not an exposed Tiger tank here and an occasional 88mm gun there. Captain Merv Anderson of the 389th Squadron flew four missions on 22 September, and each time his flight bombed a bunker they "blew the top layer of masonry from the roof, and maybe we exposed rerod steel, but never did we really dent the structure. Even direct hits with 500-pound bombs only cracked the exterior."[20]

Other groups had similar experiences. Early on 23 September, 187 Thunderbolts and Mustangs attacked sections of the West Wall that had proved especially troublesome to the ground forces. Striking at emplacements between Monschau and Lammersdorf and in front of Schmidt, these planes dropped ninety tons of carefully placed ordnance on individual bunkers. "None had much impact," a post-action survey stated.[21]

Indeed, in one celebrated incident, eight flights of four dive-bombers dropped over 25,000 pounds of general-purpose ordnance on a single pillbox with virtually no effect. "We could hear the explosions outside, and our sleeping bunks fell down," one German occupant later reported, "but we never feared destruction or death from the *Jabos*." Of forty-three specific strongpoints targeted by Quesada's fighter bombers on 23 September, just seven suffered major damage, and U.S. troops overran only four within forty-eight hours after the attack. The effect of the initial armored-column cover the day before had been disheartening; these new attacks along the Siegfried Line merely heightened the sense of failure.[22]

On 24 September Quesada and Collins conferred about future plans. Both men now realized that the West Wall, increased numbers of German defenders, and the forested terrain made the attack on Aachen different from the summer campaigns. "This is not St. Lô," Lightning Joe Collins cautioned his own G-2 after the staffer expressed disgust at the air effort. Still, the best American corps and tactical air commander of the war failed to develop any new strategy. "I think the defenses might be weakening," Collins ended the conference optimistically, "and we'll continue to blast away until they crumble." Oftentimes in war there is no other tactic available, and both Collins and Quesada had few alternatives available but to plug onward.[23]

It took a long time for the Germans to collapse. From 25 September to 7 October, the German Seventh Army committed two Wehrmacht corps and the elite First SS Panzer Corps to the Aachen battle. On 1 October there were over fifty thousand defenders organized into six divisions around the city. Although disinterested observers could see the long-term futility of the defense, the Reich's soldiers in Aachen were determined to hold out as long as possible and inflict as much damage as they could on the attackers. "I expect each and every defender of the venerable Imperial City of Aachen to do his duty to the end, in fulfillment of our Oath to the Flag," the commander of the city's garrison decreed. "I expect courage and determination to hold out. Long live the Führer and our beloved Fatherland."[24]

Faced with such fanatical opposition, Hodges committed yet another corps to the fight, altered the direct frontal approach to the city, and asked for even more air support. He directed the XIX Corps to encircle Aachen from the west and north while he ordered the VII Corps to ring around to the south and east. If the set defenses of Aachen were too great for a direct combined arms assault, Hodges figured, a pincers movement by two corps just might isolate the city and choke it into submission. He received two additional fighter-bomber groups for the task, raising the air effort to seven groups from both the IX and XIX TACs. On 7 October, the Thirtieth and First Infantry Divisions attacked from opposite sides of Aachen, hoping to join hands soon behind the ancient fortress city.[25]

With the armored ground divisions no longer participating, the accompanying tactical-air effort was relegated to the close support of foot soldiers. From 8 to 18 October, 525 Thunderbolts and Mustangs sortied over 5,000 times and dropped 2,000 tons of general-purpose and fragmentation bombs on Aachen's outer defenses. The strategic Eighth Air Force, too, participated on three separate days, dumping 1,800 tons of explosives on the city center. On only two days, the 12th and 14th, did clouds and rain preclude flying. If ever there was a laboratory to measure the effectiveness of close air support, the later stages of the Aachen fight was it.[26]

But despite such efforts the going on the ground was extraordinarily slow, with advances averaging just under a thousand yards a day. As the two prongs of the pincers approached one another behind the city,

Quesada advocated a reduction in the air support, fearing accidental attacks on friendly troops. Hodges was conscious of such dangers but felt that the benefits of air action outweighed the potential accidents; he convinced Vandenberg to continue the tactical air strikes. Quesada protested the decision, telling both Hodges and Vandenberg that he "could not guarantee the safety of soldiers" as the two corps closed the gap. Both the Army and Ninth Air Force commanders acknowledged Quesada's conviction, but decided to proceed with the close air support. When, on the 16th, five of Quesada's pilots strafed elements of the 120th Regiment, Quesada pleaded innocent of the more than fifty casualties and eight deaths among the U.S. troops.[27]

The calamity did not garner the attention of earlier mishaps because the same day also marked the long-awaited link-up of units behind Aachen. At 1615 hours, elements of the 119th and 18th Regiments finally completed the inexorable ring around the city. At first a frail perimeter, within two days the Allied isolation of Aachen was firm and resolute. Thirteen thousand Germans had been snared inside the jaws around the city, and by 21 October all organized resistance in the city ceased. Aachen, first attacked by VII Corps on 12 September, was finally in Allied hands.[28]

The assault had been in equal measure costly and revealing. The Germans had suffered a tactical defeat, to be sure, but they had also mustered a formidable defense which marked the end of Germany's pell-mell retreat across France. Now, on the soil of their homeland, the soldiers of the Reich fought with more determination and resiliency. Casualties in the U.S. Thirtieth Division alone topped 3,000, and for J. Lawton Collins it had been the "toughest fighting since the *bocage* days in Normandy." The slow battle cost the XIX Corps Commander, Charles Corlett, his job. Like Hodges after him, Corlett coped poorly with the transition from the open flanks and light casualties of late summer to the close-order combat of the autumn. On 18 October he returned to the United States on recuperation leave. Not even the introduction into the line of another American Army, the Ninth led by Lieutenant General William Simpson, and another Tactical Air Command, led by Brigadier General Richard Nugent, altered the Allied situation as the days shortened.[29]

Way back on 4 September, the First Army had estimated that the capture of Aachen would take one corps, possibly three divisions, and fifteen days. In the end, Aachen devoured two corps with five divisions and stood free of U.S. occupation for thirty-nine days. This must have been little consolation for the attackers when they entered the first German city to fall in the war and beheld a ruin of rubble.

The battle was costly for the tactical air commands, too. Quesada lost seventy-nine planes and fifty-eight flyers in the Aachen campaign. His remaining pilots flew over 10,000 sorties to Aachen in September and October, and spent 8,618 bombs on the attack. Given the general shortage of war material throughout the Allied forces, such an expenditure meant neglect of other tasks. Interdicting the entry of German defenders into the Siegfried Line was supposed to receive 39 percent of the IX TAC's effort in October, but the attention to Aachen siphoned off over half of that commitment. Likewise, Quesada was able to mount less than half of the fighter sorties initially scheduled to escort heavy and medium bombers. General Sam Anderson, the IX Bomber commander, believed that this reduced protection was in part responsible for a twofold increase in the number of B-25s and B-26s lost to the Luftwaffe in October. Over in the Third Army zone, the XIX TAC lost two groups to the Aachen offensive, which George Patton thought seriously "derailed attempts to reach the important city of Nancy."[30]

All of this, of course, might have been deemed worthwhile if air power had exercised a profound influence in the Aachen attack. But it did not. On no day of the assault did an air strike actually make a ground advance possible, and rarely did even a concentrated air strike destroy a pillbox or bunker. Armored-column cover, like the tanks they protected, did not reproduce the spectacular results of late July and early August.[31]

After the ancient city fell, a conference convened by the Twelfth Army Group's air-operations liaison officer, Colonel Sheffield Edwards, sought answers for the apparent failure of tactical aviation. Composed of corps, division, and command air-liaison officers, the conferees interviewed numerous company and regimental officers as well as members of tactical air commands. It was a noble attempt to codify the lessons of the war, and its report identified the dense forests and the reinforced West Wall as the primary factors limiting tactical air efficiency in the Aachen battle. "Tactical air works well in open terrain against a retreating foe," Edwards wrote, "but its effectiveness in tight situations against fortified defenders remains today an open question." Indeed. And it would remain an open question into the next months as everyone from George Marshall to Pete Quesada sought solutions to the stalled tactical air war.[32]

At IX TAC, ideas to jump-start tactical aviation ran the gamut from small adjustments in procedure to a complete overhaul of the system. Quesada's chief of staff, Brigadier General Alvin Kincaid, convened his own conference of group commanders and staffers to tackle the problem. Meeting on three bad-weather days in early November, the group produced a hodgepodge of recommendations. Colonels Ray Stecker and Frank Perego of the 365th and 368th Groups advocated only minor procedural changes, such as issuing daily operational orders the night before instead of at 0400 hours. "We can then have more time to prepare our briefings and coordinate with the squadrons," Perego believed.[33]

Lieutenant Colonel Seth McKee of the 370th thought the distance from airfields to the front lines was responsible for the decline in tactical-air operations. He was in part right. The movement of fighter groups to forward bases had not kept pace with the fantastic advance of the ground forces in August, and the logistical shortages of autumn precluded a quick remedy for that situation. By early November, the average distance between tactical airfields and the front was over a hundred miles, just under the distance that existed on D-Day.[34]

Other participants supported broader changes in the tactical-air command. Harold Holt urged Quesada to bar all P-38 Groups from armored-column cover, believing that the Lightnings offered poor visibility and were more vulnerable than the sturdy Thunderbolts to small-arms ground fire. Colonel Clinton Wasem of the 474th supported barring them, and went even further, stating that P-38s ought not be part of the tactical air war at all; "They should be traded to the VIII Fighter Command [which escorted heavy bombers] or sent back to the States."

To Colonel Ed Chickering, the problem stemmed not from inadequate equipment but from outdated tactics. He wanted Quesada to discard the "willy-nilly" improvisation that the summer had demanded in favor of the more careful and meticulous stratagems that had been in place before D-Day. He urged a shift away from 100-pound fragmentation bombs, which had worked well in armored-column cover operations, and recommended a greater use of heavier ordnance to combat the concrete emplacements of the Siegfried Line. He advocated less glide-bombing, which was effective in areas of light flak, and more dive-bombing, to minimize the effect of increased ack-ack from fixed enemy batteries. "Different ground situations," he observed with some insight after the war, "required different air setups. What one campaign needed was not necessarily the best for another kind of campaign."[35]

Staff officers at Kincaid's conference focused less on operations and more on procedure. Blair Garland and Bill Cowart were convinced that the communications network, with which they had tinkered constantly, required still more changes. They wanted to move the SCR-584 equipment from the IX TAC operations trailer to forward fighter-direction posts, thus eliminating another administrative layer in the control of planes. Colonel John Taylor, Quesada's new operations officer, believed the IX TAC could do with fewer bureaucratic layers, too, and targeted the entire wing-organization tier for elimination. Since D-Day, the 70th and 84th Wings had passed orders from IX TAC to the groups and acted as a filter for all direction between the Tactical Air Command and its groups. As long as Quesada commanded a dozen or more groups, such conduits performed a necessary function, but in the autumn as few as four and no more than nine groups comprised the entire IX TAC. Taylor figured that the time was ripe to streamline.

In ways, all these recommendations were valid. Getting operational orders to groups earlier than 0400 hours on the day of a mission would undoubtedly lessen the strain on group preparations. Moving their airfields closer to the war would clearly increase the time that small fighters could spend over the fighting front. The P-38 was not as fit as the Thunderbolts and Mustangs for close air support. The West Wall presented new tactical problems to fighter-bombers, and Chickering's advocacy of longer-fused, heavier bombs made logical sense. Communications and signals use were never completely satisfactory in World War II, and required constant modification. And eliminating wings as tactical organizations appeared a shrewd move now that the IX TAC no longer controlled the eighteen groups it had at the height of summer. So Quesada, who sat in all the meetings but had worked hard to keep quiet, implemented some of the recommendations. He requisitioned more 500- and fewer 100-pound bombs for December, cut his two wings from the chain of command, and made minor changes in the signals scheme at his headquarters in Verviers.[36]

But the greater truth behind efforts to fine-tune the tactical air war was that the airmen missed the forest for the trees. Overall, their counsel would not and did not materially affect the conduct of the Siegfried Line campaign. In November, there were only two P-38 groups in the Ninth Air Force, and they were employed almost exclusively on armed reconnaissance missions anyway. Changing the signals system yet again and eliminating the two wings made no difference in the response time for ground support, which was on average seventy-four minutes in September, seventy-one minutes in October, and seventy minutes in November. Even the efficiency benefits of moving the airfields closer to the fighting were negated by the severe supply shortages along the front. When Quesada asked, he found that no Army logistician would earmark vital transportation resources to move a fighter group when foot soldiers and tank drivers had little ammunition, fuel, or winter clothing.[37]

Although they did not recognize it, like their brethren in the strategic air forces, the tactical airmen had by then come to believe implicitly in the power of airplanes. In the discussions chaired by Kincaid, no pilot acknowledged the intrinsic limits of air power. It occurred to no one that the strength of the West Wall, the forests of the Ardennes and Hürtgen, and the increased German presence along the front were obstacles that perhaps bombers and fighters could not conquer.

In fact, American ground leaders were coming to these very conclusions as the IX TAC met in conference. On 4 November, Bradley's chief of staff at the Twelfth Army Group, Major General Leven Allen, told Sheffield Edwards that "the air cannot hope to be everything to us, and I am inclined to count on less help from them in the future." At First Army, Chief of Staff Bill Kean echoed the sentiment.[38]

But within IX TAC—among the very men who had cast off the wild assumptions of an independent bombardment strategy—the pilots failed to see the less-than-spectacular results of that autumn as a function of their own imperfect ability to influence the battle. Pete Quesada clearly expressed their faith in air power's omnipotence. "We are trying about everything we know," he wrote to his old mentor Trubee Davison on 14 November, "but nothing is working yet. With more trying we will find something to blast these Hun right out of their positions and end this war."[39]

The exploration for new tactics and procedures obscured for Quesada and others the fact that tactical aviation was in fact operating at a high degree of efficiency. October 1944 was in many measures a high point for the IX TAC. In that month, the command had more sorties per plane, fewer mechanical and accidental mishaps, the highest rate of Luftwaffe kills, the greatest number of successful SCR-584 blind-bombing missions, and the fewest incidents of friendly fire of any month in the war. Weyland's XIX TAC had a similar October in every category save blind bombing. But the flyers, whose hopes for the war were so high, remained unaware of such accomplishments and persevered in their search for a new approach to the air war.[40]

Quesada himself had perhaps the most ridiculous brainstorm in this pilgrimage of faith. On 8 November he explained to Blair Garland what he called his "Jeb Stuart" plan. In order to collapse Germany's dwindling transportation network and impress her people with the might of Allied air power, Quesada wanted every Allied plane to swarm across the Third Reich and attack a thousand objectives in a hundred towns that had not yet been molested by the air forces. The sheer mass of the attack, he believed, would crumble Germany's rail and roadways, and would create such mayhem in the streets that Hitler would have no choice but to surrender. Garland was scheduled to return to the United States the very next day on a fact-finding mission, and Quesada instructed him to broach the plan with officers in the War Department. To be certain he got Hap Arnold's ear, Quesada also detailed the plan to David Griggs, a civilian technology expert on Arnold's staff who was then in Europe.[41]

Garland and Griggs both related Quesada's scheme to Arnold, and it is a measure of the frustration of the fall campaign that George Marshall and even Roosevelt actually considered the notion. Marshall sent the plan back to SHAEF for consideration, telling Eisenhower that "this plan looks like something we ought to look into." Fortunately for everyone involved, SHAEF's Psychological Warfare Division denounced the plan as terroristic, and the plan was dropped.[42]

Beyond that objection lay other, maybe better, reasons to kill Quesada's brainchild. Given the resiliency of the German population under three years of persistent day-and-night bombardment, "Jeb Stuart" would not have pummeled the enemy into submission and would only have diverted the strategic air forces from their important offensive against oil-tank targets. In fact, the whole plan was poorly conceived and lacked any doctrinal integrity. It would have involved a diffusion of effort over wide areas of central Europe, and was a strange conglomeration of strategic and tactical precepts without an underlying foundation. That it garnered the attention it did speaks volumes of the lack of developed doctrine in the tactical air war. Better than any single battle of the campaign, Quesada's plan suggests that by November the Americans were flailing about in an effort to improve tactical aviation.

Eventually, ground and air officers returned to the principle of Operation COBRA, of an overpowering air onslaught to puncture the tough Siegfried Line at one small point. Courtney Hodges seemed to have first proposed a COBRA repeat, although the idea undoubtedly germinated in many minds before the conference at First Army on 1 November, when Hodges presented his idea to ground and air officers. On the surface, it was simple: 4,000 Allied planes from every air force were to blast German strongpoints around Eschweiler, to be followed by an aggressive ground offensive to, in Hodges' words, "break out of the Hürtgen Forest and into the rolling German plains." There was no doubt that he patterned his plan—and his hopes—after COBRA. After securing Quesada's enthusiastic cooperation, both men sold Omar Bradley, Hoyt Vandenberg, and Dwight Eisenhower the scheme at a SHAEF conference on 3 November. "I am of the opinion we might as well try this new angle of attack," the Supreme Commander wrote to Marshall.[43]

A special planning session was held the next day with representatives of the U.S. Eighth and Ninth Air Forces, the British Second Air Force and Bomber Command, and the First Army. Three divisions of the Eighth's heavy bombers were assigned targets in the Langerwehe area; Bomber Command was slated to attack in the vicinity of Düren; eleven Ninth Air Force medium bomber groups were to destroy the myriad villages beyond Eschweiler; and the IX TAC received the dual task of supporting VII Corps and attacking gun positions and observation posts near the front lines.[44]

To avoid the short bombings that had marred COBRA, the strategists established an elaborate marking plan. Ground soldiers were to place football-field-sized cerise panels at one-mile intervals 500 yards behind the front, and artillery batteries were to fire red burst shells to explode at 5,000, 10,000, and 15,000 feet, in effect marking a bomb line in the sky. Moreover, the Ninth Air Force Signals section established special homing frequencies to aid in the heavy-bomber approach and gained temporary control over every navigational aid in the European theater. If nothing else, the preparations indicated that the planners were not content to rely this time on any highway, no matter how prominent, to mark the bomb line.[45]

Contingent upon weather, the planners set 10 November as D-Day, with delays possible until the 16th. After that date, the First Army would jump off even without the benefit of the largest air-support operation of the war. Predictably, overcast skies did postpone QUEEN for days. On 11 and 12 November, the weather in England was too poor for the heavies to get off, and then on 13 and 14 November the same cold front that had dogged Great Britain wafted over the Continent and grounded Quesada's planes. Finally, at the nightly air-ground conference on the 15th, Courtney Hodges decided to attack the next day with or without aerial support. We'll be in the air tomorrow," Quesada promised Hodges, "if I have to crash-land every goddamm plane on the way home to do it."[46]

At least one pilot resented such a pledge, but as it turned out dawn broke on 16 November with decent weather on the Continent, although 500 heavies and 300 mediums could not participate due to fog at various airstrips. The big bombers that did make the crossing arrived over their targets between 1113 and 1248 hours and dropped 9,760 tons of fragmentation bombs. Medium bombers flew into the battle zone as soon as the heavies vacated the area, and they, too, salvoed hundreds of tons of ordnance.[47]

Starting at 1305 hours, 350 fighter-bombers placed their bomb loads along the leading edge of the front, knocking out some emplacements. Planes of the 365th, 366th, 376th, and 368th Groups managed to attack positions in front of the First and 104th Infantry Divisions. Although the 370th and 474th Groups failed to locate their targets and instead carried out routine patrols beyond the battle area, Quesada pronounced himself pleased with the day's effort. All together, these attacks achieved a remarkable degree of surprise; only one Luftwaffe plane appeared all day to contest the Allied air fleets, antiaircraft fire was meager, and just ten of 2,809 planes were lost to enemy action all day. Unfortunately, the bombing was less accurate than expected. Clouds, haze, smoke, and snow in some areas effectively hid certain targets, but only a single case of short bombing marred the day. Quesada and Hodges were both particularly proud of that, and congratulated each other by phone at 1654 hours.[48]

When four divisions of VII Corps launched their attack at 1345 hours, foot soldiers harbored none of the animosity that marked their brethren in COBRA. At first they met light resistance as they reached the outer German defenses just fifteen minutes after the last fighter-bomber released its ordnance. But as the day wore on, it became increasingly clear that the bombardment had not delivered all it promised. Casualties among the dug-in and protected Germans were "remarkably light" in the words of one post-action summary, though officers more versed in air attacks along the West Wall would not have characterized the absence of damage that way.[49]

Among the regiments of the German Forty-seventh Division, which received the brunt of the air attacks, casualties averaged 3 percent. Elsewhere, the defenders endured losses of just 2 percent. Only in the 984th Regiment of the 275th Division did casualties top 10 percent. For individual defenders, the bombing was something to behold, though not necessarily something to fear. "The blasts were tremendous, and I never experienced anything like it," recounted one German. "I organized shows of fireworks before the war, and that is the only thing I can compare the blast of bombs to."

By nightfall, his impression—and the low casualty figures—would have surprised no American foot soldier. The typical gain of the day was 3,000 yards. Nowhere did the front move forward more than a mile. Although 10,000 tons of bombs had been delivered by nearly 3,000 planes, bringing much destruction in the villages surrounding Eschweiler, it made little difference to the real defenders of the German border.[50]

Weather on 17 November precluded any air support whatever, and advances were less striking than even the previous day's progress.

From 18 to 23 November Quesada's planes sortied a total of 1,215 times in support of the First Army offensive, and each day advances continued to be measured in yards, not miles. On the 24th, the day after Hodges and Quesada had their private dinner to discuss QUEEN's apparent failure, the 367th and 368th Groups attacked strong points near the small towns of Hürtgen and Merode. These were the exact positions that both groups had attacked on the opening day of the offensive, and nothing could have been a more stark reminder to pilots that the First Army thrust had miscarried. On top of that sobering realization, Colonel Ed Chickering recalled, "We did not do much better at Merode the second time around than we did on the first."[51]

On 2 December, the First Army issued its own postmortem on QUEEN. Based on an intensive investigation of bombed sites, POW interviews, and regimental after-action reports, the report concluded that air power had done as much as it could in the attack. The bombardment succeeded by almost every measure. No close-support effort ever involved more bombs or planes; there had been no friendly-fire mishaps; the pilots had aimed their ordnance well; virtually no planes had been lost; and the Luftwaffe did not challenge the Allied air armada.

Yet QUEEN had failed to break the ground troops out. In the end, the First Army Report surmised what truly disinterested observers might have told the Americans all along: that air power's ability to affect the war was "not total or complete. When the enemy has time to organize effective defensive positions and when his supply lines are more stable than ours, tactical and strategic air power, in whatever quantities, can exercise at best a corollary influence on the battle."[52]

It was a tragedy of the air war in Europe that it took many officers until the fall of 1944 to arrive at this conclusion. Quesada and others, involved in the daily minutiae of war, were slow to grasp the war's broader picture. So it was December before most ground and air leaders in the European theater explicitly recognized the limits of air power. On 5 December, Hodges told his aide, William Sylvan, "We can't continue to count on air magic." Quesada, too, suggested as much in letters to friends and officers. "We are not everything in this war," he wrote to Momyer in Florida. He told his old North African aide Jimmy Mills, "We've had a few kicks in the teeth recently. . . . I think we sometimes ask too much of the fighter-bomber boys." For their part, Eisenhower and Bradley learned to push less for massive air attacks than they had in previous months, and even Arnold told President Roosevelt that "our air forces are not able to cut the Nazis at the knee with impunity."[53]

In due time, the Americans would learn another lesson of the air war. As Arnold, Eisenhower, Bradley, Hodges, and Quesada came to understand the limitations of planes and bombs, the Germans were hatching a last-ditch effort to turn the tide of the war. Deep in his East Prussian headquarters, Adolf Hitler ordered a final counteroffensive aimed at the seams between the British and American armies. Since September, he had been harnessing fuel, planes, tanks, men, and food for the thrust. In mid-December, four well-equipped, well-manned, and well-prepared German armies would crash across the Allied lines in Belgium, concentrating their early push in the First Army/IX TAC area.[54]

If the American leaders now understood better the limits of air power in offensive action, they were about to learn both the potency and the weakness of airplanes in defensive warfare.[55]

Chapter Ten

We Took a Bit of a Beating on the Ground But Boy Did We Dish It Out in the Air

ST. DIZIER, THE ARDENNES FOREST. 16 DECEMBER 1944. 0230 HOURS. The tele-type brought startling news to the 405th Fighter Group airfield outside St. Dizier. Just moments before, German paratroopers had reportedly dropped to the ground near Nancy. After reading the communiqué, group commander Colonel Garrett Jackson roused his men from their sleep to defend their airfield. With each passing moment, his shock at a German offensive in the dead of winter grew. Surely, Jackson thought, the Germans could not be launching a counterattack in a sector that had been quiet for weeks, in an area that one Allied report had de-scribed as "the quiet place for weary troops." If they were, his airstrip and his pilots were in trouble.

Groggy, Sergeant Gilbert Parass and others stumbled down to the field's gasoline dump, where they lay in the snow for five hours. "The gasoline tanks were in open pits," Parass recalled. "Some idiots across the field started firing and the bullets were cracking over our heads so we slid down the sides of the pits for cover. Someone suggested that maybe this wasn't the best idea should a bullet hit one of the gasoline tanks, so we scrambled out en masse, and lay on the flat ground again. Our brave Flight Chief said we would make our stand here should the Germans appear. We told him he could make a stand and we would be right behind him—as far away as possible."[1]

Just hours later the same sort of confusion emerged all along the front. At 0530 hours the first thunderclap from German artillery punctuated the fog-shrouded silence of the U.S. First Army line. Each volley spewed dirt skyward and sent shell fragments in every direction. American soldiers suffered few casualties in their well-fortified positions, but, like their brethren at St. Dizier, they struggled to decipher what the German activity meant. The unusual enemy tactic of using searchlights for illumination indicated that something special was starting. Just what, however, no one knew.[2]

The German assault made good headway. By midmorning every regiment in the American Ninety-ninth Division had been hit, and division commanders in both V and VIII Corps were busy plugging holes in their lines. By noon the German tide had overrun outposts in the Twenty-eighth and 106th Divisions, and the Fourth Division barely clung to positions near Echternach. By late afternoon fourteen German divisions were operating in the Ardennes, a tally that would soon grow to twenty-five divisions, 600 tanks, and 1,000 aircraft. Although there was no large-scale breakthrough by nightfall, American soldiers sensed that harder blows would be dealt on the morrow. "Nobody able to sleep and no hot meals today," one wrote in his diary. "This place is not healthy anymore." For the first time since invading Normandy some six months before, the Americans felt like defenders. The Battle of the Bulge, Germany's last attempt to win the war, had begun.[3]

Allied leaders were slow to react to Hitler's mad dash to drive through to Antwerp and split the American and British forces on the Continent. The weather was overcast; the impossibility of tactical reconnaissance flights shrouded the scope of the German gamble. In Paris, Eisenhower and Bradley dallied at a wedding reception for hours. At First Army headquarters in Spa, Courtney Hodges believed that the German thrust was a mere spoiling attack. In Verviers at IX TAC, Pete Quesada agreed and issued no general alert. George Patton of the Third Army was one of the few commanders who sensed that something bigger was in the air, but he did not push his views with vigor in the battle's early hours. At most higher headquarters, it would take a while for the hard fighting in the trenches to translate into decisive action.

By midnight on 16 December the offensive could no longer be dismissed as a local skirmish. The Germans had committed the Fifth and Sixth Panzer armies and the Seventh Army on a sixty-mile line through some of Europe's most rugged country. Aimed squarely at Hodges' First Army, which was now arrayed from Aachen in the north to Echternach in the south, Hitler's brainchild already threatened the huge Allied supply installations that had been built up through the autumn to support the springtime drive to the Rhine. The First Army headquarters at Spa, for instance, was surrounded on every side by service groups and supply dumps. Liège, twenty miles northwest of Spa, was one of the greatest U.S. logistical centers on the Continent. Verviers, an important and densely-stocked Belgian railhead, lay eleven miles north of Spa. All these depots were now in danger of capture by German forces, and at last U.S. leaders took action.

In an effort to contain Hitler's thrust, Eisenhower and Bradley moved armored divisions to the northern and southern flanks of the attack. At First Army, Courtney Hodges shifted some divisions from quiet sectors to areas of intense fighting. He also began thinking about falling back from Spa to safer environs. Luftwaffe planes had already bombed his command post twice, and there were reports of planes full of German paratroopers headed for Spa. At the various tactical air commands, Pete Quesada, O. P. Weyland, and Richard Nugent placed their fighter groups on operational alert, and laid plans for the defense of airfields closest to the fighting.[4]

When morning came on 17 December the German assault had created the start of a giant salient in the battle line. There was no panic in the Anglo-American camp, but the onslaught had clearly ambushed the Allies. "The German attack came as a complete surprise to us," one officer in the beleaguered Fourth Division recalled. Indeed, since 1 November the Germans had been planning this, their first offensive in nearly three years, with great care. They had hidden their reserves from prying eyes, they had taken full advantage of the forested terrain, and they had attacked at a point where American troops were either green or tired. Even though some clues had hinted at Hitler's intentions in the weeks before 16 December, no one in the Western Alliance believed that the Germans could or would now mount a serious push to turn the war in their favor. But as 1944 came to an end, Adolf Hitler surprised the world one last time.[5]

For U.S. soldiers, the Battle of the Bulge would be the most severe test of all the European fighting. For Pete Quesada and the men of the tactical air forces, the campaign would mark the first and only time when American air power was used in an unplanned and large-scale defensive operation. The previous summer, they had learned of air power's potency in a planned offensive. In the autumn, they had learned of aviation's limits in a stalemated campaign. Now they would learn what airplanes could do in yet another circumstance of war. The outcome could well be the capstone to the wartime service of the tactical air forces.

Courtney Hodges convened a war conference in the wee hours of 17 December to fashion a defense for his sector. William Simpson, commanding the Ninth Army to the north, various corps commanders, Hoyt Vandenberg, Richard Nugent, and Pete Quesada all attended the meeting. Simpson and Nugent agreed to slacken any offensive operations in the Ninth Army zone, a move that allowed Quesada to bleed two fighter groups from Nugent for the emergency confronting Hodges' men. For his part, Hodges moved a battalion from here to there, exhorted division commanders to hold their ground, and requested reserves from Bradley's Twelfth Army Group and Eisenhower's headquarters. But the conferees knew that these were mere stopgap measures designed to prevent a rupture in the First Army line. All the generals hoped for another forty-eight hours to better assess the situation and design a counterattack.[6]

When the meeting adjourned, Quesada returned to Verviers to direct the air battle above the First Army. He immediately mustered every available plane for armed reconnaissance flights above the confused and anxious ground soldiers. Within thirty minutes pilots at a dozen airfields were scurrying into their airplanes.

At one airstrip in northern France, Major John Motzenbacker lifted into the air and pointed his flight of sixteen Thunderbolts toward the Roer River south of Düren. In the calm before the storm of battle, the river looked pretty and peaceful as it wound through the white snow and green firs. "There is the main road down there," Motzenbacker radioed his wing man. "Give me some top cover and I'll go down and have a look."

Dropping in lazy circles, Motzenbacker drew closer to the ground. What he saw made his head bounce back against the canopy. The road was clogged with hundreds of tanks, half-tracks, and motor transport. The wrecked convoy sprawled across four miles. Climbing back to altitude, Motzenbacker called IX TAC. "There is a hell of a big convoy heading into our lines just south of Monschau. . . . Could that be us or is it the enemy?" The flight controller said they were Germans. "Then send some reinforcements. We are going down."[7]

Motzenbacker split his squadron into four flights of four planes each. As they dove toward the ground the enemy column dispersed into the woods and side roads. Fifty big trucks remained in the open, however, and the pilots blasted them with 50mm cannon fire. With the trucks burning in the roadway, Motzenbacker's pilots next ranged up and down the smaller roads. One flight located a group of tanks and attacked with 500 pound bombs. The Panzers disappeared in the smoke, and their guns stopped firing. When the pilots could see the ground again, the earth was strewn with ruined tanks lying upside down.

"There they are again, those Thunderbolts and Lightnings," lamented one veteran German soldier huddling in the wreckage. "Their order is perfect . . . they are always here when there is something interesting to dive on." By then, his German comrades had recovered enough to throw up a barrage of flak, claiming three planes and the lives of two pilots. Still, it was a good raid for the American pilots. They had destroyed 107 vehicles of all descriptions and fifteen of the prized 88mm guns; in one place the wreckage stretched for over a mile. The surviving Germans were now bunched in little groups of four or five vehicles.[8]

Flyers from other groups patrolled closer to the actual fighting. Five miles to the south, near the hamlet of Bullingen, the 366th Group attacked elements of the First SS Panzer Division surging toward Malmédy and Stavelot. These Germans had already bypassed U.S. strong points on the front and were about to envelope the Second and Ninety-ninth Divisions. But the air strike, along with determined fighting by the American Seventh Armored Division, forced the Panzers to the southwest, saving thousands of Americans from isolation. As the pilots turned to chase the Germans, 150 Luftwaffe planes appeared through the clouds. Although the Thunderbolt pilots managed to claim seven German planes against three losses, the dogfighting distracted them from the important ground targets, and the German column escaped without further injury.[9]

Despite these air operations, there were too few sorties, too few guns, and too few troops to keep the German assault immobilized for long on 17 December. On the ground, lingering artillery shortages and poor communications among American divisions hamstrung Hodges' response to Hitler's strike. In the sky, the Luftwaffe at last managed to offer at least some cover for their brethren on the ground. "The German air forces," recorded one surprised officer in Collins' VII Corps, "were putting up their first great offensive operation." Compounding matters, some German columns were sporting American insignia, making identification of enemy forces difficult for Allied fighter pilots. Throughout the day the story was the same; despite momentary setbacks here and there, Hitler's war machine simply rumbled onward.[10]

By nightfall the state of the battle was worse than it had been in the morning. "The situation developed badly during the day," Hodges' aide wrote, "and may be considered tonight to be serious if not yet critical." The Belgian towns of St. Vith and Bastogne, with their important road nets, were in danger of falling. Along the northern edge of the German attack, the Sixth Panzer Army was in striking distance of the important supply centers around Spa. In the south, Hitler's Seventh Army was providing effective flank security for the Panzer attack. Forty-eight hours earlier, few would have believed the battle summaries now filtering into various American headquarters. But the reports were real enough, and confusion and disbelief were on every face at many Allied command posts. As Omar Bradley muttered to nobody in particular when he arrived at Hodges' headquarters late on the seventeenth: "Where in the hell is this son of a bitch getting all his strength?"[11]

Worst of all, the next day brought more of the same. On the morning of 18 December Colonel Joachim Peiper of the First SS Panzer Division aimed a considerable column of tanks and half-tracks toward the hamlet of Stavelot, an Allied storage point for over three million gallons of gas just south of Spa. Hitler had begun his campaign with meager petrol reserves, and his attack depended on skimming fuel from American supply centers. More crucial than the gasoline, however, if Peiper and his follow-up forces secured Stavelot, they would be just twenty miles from the vital supply point at Liège. If Liège fell, the U.S. First Army would be compelled to retreat from the whole Aachen-Düren area. Just like that, an entire season of hard campaigning lay in the balance for the Allies.[12]

Kampfgruppe Peiper made good progress in the morning. Time and again the Panzers overwhelmed American positions, though some U.S. soldiers bravely held onto isolated places and continued to hamper the Nazi spearheads. To even the fighting odds, Hodges determined to commit the Eighty-second and 101st Airborne divisions to the fray. But the paratroopers could not be deployed until evening or later. So by noon only air power and a few fighting troops stood between Peiper and his goal of fuel. Unfortunately, the small artillery planes swirling above the German armor could do little more than report the deepening crisis, and fog kept Pete Quesada's powerful fighter-bombers firmly on the ground. The situation was desperate.[13]

At IX TAC Headquarters, Quesada made a fateful decision. For the first and only time in the war, he explicitly traded lives for a tactical objective. He asked Colonel George Peck of the 67th Reconnaissance Group for volunteers to brave the thick overcast and find Peiper's surging column. At about 1200 hours, Peck sent Captain Richard Cassady and Lieutenant Abraham Jaffe into the soup. The flyers gingerly made their way through the Amblève River valley near Stavelot. Flying their P-51s as low as 100 feet above the ground, they at last located sixty Nazi tanks and armored vehicles moving through the mist. "We made three runs over that column," Cassady recalled, "and the Germans were so surprised to see us that they didn't fire until the last run." Then the Panzers aimed everything from rifles to 20mm cannon at the Mustangs.[14]

Cassady and Jaffe climbed into the safety of the clouds and radioed their luck to IX TAC. Quesada directed his operations chief, Colonel Gil Meyer, to get as many Thunderbolts over the Germans as possible. Meyer, in turn, called Colonel Ray Stecker of the 365th Group. "A Jerry column has broken through our lines at Stavelot," he began. "In fact, there is now nothing between it and the English Channel but service troops and cooks and bakers." That was an exaggeration, but not by much.

Stecker at first begged off the mission, citing concern about the atrocious overcast. "I know," replied Meyer, "the weather is down on the deck and it probably will be suicide but Goddamn it, the Army says we've got to get something in there or the bastards will be in Liège." On the other end of the line, Stecker winced. "See what we can do," he said as he put the phone down.[15]

Ray Stecker laid plans to send four-plane flights into the fog at twenty- to thirty-minute intervals. The first flight to find the Germans, he told his pilots, would direct the entire group down through the dangerous gray sky to the prize targets. How they would all land again in such thick fog, however, was anybody's guess.

Major George Brooking led the first flight off the runway at 1305 hours, a second flight left at 1330, and a third prepared to climb into the air at 1400. Brooking directed his Thunderbolts directly over the battle area. He had been there the day before, but now the 2,000-foot Belgian foothills were covered with fog. The pilots could not see a thing. "I'm going down to poke around by myself. There must be a break somewhere in those mountains," Brooking called to the others. "You're crazy," radioed his wingman.[16]

Brooking pushed down through the clouds, narrowly missing ridges as they loomed suddenly into view. At the floor of one valley he found an opening in the overcast that was just large enough for a Thunderbolt to squeeze through and still remain above the trees. As he threaded his bird deep into the small canyon, he searched for the elusive Panzers of *Kampfgruppe* Peiper. The roads were empty. There was no enemy there.

Brooking pointed his Thunderbolt skyward, pushing on to the next ridge and the next valley to the west. Feeling his way over the crest and down the gorge, he expected to crash his plane into the ground at any moment. Instead, he suddenly burst through the clouds and stared squarely at a huge concentration of Nazi armor. The Germans were moving serenely along the road as if, Brooking recalled, their weather officer had told them not to "worry your little heads at all about enemy aircraft today. Nothing can fly in weather like this." Brooking looked at the Germans, and the Germans looked at Brooking. The surprise was mutual. Not a single shot was fired.[17]

Brooking scooted up the valley and called his flight down. Gingerly the other Thunderbolts descended through the solid overcast. In single file they roared up the valley, only a few feet above the ground and a few feet beneath the clouds. A barrage of flak rose to meet them. Captain Jim Wells managed to drop his 500 pound bombs in the middle of a cluster of tanks, sending six Panzers tumbling down an embankment. Right behind him, Brooking and another flyer strafed a group of half-tracks. With fires burning on the road, the Thunderbolt pilots then climbed back into the clouds and called for reinforcements.[18]

Flyers came from all over northern France. Ray Stecker arrived with sixteen Thunderbolts. After Brooking led them into the gorge, Stecker's flyers snaked through the hills and plastered the enemy column. Squadrons from the 366th and 404th Groups soon joined the fray. Major Arlo Henry found a gaping hole in the clouds and dive-bombed a line of tanks that had peeled off the main road. Captain Neal Worley's flight found the same hole and accounted for over a dozen tanks. All together, over 300 fighter-bomber sorties netted thirty-two armored and fifty-six motor vehicles.[19]

On the ground, *Kampfgruppe* Peiper lay scattered along a maze of rural roads that were sometimes no more than paths through the woods. Although Peiper and his follow-up forces would still constitute a legitimate danger to Stavelot for days afterward, the threat to Liège and the huge Allied petrol stores diminished after 18 December. "It is now established," reported a First Army report the next day, "that the fighter-bomber attack on the column heading westward from Stavelot inflicted damage which caused it to change direction to the south."[20]

Elsewhere the news was not so good on 18 December. In the south, the Germans were near a breakthrough at Bastogne. To the north, the garrison at St. Vith drew closer to surrender. In between, Allied signals communications were so bad that leaders had little real understanding of the German assault. Everywhere there were rumors of German assassination squads roaming through Allied camps, looking to kill Eisenhower and other leaders. As Major General Ernest Harmon of the Second Armored Division recalled, in such circumstances "your rumor is as good as mine," so military police put many commanders under tight guard. Still, one fact stood out as the defenders hunkered down for the night: without the success of isolated air operations and the bravery of small units here and there, the day could have been much worse.[21]

Compounding matters, a nasty weather front seeped over the battle during the darkness and grounded virtually every Allied plane on the continent for days. From 19 to 22 December, aircraft from Quesada's IX TAC, Weyland's XIX TAC, and Nugent's XXIX TAC managed only a few close-support sorties, several strafing attacks, and a small number of strikes against defended villages. All along the front, low ceilings and snow prevented the fighter bombers from massing in any substantial strikes against the German columns. In an effort to beat the weather, on 20 December Quesada gathered his group commanders to "explain the crying need for resourcefulness and initiative among all officers of my command." But these urgent words were powerless against an angry sky. As one officer at IX TAC recalled, "Never had weather meant so much to the air forces and their supported units, and never were we more prostrate to do anything about it."[22]

The Germans used the overcast to good advantage. They continued to pound at the critical road junctions of St. Vith and Bastogne. Each day the local U.S. commanders in these towns pleaded for air support, but to no avail. With every hour, the Germans made deeper penetrations around the towns. St. Vith finally fell to them on 22 December. Bastogne continued to hold out, although even there the story was bleak. The sporadic reports that reached higher headquarters only increased the Allied gloom and confusion. "It is impossible to tell where we stand at this point," Hodges' aide wrote on 21 December. "One minute things look good and the next minute bad."[23]

Units fell back in retreat throughout the First Army zone during these dark days. Hodges moved his command post from Spa to St. Trond. The battle had wrecked him; he was bedridden, exhausted. At IX TAC, Quesada authorized numerous outfits to vacate their positions, including his MEW radar outpost and most support personnel in his own headquarters at Verviers. German combat teams had attacked his fighter control center, and three of his fighter groups stood ready to retreat from their air bases on twelve hours' notice.[24]

The situation during these foggy days compelled Eisenhower to take drastic action. The "Bulge" into the Allied line had split Bradley's

Twelfth Army group in two, with Patton's Third Army now along the southern shoulder of the salient and Hodges' First Army and Simpson's Ninth Army along its northern edge. Eisenhower believed that if he hoped to improve his overall communications and mount an effective counterattack, he would have to peel the northern forces from Bradley's command and merge them with Montgomery's British Twenty-first Army Group. Bradley could then concentrate on first holding and then attacking the southern shoulder of the salient while Montgomery did the same in the north with a combined Anglo-American force.

Although such a shift in command structure would have delicate political implications for the Western Alliance, Eisenhower felt that the military situation demanded the switch. On 21 December he ordered Hodges' and Simpson's forces transferred to Montgomery's command, a decision that made Bradley "livid," recalled his aide Chester Hansen. Bradley "walked up and down and cursed Monty. Was startling to see Brad like this." In fact, only Bradley's personal loyalty to Eisenhower kept him from quitting.[25]

The rearrangement included corollary shifts in the tactical air forces. Quesada's IX TAC and Nugent's XXIX TAC, the supporting arms for Hodges' and Simpson's troops, were transferred to "Maori" Coningham's British Second Tactical Air Force. But if in the ground forces these changes meant real shifts in operational control over soldiers, among the airmen an unwritten agreement preserved the authority of U.S. leaders and even increased it. On 21 December Quesada met with Coningham, Nugent, and several American and English group commanders at a IX TAC airfield. There, Coningham placed all his fighter-bombers under Quesada's control, "as General Quesada's units were located in the immediate vicinity of the battle area, and he, as the closest air commander to the scene of activity, was in the best position to draw up a plan and close control of the important air phase of the Bulge Battle."[26]

Coningham's action was a great example of trust and cooperation among the Allies in a war often marked by intrigue within the halls of leadership. "Mary did it, gave me his planes, right on the spot," Quesada recalled. "It was very wise of him because he was right in his reasoning. It made me completely rethink my impressions of him from when we served in North Africa together, where I thought he was a prima-donna. In the Ardennes he did what he had to do, and it helped tremendously."[27]

As far as Quesada was concerned, the only down side to the whole arrangement occurred the following day. On 22 December Vandenberg took three fighter groups from IX TAC and gave them to O. P. Wey-land's XIX TAC to support George Patton's drive toward the now-isolated Americans at Bastogne. Quesada complained, but Vandenberg's action was justified. Patton would need plenty of help plowing through the enemy forces surrounding Bastogne. Besides, although the move left Quesada with only three groups of his own, he now had Coning-ham's planes; the next day he would also take temporary control of two Eighth Air Force P-51 groups on the Continent. Given the thin layer of Allied resources in the Ardennes, Quesada had his fair share of fighters.[28]

Who commanded the planes mattered little, of course, as long as the weather kept them on the ground. As the days of fog merged together, flyers and soldiers of all ranks hoped for blue skies. "For Christmas I want some good weather so the fighter-bombers can come over and give us a hand," one corporal told a war correspondent on 21 December. Bradley and his staff likewise waited for a decent patch of high pressure to clear the overcast, to end what Bradley later called the Germans' "conspiracy with the weather." As his aide Chester Hansen wrote on 20 December, "With two good days in the air we could decimate his [Hitler's] supply lines, arrest road movement, and knock out his troop-carrying transport." In Paris, Eisenhower wrote that "the Boche has certainly been lucky in the help he has gotten out of weather. . . . about four-fifths of the time we have been fighting weather as seriously as we have the Hun." At IX TAC, Quesada went one step further, claiming he "was starting to think the Germans had God on their side."[29]

The clouds at last cleared on the morning of 23 December. At air bases in England, France, and Belgium, pilots rose early. When light came they took to the sky in droves, anxious to offer close air support for the beleaguered troops and to interdict the German supply lines behind the front. All day long planes from the IX and XXIX TACs concentrated on the middle and northern portions of the Bulge. While the 370th Group supported the Eighty-second Airborne Division's attempt to recapture St. Vith, other groups helped the Third and Seventh Armored Divisions' effort to hold the northern flank of the salient.

These missions encountered unusual Luftwaffe opposition. For the day, the Allied fighter bombers lost nineteen birds against claims of over ninety German planes shot down. But more significant than that tally was the destruction of Hitler's men and machines on the ground. In total, 669 sorties netted over 320 German motor transports and armored vehicles. The American pilots also managed to ruin many buildings occupied by enemy troops, a sizeable number of gun positions, much rolling stock, and seven rail lines. So much destruction heartened American soldiers on the ground. December 23 was a "red letter day," recalled one observer, because friendly planes "once more streamed overhead like shoals of silver minnows in the bright winter sun, their sharply etched contrails making a wake behind them in the cold air."[30]

Medium and heavy bombers were busy, too. Over 1,000 big planes of the IX Bomber Command and the Eighth Air Force targeted railroad bridges and marshaling yards behind the front. Again the Luftwaffe defended these supply centers in atypical strength; the 391st Bombardment Group lost sixteen planes and their crews on a single mission to Ahrweiler. Still, the strikes slowed important German stores heading to the front to feed Hitler's push. At the same time, American cargo planes were finally able to deliver critical material to the surrounded 101st Division at Bastogne. Throughout the entire battle area only an accidental attack by U.S. fighters on five U.S. bombers loaded with gasoline for Patton's troops marred the air effort on 23 December.[31]

The next day was similar. Quesada's and Nugent's pilots again flew armed reconnaissance missions over the St. Vith-Stavelot sector. At about midday they located what was left of *Kampfgruppe* Peiper. "The once so arrogant SS battlegroup Peiper collects its sad-looking remnants," one disgruntled German later recounted in his diary. "We stumble along, but then our troubles start multiplying, for the *Jabos* circle above and apparently take an interest in us." Pouncing like hungry animals, the fighter pilots racked up over 500 motor transports and dozens of tanks and armored vehicles. As the local German commander later admitted, the air was so thick with Allied planes that his tactical units could not move during the later part of the day.[32]

Again attacks by heavy and medium bombers compounded German

difficulty. An even 1,400 heavy bombers from England blasted eleven German airfields east of the Rhine, greatly reducing the Luftwaffe's operations in the Bulge. Meanwhile, B-25s and B-26s of the IX Bomber Command pounded the logistical lines winding through southern Germany to the Panzer spearheads in Belgium. One of these strikes knocked out an entire flak battery and the only tank-recovery vehicles of the rebuilt Panzer Lehr Division, losses described as "catastrophic" by the division commander. Another strike late in the day forced a German troop train to take refuge in a tunnel. It stayed there for three days, denying Panzer commanders crucial reinforcements.[33]

By Christmas Eve the tide had begun to turn in the Ardennes. Effective air strikes, dogged small-unit combat, and the determined resistance at Bastogne had all combined to delay the German columns moving west. More than that, by forcing the attacking tanks onto narrow rural roads with few exits, the American defenders had actually increased German vulnerability to air attack. Time and again, Allied pilots first blocked entire columns with solitary strikes aimed at the lead vehicles, and then blasted the remaining armor. Watching these tactics, most of Hitler's tank commanders soon gathered that they would not reach Antwerp. Indeed, they would now be lucky to even cross the Meuse River.

In the American camp, leaders breathed a small sigh of relief on 24 December. Omar Bradley was, according to his aide, "ebullient . . . [about] the fighter bombers thickly over the front where they are ripping savagely into enemy supply columns and destroying his shrinking armor reserves." At XXIX TAC headquarters, Richard Nugent exclaimed that his "fighter bomber squadrons have been having a field day." In a Christmas Eve letter to his mother, Pete Quesada echoed Nugent's enthusiasm. "The weather has been very cruel to us but today is a fine one," he wrote. "If you go back and read the events that took place you might find that today and the few days following are historic ones."[34]

Good weather held on Christmas Day, making Quesada a prophet. The day before, J. Lawton Collins' VII Corps had uncovered huge elements of the Second Panzer Division just five miles from the Meuse River outside Celles. The Panzers, nearly out of gas and unable to maneuver effectively, were vulnerable. Collins directed his corps to strike the Germans in a coordinated attack with fighter bombers. At dawn, Quesada sent the first of three groups to the area. Together with Collins's troops, the flyers bagged hundreds of hapless German armored vehicles in an action recalling the heyday of the summer campaign. "Quesada's wonderful fighter-bombers," Collins remembered, greatly aided his men. "The attack was brilliantly executed," added Major General Ernest Harmon of the U.S. Second Armored Division, "and by 5 PM Celles was taken." The action at Celles was important, for at no time during the battle would the Germans advance farther west. Hitler's drive on Antwerp had reached its high-water mark.[35]

Elsewhere that day, over eighty Lightnings from the 370th Group flew continuous armed reconnaissance missions along the First Army–Third Army seam, freeing ground forces that were typically assigned to flank security to fight crucial battles at other places. Coningham's Second Tactical Air Force contributed over 370 aircraft for similar sorties along the northern edge of the salient. Their efforts near St. Vith netted 170 motor transports and seven armored vehicles. All together, fighter bomber pilots wrecked over 500 vehicles of all kinds, knocked out fifty gun positions, and attacked thirty-two towns and German strongpoints on Christmas Day. For American pilots, it was a satisfying way to spend the holiday. As Nugent succinctly recorded in his diary: "Today is Christmas. The weather is clear. The XXIX Tactical Air Command Santa Clauses are delivering presents to the German army in the penetration area." That night Quesada traveled to Hodges' headquarters to report that "his people had had probably their finest shooting since the war began."[36]

American and British fighter bombers continued to mop up the Celles pocket on 26 December. Around midday a strong German thrust to free the trapped Panzers threatened to overwhelm U.S. troops. British Typhoons were the only planes immediately available to help the ground troops, though their radios were incapable of communicating with the American units. But small Cub planes, used as artillery observers, did know the location of the German relief column and could radio U.S. troops on the ground. So one small unarmed Cub led a squadron of Typhoons loaded with rockets into the battle zone. "It was like a butterfly leading a squadron of buzzards," recalled Ernest Harmon. "The Typhoons screamed down, rockets sizzling from their wing runners, and left devastation in their wake. What was left of the German column retired with our troops in hot pursuit."[37]

While all this action took place along the northern edge of the salient, to the south O. P. Weyland's flyers were marching in lockstep with Patton's Third Army toward Bastogne and its beleaguered garrison. Already troop carriers had sustained the isolated defenders for days, and already Brigadier General Anthony McAuliffe, in temporary command of the 101st Airborne Division, had replied to a German surrender ultimatum with his famous "Nuts!" Now, on 26 December, Patton was close to breaking through to the city.

Early that morning an American armored-combat command began pushing toward Bastogne from the southeast. The ground was frozen, and at first the tank going was even better than it had been during the summer pursuit across France. But two hours after starting out the column met determined resistance from German troops ensconced in the outskirts village of Remichampagne. The tankers called for air support. Two Thunderbolt squadrons roared through the air twenty minutes later, bombing only a few hundred yards in front of the U.S. armor. The P-47s shook any notion of resistance from the Germans, and the U.S. tanks rumbled onward.[38]

Behind Remichampagne lay the twin towns of Clochimont and Assenois, where the Germans had constructed their main holding line southeast of Bastogne. Assenois, an assemblage of perhaps forty buildings that controlled an important roadway, was especially well fortified. Germans there had bedeviled American attempts to advance for over twenty-four hours, and now they blocked the American combat command. Frustrated, O. P. Weyland directed an entire group loaded with napalm to fire the town.

At about midday Thunderbolts and Lightnings howled from the horizon, dropped to 1,000 feet, and approached the target in eleven flights of four. The first bomb fell in the town square at 1410 hours, sending red flame and black smoke billowing into the sky. Other fires soon broke out elsewhere. The strike completely destroyed ten buildings, and spared only the masonry walls of an additional dozen. More important, the heat and smoke forced the Germans from their hidden positions, exposing them to American ground fire. After that, Assenois was not so difficult to pass.[39]

Patton's troops finally made contact with elements of the Bastogne garrison at 1645 hours on 26 December. Air support and effective tank-infantry action had accounted for much of the progress that day. Napalm attacks had proved particularly effective. Even inside the garrison, soldiers could discern the value of the fire strikes. "We were glad to see the squadron mission loaded with Napalm," remembered the 101st Airborne Division air-support officer. "The General [Brigadier General Anthony McAuliffe] and the G-2 and G-3 [intelligence and operations officers] had never seen Napalm used before and asked what it was and all about it. . . . they were well pleased with the effects of Napalm attacks in our area."[40]

In fact, these napalm strikes produced good results in every sector during the Battle of the Bulge. This was in marked contrast to the autumn campaign, when napalm was no better than bombs or machine guns against well-fortified positions. In the Ardennes the Germans were often hidden from view, but they were rarely ensconced in concrete pillboxes or bunkers. As a result, napalm's blunt effect made it an especially valuable weapon for the Allied air forces in late December.[41]

Although Patton's breach in the German ring around Bastogne was tenuous for days, the enemy was not able to surround the city a second time. The defense of Bastogne had cost the Americans plenty; casualties numbered over 2,000 men. But holding the city had denied the Panzer columns important roads and had become, as early as 23 December, the symbol of Allied resolve in the Ardennes. The garrison had fought magnificently, and so had the supporting pilots of the Ninth Air Force. Afterwards, Anthony McAuliffe thanked Hoyt Vandenberg for "the tremendous support we received from the fighter-bombers of the Ninth Air Force. Despite intense flak, these fighter pilots repeatedly attacked and disrupted German formations preparing to act against the town. They were a tremendous boost to our morale and were a vital contribution to the successful defense of Bastogne." Another general who had been trapped inside the city went even further, stating that "the fighter bombers did work equivalent to the employment of two U.S. Infantry Divisions." In a battle that was often waged by platoons and companies, that was more than a sizeable contribution. That was the critical margin of power which allowed Americans first to hold Bastogne and then to rescue its isolated garrison.[42]

Lest Quesada and others in the air forces build too much confidence from these words of praise, instances of friendly fire now underscored again the intrinsic limits of tactical aviation. Medium bombers had already struck at American troops near Malmédy, and Quesada warned against accidental attacks due to overcast skies and a fluid front on the very day Patton reached Bastogne. Three hours later twenty of his P-47 Thunderbolts killed thirty-seven Allied soldiers and a considerable number of civilians in three separate incidents.[43]

As usual, pilots did not have a monopoly on human error. American flak crews shot at Allied aircraft on at least four different occasions in the last week of December. These accidents prompted both Hodges and Patton to forbid any battery fire at planes unless their pilots initiated an attack. Beyond that, the army commanders began "an intensive program to stamp out [the] rumor that the Germans are flying American aircraft." In fact, the Luftwaffe had used captured planes on a few occasions, but Vandenberg, Quesada, Weyland, Hodges, and Patton all agreed to squelch such talk so that jumpy gunners in the air and on the ground would not poison effective interservice cooperation.[44]

In the end, these ongoing accidents did not substantially affect the Ardennes fighting. The Allies were gaining momentum with each passing day, and by this point in the battle fighter-bombers had reasserted their near total control over the ground forces. Increasingly, Wehrmacht soldiers began ignoring orders to fire at planes with every available weapon and took cover whenever fighter bombers screamed overhead. One wrote in his diary of the "never ceasing array of airplanes" as he watched American fighter pilots attack St. Vith. "The thunder of motors resounds in my body. How often have I witnessed such a modern Pompeii." Even the Luftwaffe's sporadic nighttime raids did little except annoy the Allies as they moved from the defensive to the offensive in the last days of December.[45]

With the New Year approaching, Patton's Third Army continued its push up from the south while Montgomery organized his Anglo-American line and began marching southward. Like a giant vise, the two forces planned to squeeze the Germans from Belgium and bag thousands of prisoners in the process. Von Rundstedt and his field commanders sensed this strategy and hoped to fall back across the Rhine, where they could still construct a formidable defensive barrier. But in Berlin Hitler would not hear of retreat. Although it was clear who would win the battle, the Führer refused to admit reality. Now conducting what Fifth Panzer Army commander Hasso von Manteuffel later called "a corporal's war," Hitler committed some twenty-one swiftly-organized and poorly-trained divisions to the fray.[46]

The steady flow of German men and materials marching into the Ardennes meant rich targets for Allied air forces. Heavy and medium bombers attacked communication centers, supply depots, and rail bridges. On 29 December 200 B-17s dropped bombs on Siegburg, destroying the town's business district, marshaling yards, passenger train station, and a large residential section. The strike wiped out the region's entire rail system and stranded two Panzer Grenadier regiments. Instead of fighting the Allies at the front, Gerhard Jockwehr and 2,000 of his comrades of the Eleventh Panzer Grenadier Regiment were drafted into a makeshift repair force and spent three days clearing the town of debris.[47]

The story was the same in Prüm, an important road junction. The town had endured air raids on 25, 27, and 29 December. By the last of the attacks, bomb craters filled the streets, most buildings were crumbled wrecks, and the town fathers would soon evacuate the place. On New Year's Eve, not even a single German soldier on a bicycle could pass through the town.[48]

Closer to the front the tactical air commands did not have the kind of luck that the medium and heavy bombers experienced. After 27 December poor weather returned to Belgium, greatly reducing fighter bomber operations. Quesada's IX TAC and Nugent's XXIX TAC, stationed to the north of the shrinking German Bulge, flew no missions on 28 December and managed only limited sorties the last three days of the month. O. P. Weyland's XIX TAC, supporting Patton's army to the south, flew more often. But even there clouds shrank the usual harvest of destruction for the pilots.[49]

A last-ditch Luftwaffe effort to destroy Allied planes in the Bulge compounded matters. On the morning of New Year's Day over 600 German planes of all types bombed Allied airfields in France, Belgium, and Holland in a stunning attack. It was an ugly surprise for the Anglo-Americans, who had grown complacent through months of relative immunity from these raids. At least 156 planes were destroyed on the ground, and although the German Air Force lost upwards of 200 aircraft, the raid was an embarrassment for all Allied airmen. In an unbecoming attempt to claim credit for many of the GAF losses that day, Quesada wrote to a friend that he had "anticipated such an attack as it was the logical thing for the Boche to do." But in truth the raid took even Quesada by surprise, and the Allied loss in planes temporarily exacerbated a shortage of U.S. fighters on the heels of a hard week of campaigning.[50]

Still, neither the return of poor weather nor the Luftwaffe's major raid seriously prevented the Allies from smashing the German Bulge in Belgium. In fact, just hours after the German planes retreated from the sky on 1 January, Generals Hodges, Spaatz, Vandenberg, Doolittle, and Quesada met at First Army headquarters to plan a new attack. In line with Eisenhower's directive to destroy the enemy forces in the Ardennes, four American corps, the VII, VIII, XII, and XVIII Airborne, would keep pushing against the Bulge's southern and northern shoulders while the British Thirtieth Corps hammered away at the nose of Hitler's forces. A diversionary attack by German troops in the Alsace-Lorraine region failed to divert Allied pressure from the Ardennes operations, and on 3 January Hodges' army renewed its forceful plunge into the German salient.[51]

The attack was a true combined-arms strike. At the crux of the fighting, artillery, tank, and infantry teams made good headway against an increasingly weary adversary. Above them, fighter-bombers flew continuous armed reconnaissance missions despite a temporary shortage of P-47 aircraft. To the enemy rear, heavy and medium bombers redoubled their efforts to plaster German transportation choke points, once again blurring the neat theoretical divisions between strategic and tactical air power. On 16 January Eighth Air Force B-17s bombed the U.S. 104th Division, but even this accident failed to diminish the value of air support. "So fast is our advance and so difficult to trace our front lines," Chester Hansen explained, "that we do not particularly complain" about friendly fire. On each clear day in January, the horizon was literally full of Allied aircraft, a fact not lost on even the most veteran soldiers.[52]

Particularly if they were Germans. One Wehrmacht sergeant later said that there was "seldom a moment during the day when Allied planes were not overhead West of the Rhine." Another told of entire villages blasted across roads. Some German soldiers even compared napalm attacks to the terror of their own V-1 and V-2 weapons. To combat the swarms of Allied birds, German generals had reiterated their order to shoot at them with every available weapon, including pistols. But the troops routinely disregarded such foolishness and took cover. "Soon they will tell us to fight *Jabos* with pocket-knives," Karl Laun wrote in his diary.[53]

Constant air strikes sapped German morale and compelled many to desert. After one strafing attack near Gordendorf, thousands of soldiers refused to leave their pillboxes and dig foxholes. By the middle of January Karl Laun was among those who had had enough. Escaping army life with a comrade through the Saar Valley, Laun reflected on the war and railed against his nations's leaders. "It's peaceful along the highway here. The sun shines from a steel-blue sky and the snow reflects the beams, bathing the whole scenery in an ocean of light. Why did these loons have to start this war? The murmuring forest and the gay song of the Nahe River symbolize the frustration of a world born to live in peace. In my imagination I still hear the thud of bombs, the screaming of Artillery shells, the detonation of mortars, and always, always, the roar of fighter bombers." With each passing day, fewer subjects of the Third Reich, in uniform or not, believed in the fantasy of victory.[54]

A new Russian offensive in the East combined with plummeting German resolve to quicken the Allied advance from the west into southern Germany. By 14 January VII Corps troops had cut deep into enemy lines near St. Vith. On 16 January patrols from Hodges' and Patton's armies linked up in Houffalize, Belgium, eliminating the western tip of the German offensive. January 22 and 23 were bright, clear, crisp days, and the tactical air commands bagged nearly 2,000 motor vehicles of all descriptions. "So many aircraft were out," Quesada told Hodges, "that you couldn't see the sun." On 23 January St. Vith fell to the American Seventh Armored Division, the same unit that had made a gallant stand at the same place a month earlier. Five converging corps then swung to the east, and by 31 January they had completely eliminated the German salient in the front. The Battle of the Bulge was over.[55]

Hitler had hoped to deliver a lethal blow to the Allies in the Ardennes. In the end his scheme only served to wound his own forces. The Anglo-Americans could afford to replace their losses, but Germany had neither the equipment nor the personnel reserves to make good their own costs. As Dwight Eisenhower told Winston Churchill, "The enemy took us for quite a surprise, but in the end the Battle of the Bulge will go down in history as the greatest victory of the Western Alliance in this war. Germany has very little left now, and the war will be finished soon." Closer to the front, Chester Hansen seconded Eisenhower's views. "The German command had vast resources of men and material in the battle and has lost irrevocable portions of both." Pete Quesada offered his own spin on the fight in letters to friends back home, writing that "the last month has been a bit rugged, however everything is alright now. We have got those nasty old Germans sorry for having been so impertinent. We in the Air Force gave them a hell of a drubbing and the Ground Forces didn't do so badly, either."[56]

Air power, particularly that of the U.S. Eighth and Ninth Air Forces, had indeed helped turn back the German attack. Omar Bradley believed that heavy and medium bombers had "strangled" Hitler's supply routes and "helped in no small measure the counter-attack of the First and Third Armies which caused him [Hitler] to retreat." Although Panzer columns were never wholly cut off from logistical support, only the most determined efforts kept their materiel moving forward. Even then, most supplies did not reach the front. To at least one American division commander, Allied air forces had "completely choked off the supplies needed badly by the Nazi spearheads. German prisoners were taken who had had practically nothing to eat for several days and who were inadequately supplied with clothing and ammunition."[57]

Close air support and armed reconnaissance missions did their part as well. All together, fighter bomber pilots in the Ardennes claimed 299 gun positions, 751 tanks and armored vehicles, over 6,000 motor transports, nearly 1,200 buildings, and countless locomotives and rail cars destroyed. After-action surveys cut these figures by perhaps a third, but the tallies still represented a mortal blow to Hitler's dream to reverse the war's course. Division and corps commanders unanimously praised the fighter pilots, crediting them with slowing Panzer spearheads, wreaking havoc on roads, and forcing entrenched Germans from fortified positions. Bradley felt that the fighter-bombers played as important a role in the Ardennes as they had in Normandy. That was a conclusion that Quesada was not inclined to question. "We took a bit of a beating on the ground but boy did we dish it out in the air, we up here in particular," he wrote to Jimmy Lee on 26 January. "We have had more success by comparison than anyone could expect. Things are now back to normal and the German has been hurt very badly."[58]

With only depleted reserves and home-guard units of old men and young boys, Germany began to collapse under the weight of Russian advances in the east and renewed Allied attacks in the west. In early February the young leader of the Luftwaffe's Fighter Command, Adolf Galland, flew out over the Western Front on a personal reconnaissance. Four P-51s immediately jumped him, and the five planes raced all the way back to Berlin. Galland reached safety, but the episode "convinced" him the end was near. "The Third Reich received its death blow in the Ardennes offensive," he recalled. "In unfamiliar conditions and with insufficient training and combat experience, our numerical strength had no effect. It was decimated while in transfer and devastated while in action, and the Jabos were especially proficient at intercepting much needed reinforcements at critical times. The American fighter-bomber destroyed us."[59]

Quesada did not learn of Galland's comments until well after the war, but he shared his adversary's conclusions about Allied fighter planes. The Battle of the Bulge convinced him that World War II had carved a niche for fighter planes beyond aerial combat and escort duty. With the war now in its final stages, Quesada directed his IX TAC staff to conduct tests, collect data, and compile standard operating procedures for the close support of ground troops. In February and March he placed considerable importance on this task, explaining to his old friend William Momyer that "we've got to write these lessons down for future generations."[60] In the last weeks of war, then, Quesada produced a written legacy of the part played by tactical air power in World War II.

Not surprisingly, these reports described IX TAC signal systems in great detail. From the very beginning, radars and radios had been central to the success of fighter bombers, and during the summer of 1944 it had became axiomatic that close air support was only as good as the communication links between ground and air forces. IX TAC's control chain for fighter planes, which ran from forward director posts to radar centers, to fighter control stations, to a combat command post, and finally to each fighter group, was a model of efficiency. Although Quesada recognized "we have only begun to master the art of close control of aircraft," he took great "pride" in this system.[61]

Everybody lauded microwave early warning radar. Since the rainy days of summer, MEW had directed planes to and from targets, linked bombers with their fighter escorts, and tracked what few birds the Luftwaffe managed to hurl at the Allies. "Without that radar," Quesada recalled, "we would have been dead in the water. Very much of what happened on the Continent would not have happened without that radar." Colonel Blair Garland concurred: "MEW radar was the single most important development in the tactical air war."[62]

Garland and his technical experts did, however, find fault in using MEW and SCR-584 radars to direct fighter planes on blind bombing runs. By February 1945 they knew that even modest shifts in humidity and temperature inside radar huts could skew intricate calibration equipment by as much as a quarter-inch. The results could be disastrous; a mere eighth-inch error on a radar chart easily translated into a bombing error of a half-mile on the battlefield. More than that, entering the airspeed, altitude, wind, and barometric pressure into the Norden computers at the control stations had proved a lengthy process. Oftentimes, there was little chance for pilots to change course or altitude after controllers had plotted their bomb runs. Together, these deficiencies forced Quesada to conclude that "the Norden bombsight as currently used in the close-support 584 equipment still leaves much to be desired."[63]

Garland recognized this and remained "completely open-minded to any recommendations" regarding blind bombing methods. As he saw it, part of the problem lay in a persistent shortage of qualified radarmen. But with the war in its final stages Garland saw little chance to get more technicians and instead focused on increasing the efficiency of his present troop complement. In late February operational tests suggested that better coordination between the radar centers and the directing posts would improve radar control, so Garland issued new guidelines to streamline the flow of information through the various cogs in the control system.[64]

He also instituted a new course to train fighter pilots for six-week rotations as flight controllers. Begun on 12 February at the 70th Fighter Wing, Garland hoped the practical course would introduce airmen to the innards of radar control and help them "understand the limitations of the control system so they would know what aid they may expect" after they returned to flying. For Garland, bringing pilots into the radar centers not only alleviated manpower shortages but also exposed flyers to a broader view of the air war. "In combat as complicated as close air support could be, that was always an advantage," he remembered. Although no endeavor would ever eliminate the effects of poor weather and human error, placing pilots at forward directing posts did make close air support even more effective as the war wound down.[65]

In fact, accolades now poured into the various tactical air commands. Major General Matthew Ridgeway of the XVIII Airborne Corps told Quesada that "Your people did for us all that could be asked on all occasions." The best U.S. corps commander of the war, J. Lawton Collins, wrote to "express my deep appreciation for the part played by the Air Force, particularly the fighter-bombers, in support of the VII Corps. We could not possible [*sic*] have gotten as far as we did, as fast as we did and with as few casualties, without the wonderful air support that we have consistently had." Perhaps the finest endorsement of tactical air power came from the American army commanders. Courtney Hodges of the First Army, George Patton of the Third Army, and William Simpson of the Ninth Army responded alike when asked how they would have deployed fighter-bombers if they had been given operational control of them: "No change."[66]

Together these sentiments reflected a dramatic shift in attitude among air and ground officers. Prewar squabbles in America over airpower policy and debates early in the war over air support had been intense. To anyone who cared to recall these old fights, this new spirit of good will was remarkable. "If you could see your way clear to do it, I think you should make a visit here at the earliest possible moment," Eisenhower urged George Marshall in the spring of 1945. "You would be proud of the Army you have produced. In the first place, the U.S. ground and air forces are a unit; they both participate in the same battle all the way down the line from me to the lowest private. I can find no evidence whatsoever of any mutual jealousy, suspicion or lack of understanding. In fact, I know of one or two Major Generals in the Air Force that one of my Army commanders would accept as Division Commanders today."[67]

Quesada echoed the importance of this good will. "Of all the lessons we learned about tactical air operations, perhaps the most important is that the air commander [and] his group and squadron commanders must have [a] sincere desire to become part of the ground team. The Army must, of course, have the same dedication to reciprocate, and this close liaison can only come from close day-to-day contact—especially at command levels."[68]

It had been an amazing journey for both the pilots and the soldiers. From contentious conflict before the war, to crude adjustments in North Africa, to a laboratory of learning in France, to the difficult lessons of the autumn of 1944, and finally to the triumph in the Battle of the Bulge, tactical air power had come of age. Although few would have predicted it, by the end of the war just 24 percent of the U.S. Army's air effort was dedicated to strategic bombardment; the vast majority of the rest was devoted to tactical air operations. More than that, close air support had played a key role through every stage of the European campaign. In a speech shortly after the war Dwight Eisenhower drove that idea home: "Don't think for a moment that the tactical air units supported us in this past war," he told a group of officers at the Army's Infantry School at Fort Benning. "Rather did we support them by capturing air fields from which they could operate so effectively ahead of us." That was hyperbole, but Eisenhower had made his point.[69]

It was supreme irony and great tragedy of the air war that, on the heels of the Battle of the Bulge and amid this praise, air arm leaders began to slight their own contributions on the battlefield and renewed their struggle for a separate Air Force predicted on independent strategic air power. Ninth Air Force Commander Hoyt Vandenberg was quick to discern this shift as the war entered its final stage. Immersed as he was in high-command intrigue, he understood that while senior airmen had bowed to the tactical demands of the war, they had never forgotten the importance of strategic bombardment in the struggle for their own Air Force.

He knew, too, that with victory in Europe assured the air arm would return to its historic devotion to big bombers. As a result, he worried that his service at the head of America's largest tactical air force might leave him outside the inner circles of the postwar air arm. His anxiety grew when the 15 January issue of *Time* magazine hailed his work with the ground forces. So in the war's waning weeks he hatched a plan to align himself with the strategic bomber barons.

As Vanderberg's intelligence chief, Colonel Richard Hughes, re-called: "The *Time* article was mainly complimentary to Vandenberg and his Ninth Air Force. However, one paragraph made the general almost frantic. Largely by inference, it accused him of being too closely tied to the wishes of the ground force generals, and possibly lacking in the breadth of strategic thought so desirable in an Air Force commander, as compared to the thinking of the pedestrian slow-moving ground sol-diers! There was no validity in this implied criticism whatsoever, but the printed, published, word scared the insecure Vandenberg almost to death. His reaction was violent. It assumed two aspects. First, who could have inspired the paragraph, General Spaatz, General Arnold, or who? Secondly, what could he do quickly to disprove the accusation? I was sent for in a hurry, the situation rapidly explained to me, and an ap-peal made to me to dream up some semi-strategic operation immedi-ately."[70]

For Hughes the trick was to assuage Vandenberg's vanity without "getting anybody hurt." Hughes thought an operation interdicting the industrial Ruhr Valley by tactical air power would meet both criteria. Although Allied ground forces were close to surrounding the Ruhr and bagging tens of thousands of Germans troops, Hughes concluded that "just enough time probably remained for General Vandenberg to make a grand-stand play."

While Hughes prepared this folly, Vandenberg took additional mea-sures to recoup some strategic-air-power credentials. In late January he began refusing requests for air support that came directly from Bradley's Twelfth Army Group, insisting that requests first route through and be approved by the responsible tactical air command. This new procedure added a cog to the chain of command for air support, something tactical airmen had worked hard to avoid. But Vandenberg felt it would help isolate him from close-support missions. To shore up his image with Arnold and Spaatz, he also sought "negative reports" of air support missions and photographs showing fighter-bomber destruction in German cities. He intended to use both the reports and the pictures in his weekly briefings with Spaatz and Eisenhower.[71]

By early February Hughes had completed his target list of cities, bridges, and roads along the perimeter of the Ruhr Valley. Hughes recalled that Vandenberg "pounced on the plan like a starving lion, and immediately ordered his personal pilot to fly us down to Paris to General Eisenhower's headquarters." There the idea met with enough interest to garner approval. "Strategic bombers in a tactical role is an old story," one Eisenhower staffer wrote, "but Tactical Air Forces in a strategic role is, I believe, a trend which requires close watching."[72]

By the time Vandenberg and Hughes returned to the front their plan had been absorbed by a much larger fantasy to destroy German morale in this, the sixty-sixth month of total war for the Third Reich. Operation CLARION was a longstanding scheme that called on all available Anglo-American aircraft to range over Germany and attack a host of transportation targets: roads, rails, barges, docks, marshalling yards, bridges. Allied air leaders believed that this strike, unlike others throughout the war, would produce a stupefying effect on German communications and morale.[73]

Quesada recognized CLARION as his old "Jeb Stuart" proposal from the previous autumn and now thought it was a poor idea. "The fighter-bombers are not adapted to this type of employment," he argued at one Ninth Air Force meeting. "If used properly in their own niche ... [fighter-bombers] can be of tremendous value, but if frittered away in these operations their value will be almost nothing." Ira Eaker, commanding the Fifteenth Air Force in Italy, agreed with Quesada and questioned CLARION's broader doctrinal integrity. Beyond that, Eaker criticized the ethics of what amounted to area bombardment so late in the war: "We should never allow the history of this war to convict us of throwing the strategic bomber at the man in the street." Nonetheless, CLARION dovetailed with the hope to end the war on a high note for strategic air power, and with Spaatz's support it won Eisenhower's approval.[74]

Operation CLARION was launched on 22 and 23 February, the first clear days in weeks. The strategic bombers of the Eighth and Fifteenth Air Forces as well as Bomber Command attacked over a wide region in north-central, southern, and eastern Germany. The tactical air forces, including both the American Ninth and British Second, aimed for targets closer to the front in western and northwestern Germany. Only seventy-odd planes of the increasingly crippled Luftwaffe rose to challenge the vast air armada. The bombing was good. The heavies, some 2,125 in number, dropped over 6,000 tons of bombs on more than eighty separate targets. The tactical forces added another 2,500 tons to thirty-seven targets.[75]

As the sun set on the 23rd, all the news seemed good for the Allies. Bombing accuracy was unexpectedly high, losses numbered just eleven planes, and the German people had received an unforgettable demonstration of Allied air power. If the bomber generals wanted to end the war with a great demonstration, CLARION appeared to have fit the bill.[76]

Yet CLARION failed in its bid to cow Germany from the air. Although it was never possible to evaluate all of CLARION's damage, there were no signs of a general breakdown and no evidence that the Reich's remaining industries had been destroyed. As it was throughout the war, high-priority military traffic was not stopped, and the bombings had only local and temporary effects. Perhaps CLARION was a case, as the Air Forces's official historians argued, of "trying to injure the morale of a people who had no morale."[77]

But more probably CLARION failed because it stemmed from the fantasy that air strikes could win wars alone. The Allied Joint Intelligence Committee concluded that CLARION had not seriously affected Germany's capacity or will to wage war, and many British air leaders echoed the opinion. Spaatz, Vandenberg, and other American airmen disagreed with the judgement, but they never again tried CLARION-like projects. For his part, Quesada thought the whole affair resembled the air assault on Pantelleria in June 1943: "operational masturbation."[78]

Better than any other operation, CLARION revealed the renewed stress on bomber theory among the airmen and foretold the post-war restoration of strategic air power theory. But in the spring of 1945 it was quickly forgotten as the Allies marched into Germany. By early March Eisenhower's troops had advanced to the Rhine River. The chance discovery of an intact bridge over that river at Remagen spirited the Anglo-Americans across the water. Over 6,000 fighter-bomber sorties then helped push the Allies deep into Hitler's Reich. Patton's Third

Army crossed the Rhine on both sides of Weisbaden on 23 March, pushing all the way to Frankfurt in four days. And on 24 March Simpson's Ninth Army forded the river with Montgomery's troops near Wesel.[79]

By late March there was a chance to bag tens and perhaps hundreds of thousands of German troops caught in the Ruhr Valley by the Allied thrust. The end was very near for Germany. As the Anglo-Americans marched deeper into the Fatherland, soldiers of every rank told of the vast destruction to Hitler's Reich. Bradley's erstwhile aide Chester Hansen wrote of gaping craters and decaying cattle everywhere. Entire towns lay in ruin. "I wish you could all see Germany," Quesada wrote a friend in America. "The destruction is beyond your imagination. I have never seen anything like Düren, in fact I had no idea such destruction could ever in fact take place. Cologne, of course, is destroyed." To his mother, Quesada wrote that the Germans had "received the beating that was coming to them. I don't see how they take it—it's terrific."[80]

Allied air power was everywhere, a fact not lost on the Germans in the last days of their war. Von Rundstedt termed the aircraft arrayed against the Reich *"katastrophal."* Another German Field Marshal, Albert Kesselring, believed air strikes "proved our undoing. . . . Allied air power was the greatest single reason for the German defeat." The head of the Luftwaffe, Reichsmarschall Hermann Goering, offered yet one more testimonial to the airplanes aimed against him: "The Allies must thank the American Air Force for winning the war. If it were not for the American Air Force the invasion would not have succeeded. Even if it had succeeded it could not have advanced without the American Air Force. Further, without the American Air Force Von Rundstedt would not have been stopped in the Ardennes. And who knows but that the war would still be going on."[81]

Everyone save for Hitler and a few deluded cohorts knew the war was over. In the Allied camp the celebrations commenced. Quesada made time to attend a party at the 365th Fighter Group. One officer there noted that everyone was on their best behavior despite the evening's entertainment: "The girl with her scanty black gown and snake-like hips caused male eyes to open wide and mouths to drop open in appreciative wonderment. Cut low in front and lower in back,

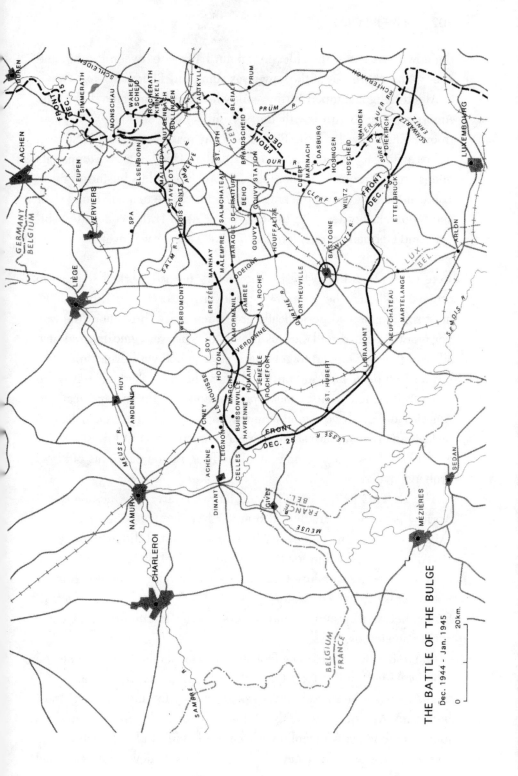

THE BATTLE OF THE BULGE

Dec. 1944 - Jan. 1945

the gown was slit at the sides to a point halfway between the hip and knee. What there was of the gown was admirably filled."[82]

Allied delight jumped further still when the Ruhr Valley fell to the Americans on 18 April with the surrender of over 300,000 German troops. Eight days later the First U.S. Army made contact with Russian troops at Torgau on the Elbe River. With that, Hodges' army stopped its offensive operations and Quesada's IX TAC finished its business of war. Later in the same week the entire Allied line came to a halt along river and mountain borders. On the last day of April Hitler committed suicide, and Germany surrendered on 7 May. The war was over.

Pete Quesada did not stay for the victory he had worked so hard to achieve. Although he took great pride in his service in Europe, like most soldiers he had periodically grown homesick throughout the war. For months he had told various friends that he was "getting tired of it all" and that he "longed to get home, say the hell with everything, and buy a ranch in Nevada and raise cattle." So he had mixed feelings when Tooey Spaatz told him to make preparations for thirty days' leave in America and a subsequent assignment in the Pacific Theater. "I hate to be leaving just as we are about to make a touchdown but I must admit I am looking forward to seeing my many friends," he wrote his old boss Trubee Davison.[83]

The IX TAC held a birthday and farewell party for Quesada on 13 April. Eisenhower, Bradley, Patton, Arthur Tedder, Miles Dempsey, "Maori" Coningham, and even Montgomery toasted the man many believed most responsible for the close air support of American ground soldiers. "Hodges worships Quesada, as does Bradley," Chester Hansen noted in his diary the day after the party. "I have never seen so much affection between air and ground officers as I saw last night when General Quesada left us."[84]

Omar Bradley, Quesada's first ground partner in France some ten months earlier, understood Quesada's contributions to the war better than anyone. When Eisenhower asked Bradley to rank the thirty most important American generals of the campaign, he placed Quesada fourth, behind only Eisenhower's chief of staff Walter Bedell Smith, Tooey Spaatz, and Courtney Hodges. Bradley believed Quesada had contributed more to the war effort than George Patton, who was sixth; J. Lawton Collins, who was seventh; Leonard Gerow, who was eighth; and William Simpson, who was sixteenth. Perhaps most important, Bradley rated Quesada far above most other air force commanders. Jimmy Doolittle was seventeenth, Ira Eaker was twenty-second, and Quesada's own boss Hoyt Vandenberg was a lowly twenty-sixth. For his part, Eisenhower described Quesada a "dashing, cooperative leader." If wartime service would mean anything in the postwar air forces, then Quesada's future looked bright indeed.[85]

But already different criteria were being applied to air force generals. Just as Hoyt Vandenberg had discerned, with the war over air leaders were now looking toward an independent Air Force. Most had already reaffirmed their faith in strategic bombing. Quesada did not know any of this as he was flying home after being knighted by King George VI. But all of it would profoundly affect his future.

Chapter Eleven

There Was Great Arrogance in Victory

THE PENTAGON. 28 APRIL 1951. 1115 HOURS. Air Force Chief of Staff Hoyt Vandenberg welcomed Lieutenant General Pete Quesada into his office. Their friendly handshake masked deep ill will. The two men had been at odds since the campaign for France in the summer of 1944, when Vandenberg had taken command of the Ninth Air Force. Their relationship had strained further when Vandenberg pushed the misguided CLARION air strikes against a vanquished Germany in the spring of 1945, and feelings between the two men had deteriorated yet more in the years following the war. In 1949, shortly after becoming the ranking officer in the Air Force, Vandenberg stripped Quesada's cherished Tactical Air Command of most of its planes and pilots. For Quesada, that was not only a clear repudiation of the lessons of World War II, but also the last ignominy.

Quesada had first asked Vandenberg for permission to retire in the fall of 1949. Vandenberg had denied the request, and for twenty months he and Secretaries of the Air Force Stuart Symington and Thomas Finletter had tabled Quesada's desires. In part, these men feared Congressional and Army reaction if Quesada, the air arm's most prominent advocate of close air support, prematurely left the service. The Air Force had won its independence from the Army in 1948 only after its leaders had promised to keep tactical aviation a high priority, and Quesada's presence in uniform had been a visible symbol of that commitment. As the years passed, however, Quesada began to feel like a pawn in this strategy, and it only increased his yearning for civilian life. Now, in the spring of 1951, Quesada determined to "state my case without reservations and to hell with the consequences." Just days before leaving for a four-month tour directing the Eniwetok atomic-bomb tests in the South Pacific, he asked to see Vandenberg at the Pentagon. Vandenberg, knowing full well what Quesada wished to discuss, agreed to see him.[1]

"Here is a blow by blow account regarding how I made out with my desire to retire," Quesada wrote his old friend Ira Eaker after the meeting. "I had a long talk with Van [Vandenberg], in which I expressed myself freely and forcefully. He was pleasant but I can't say he confined himself at all times to the facts. Upon leaving him I did not think I had much of a chance. . . . As Mr. Finletter is the deciding one, I asked to see him and did on Tuesday morning, early. I saw him at 9 and was on my way to Eniwetok at 9:30. I made a forceful and articulate presentation of my case which attracted, in his own words, his complete sympathy."[2]

Quesada's visit with Finletter did the trick. A week after Quesada arrived in the Pacific he received a wire message from Vandenberg. After further thought, Vandenberg wrote, he had decided he would "no longer stand in the way" of Quesada's retirement. Quesada was ecstatic, telling Eaker that "This, of course, settles it once and for all and I am more than happy because come July I will be on my own."[3]

Just as Vandenberg and Finletter had feared, members of Congress asked difficult questions when news of Quesada's resignation spread in the early summer of 1951. The nation was then locked in the Korean War, a conflict that underscored the Air Force's lack of tactical aviation. Many officials thought this was an odd time to retire a celebrated close-support warrior. Carl Vinson, the powerful chairman of the House Military Affairs committee, proposed a public hearing to uncover, in his words, "why the forty-seven-year-old three-star general with the best tactical-aviation credentials in the country would want to, and why we are letting him, retire in the middle of a new war in Korea." Quesada swiftly made it clear to everyone involved, however, that he would not engage in any mud-slinging at the end of his career. Without Quesada's cooperation the matter could not go forward, and Vinson dropped his threatened investigation.[4]

There were the usual rounds of retirement parties in September. The usual toasts followed the usual accolades; the usual stories followed the usual nostalgia. But these polite rituals hid deep tension. Although Quesada had refused to discuss his dissatisfaction in a public forum, he had in fact grown concerned about the air arm's turn away from tactical air power following World War II. Since at least 1948 he had been a vocal if private critic of the bomber barons, arguing that the renewed stress on strategic aviation had left Army troops more prone to defeat and death in the field. These quiet debates had alienated Quesada from other air leaders, and now that the Korean experience had buttressed Quesada's belief, the tension between him and other generals was palpable.

Quesada himself doubted that many air leaders were sorry to see him leave the service. "I knew that as long as Van [Vandenberg] was the chief, my career could go no further," he recalled years later. After the genteel farewells, Pete Quesada wore a military uniform for the last time in October 1951. In a small ceremony attended by more Army officers than Air Force officers, Quesada bid the military life good-bye. It had been a hard fall from the glory days of the war, when he and tactical air power had enjoyed praise from every quarter.[5]

Pete Quesada had relished a hero's welcome home from the war in Europe in April 1945. There were marches, dinners, and speeches. A victory parade in Philadelphia attracted over 500,000 people and featured the role his IX TAC had played in the war. Tooey Spaatz told Hap Arnold that Quesada was "one of our most enthusiastic young General Officers, whose command services in World War II were outstanding." For his duty overseas, Quesada was awarded the Distinguished Service Medal, the Legion of Merit, the Distinguished Flying Cross, the Air Medal with two Silver Stars, and a host of foreign awards, including a companion degree in the British Order of the Bath, the French Legion of Honor, and the French Croix de Guerre with Palm. "The outpouring of gratitude is just amazing," Quesada wrote one friend, "and I must admit to feeling a bit overwhelmed by all the attention." With the exception of a brief vacation to Georgia, for Quesada the first weeks back in the United States flashed by in a series of "Victory in Europe" celebrations.[6]

The war, of course, was not over. In the Pacific the Japanese were still battling to the fierce end. In May Arnold appointed Quesada his Assistant Chief for Intelligence, making Quesada the ranking intelligence officer in the Army Air Forces. The position surprised Quesada. "It's much too big a job and requires a type of mind that I am afraid I do not possess," he wrote his mother. "I am not very good at dealing with the big-wigs but I suppose I will have to do my best."[7]

This new duty gave Quesada a leading role in codifying the lessons of the European campaign. As a result, tactical aviation seemed to have a secure place in the air arm's postwar doctrine. But the job also introduced Quesada to the Manhattan Project, the supersecret undertaking to produce an atomic bomb. By the early summer of 1945 scientists had produced working atomic weapons, and in July President Harry Truman agreed to drop the bombs. The Twentieth Air Force then launched atomic strikes on Hiroshima and Nagasaki on 6 and 9 August. The Japanese capitulated, the war ended, and the world of air power changed forever.

Atomic power added a new dimension to warfare and fueled the move away from tactical air power within the Army Air Forces. The atomic bomb seemed to make the bomber theorists of the 1920s and 1930s prophets. Hap Arnold believed that nuclear fission had made air power "all-important" and wrote George Marshall that "we are on the threshhold of a true scientific revolution in the air. The next war may be fought by jet- and rocket-propelled airborne missiles guided by men sitting in concrete emplacements." As a result, Arnold argued, the nation ought to funnel the lion's share of defense spending to the air arm to maintain it in a state of immediate readiness. Even officers outside the Air Force agreed that atomic power made previous notions of war obsolete. When General Douglas MacArthur learned of the weapon he said simply, "This changes warfare." Ironically, after spending nearly thirty years developing big bombers to justify an independent air force, airmen finally found their vindication not in planes but in ordnance.[8]

Arnold and MacArthur reflected the common view of the age, but they were only partially right. Their views were persuasive as long as air-planes were the only way to deliver nuclear weapons and as long as America held a monopoly on atomic power. But the importance of the air arm would diminish when the ground Army or Navy developed their own means to launch atomic bombs, and the promise of U.S. military dominance would disappear as soon as other nations mastered nuclear fission.

More immediately, America's meager atomic capability should have blunted the belief that atomic power meant a revolution in warfare. The U.S. had two bombs in 1945, nine in 1946, thirteen in 1947, fifty in 1948, and 250 in 1949. As late as 1947 there were just sixteen B-29s modified for atomic missions. In terms of both bombs and planes, the U.S. did not have the capacity to carry forward an atomic offensive against a well-fortified foe.[9]

Few men recognized these limits in 1945, however. One astute ob-server, Alexander de Seversky, rejected the concept that national secu-rity had been reduced simply to a race to stockpile atomic weapons. He believed that nuclear warheads were of measurable dimensions with known potential and known limitation. "There is still no reason for the assumption in some quarters that basic concepts of strategy in military installations can be scrapped," he wrote to the Secretary of War. "Such talk is mere hysteria."[10]

But De Seversky's was an unusual voice of careful thought, and most men held fast to the idea that nuclear fission had changed warfare forever and placed an absolute premium on strategic air power. In the catbird seat as the Air Forces' chief intelligence officer, Quesada recalled with under-statement that "The advent of nuclear weapons resulted in a greater em-phasis being put on strategic warfare and a lesser emphasis on tactical warfare." Even Quesada's magnificent achievements in World War II would soon be obscured by the mushroom clouds of the new bombs.[11]

Rethinking the future of war in the nuclear age also meant reassessing the lessons of past conflicts. To support their renewed enthusiasm for strategic bombing, air leaders sought to recast World War II in a light favorable to big-bomber operations. Nothing better illustrated this re-habilitation of independent-air theory than the United States Strategic

Bombardment Survey (USSBS). The USSBS was Franklin Roosevelt's brainchild and was supposed to be a small committee of civilians charged with evaluating the effects of the strategic-bomber offensive against Germany. In the president's mind, the survey was necessary in light of the cost, publicity, and share of the nation's war resources that the bombers had consumed.[12]

In late 1943 Roosevelt appointed Franklin D'Olier, president of the Prudential Insurance Company, to head the committee. D'Olier began his ground work in early 1944 and went to Europe later that year with a letter from Roosevelt instructing Tooey Spaatz and others to "do everything necessary to assist Mr. D'Olier in producing an unbiased appraisal on the bomber offensive." Spaatz quickly grasped the importance of D'Olier's work and made officers from his strategic air forces available as technical experts to help the panel of civilians. As often happens, the original notion of a small, nonuniformed board grew to a large group with a staff of over 300 military men, almost all from Spaatz's command. From the outset, then, Spaatz and the strategic enthusiasts had an ample influence in the USSBS's work.[13]

The USSBS produced its initial report in August 1945. The summary exposed mistakes in the air war. It identified the failure to destroy German submarine pens, the ill-advised campaign against ball-bearing plants, the poor bombing accuracy of B-17s and B-24s, the occasional failures of intelligence inside Spaatz's command, and the lamentable lack of continuity in the one great success of the bombers—the attacks on oil refineries.[14]

But while the USSBS acknowledged the failures of bombing, it also placed great stress on the few accomplishments of the big planes. For example, the committee devoted nearly two fifths of its written report to the attacks on Hitler's oil refineries. More than that, the USSBS actually appropriated achievements of tactical air planes to buttress the contributions of strategic air power. Among these were the near-total wreckage of Germany's transportation network, the interdiction of various battlefields, the annihilation of Europe's railroads, and Allied air superiority. These accomplishments were the product of tactical aviation as much as they were the result of bomber-pilot efforts; yet the USSBS claimed that they were victories in the strategic-air war.

Only by shifting the definitions of strategic and tactical aviation could the USSBS say in the end that air power was a determining factor in the outcome of World War II. "Allied air power was decisive in the war in western Europe. . . . Its power and superiority made possible the success of the invasion. It brought the economy which sustained the enemy's armed forces to virtual collapse. . . . It brought home to the German people the full impact of modern war with all its horror and suffering. Its imprint on the German nation will be lasting." Few military men could have argued with this conclusion, but in merging the contributions of strategic and tactical aviation D'Olier's committee relegated the contributions of Fighter-bomber planes to the shadows of bigger planes on bombing missions.[15]

Strangely, many of the most ardent supporters of bomber theory did not read the report. Tooey Spaatz stated simply that "we won the war" and that he was "never that interested enough to read it." For bomber barons there was little motive to identify individual successes and failures from a context of broader victory. They had prevailed against the Axis nations and that was enough. But for the men of the tactical-air war such an attitude was appalling. To Pete Quesada "there was a great arrogance in victory—an arrogance that the U.S. would pay for in lives in future wars." Tactical airmen were rare in the immediate postwar era however, and by early 1946 careful observers knew that tactical lessons would find little reflection in peacetime military organizations.[16]

From his position in Washington Quesada was certainly aware of this new trend, though he did not realize how pervasive the fall of tactical aviation had become. In that same month Arnold's staff published the official history of the wartime Ninth Air Force. On the surface it praised the work tactical pilots did in World War II: "The Ninth Air Force was the single extra-ordinary air force which made possible the great invasion of the European war. . . . In the end, through its flexibility, innovation, and superb leadership, it was the one air force that did the most to assist in the end of the ground fighting in Europe."[17]

But such acclaim was double-sided. Air Staff historians were careful to portray the Ninth Air Force as exceptional and not a model upon which to base postwar organization. "The tactical air forces, although they performed marvelously the tasks assigned them, are not considered good prototypes for future air units," they concluded succinctly. Although Quesada protested the judgment of the study, it won the official approval of the new air chief, Tooey Spaatz, in June 1946.[18]

After that the structure of the peacetime air arm began to reflect the effort to recast the lessons of the war. In its first demobilization estimates in September 1945, the Army Air Forces contemplated a reduced force of 112 heavy bomber groups and ninety-five light- and fighter-bomber groups. By the end of 1946, these figures had changed to eighty-eight heavy bomber and forty-five light- and fighter-bomber groups; the ratio changed yet again in 1947 when the air arm established its final demobilization at seventy-five groups assigned to the strategic air forces and a mere twenty-five groups assigned to the tactical air forces. All the while, Pete Quesada complained that the new balance of strategic and tactical units was out of step with the experience of World War II. "We were forgetting the teachings of the war in Europe," he remembered years later.[19]

Be that as it may, air arm leaders were able to leverage its bombers to help gain their cherished independence from the Army in 1947. As a condition of this new autonomy Tooey Spaatz promised Army Chief of Staff Dwight Eisenhower a firm commitment to tactical aviation, and for a time the fighter pilots of the war won a reprieve from their swift decline. In 1948, the number of tactical groups increased from twenty-five to forty-eight, and Spaatz created the Tactical Air Command (TAC) as a coequal headquarters with the Strategic Air Command (SAC). Composed of the Third, Ninth, and Twelfth Air Forces, TAC was indeed an adequate pledge to the Army for ongoing close air support. To buttress this commitment even further, Spaatz gave Pete Quesada, the most prominent tactically-minded air officer, a promotion to lieutenant general and command of the new organization.

Quesada placed TAC headquarters at Langley Field, Virginia, to be near the Army Ground Forces Command at Fort Monroe. Together, he and the ground forces commander—first General Mark Clark and later General Jacob Devers—toiled to preserve the air-ground battle teams that had marked the European campaign. But Quesada could never get the necessary resources for simple maneuvers. The centerpiece of his efforts to maintain tactical air power were three exercises in 1947 and 1948 dubbed COMBINE I, II, and III, and even these operated on a shoestring account while General Curtis LeMay's SAC received fully 65 percent of the air arms's first independent budget. "If we are to be treated like this," a disgusted Quesada once told his deputy, Major General Robert Lee, "I do not want to be here."[20]

Toward the end of 1948 Quesada became so disillusioned with the decline of tactical aviation in the Air Force that he privately told young pilots to leave TAC if they harbored high ambitions. "He said to me, rather bitterly, that if I wanted to be a general I had better find a way into LeMay's SAC, or I would stay a colonel until retirement," one officer recalled. But if Pete Quesada had grown frustrated by the end of 1948, what happened the next year would truly dishearten him.[21]

Hoyt Vandenberg had become the Air Force's Chief of Staff upon Tooey Spaatz's retirement in April 1948. Later that summer the new chief began a reassessment of the Air Force's pledge to close air support. Reasoning that tactical air power would only be useful in a major war if an atomic offensive failed, Vandenberg decided to downgrade TAC. In December 1948 he stripped TAC of most of its planes and pilots and recast it as a "planning headquarters, charged with writing joint doctrinal manuals and organizing joint training exercises." At Langley, Pete Quesada resented the change, viewing it as a violation of the pact between Spaatz and Eisenhower to maintain tactical air support as a major function of the Air Force. Vandenberg disagreed, and not surprisingly the chief of staff won the argument.[22]

Quesada believed that his continued service as TAC commander would make him a "conspirator in an ugly mistake" and asked to be reassigned to a new duty. Vandenberg consented; he appointed Quesada to head a committee charged with combining the Air Force Reserves with the Air National Guard to save money. The job was fraught with pitfalls. Officers in the Reserves and the Guard had reason to fight the proposal and could make life difficult for those who sought to implement it. Indeed, combining the two forces, if it was possible at all, would require patience, tact, and diplomacy. Pete Quesada had many attributes, but these were not among them. As one general recalled of Quesada's new posting, "That job was political suicide."[23]

Foes of this integration soon ran Quesada out of the post. After two months at the task, leaders in the National Guard called for Quesada's resignation, citing his "authoritative and arrogant manner." This charac-

terization was consistent with the opinions of others, but the Guard
leadership no doubt also feared Quesada's reputation for accomplishing
tasks. They had no desire to see themselves subsumed into the inactive
reserves, and with political clout reaching into the Congress and White
House, the Guard successfully removed Quesada from the job in late
1949.

In other circumstances Quesada might have been despondent over
the firing, but by then he had already requested early retirement. Not
only was he frustrated at the turn away from tactical aviation, but he
had married Joseph Pulitzer's daughter Kate Davis (a war widow) in
1946 and now had two step-daughters and two sons of his own. After
years of service to his country Quesada felt he ought to provide for his
family. For him, then, 1949 marked the end of a promising career. For
the Air Force, 1949 underscored the postwar neglect of close air support. And for the nation, the changes made in 1949 fated the country to
serious doctrinal and tactical mistakes in Korea and Vietnam.[24]

In June 1950 North Korea invaded South Korea, sparking the Korean
Conflict. The early fighting underscored the atrophy of close air support in the American military, and the first months of war were marked
by all the failures that had visited the air arm in early World War II. As
Quesada prepared to retire, his old friend O.P. Weyland went to Korea
to fix the problems. But Weyland would not be able to remedy years of
neglect and indifference easily, and by the Korean Armistice no effective system had been established. In fact, throughout the Cold War
era—with its great emphasis on strategic nuclear deterrence—no good
system of close support would re-emerge. Most importantly, the Korean War revealed that as long as there was nuclear parity between the
U.S. and the USSR, atomic power, which had been the supreme justification for SAC just a few years earlier, was a virtual nonweapon. No nation would use it, and the Cold War's "hot" conflicts were in fact very
conventional in terms of ordnance.[25]

Pete Quesada continued an active life after leaving the Air Force,
serving in numerous capacities at defense contracting firms and, in the
Eisenhower Administration, as the first head of the Federal Aviation
Administration. But he was rarely involved in Air Force matters after
his retirement, even in an informal or unofficial capacity. No ranking

Air Force officer sought his advice when the Air Force re-emphasized its tactical air arm in the 1970s, for example. Although Quesada was ready to participate in whatever capacity air leaders deemed wise, no one came to him. After a long and both full and unfulfilled life, he died in February of 1993. The end had come for Pete Quesada.[26]

The story continues in the Air Force to this day. In 1982 the Department of Defense issued a doctrinal blueprint called "Airland Battle 2000." It envisioned a war of high mobility, small-unit innovation, and closer ground cooperation with an Air Force that would strike at enemy columns two to three days from an active front—just the kind of war Quesada fought fifty years ago. As recently as 1991, the Air Force underwent a major reorganization, eliminating both SAC and TAC and molding all aircraft into a single unit with the realization that tactical and strategic operations often meld together in war—just the insight Quesada's career foretold. And today, after the Persian Gulf War, the Army, Navy, and Air Force struggle to envision combined-arms conflict in the modern age. Although the technology is vastly different from that of World War II, these officers would do well to learn from Quesada's career.[27]

Notes

Introduction. History May Show They Saved the Day

1. Quesada interview with Steve Long and Ralph Stephenson, May 1975, USAMHI (hereafter cited as Quesada interview 1).
2. Quesada to Helen Quesada, 4 June 1944, Quesada Papers, Library of Congress (hereafter cited as LC); Quesada interview with Tom Hughes, May 1990 (hereafter cited as Quesada interview 2).
3. Unit History, 370th Fighter Group, June 1944, GP-370-HI, Air Force Historical Research Center (hereafter cited as AFHRC); Unit History, 404th Fighter Group, June 1944, GP-404-HI, AFHRC.
4. Quesada cited in *Impact: U.S. Tactical Airpower in Europe* (May 1945), xiv; Ferguson cited in Richard Kohn and Joseph Harahan, Eds., *Air Superiority in World War II and Korea: An interview with Generals James Ferguson, Robert M. Lee, William Momyer, and Lieutenant General Elwood R. Quesada*, 54; Chester Hansen War Diary, United States Army Military History Institute (hereafter cited as USAMHI); *The Public Papers of Dwight D. Eisenhower*, 5 June 1944.
5. Harold Holt, "Column Cover: The 366th Fighter Group In World War II," *American Aviation Historical Society*, Fall and Winter 1983; 235; 71st Fighter Wing History, June 1944, WG-71-HI, AFHRC.
6. A good description of Uxbridge on D-Day is in James Howard, *Roar of the Tiger*, 279–281.
7. Quesada interview 2.
8. W. F. Craven and J. L. Cate, *The Army Air Forces in World War II*, III, 186; Omar Bradley, *A Soldier's Story*, 259.
9. For detailed discussions on the landings, see Gordon Harrison, *Cross Channel Attack*.
10. Craven and Cate, *The Army Air Forces in World War II*, III, 190; Charles Gerhardt and Leonard Gerow cited in "Answers to Questionnaire for Key

Army Commanders on the Effects of Strategic and Tactical Air Power on Military Operations ETO," 533.4501-2, AFHRC (hereafter cited as Questionnaire).

11. Charles Gerhardt Memoirs, USAMHI; Harrison, 309; After Action Reports, V Corps, June 1944, Record Group 407, National Archives (hereafter cited as NA).

12. Max Hastings, *Overlord*, 94; Carlos D'Este, *Decision in Normandy*, 114; Harrison, 319.

13. Hastings, *Overlord*, 96.

14. Blair Garland interview, K239.0512-1806, AFHRC.

15. Cited in Hastings, 95.

16. Cited in Questionnaire, 533.4501-2, AFHRC.

17. Bradley, *A Soldier's Story*, 270; unidentified officer and Heubner cited in Hastings, 92, 152.

18. Nigel Hamilton, *Monty: Master of the Battlefield*, 623; Kean cited in Chester Hansen War Diary, 7 June 1944, USAMHI.

19. Quesada interview 2; "Signals Planning for OPS Neptune," Fall 1944, 533.4501-8, AFHRC; "Communications Aboard the Headquarters Ships," IX Tactical Air Command Plans for Neptune, 15 May 1944, 536.02, AFHRC. See also memo on Fighter-bomber control for D-Day, 533.4501-8, AFHRC.

20. Colonel Lorry Tindal interview, K239.0512-1776 AFHRC; Hoyt Vandenberg War Diary, Vandenberg Papers, LC.

21. Ninth Air Force Daily Journal, 6 June 1944, 533.305-2, AFHRC; "IX Tactical Air Plan, Signals Annex," 536.01 AFHRC; "Communication Facilities on the Headquarters Ships"; Craven and Cate, III, 192.

22. Quesada interview 2.

23. Biggers to Tom Hughes, 27 April 1992.

24. Holt, 234; Chief of Staff Daily Journal, Ninth Air Force, 6 and 7 June 1944, 533.305-4, AFHRC.

25. Holt, 236.

26. Chief of Staff Daily Journal, Ninth Air Force, 6 and 7 June 1944, 533.305-4; AFHRC; Unit Histories, June 1944, GP-365-HI, GP-366-HI, and GP-368-HI, all in AFHRC.

27. Office of the Chief of Staff, Intelligence, *Sunday Punch in Normandy*, 24, Air University Library (hereafter cited as AUL); "Summary of Operations: Ninth AF, June 1944," 533.4501-18 and 536.3061-2, AFHRC.

28. Harrison, 333; *The Public Papers of Dwight D. Eisenhower*, 8 June 1944.

29. Ninth Air Force telephone journal, 7, 8 June 1944, 533-3501-4, AFHRC.

30. IX TAC Unit History, June 1944, 536.02, AFHRC; pilot cited in *"Jabos Achtung*," 536.02, AFHRC; 365th Group History, June 1944, GP-365-HI, AFHRC; Chester Hansen War Diary, USAMHI. Sources do not agree on

the number of sorties flown by IX Fighter Command during the invasion. The figures here are composites from three sources: "Operational Summary for the Ninth Air Force, 6 June to 9 June 1944," 533.308-1, AFHRC; "Ninth Air Force Activities," 533.306-2, AFHRC; and the IX TAC Unit History. The totals only apply to sorties of direct support. All together in the two-day period, Quesada's planes flew 568 sorties covering the invasion navy, 464 sorties escorting the IX Troop Carrier Command, 3,303 air support sorties, and 195 antisub patrols.

31. Chester Hansen War Diary, 8 June 1944, USAMHI; Bradley to Eisenhower, 8 June 1944, *The Public Papers of Dwight D. Eisenhower*.

32. Bradley cited in Sheffield Edwards Papers, USAMHI; Collins and Gerow cited in Questionnaire, AFHRC. For the views of ordinary soldiers see Veteran Questionnaires, USAMHI, especially those of Colonel Kenneth Lord and Staff Sergeant Randolph Ginman.

33. Panzer commander cited in Gerd von Rundstedt interview, Sheffield Edwards Papers, USAMHI; German Seventh Army War Diary, 11 June 1944, 533.55-3, AFHRC; von Rundstedt interview with Tooey Spaatz, May 1945, Spaatz Papers, box 134, LC.

34. Cited in IX TAC Unit History, June 1944, 536.02 AFHRC.

35. *Report of the Commanding General of the Army Air Forces to the Secretary of War*, January 1944, 42; Hap Arnold, *Global Mission*, 290.

36. Arnold cited in United States Army Air Forces Historical Study, *The Eighth Air Force, April 1944 to May 1945*, 23, 218; Commanding General's Statistical Notebook, Arnold Papers, bx 78, LC.

37. Cited in United States Army Air Forces Historical Study, *The Tactical Use of Heavy Bombers in the Invasion of Normandy*, 1.

38. For an overview of air power in these wars, see Mark Clodfelter, *The Limits of Air Power*.

39. Bradley, 122.

40. Blair Garland interview, K239.0512-1806, AFHRC.

41. O. P. Weyland interview, K239.0512-1421, AFHRC.

42. Rice cited in *Time*, 30 September, 1991.

Chapter One. Unusual, Offbeat Assignments

1. Quesada interview 1; Quesada interview 2. Quesada's early history is drawn from these two sources, and quotations reflect his verbatim recollections.

2. For a firsthand account of the early history of army aviation, see Henry Arnold, *Global Mission*, 21–39.

3. For an excellent overview of American air power in the war, see Edward

Coffman, *The War to End All Wars: The Military Experience in World War I*, 187–211.

4. Irving Holley addresses the command structure and role of World War I aviation in *Ideas and Weapons*.

5. Ira Eaker interview, K239.0512-829, AFHRC, 103.

6. Maurer, 51–53; For Billy Mitchell's own thoughts on his court-martial, see William Mitchell, *Winged Defense*, 76–78, 167–170.

7. The exact number of aircraft in the Air Service in this period is not known, further reflecting the air arm's state of disarray in 1925. The figures cited are from a Presidential investigation known as the Morrow Board, cited in Holley, *Buying Aircraft*, 96–97.

8. Robert Mueller, *History of Air Force Installations*, 49–51.

9. Gordon Swanborough and Peter Bowers, *United States Military Aircraft Since 1909*, 203–208; Quesada interview 2.

10. Quesada interview 1; Maurer, 55–59.

11. Quesada interview 1.

12. Quesada interview 2.

13. Swanborough, 706; Quesada interview 2.

14. Cadet class list, Quesada Papers, LC; Quesada interview 1.

15. Aircraft Accidents Reports, Elwood R. Quesada, 14 July 1925, 200.3912-1 AFHRC.

16. Quesada interview 1; Aircraft Accident Reports, Elwood R. Quesada, 20 August 1925, 200.3912-1, AFHRC.

17. Quesada interview 1.

18. Quesada interview with Tom Hughes, June 1990 (hereafter cited as Quesada interview 3).

19. Quesada interview 3; Swanborough, 207–209.

20. Maurer, 197.

21. Quesada interview 1.

22. Mueller, 31-24, Quesada interview 3; Swanborough, 659; Quesada interview 1.

23. Eaker to Richard Witkin, 27 January 1950, in Eaker Collection, microfilm #260, AFHRC; Aircraft Accident Reports, Elwood R Quesada, 15 March 1928, 200.3912-1, AFHRC.

24. Except where specifically noted, the following account is a composite taken from Quesada interviews 1 and 2 and Air Corps Newsletter accounts.

25. Eaker to Richard Witkin, 27 January 1950, in Eaker Collection, microfilm #260, AFHRC.

26. DeWitt Copp, *A Few Great Captains*, 189.

27. Quesada interview 3.

28. Quesada interview 2; Aircraft Accident Reports, Elwood R. Quesada,

200.3912-1, AFHRC; Eaker to Quesada, 15 January 1948, and Quesada to Eaker, 20 January 1948, in Eaker Collection, microfilm #260, AFHRC.

29. Eaker interview, K239.0512-829, AFHRC; Spaatz interview, box 149, Spaatz Papers, LC.

30. Eaker to Richard Witkin, 27 January 1950, in Eaker Collection, microfilm #260, AFHRC.

31. Cited in undated and unnamed newspaper article, 536.08, AFHRC.

32. Air Corps Newsletter, 31 January 29 (hereafter cited as ACNL).

33. *Time*, 11 January 1929, 24.

34. Cited in undated and unnamed newspaper article, 536.08, AFHRC; ACNL, 31 January 1929; Quesada remarks in *Los Angeles Examiner*, 5 January 1929.

35. Quesada cited in Spaatz Papers, box 10, LC.

36. ACNL, 23 February 1929; Spaatz cited in undated and unnamed newspaper article, 536.08, AFHRC.

37. ACNL, 10 and 31 January 1929; New York Times, 11 January 1929, 1; Blair Garland interview, K239.0512-1332, AFHRC.

38. Quesada interview 1.

39. Quesada interview 1.

40. "Statement of Trubee Davison" before the Baker Board, cited in the *Baker Board Report*, 167.66-81, AFHRC.

41. John Shiner, *Foulois and the U.S. Army Air Corps, 1931-1934*, 147–150; Quesada interview 3.

42. Shiner, 147–158; Quesada interview 2; Maurer, 191–221.

43. For Davison's firsthand accounts of the safari to Africa, see *Saturday Evening Post*, 7 July 1933, 12–19, and "Elephants, Lions, and Airplanes," *Natural History*, March–April 1934.

44. Quesada interview 2.

45. Benjamin Foulois, *From the Wright Brothers to the Astronauts*, 235; press statement, Benjamin Foulois, 15 March 1934, Foulois Papers, box 15, LC. Foulois remembered the air mails as one of the three most important aerial events of his lifetime (along with the Wright Brothers' Kitty Hawk flight and the tactical use of airplanes during the Pershing expedition to Mexico). He overstated the air-mail mission, but his belief reflected the importance airmen placed on Roosevelt's mandate. For a detailed study of the air-mail episode, see John Shiner, *The Army Flies the Mail*.

46. Rickenbacker cited in Baker Board Hearings, in Senate Document 23, 31st Congress, 1112–1118; Swanborough, 196; Rogers cited in *Congressional Record*, LXX-VII 4501. See also Foulois, *Memoirs*, 242–43; *Los Angeles Times*, February 17, 1933, 1; Copp, 187–189.

47. Shiner, *Foulois*, 130; Copp, 190.

48. Pilot rosters, Foulois Papers, box 15, LC; Copp, 182; Foulois, *Memoirs*, 127; Quesada interview 1.

49. Quesada interview 1; Jones cited in Copp, 190; Foulois cited in *Los Angeles Examiner*, 18 February 1934.

50. Quesada interview 1; Swanborough, 249.

51. Copp, 202.

52. Quesada interview 3; Copp, 202.

53. Shiner, *Foulois*, 130.

54. Foulois, *Memoirs*, 213.

55. Roosevelt to Dern, Arnold Papers, box 223, LC.

56. James, 382–384; memo, MacArthur to Hurley, 14 March 34, cited in "Jones Chronology," 384.10 AFHRC; Shiner, *Foulois*, 133; Foulois, *Memoirs*, 245–46. Weather was not the only variable contributing to the Air Corps' initial air-mail failures. The Post Office had issued a special cancellation stamp to commemorate the event. As February 19 due near, philatelists deluged post offices throughout the country with huge bundles of letters. This completely upset the original sortie rates based on previous daily volume (Baker Board hearings, 2231–2233; Eldon W. Davis, "Army and the Air Mail," *Airpower Historian*, IX, 35–51).

57. Arnold cited in Harold Bowman manuscript, Murray Green Collection, United States Air Force Academy Library Special Collections (hereafter cited as USAFA); Foulois, *Memoirs* 118; *Washington Evening Star*, February 22, 1; *Washington Post*, February 22, 1.

58. Shiner, *Foulois*, 220; "Final Report of the Army Air Corps Air Mail Operations," 6 October 34, 111.23-40, AFHRC.

59. Shiner, *Foulois*, 220; "Final Report of the Army Air Corps Air Mail Operations," 6 October 34, 111.23-40, AFHRC; Copp, 219; Quesada interview 3; Foulois, *Memoirs*, 200.

60. Quesada interview 3.

61. Maurer, 187; Shiner, *Foulois*, 134.

62. Cited in *Congressional Record*, LXXVIII, 3615.

63. Copy of Drum's testimony before the Rogers Committee, June 5, 1934, 81, 84–86, 89, *Hearings-F*, 313.23–41, AFHRC (Benjamin Foulois Collection); Shiner, *Foulois*, 134–147; Foulois, *Memoirs*, 243; *Washington Post*, 22 July 34, 1.

64. Maurer, 139–141.

65. *Congressional Record*, LXXIX, 9392, Foulois, *Memoirs*, 272.

66. Eaker interview, K239.0512-829, AFHRC; Quesada interview 3.

67. "Eastern Zone Summary Report of the Air Mails," 141.10A, AFHRC.

68. Quesada interview 3.

69. Quesada interview 3.

70. Quesada interview 3. For a good account of Marshall during these years, see Forrest Pogue, *Education of a General*.

71. Pogue, *Marshall*, 123; Quesada interview 3.
72. Quesada interview 1; Frank Killigrew, "Impact of the Great Depression on the Army," *Perspectives*, XII, 1–12; "Reduction of other Army Services under the Air Corps Five Year Program," undated chart, DEF C-2B, in Foulois Collection, box 18, AFHRC; "Relation of Air Corps Expenditures to Total War Department Expenditures, 1925–1938," 167.65 AFHRC. Specifically, Infantry lost 3,108 men to the air arm; Cavalry, 1,342; Field Artillery, 826; Coast Artillery, 285; Engineers, 243; and Miscellaneous, 63. Although the air arm complained vigorously about the General Staff's meager support of the five-year program, ground generals in fact spent 94 percent of all the money Congress allocated for the project—a high level of funding in light of the nation's economic woes.
73. James, I, 162–166; Quesada interview with Tom Hughes, October 1990 (hereafter cited as Quesada interview 4).
74. Quesada interview 4.
75. Quesada interview 3; Maurer, 412. For firsthand background on the GHQ Air Force, see Frank Andrews, "The GHQ Air Force as an Instrument of National Defense," *Army Ordnance Magazine*, 18:15 (November–December 1937).
76. Quesada interview 3; Shiner, *Foulois*, 204.
77. Quesada interview 1.

Chapter Two. They Allowed Their Doctrine to Become Their Strategy

1. Quesada interview with Tom Hughes, July 1990 (hereafter cited as Quesada interview 5).
2. Quesada interview with Major Ken Leisch, July 1960, K146.34-84 AFHRC (hereafter cited as Quesada interview 6); Quesada interview with Edgar Puryear, September 1977, K239.0512-1485, AFHRC (hereafter cited as Quesada interview 7).
3. For a detailed listing of classes at the ACTS, see Robert Finney, *Air University Historical Study Number 100: History of the Air Corps Tactical School, 1920–1940*, Appendixes 2 and 3.
4. For details on the specific building projects, see Meuller, 118–120.
5. Finney, 7, 18–20; Quesada interview 4.
6. ACTS Lecture, "An Inquiry into the Subject of War," 1935, 248.11-19, AFHRC.
7. Copp, 212–213; memo, Director of Instruction, ACTS, 30 March 35, 245.111, AFHRC. For a good but brief treatment of Harold George, see Haywood Hansell, "Harold George: Apostle of Air Power," in Frisbee, 73–98.
8. ACTS Lecture, "The Air Force," General, 1935–1936, 248.101.1, AFHRC;

Quesada interview 3. For fuller accounts of Wilson and his ideas, see Finney, 31–37, and Frisbee, 79–83.

9. Walker cited in Finney, 33; Frisbee, 77–78.

10. Wright Brothers cited in Arnold, *Global Mission*, 149.

11. Hansell interview, Murray Green Collection, box 43, USAFA.

12. Arnold, 154; "Report of the March Field Exercises, March 1932," B78.A20-F9, AFHRC; memo, Colonel Harmon to Lieutenant Colonel Wilson, 1 May 39, with attached comments, 245.282.21, AFHRC; Thomas Greer, *The Development of Air Doctrine in the Army Air Arm, 1917–1941*, 150–152. For a detailed description of Chennault's time at the ACTS, see Jack Sampson, *Chennault*, Chapter 3. The best single biography of Chennault is Martha Byrd, *Chennault: Giving Wings to the Tiger*.

13. Claire Chennault, "Why Pursuit?" *The Coast Artillery Journal*, 15.2, 7.

14. Claire Chennault, "Why Pursuit?" *The Coast Artillery Journal*, 15:1; 15:2; 15:3; Chennault, *Way of a Fighter*, 36–38.

15. Lecture, Haywood Hansell, "Development of the U.S. Concept of Bombardment Operations," 16 February 1951, 13, 89F.314-39 AFHRC.

16. Chennault, *Way of a Fighter*, 40–47. Chennault's memoirs, written with bitterness in 1947, must be treated with care. His recollections here are corroborated by academic biographies and Quesada (Quesada interviews 1, 4).

17. Lecture, "The Air Force," General, 248.101.1 AFHRC; memo, Brigadier General Hume Peabody to the Director, Research Science Initiative, 19 April 1954, 312.43.40, AFHRC.

18. Lecture, "Combined Operations," 1936, 240.136-4, AFHRC; memos to Assistant Commandant from Director of Instruction, 21 December 1934 and 31 January 1935, both in 145.93-116, AFHRC; Finney, 30. Ground and general subjects, which had comprised 54 percent of instruction in 1927, received only 15 percent of class time in 1935. Air subjects not associated with bombardment, which totaled 716 hours in the early 1920s, received a scant 204 hours.

19. Finney, 20 and Appendixes 2 and 3. The four students from outside the Air Corps during Quesada's year at the ACTS came from the Infantry and the Field and Coast Artillery.

20. Finney, 22–24; Quesada interview 4; Lecture, "Naval Operations," 1936, 169.234-10A, AFHRC.

21. Quesada interview 1.

22. Quesada interview with Michael Reed, K239.0512-1813, AFHRC (hereafter cited as Quesada interview 8).

23. Lecture, Oscar Westover, 26 April 35, 541.127-134, AFHRC.

24. Quesada interview 4; Accident Report File, Elwood R. Quesada, 200.3912-1, AFHRC. For a good account of the Command and General

Staff School in the interwar years, see Timothy Nenninger, "Leavenworth and its Critics: The US Army Command and General Staff School, 1920–1940," *The Journal of Military History*, April 1994.

25. Class rolls, Command and General Staff School (CGSS), Research Floor, CGSS Library. For more information on Kepner, see Paul Henry, "William Kepner: All the Way to Berlin," in Frisbee.

26. Westover to Chief of Staff, 7 August 1937, cited in Nenninger, 223.

27. Quesada interview 4. At Leavenworth in 1936 there were seventy-one Infantry officers, thirty-nine Artillery officers, and eighteen Cavalry officers.

28. Nenninger, 219.

29. Cited in Pogue, *George C. Marshall: Education of a General*, 101.

30. Quesada interview 4. In early spring 1944, while Quesada was preparing his IX Tactical Air Command for the Normandy invasion, he visited Rose, then commanding a cavalry brigade in Italy. There a German sniper shot Quesada in the buttocks. Afterwards, Quesada delighted in referring to Rose as "one pain in the ass friend" (Quesada interview 2).

31. Quesada interview 8.

32. CGSS course text entitled "Attack," 1934, 75.

33. "Attack," 129.

34. Quesada notebook courtesy of Kate Davis Quesada.

35. Quesada interview 4.

36. Quesada 201 File, Quesada Papers, LC.

37. Annual Report of the Secretary of War, 1920, 147.35–38, AFHRC; Futrell, 20; Holley, 124.

38. Swanborough, 210–211; Eastman, 217; Maurer, 289. For a fuller account of Navy–Army infighting than is possible here, see Frisbee, 127–139; 156–167; and Copp, Chapter 7.

39. Quesada interview 3; Swanborough, 212; Copp, 423–24; ACNL, 7 May and 14 May 1938.

40. Copp, 232, 423.

41. Copp, 423; Copp, 231; Maurer, 247.

42. Arnold, 176.

43. Edward Haley, *Makers of U.S. Naval Policy*, 300–321.

44. Quesada interview 4; Quesada 201 File, Quesada Papers, LC; Frisbee, 167; Swanborough, 210.

45. Quesada interview 4; Haley, 189–191; Quesada interview 1; Frisbee, 168.

46. Quesada interview 8.

47. Quesada interview 8.

48. Copp, 452; Mark Watson, *The War Department: Chief of Staff, Prewar Planning and Preparations*, 136–137.

49. Arnold, 132; Wesley Craven and James Cate, Eds., *The Army Air Forces in World War II*, I, 104; Maurer, 411; Arnold, 179.

50. Marshall cited in Pogue, *Ordeal and Hope*, 77; Watson, 107, 132–137; Copp, 456.

51. Annual Reports, Chief of the Air Corps, 1938, 1939, 145.111, AFHRC; Robert Boylon, *Development of the Long-Range Fighter Escort*, 22–24. The research programs begun in 1939 led to some of World War II's most illustrious planes: the North American B-25, the Martin B-26, the Douglas A-20, and the Boeing B-29.

52. Copp, 234; Quesada interview 4.

53. Quesada interview 4.

54. Quesada interview 4.

55. Cited in David Mets, *Master of Air Power: General Carl A. Spaatz*, 119. For more on Arnold's leadership style, see Thomas Coffey, *Hap*, especially Chapter 3.

56. Craven and Cate, I, 126; Watson, 397.

57. Quesada interview 4; Craven and Cate, I, 103.

58. Quesada interview 4; Coffey, 98–101; Pogue, 137; *Army Air Force Reference History No. 6: Distribution of Air Materials to the Allies*, 18.

59. *Army Air Forces Historical Study No. 22: Legislation Relating to the AAF Material Program*, 19–20; Craven and Cate, I, 135; *Army Air Forces Reference History No. 6: Distribution of Air Material to the Allies*, 56–57.

60. Arnold, 154; draft, "Army Air Forces Historical Study: Logistical Plans and Problems, 1941–43, with Special Reference to Build-up of the Eighth Air Force," 3; Boylon, 26; Craven and Cate, I, 148–14.

61. Quesada interview 4; Arnold, 212; Copp, 413; *Army Air Forces Historical Study No. 22: Legislation Relating to the AAF Material Program*, 34.

62. Watson, 286; Candee cited in Quesada 201 File, Quesada Papers, LC; Quesada interview 4.

63. Watson, 230; Craven and Cate, I, 124; memo, Stimson to Arnold, 14 April, 41, cited in *Army Air Forces Reference History No. 6: Distribution of Air Material to the Allies*.

64. Arnold Trip Diary, Arnold Papers, box 271, LC (hereafter cited as Arnold Trip Diary).

65. Arnold Trip Diary, 12 April 1941.

66. Craven and Cate, I, 135; Frisbee, 184; *Army Air Forces Historical Study no. 40: The Ferrying Command*.

67. Arnold Trip Diary, 15 April 1941.

68. Arnold Trip Diary, 15 April 1941.

69. Arnold Trip Diary, 18 April 1941.

70. For more information on the war's early efforts at bombing, see Max Hastings, *Bomber Command*, especially 99–115.

71. Arnold Trip Diary, 21 April 1941.

72. Kepner interview, AFHRC; Quesada to Helen Quesada, 20 April 1941,

Quesada Papers, LC. The best account of the Battle of Britain is Hough and Richards, *The Battle of Britain.*

73. Craven and Cate, I, 146; Watson, 156.

74. Citations of AWPD-1 taken from Craven and Cate, I, 148.

75. Craven and Cate, I, 148.

76. Marshall cited in Pogue, *George C. Marshall: Ordeal and Hope,* 290; memo; Marshall to Arnold, 22 June 41, cited in Watson, 163.

77. Stimson cited in Arnold, 199; Craven and Cate, I, 146.

78. Quesada interview 4; draft, "Army Air Forces Historical Study, Logistical Plans and Problems, 1941–1943, with Special Reference to Build-Up of the Eighth Air Force," 3; Copp, 407–409; "Biographical Sketch of Pete Quesada," USAF Press Release, 23, July 47, 333.213–220, AFHRC.

79. Swanborough, 319–320; Quesada interview 1.

80. Quesada interview 4; Frisbee, 132; Copp, 312, 356.

81. Swanborough, 234–236.

82. Quesada interview 1; Craven and Cate, I, 154.

83. Arnold, 187; Unit History, 33rd Fighter Group, 39, AFHRC.

84. Copp, 444; News Briefs, The Coast Artillery Journal, 21:5 (May 1942); Quesada interview 1; Glenn Barcus interview, K239.0512-908, AFHRC, 89.

85. Frisbee, 169; Quesada interview 4.

86. Quesada interview 1.

87. Cited in Pogue, *George C. Marshall: Ordeal and Hope,* 96, 103.

88. Quesada interview 1.

89. Quesada interviews 1; 4; Craven and Cate, I, 113–130.

90. Quesada interview 8.

91. Quesada interview 2.

Chapter Three. We All Learned a Hell of a Lot

1. Quesada interview 1; War Diary, First Air Defense Wing, December 1942–September 1943, WG-62-HI, AFHRC.

2. Quesada interview 1; War Diary, First Air Defense Wing, December 1942–October 1943, WG-62-HI, AFHRC.

3. Quesada interview 1; War Diary, First Air Defense Wing, December 1942–October 1943, WI-62-HI, AFHRC.

4. For a concise account of the mounting fight in Africa, see Peter Calvocoressi, *Total War* I, 68–84.

5. For a discussion of the American supply situation in early 1942, see Craven and Cate, II, 7. The Air Corps supplied the initial American forces to ensure safe passage of Allied supplies through Africa. The Arnold-Portal

Agreement, signed on June 21, assigned a total of nine combat groups to the Middle East and Egypt to safeguard the air routes (Craven and Cate, II, 14).

6. Montgomery cited in Nigel Hamilton, *Monty's War Years*, 145, 148, 213; Eisenhower to Thomas Handy, 7 December 1942, Eisenhower Papers, Pre-Presidential file, Dwight D. Eisenhower Library (hereafter cited as DDE); Quesada interview with Eisenhower Library, 1973–1975, Eisenhower Library, 28–29 (hereafter cited as Quesada interview 10).

7. Arnold, *Global Mission*, 326; Arnold to Spaatz, 3 January 43, Spaatz Papers, LC.

8. Eisenhower cited in Diary of Harry Butcher, 4 January 1943, in Eisenhower Papers, Pre-Presidential files, DDE. Craven and Cate, II, and George F. Howe, *Northwest Africa: Seizing the Initiative in the West* both detail air operations in the African campaign.

9. War Diary, First Air Defense Wing, January 1943, in WG-62-HI, AFHRC. The permanent echelons of an Air Defense Wing included a headquarters squadron, two fighter control squadrons, and a signal aircraft warning battalion.

10. Cited in War Diary, Second Air Defense Wing, January 1943, in WG-63-HI, AFHRC; War Diary, First Air Defense Wing, January 1943, WI-62-HI, AFHRC.

11. Quesada interview 7, 28–29; Quesada to Alice Mills, 3 May 1943, Quesada Papers, LC.

12. Unit History, 52nd Fighter Group, April 1943, GP-52-SU-RE-D, AFHRC, 74; Craven and Cate, II, 295; Unit History, 52nd Fighter Group, April 1943, GP-52-SU-RE-D, AFHRC, 65.

13. Craven and Cate, II, 162; Spaatz to Hap Arnold, 14 January 1943, in Spaatz Papers, LC. For a good discussion of these changes, see both Howe, 354–356, 492–497; and Craven and Cate, II, 162–166. Eisenhower named Britons to the other posts as well. Earl Anderson and Andrew Cunningham commanded the ground and sea forces respectively.

14. Quesada interview 3.

15. Craven and Cate, II, 416; NAAF General Order #1 cited in "Minutes of the Air Officer Commanding, Northwest African Coastal Air Force (NACAF), AIR24/1239 Public Record Office (hereafter cited as PRO).

16. Churchill to Hugh Lloyd, no date, Lloyd Papers, box 1127, RAF Museum, Hendon, London; Roosevelt to Hugh Lloyd, 27 January 1943, Lloyd Papers, box 1127, RAF Museum, Hendon, London; "Notes on Africa, in photo album, Lloyd Papers, RAF Museum, Hendon, London. In full Parliamentary session, Churchill declared Lloyd the "architect of the brilliant defense at Malta." So heroic did the King consider the Malta defense, in fact, that he eventually bestowed on the entire island the civil Victoria

Cross, the first time that decoration had been given to a part of the Empire.

17. "Notes on Africa," in photo album, box 1722, Lloyd Papers, RAF Museum, Hendon, London.

18. NAAF General Order #1, 18 February 1943, Spaatz Papers, box 142, LC; "Brief Outline History, NACAF," 618.01-1, AFHRC.

19. Quesada to Elise and Harriet (no last names found), 26 April 1943, Quesada Papers, LC.

20. Kenneth Wade to Tom Hughes, 11 February 1992.

21. D. B. Harris to Tom Hughes, 11 January 1992; Richard Carter to Tom Hughes, 27 January 1992. Fourteen former pilots of the 81st Fighter Group sought out the author some fifty years after these events to register their utter distaste for Quesada. In 1992, General Quesada did not recall Kenneth Wade or these incidents. Still, the consensus of these men after over five decades of reflection constitutes compelling historical evidence.

22. Wade to Tom Hughes, 11 February 1992.

23. Redline messages, Lloyd via Quesada to Spaatz, 28 August 1944; Quesada to Tooey Spaatz, 29 August 1943, Spaatz to Quesada, 24 August 1943, Spaatz to Quesada and Lloyd, 29 August 1943, all in Spaatz Papers, box 44, LC. Lloyd to Mrs. Lloyd, 23 August 1943, Lloyd Papers, RAF Museum, Hendon, England.

24. Operation Order #13, NACAF, 618.512, AFHRC.

25. Unit History, 15th Fighter Control Squadron, January 1943–February 1944, SQ-FI-CONTL-15-HI, AFHRC; Quesada interview with Tom Hughes, January 1991 (hereafter cited as Quesada interview 9).

26. Quesada interview 3.

27. Albert Garland and Howard Smyth, *Sicily and the Surrender of Italy*, 69. In fact, in ways HUSKY was the largest amphibious operation of the war. It employed more assault troops on beaches farther apart than the men who waded into Normandy eleven months later.

28. Quesada interview 4; Arnold to Spaatz, in Murray Green Collection, box 56), USAFA; Craven and Cate, II, 430. Flyers were not the only ones to view Pantelleria as an experiment in independent bombardment. Eisenhower had told Marshall the operation could reveal whether air power can take territory "the same way as ground forces" (Eisenhower to Marshall, 13 May 1943, cited in Garland and Smyth, 70).

29. Garland and Smyth, 70; Allied intelligence estimates cited in NACAF *Daily Staff Journal*, April 1943–September 1943, 6–9 June 1943, AFHRC.

30. Quesada interview 4; cited in War Diary, 350th Fighter Group, June 1943, GP-350-HI, AFHRC, 40.

31. Cited in Unit History, 52nd Fighter Group, June 1943, GP-52-SU-RE-D, AFHRC, 66.

32. War Diary, 81st Fighter Group, June 1943, GP-81-HI, AFHRC; Operations Record Book, RAF 323 Wing, June 1943, AIR26/26, PRO; German commander cited in "Minutes of the Air Officer Commanding, NACAF, June 1943, AIR24/1235 PRO; Quesada to Margaret McGee, 18 June 43, Quesada Papers, LC.

33. Garland and Smyth, 69; Craven and Cate, II, 428.

34. Craven and Cate, II, 421; War Diary, First Air Defense Wing, June 1943, WG-62-HI AFHRC. The little island was also well covered by pillboxes, machine-gun nests, trenches, and barbed wire.

35. Arnold and Spaatz reactions cited by Lawrence Kuter in an interview with Murray Green, Murray Green Collection, USAFA; Spaatz cited in Spaatz War Diary, Spaatz Papers, LC; Unit History, 52nd Fighter Group, June 1943, GP-52-SU-RE-D, AFHRC, 66.

36. Craven and Cate, II, 422–432. Spaatz to Arnold, 19 June 1943, copy in Eisenhower Papers, Pre-Presidential files, Principal File, box 5, DDE. American intelligence estimates of "doubtful" esprit de corps on the islands only hinted at the low morale on Pantelleria and Lampedusa. Planners had estimated that 10 percent of the aerial ordnance would fall within a 100-yard radius of the targets, but in fact the planes only averaged between 2.6 percent and 6.4 percent. Certain British records are the only contemporaneous records that record some reservations about the Pantelleria operations. See "Narrative of Events," (Form 540), NACAF, 1 July 1943, AIR24/1235, PRO; Operation Record Book, RAF 323 Wing, 29 June 1943, AIR26/426, PRO.

37. Quesada interview 2. The misinterpretation of CORKSCREW was indeed unfortunate. Airmen could have drawn important lessons from it. For example, CORKSCREW revealed inadequate communications between the three armed services and the importance of well-defined bomb lines, bomb size, and fuse duration. The Allies paid for their obstructed perception in future operations.

38. For a fuller discussion of Allied planning for HUSKY, see Garland and Smyth, 52–62.

39. "Narrative of Events" NACAF (Form 540), June, 1943, Appendix C, AIR 24/1235, PRO; "Hours Flown by A/C and Crew" NACAF, Our Victory, 618.01, AFHRC.

40. "Convoy Defense in NACAF," NACAF Our Victory, 7, 618.01, AFHRC.

41. "Convoy Defense in NACAF," NACAF Our Victory, 7–8, 618.01, AFHRC; "Allied Ships, Planes Score Vital Victory" War Diary, 52nd Fighter Group, June, 1943, GP-52-SU, AFHRC.

42. "Allied Ships, Planes Score Vital Victory" War Diary, 52nd Fighter Group, June, 1943, GP-52-SU, AFHRC; Quesada interview 2; "Convoy Escort"

Unit History, June 1943, XII Fighter Command, June–September 1943, 654.01, AFHRC.

43. Operations Record Book, 323 Wing, 27 June 1943, AIR26/426 PRO; pilot cited in Unit History, 350th Fighter Group, GP-350-HI, AFHRC.

44. Spaatz cited in Operations Record Book, 323 Wing, 27 June 1943, AIR26/426, PRO. In the context of the war, defending TEDWORTH was a very minor episode. It appears in only the most detailed official histories of the Mediterranean Theater. Nevertheless, it was an important part of Quesada's own journey to a tactical leader, and here merits attention.

45. "Anti-Submarine Effort, March 26–October 6," NACAF, *Our Victory* 618.01, AFHRC; Quesada interview 6; "Anti-Submarine Intelligence Summary," July 1943, Narrative of Events (Form 540), NACAF, AIR24/1235, PRO.

46. "U-Boat Menace," 12, NACAF, *Our Victory*, 618.01, AFHRC; War Diary, XII Fighter Command, July 1943, 654.01, AFHRC. Operations Order #1, NACAF, Appendix A: Operation HUSKY, AIR24/1237; Operation Order #3, NACAF, Appendix C: Operation AVALANCHE AIR24/1237; Unit History, 350th Fighter Group, July, 1943, GP-350-HI AFHRC; War Diary, XII Fighter Command, July 1943, 654.01 AFHRC. Tallies of ships participating in HUSKY vary from about 1,000 to over 2,000. The numbers here represent a median estimate of the vessels involved in the invasion of Sicily. HUSKY forces lost an additional six ships once off the coast of Sicily to naval and shore fire.

47. Quesada interview 2.

48. The following narrative is from "African Incident," a formal report and transcript of radio calls sent and received by the 15th Fighter Control Squadron, in SQ-FI-CONTL-15-HI, 9 January 1942–February 1944, AFHRC. Quotations are taken directly from this transcript.

49. Quesada interview 4.

50. Garland and Smyth, 156, 423.

51. Redline message, Quesada to Spaatz, n.d. (week of July 12), Spaatz Papers, LC. Quesada cited in "African Incident," SQ-FI-CONTL-15-HI, AFHRC.

52. Garland and Smyth, 421; Craven and Cate, II, 486; McNair to Brigadier General Henry Reilly, 21 September 1943, McNair Papers, USAMHI.

53. "Summary of Events" Minutes of the AOC, NACAF, July, 1943, AIR24/1239, PRO; Unit History, XII Fighter Command, July 1943, 654.01 AFHRC; Unit History, 52 Fighter Group, August, 1943, 71, GP-52-SU-RE-D AFHRC; pilot cited in Unit History, 52nd Fighter Group, August 1943, 72–73, GP-52-SU-RE-D, AFHRC.

54. Smyth and Garland, 262; Craven and Cate, II, 499, 503. The respective navies also realized the importance of effective air cover, and ponied up

four escort carriers to bolster Coastal's protective umbrella. HMS *Hilary* acted as an auxiliary control ship, and USS *Samuel Chase* and HMS *Ulster Queen* performed back-up duties.

55. Craven and Cate, II, 512. Daily Journal, NACAF Advanced Command Post, July 1943–August 1943, 618.13/microfilm roll A6015, AFHRC.

56. Quesada letters to Helen Quesada, 11 July 1943, 14 August 1943, 1 September 1943, 9 September, 1943; all in Quesada Papers, LC.

57. Quesada to Buddy Quesada, 18 October 1943, Quesada Papers, LC.

58. Quesada interview 3; Craven and Cate, II, 520; Operational Order #3, NACAF, Appendix C: Operation AVALANCHE, AIR24/1237, PRO. LST 305 controlled the Coastal planes over the various convoys.

59. Cited in Craven and Cate, II, 520.

60. Craven and Cate, II, 523, 537–538, 544, 585.

61. Cited in Craven and Cate, II, 536; 542, 544.

62. Craven and Cate, II, 538.

63. Quesada interview 7; Operations Record Book, 323 Wing, AIR26/426, PRO; Unit History, XII Fighter Command, August and September 1943, 654.01, AFHRC; Unit History, 52nd Fighter Group, 72, GP-52-SU-RE-D, AFHRC; War Diary, 52nd Fighter Group, September 1943, GP-52-SU, AFHRC. The RAF units assigned to Coastal also reflected this inactivity. "The month provided our anti-shipping aircraft with little or nothing in the way of targets—Corsica and Sardina had fallen and enemy shipping kept close in to German occupied shores where it could enjoy fighter protection. . . . in addition, with the Allied occupation of southern Italy and Sardina, the enemy has been denied the use of forward air fields and as a result, there has been an absence of attacks on the vast majority of cities we defend."

64. Quesada to Colonel Trubee Davison, 7 August, 1943; Quesada to Eaker, 29 August 1943; Quesada to Helen Quesada, 1 September 1943, Quesada Papers, LC. For more on Quesada's transfer to England, see redline message traffic between Spaatz and Eaker, September 1943, Spaatz Papers, LC.

65. War Diary, XII Fighter Command, October 1943, 654.01, AFHRC; Quesada to Lloyd, 22 October 1943, Quesada Papers, LC; Lloyd to wife, 8 August 1943, Lloyd Papers, RAF Museum, Hendon, London; Spaatz cited in Quesada 201 File, Quesada Papers, LC.

66. Quesada to Larry Bell, 16 July 1944, in Quesada Papers, LC; Paul Christy to Tom Hughes, 12 March 1992.

67. For Lloyd's assessment of Coastal's performance through September 1943, see NACAF, *Our Victory*.

68. Arnold to Eisenhower, ? June 1943, Dwight D. Eisenhower Pre-Presidential Papers, Principal File, box 5, DDE.

69. Field Manual 100-20 "Command and Employment of Air Power."

70. William Momyer cited in Richard Kohn, *Air Superiority in World War II, Korea, and Vietnam: An Interview with General James Ferguson, General Robert Lee, General William Momyer, and Lieutenant General Elwood Quesada*, 36; *Condensed Analysis of the Ninth Air Force in the European Theater of Operations, 1946*, 13. For a detailed account of the doctrinal changes in close air support in Africa, see Dan Mortensen, *A Pattern for Joint Operations: World War II Close Air Support North Africa*. Arnold's vocal prewar and postwar advocacy of strategic bombardment and an independent air force obscure his wartime actions. As his foremost biographer Murray Green suggests in an unpublished manuscript, Arnold was more balanced in his views about tactical aviation during the war (Green to Tom Hughes, 29 June 1992).

71. Quesada interviews 4, 7.

Chapter Four. All That I Can Do Is Far Short of That Which Is Required of Me

1. Joint Commander Meeting minutes, 12 October 1943, 533.02 AFHRC.

2. The discontinuous and oft-interrupted planning of the invasion is well told elsewhere. The principal pre-OVERLORD conferences were ARCADIA (Washington, January 1942), SYMBOL (Casablanca, January 1943), TRIDENT (Washington, May 1943), QUADRANT (Quebec, August 1943), SEXTANT (Cairo, November 1943), and EUREKA (Tehran, November/December 1943). The seven invasion plans were ROUNDUP (various 1941–1943 plans for an attack in the waning moments of war), SLEDGEHAMMER (a limited-objective plan in 1942 designed as a sacrifice operation to aid Russia), COCKADE (a more developed version of SLEDGEHAMMER for 1943), SKYSCRAPER (a plan by the Combined Commanders for a full-fledged assault in 1943), JUPITER (a 1942–1943 plan to invade Norway), BUCCANEER (an operation planned against the Andaman Islands in the Bay of Bengal for fall 1943), RANKIN (a contingency plan for returning to the Continent in the event of German internal collapse), and OVERLORD. These conferences and plans are detailed in Gordon Harrison, *Cross Channel Attack*, Chapters 2, 3.

3. Eaker to Arnold, 6 September 1943, box 16, Eaker Papers, LC. By spring 1944, the Ninth Air Force consisted of an Engineer Command, Bomber Command, Fighter Command, two Tactical Air Commands, Troop Carrier Command, Service Command, and an Air Defense Command.

4. War Department Press Release, 25 May 1943, Brereton Papers, DDE; Eaker to Arnold, 12 October 1943, Eaker Papers, box 16, LC.

5. Joint Commanders Meeting minutes, 12 October 1943, 533.02, AFHRC.

6. Joint Commanders Meeting minutes, 12 October 1943, 533.02, AFHRC; Quesada interview 2; Eaker remarks recounted in Arnold, *Global Mission*, 375.

7. Joint Commanders Meeting minutes, 12 October 1943, 533.02, AFHRC.

8. Joint Commanders Meeting minutes, 12 October 1943, 533.02, AFHRC; William Kepner interview, 15 July 1944, Spaatz Papers, box 136, LC.

9. Unit History, IX TAC, May 1944, 536.02 AFHRC; IX TAC A-4 History, Quesada Papers, LC; IX TAC Movement Control History, Quesada Papers, LC.

10. Quesada to Francis Perkins, 17 November 1943, Quesada Papers, LC.

11. Morton Magoffin to Tom Hughes, 13 March 1992; Reports of Staff Meetings, IX TAC, 23 November 1943, 536.02, AFHRC; Quesada to Dixon Allison, 14 April 1944, Quesada Papers, LC; Reports of Staff Meetings, 25 December 1943, 536.02, AFHRC.

12. Blair Garland interviews, K239.0512-1332 and K239.0512-1806, AFHRC.

13. Garland interview, K239.0512-1332, AFHRC; Quesada to Ken Martin, 1 December 1943, Quesada Papers, LC (Identical letters were sent to each group commander as they arrived in theater); Quesada interview 8.

14. Garland interviews, K239.0512-1806 and K239.0512-1332, AFHRC.

15. Unit History, 354th Fighter Group, December 1943, GP-354-HI, AFHRC. The fighter groups (with aircraft type), arranged in order of arrival in England (and operational dates), were:
354th (P-51) 2 November (13 December)
357th (P-51) 7 December (27 January)
362d (P-47) 7 December (8 February)
363d (P-51) 30 December (22 February)
365th (P-47) 30 December (22 February)
366th (P-47) 8 January (14 March)
368th (P-47) 8 January (14 March)
358th (P-47) 1 February (3 February)
370th (P-38) 14 February (1 May)
405th (P-47) 7 March (11 April)
371st (P-47) 7 March (12 April)
474th (P-38) 11 March (25 April)
36th (P-47) 11 March (8 May)
373d (P-47) 11 March (8 May)
48th (P-47) 31 March (20 April)
50th (P-47) 4 April (1 May)
367th (P-38) 4 April (9 May)
404th (P-47) 4 April (1 May)
406th (P-47) 10 April (9 May)

Data from "Statistical Binder," IX Tactical Air Command, Quesada Papers, LC; and Maurer Maurer, *Air Force Combat Units of World War II*.

16. Unit History, 354th Fighter Group, January 1944, GP-354-HI, AFHRC.

17. James Howard interview with Tom Hughes, 17 August 1992. Quotes are from *Time*, 31 January 1944, 66–67.

18. Pilot cited in Unit History, 354th Fighter Group, February 1944, GP-354-HI, AFHRC; Unit History, 354th Fighter Group, March 1944, GP-354-HI, AFHRC; James Howard interview with Tom Hughes, 17 August 1992. Martin actually survived his ordeal and became a prisoner of war. His aerial clash was no random event, for in the spring of 1944 the German Air Force began a concentrated effort to attack the menacing bombers aggressively, even to the point of ramming them. Code-named STURM, this activity continued into the summer (Adolf Galland interview, Spaatz Papers, box 134, LC).

19. Adolf Galland interview, Spaatz Papers, box 134, LC; Craven and Cate, III, 43; Eighth Air Force leaders cited from "Miscellaneous Newspaper Clips," Brereton Papers, DDE; Quesada to Helen Quesada, 7 March 1943, Quesada Papers, LC.

20. Craven and Cate, III, 43–45; memo, "Training Summary," Ninth Air Force Headquarters, 21 February 1944, 533.711-1, AFHRC.

21. Memo, "Lessons Learned, Operation Duck," 329-3.01, box 8642, RG 407, NA. As early as 1942 Army Ground Forces commander Leslie McNair griped to Hap Arnold about the deficiency in joint training. Arnold admitted the condition existed, but blamed "special commitments, special diversions, and restricted flow of aircraft" for the problem (Mortensen, 19).

22. "Training Document, KNOCKOUT," 536.717C, AFHRC; "Summary of Operation FOX," 536.717A, AFHRC; memo, "Operation FOX," 14 March 1944, 536.717A, AFHRC.

23. Stecker cited in "Training Document, DUCK," 535.717 AFHRC; Gerhardt cited in an unpublished memoir, Gerhardt Papers, USAMHI, 36; Quesada interview 2.

24. Unpublished memoir, Gerhardt Papers, USAMHI; Quesada to Gerhardt, 3 February 1944, Quesada Papers, LC.

25. Unpublished memoirs, Gerhardt Papers, 36, USAMHI; Spaatz interview, 20 May 1945, Spaatz Papers, box 136, LC. For a detailed exposition of these unruly relationships, see Carlos D'Este, *Decision in Normandy* and Nigel Hamilton, *Monty: Master of the Battlefield, 1942–1944*. For Eisenhower's continuing doubts about Brereton, see Eisenhower to Portal, 22 July 1944, *The Public Papers of Dwight D. Eisenhower*.

26. Gerow to Bradley, 19 February 1944, "Bradley Correspondence with Major Historical Figures," USAMHI; Bradley cited in Bradley Commen-

taries, USAMHI; Eisenhower to Marshall, 29 March 1944, *The Public Papers of Dwight D. Eisenhower*.

27. Blair Garland interview, K239.0512-1806, AFHRC; Quesada interview 2; Bradley Commentaries, USAMHI. In postwar interviews, numerous other ground generals mistakenly refer to Quesada as commander of the Ninth Air Force during this period.

28. Eisenhower to Marshall, 3 and 22 March 1944, *The Public Papers of Dwight D. Eisenhower*. For Eisenhower's earlier worries regarding air organization in England, see his correspondence with George Marshall, 17 and 30 December 1943, 31 December 1943, and 29 February 1944, and memo of Dwight Eisenhower, Pre-Presidential Papers, Principle File, box 110, DDE.

29. Arthur Tedder, *With Prejudice*, 564–565; Spaatz interview, 20 May 1945, Spaatz Papers, box 136, LC. For a fuller exposé of the incredible personal feuds among the major airmen, see Russell Weigley, *Eisenhower's Lieutenants* and Max Hastings, *Overlord*.

30. Harris cited in Harrison, 415; Leigh-Mallory cited in D'Este, 218.

31. Craven and Cate, III, 138; Spaatz interview, K239.0512.754, AFHRC. In the months before D-Day, Eighth Air Force dispatched 8,257 planes and dropped 21,267.7 tons of bombs on airfields, 3,469 bombers and 9,520 tons on marshaling yards, and 3,386 sorties and 9,387.45 tons on encased batteries along the Normandy coast. In the same period, just 6,813 planes dropped 16,522 tons on traditional strategic targets like aircraft factories (*Sunday Punch in Normandy: The Tactical Use of Heavy Bombardment in the Normandy Invasion*).

32. Memo, "Operation BEAVER," 3 April 1944, 535.717B, AFHRC.

33. Unit History, IX TAC, April 1944, 536.02, AFHRC; Quesada to Leigh-Mallory, 13 April 1944, Quesada Papers, LC. For further details of these impromptu meetings, see Quesada to Major General Wade Haislip, 29 April 1944, Quesada Papers, LC.

34. Unit History, 71st Fighter Wing, March 1944, WG-71-HI, AFHRC; Lloyd Wenzel to Tom Hughes, 14 December 1991.

35. Eisenhower to Marshall, 25 December 1943 and 29 March 1944, *The Public Papers of Dwight D. Eisenhower*.

36. Unit History, IX TAC, April 1944, 536.02, AFHRC; History, IX TAC Equipment Section, Quesada Papers, LC. The 354th, for example, completed its sixty-sixth mission in March, making it one of the war's most seasoned groups.

37. Biographical sketch, Brigadier General Alvin Kincaid, 533.293 AFHRC; Quesada interview 2; Unit History, IX TAC, June 1944, 536.02, AFHRC; Quesada to Gene Eubanks, 16 April 1944, Quesada Papers, LC.

38. Ninth Air Force press release, O. P. Weyland, 533.293, AFHRC; Unit His-

tory, 84th Fighter Wing, February 1944, WG-84-HI, AFHRC; Quesada interview 8.

39. Quesada interview 8; Ferguson to Tom Hughes, 19 April 1992; unpublished memoir, James Ferguson, courtesy of James Ferguson; Quesada interview 1.

40. Quesada to William Momyer, 16 April 1944, Quesada Papers, LC; Quesada to Trubee Davison, 16 April 1944, Quesada Papers, LC.

41. Quesada to Trubee Davison, 16 April 1944, Quesada Papers, LC; Morton Magoffin to Tom Hughes, 13 March 1992; Blair Garland interviews, K239.0512-1332 and K239.0512-1806, AFHRC.

42. Leigh-Mallory to Brereton, 10 March 1944, Pre-Presidential Papers, Principal File, box 110, DDE; Craven and Cate, III, 68; Unit History, IX TAC, May 1944, 536.02, AFHRC; "Impact: U.S. Tactical Air Power in Europe," 12. In 1944 northwest Europe had nearly five times the double-track miles per acre as the United States.

43. Unit History, IX TAC, April 1944, 536.02, AFHRC; Quesada to Helen Quesada, 16 April 1944, Quesada Papers, LC.

44. "Impact: U.S. Tactical Air Power in Europe," May 1945, 14; intelligence study cited in Harrison, *Cross Channel Attack*, 224.

45. For the particular aircraft problems facing the Ninth Air Force in 1943, see "IX TAC Equipment History," and "Employment of TACs in Europe," Quesada Papers, DDE. For a more general discussion of each plane's characteristics, see Swanborough and Bowers, *United States Military Aircraft Since 1909.*

46. Pilot cited in Joe Ornstein to Tom Hughes, 12 August 1992; Quesada interview 4.

47. Quesada to Joe Cannon, 20 November 1943, Quesada Papers, LC; pilot cited in "IX Tactical Air Command Technical Training," Quesada Papers, LC.

48. Reports, Daily Staff Meetings, IX TAC, 12 April, 1944, 536.02, AFHRC; Quesada to William Momyer, 12 April 1944, Quesada Papers, LC.

49. Memo, "The Development and the Technique of Low Level Bombing with P-47 Type Aircraft," Quesada Papers, LC; Unit History, IX TAC, April 1944, 536.02, AFHRC.

50. Unit History, 367th Fighter Group, May 1944, GP-367-HI, AFHRC; Craven and Cate, III, 156; Unit History, 365th Fighter Group, May 1944, GP-365-HI, AFHRC.

51. Craven and Cate, III, 157.

52. Operational Notes, "Low Level Bombing in P-47s," Quesada Papers, LC; Reports, Daily Staff Meetings, IX TAC, 11 May 1944, 536.02, AFHRC.

53. Unit History, IX TAC, May 1944, 536.02, AFHRC; Operational Notes, "Low Level Bombing in P-47s," Quesada Papers, LC; Operational Re-

search Report No. 90: "Fighter Bomber Attacks on the Seine River Bridges," Unit History, IX TAC, August 1944, 536.02, AFHRC.

54. "Impact: U.S. Tactical Air Power in Europe," May 1945, 17.

55. Brereton cited in Craven and Cate, III 160; Hermann Goering interview with Tooey Spaatz, Spaatz Papers, box 134, LC.

56. "The Development and the Technique of Low Level Bombing with P-47 Type Aircraft," Quesada Papers, LC; Quesada to Helen Quesada, 10 May 1944, Quesada Papers, LC.

57. Unit History, IX TAC, June 1944, 536.02, AFHRC; Craven and Cate, III, 140.

58. "Preliminary plans, OVERLORD plan for First U.S. Army," 18 May 1944, 101-1.5, RG 407, NA; "Air Support, Invasion of France," Fourth Infantry Division, 304-.3.0 SOR, box 6431, RG 407, NA.

59. Quesada interview 1; Garland interview, K239.0512-1332, AFHRC. For signals problems in the early years of World War II, see United States Air Force Historical Study #66: *AAF Defense Activities in the Mediterranean, 1942–1944*; Report, "Operation Husky," HQ NAAF, August 1943, Spaatz Papers, box 164, LC; Howe, *Northwest Africa: Seizing the Initiative in the West*, 231; and Unit History, 926th Signal Battalion, IX TAC, Quesada Papers, LC. For a full description of the Signal Corps between wars, see Dulany Terrett, *The Signal Corps: The Emergency*.

60. Garland interview, K239.0512-1806, AFHRC; Garland commendation, Quesada Papers, LC.

61. Quesada to Major General Roger Colton, 4 April 1944, Quesada Papers, LC; Garland interview K239.0512-1806, AFHRC.

62. Memo, "Air Force Representation on Flagships and Headquarters Ships," 533.02 AFHRC; memo "Communication Facilities on Headquarters Ships," 22 March 1944, 533.02, AFHRC; memo, Communication Requirements when Naval Aircraft are Providing Support," 4 April 1944, SHAEF ADJ-GEN DIV, box 88, RG 331, NA; memo, "Invasion of France, Fourth Infantry Division," 304-.3.0 SOR, box 6431, RG 407, NA. There were thirteen Air Support Parties in the initial infantry assaults.

63. Quesada interview 3; Unit History, 555th Signal Aircraft Warning Battalion, IX TAC, Quesada Papers, box 6, LC; Garland interview, K239.0512-1806, AFHRC; Quesada interview 2.

64. Unit History, IX TAC, May 1944, 536.02, AFHRC.

65. AEAF Historical Record, AIR 37/1057, PRO.

66. Curiously, few histories record much about this most extraordinary conference. Various diaries and memoirs contain piecemeal references, but only one work seriously addresses it: Nigel Hamilton, *Master of the Battlefield: Monty's War Years*. Fortunately, one principal, Leigh-Mallory, committed his recollections to writing just days afterwards, and the following account

is based on his "Impressions of the Meeting held at St. Paul's School on May 15, 1944," (AIR 37/784, PRO) and the AEAF Historical Record (AIR 37/1057, PRO). For a general account of the non-air planning for OVER-LORD, see Harrison, *Cross-Channel Attack*.

67. Craven and Cate, III, 143–145; Leigh-Mallory, "Impressions," AIR 37/784, PRO.

68. Quesada interview 8; AEAF Historical Record, AIR 37/1057, PRO.

69. Quesada interview, in Richard Kohn, *Air Superiority in World War II and Korea*; Quesada interview 8. As D-Day drew near, the Supreme Commander adopted Quesada's prediction as his own. While visiting members of the 82d Airborne Division scheduled for drops near Ste. Mère Église, Eisenhower told the privates, sergeants, lieutenants, and captains on whose shoulders OVERLORD then rested: "You need not worry about the air. If you see a plane, it will be ours." Long after the war, Churchill spied Quesada at a Washington dinner party. "Young man, I remember you. You are the young man who told me there would be no German Air Force over the invasion beach."

70. AEAF Historical Record, AIR 37/1057, PRO. See also D'Este, 88, and Hamilton, 567.

71. Quesada interview 3.

72. Cited in Hastings, *Overlord*, 69, 46.

73. Unit History, IX TAC, May 1944, 536.02, AFHRC; Quesada interview 3.

74. Hitler cited in Hastings, *Overlord*, 58.

75. For more on German defense measures, see Harrison, *Cross-Channel Attack*, chapters 4 and 7.

76. Operation Memorandum #54, "The Employment of Bombers and Fighter Bombers in Co-operation with the Army," 6 May 1944, Allied Force Headquarters, Norstad Papers, DDE.

77. Unit History, IX TAC, April 1944; *Impact: U.S. Tactical Air Power in Europe, May 1945*, 14.

78. William Lewis Curry to Tom Hughes, 29 January 1992.

79. Quesada interview 3; unpublished memoir, James Ferguson, courtesy of James Ferguson (Ferguson to Tom Hughes, 19 April 1992); Anne Frank, *The Diary of a Young Girl*.

Chapter Five. The Fighter Bomber Boys Are Doing More to Make This Campaign a Success Than Anyone Ever Anticipated

1. Narrative History, 555th Signal Air Warning Battalion, Quesada Papers, LC; "IX TAC Signal Section History," Quesada Papers, LC; "IX TAC Air Plan, Operation Neptune," 28 April 1944, Quesada Papers, LC.

2. "Summary of Operations, Ninth Air Force, June 1944," 533.451-18 and 536.3061-2, AFHRC. The invasion plan had called for two emergency strips on D-Day, two refueling and rearming strips by D plus 3, two more fields by D plus 4, and a total of eight landing fields in the U.S. zone just eight days after the invasion.

3. Bradley cited in Chester Hansen War Diary, 9 June 1944, USAMHI; Rommel to his wife, 18 June 1944, *The Rommel Papers*.

4. Lane cited in "The Invasion Air Force," 533.306-1, AFHRC; engineer cited in "IX TAC History of Flying Control and Mobility," Quesada Papers, LC. In an interview in 1992, Quesada clearly remembered going to Normandy on D plus 1. No historical record places him in France that early, however. This account recounts his actions according to the contemporaneous record.

5. Cited in Unit History, 70th Fighter Wing, June 1944, WG-70-HI, AFHRC.

6. Quesada interview 1.

7. Unit History, 70th Fighter Wing, June 1944, WG-70-HI, AFHRC.

8. Memo, "IX TAC in Normandy," Supplemental Histories, Ninth Air Force History, 533.01, AFHRC.

9. Unit History, IX TAC, June, 536.02, AFHRC.

10. Harrison, *Cross Channel Attack*, 189–192.

11. "Report of Missions Flown and Grounded," 533.4501-12, AFHRC.

12. Unit History, IX TAC, June 1944, 536.01 AFHRC; War Diary, Seventh German Army, 10 June 1944, Spaatz Papers, box 74, LC.

13. Unit History, IX TAC, June 1944, 536.02, AFHRC; Quesada to William Momyer, 22 August 1944, Quesada Papers, LC.

14. German cited in POW Reports, 24 July 1944, 533.4501-9, AFHRC.

15. Rommel to his wife, 10 June 1944, Hart, *The Rommel Papers*.

16. Ninth Air Force Telephone Log, 9 June 1944, 533.305-3, AFHRC; "Report of Missions Flown and Grounded," 533.4501-12, AFHRC.

17. Leigh-Mallory cited in Hamilton, 639.

18. "Report of Missions Flown and Grounded," 533.4501-12, AFHRC.

19. POW Reports, 8 July 1944, 533.4501-9, AFHRC; "The Invasion Air Force, 259–260, 533.306-1, AFHRC.

20. "The Invasion Air Force," 260, 533.306-1, AFHRC.

21. War Diary of Karl Laun, in Edwards Papers, USAMHI; War Diary of German Seventh Army, 18 June 1944, Spaatz Papers, box 74, LC.

22. Rundstedt cited in War Diary of German Seventh Army, 18 June 1944, Spaatz Papers, box 74, LC.

23. Survey Questions and Answers, "Air Power in the ETO," 533.4501-2, AFHRC (hereafter cited as Survey Answers).

24. "Report of Missions Flown and Grounded," 533.4501-12, AFHRC; Quesada to Group Commanding Officers, 26 June 1944; Quesada Papers, LC.
25. Report of Economic Warfare Division, Embassy of USA, *Movement of German Divisions into the Lodgement Area Overlord, D to D+50*, 3 October 1944.
26. *Air Historical Studies #70: Tactical Operations of the Eighth Air Force, 6 June 1944 to 8 May 1945*, 39–48; Unit History, IX TAC, June 1944, 536.02, AFHRC; Speer interview with Tooey Spaatz, 17 August 1945, Spaatz Papers, box 140, LC.
27. *"Ninth Air Force Invasion Activities: April thru June 1944,"* 57–61.
28. Report by Economic Warfare Division Embassy of the USA, *Movement of German Divisions into the Lodgement Area Overlord*, 3 October 1944; After Action Report, VII Corps, July 1944, 5, RG 407, NA.
29. POW Interrogation Summaries, Bayerlein, 19 May 1945, Spaatz Papers, box 134, LC.
30. German POW cited in Chester Hansen War Diary, 25 June, USAMHI; Rundstedt cited POW Interview, Rundstedt, 20 May 1945, Edwards Papers, USAMHI.
31. Consolidated POW Reports, box 191, envelope 3, RG 243, NA.
32. "Report of Missions Flown and Grounded," 533.4501-12, AFHRC.
33. Quesada interview 1.
34. "Report of Missions Flown and Grounded," 533.4501-12, AFHRC.
35. Ninth Air Force Telephone Log, 533.305-3, AFHRC; Richard Groh, *The Dynamite Gang: The 367th Fighter Group in World War II*.
36. Holt cited in Harold Holt, "Column Cover," *American Aviation Historical Society*, Fall, Winter 1983, 238.
37. "Report of Missions Flown and Grounded," 533-4501-12, AFHRC; Unit History, IX TAC, June 1944, 536.02 AFHRC; Unit History, 371st Fighter Group, June 1944, GP-371-HI, AFHRC.
38. Unit History, IX TAC, June 1944, 536.02, AFHRC.
39. *"Ninth Air Force Invasion Activities, April thru June, 1944,"* 68; Lt. Col. William Dunn interview, K239.0512-922, AFHRC; "A-4 Activities before the Invasion," Supplemental Histories, Ninth Air Force History, 533.01, AFHRC; Unit History, IX TAC, May 1944, 536.02 AFHRC; Unit History, "Airdrome Squadron of the IX TAC," Quesada Papers, LC. Airfield construction remains one of the war's unsung accomplishments. By the end of the campaign in Europe, Ninth Air Force engineers constructed or rehabilitated 241 air strips.
40. Quesada to Follet Bradley, 19 June 1944, Quesada Papers, LC; Bradley cited in Bradley, *The Effects of Strategic and Tactical Air Power on Military Operations, ETO*, War College Library, 16.

41. Cited in "Historical Sketch of the 365th Fighter Group, courtesy of Joe Ornstein.

42. Quesada to E. A. Deeds, 16 June 1944, Quesada Papers, LC; Bradley to Quesada, 20 June 1944, Quesada Papers, LC.

43. Quesada to Buddy Quesada, 17 June 1944, Quesada Papers, LC; Unit History, "Signal Planning for Operation Neptune," 533.451-8, AFHRC.

44. Quesada interview 1.

45. The Bradley Commentaries, The Clay Blair Collection, USAMHI.

46. Chester Hansen War Diary, 17 and 21 June 1944, USAMHI.

47. Quesada interview 1.

48. "Combat Operations History," IX TAC, Quesada Papers, LC.

49. Minutes of the Allied Air Commanders Conference, 14 June 1944, AIR 37.1057, PRO; Montgomery cited in Hamilton, 692–693.

50. Leigh-Mallory cited in D'Este, 226.

51. William Sylvan War Diary, 24 June 1944, USAMHI.

52. Chester Hansen War Diary, 19 June 1944, USAMHI.

53. Quesada interview 1.

54. Quesada interview 1.

55. Collins interview, USAMHI.

56. Craven and Cate, III, 199.

57. Quesada cited in Holt, "Column Cover."

58. Bradley to Arnold, 7 July 1944, Bradley Correspondence, Bradley Papers, USAMHI; Bradley, A Soldier's Story, 249.

59. Quesada interview 3; Joseph Collins, Lightning Joe: An Autobiography, 186.

60. Richard Groh, The Dynamite Gang: The 367th Fighter Group in World War II; "Air Force Operations in Support of Attack on Cherbourg," 533.4501-4, AFHRC. Unless specifically noted, all quotations in the following passage are from these sources.

61. Cited in Groh, The Dynamite Gang.

62. Collins, 218–219; Craven and Cate, III, 200.

63. Collins, 219; Fourth Division Commander cited in Survey Answers.

64. Patton and Bradley both cited in Bradley, The Effects of Strategic and Tactical Air Power on Military Operations, ETO, 202, 12.

65. Pilots cited in "The Invasion Air Force," 533.306-1, AFHRC.

66. "Air Force Operations in Support of Attack on Cherbourg," 533.4501-4, AFHRC.

67. These and following quotations are taken from "The Invasion Air Force," 267–273, 533.306-1, AFHRC.

68. Quesada to Charles Crockett, 29 June 1944, Quesada Papers, LC.

69. Reginald Nolte, Thunder Monsters Over Europe: A History of the 405th Fighter Group in World War II.

70. Memo, "The Cherbourg Attack," VII Corps AAR, June 1944, box 3781, RG 407, NA.
71. Unit History, IX TAC, June 1944, 536.02, AFHRC; The Bradley Commentaries, The Clay Blair Collection, USAMHI.
72. Unit History, IX TAC, June 1944, 536.02 AFHRC; Memo, "Air Cooperation with Troops in Normandy," 533.4501-4, AFHRC.
73. Quesada to Buddy Quesada, 18 June 1944, Quesada Papers, LC.
74. Cited in Nolte, *Thunder Monsters Over Europe*.

Chapter Six. *Remember That Our Work Is Really Just Starting*

1. Quesada interview; Ninth Air Force Telephone Log, 2 July 1944, 533.305-3, AFHRC.
2. Consolidated POW Reports, 24 July 1944, 533.4501-9, AFHRC.
3. Unit History, 474th Fighter Group, July 1944, GP-474-HI, AFHRC.
4. Richard Turner, *Big Friend Little Friend*, 111–113; Unit History, 474th Fighter Group, GP-474-HI, AFHRC. Turner places this event in mid-June 1944, but contemporaneous records indicate that the crash occurred on 3 July (Wing History, 70th Fighter Wing, July 1944, WG-70-HI, AFHRC).
5. Quesada to Group Commanders, 27 June 1944, Quesada Papers, LC.
6. Bradley to Eisenhower, 29 June 1944, Pre-Presidential Papers, Principal File, box 13, DDE; Unit History, 367th Group, July 1944, GP-367-HI, AFHRC; Quesada interview 4; Chester Hansen War Diary, 5 July 1944, USAMHI.
7. Bradley cited in Bradley, *A Soldier's Story*, 325; Eisenhower to Marshall, 5 July 1944; *The Public Papers of Dwight D. Eisenhower*; Quesada interview 4.
8. Chester Hansen War Diary, 3 July 1944, USAMHI.
9. Group History, 367th Fighter Group, July 1944, GP-367-HI, AFHRC; "The Invasion Air Force," 287, 533.306-1, AFHRC; Consolidated POW Reports, 24 July 1944, 533.4501-9, AFHRC.
10. Bradley to Eisenhower, 6 July 1944, *The Public Papers of Dwight D. Eisenhower*; Collins, *Lightning Joe*, 229.
11. Craven and Cate, III, 205; Consolidated POW Reports, 24 July 1944, 533.4501-9, AFHRC.
12. Unit History, 370th Fighter Group, July 1944, GP-370-HI, AFHRC.
13. Bombing studies reflected in Operational Research Section Report #12, 27 May 1944, in Unit History, XIX TAC, June 1944, 538.02, AFHRC.
14. Germans cited in Consolidated POW Reports, 24 July 1944, 533.4501-9, AFHRC, and POW Reports, 21st Army Group, 533.4501-9, AFHRC.
15. First Army medical after-action report, cited in Hastings, 246.

16. Harrison, *Cross Channel Attack*, 284; Chester Hansen War Diary, 23 July 1944, USAMHI.

17. Luftwaffe memo, "Evaluation of experience gained in operations against the landing forces," 13 July 1944, in 533.4501-9, AFHRC.

18. Eighty-third Division commander cited in Survey Answers; Memo, "Incidents of Friendly Fire," box 6121, RG 243, NA.

19. Robert Lewis, William Nelson, Clifford Cunningham, and Warren Briezacher all cited in Veteran Questionnaires, USAMHI.

20. Unit History, 67th Fighter Group, July 1944, GP-67-HI, AFHRC; Unit History, 48th Fighter Group, July 1944, GP-48-HI, AFHRC; Unit History, IX TAC, July 1944, 536.02, AFHRC; Carpenter's wing man cited by Lloyd Wenzel to Tom Hughes, 12 July 1992.

21. Eisenhower cited in *The Public Papers of Dwight D. Eisenhower*, 25 June 1944.

22. Quesada to all Commanders, IX TAC, 27 June 1944, Quesada Papers, LC; Malcolm Marshall cited in Veteran Questionnaires, USAMHI.

23. Weyland's actions are derived from "Suggested Teletype of 5 July 1944;" memo from General Schlatter with reference to Summary of Operations Report, 5 July 1944; both in Chief of Staff Daily Journal, Ninth Air Force, 6 July 1944, 533.305-4, AFHRC.

24. D'Este, 315.

25. Ninth Air Force Telephone Log, 9 July 1944, 533.305-3, AFHRC.

26. After Action Reports, VIII Corps, July 1944, 208-.3, RG 407, NA; Ninth Air Force Telephone Log, 533.305-3, AFHRC; Ninth Air Force Daily Journal, 533.305-2, AFHRC.

27. Eisenhower cited in *The Public Papers of Dwight D. Eisenhower*, 29 June 1944; Montgomery cited in Hamilton, 682; Bradley cited in Chester Hansen War Diary, 29 June 1944, USAMHI.

28. Unit History, IX TAC, July 1944, 536.02, AFHRC; Quesada to Jimmy Mills, 23 June 1944, Quesada Papers, LC.

29. Weather information derived from U.S. Department of Commerce, *World Weather Records, 1941–1950*, Washington, DC.

30. Cables, Eisenhower to Marshall, 12 May 1944; Arnold to Spaatz, 15 May 1944; Spaatz to Arnold, 28 May 1944; and memo, "Action to Defeat the Weather," 17 June 1944; all in Quesada Papers, LC.

31. Bradley cited in D'Este, 321; Eisenhower to Bradley, 8 July 1944; *The Public Papers of Dwight D. Eisenhower*.

32. Preston cited in Hastings, 248.

33. Episode related in Chester Hansen War Diary, 13 July 1944, USAMHI.

34. IX TAC History, July 1944, 536.02, AFHRC; First Division Commander cited in Bradley, *The Effects of Strategic and Tactical Air Power on Military Operations, ETO*.

35. Bradley cited in Blair Garland interview, K239.0512-1332 and K239.0512-1816, AFHRC. Bradley's views of air–ground communications are derived from a memo by Bradley, Fifth Army Headquarters, 1 March 1943: "We can't get the stuff when it's needed and we're catching hell for it. By the time our request for air support goes through channels the target's gone or the Stukas have come instead."

36. Quotations from Bradley, *A Soldier's Story*, 338; Bradley Commentaries, The Clay Blair Collection, USAMHI; and Blair Garland interviews, K239.0512-1332 and 1806, AFHRC.

37. Quesada interview 3.

38. Blair Garland interview, AFHRC; Bradley, *A Soldier's Story*, 337.

39. Unit History, 555th Signal Air Warning Battalion, Quesada Papers, LC.

40. "MEW in the Normandy Campaign," 533.0517-12, AFHRC.

41. Unit History, 555th Signal Aircraft Warning Battalion, BN-555-SU-HI, AFHRC.

42. Commendation, Lieutenant Colonel William Cowart, Quesada Papers, LC; Garland interview, K239.0512-1332 and 1806, AFHRC.

43. IX TAC History, July 1944, 536.02, AFHRC.

44. IX TAC History, July 1944, 536.02, AFHRC.

45. Operational Research Report #32, in Unit History, IX TAC, August 1944, 536.02, AFHRC.

46. Unit History, 362d Fighter Group, July 1944, GP-362-HI, AFHRC.

47. Quotations from IX TAC Control Section History, Combat Operations, Quesada Papers, LC.

48. James Tilford to Tom Hughes, 3 November 1991 and 9 January 1992.

49. Blair Garland interview, K239.0512-1332 and 1806, AFHRC.

50. Deputy Chief of Staff Daily Journal, Ninth Air Force; and Meeting Minutes, 2 July 1944; in 533.305-4, AFHRC; Ninth Air Force Daily Journal, Meeting Minutes, 12 July 1944, 533.305-1, 2, AFHRC; Deputy Chief of Staff Daily Journal, 16 July 1944; 533.305-4, AFHRC.

51. Consolidated POW Reports, 24 July 1944, 533.4501-9, AFHRC; IX TAC History, July 1944, 536.02, AFHRC.

52. Arnold quotation taken from Murray Green Collection, Index/Bibliography notes, box 43, USAFA.

53. Weyland's position related in Deputy Chief of Staff Daily Journal, Ninth Air Force, 16 July 1944; 533.305-4, AFHRC; Quesada to Lovett, 21 August 1944, Quesada Papers, LC.

54. Brereton quotation from Deputy Chief of Staff Daily Journal, 13 July 1944, 533.305-4, AFHRC; Quesada to Robert Lovett, 21 August 1944, Quesada Papers, LC.

55. Unit History, 370th Fighter Group, July 194, GP-370-HI, AFHRC.

56. IX TAC History, July 1944, 536.02, AFHRC; "Use and Effectiveness of

Napalm Fire Bomb," February 1945, box 166, envelope 317, RG 243, NA; Quesada to Robert Lovett, 21 August 1944, Quesada Papers, LC.

57. Corlett Memoirs, USAMHI; Eisenhower to Bradley, Dwight Eisenhower Pre-Presidential Papers, Principal File, box 13, DDE.

58. The reference to "smoldering" is Arthur Tedder's description of Eisenhower's attitude toward Montgomery in early July, cited at D'Este, 309; Eisenhower to Montgomery, 7 July 1944, *The Public Papers of Dwight D. Eisenhower*; Montgomery cited in Hamilton, 791.

59. Montgomery's staff attitudes cited in Hastings, 270.

60. Memo, Eisenhower to Walter Bedell Smith, 23 June 1944, *The Public Papers of Dwight D. Eisenhower*; Eisenhower telegram to his subordinates, cited in Walter Bedell Smith memo of record, Spaatz Papers, box 136, LC.

61. Brereton memo, 12 July 1944, 533.4501-10, AFHRC; Fourth Division commander cited in Survey Answers.

62. Arthur Tedder, *With Prejudice*, 559; Quesada cited in Hastings, 269.

63. D'Este, 155; Quesada cited in *Impact: The Tactical Air War*, xv.

64. Montgomery and Eisenhower cited in *The Public Papers of Dwight D. Eisenhower*, 13 and 14 July 1944.

65. Hastings, 232–233.

66. DeGuingand, *Operation Victory*, 403.

67. "Preliminary Analysis of Air Operations—GOODWOOD," July 1944, AIR 37/762, PRO.

68. Montgomery cable cited in Hamilton, 734.

69. Cited in Hastings, 235.

70. Hastings, 236.

71. Eisenhower cited in Harry Butcher War Diary.

72. Notes on Conference, First Army, 12 July 1944, 101-.05, RG 407, NA.

73. Notes of Conference, First Army, 12 July 1944, 101-.05, RG 407, NA.

74. Bradley cited in Chester Hansen War Diary, 12 July 1944, USAMHI; and Bradley, *A Soldier's Story*.

75. Chester Hansen War Diary, 6 July 1944, USAMHI.

76. Chester Hansen War Diary, 19 July 1944, USAMHI.

77. Cited in redline messages, Quesada to Spaatz, 18 July 1944, Ninth Air Force Communications Files, 533.01, AFHRC.

78. Bradley, *A Soldier's Story*, 340.

79. John Sullivan, "The Botched Air Support of Operation COBRA," *Parameters*, (March 1988), 106–108. Subsequent details of the Stanmore meeting are taken from this source unless otherwise noted.

80. Harold Ohlke, "Report of the Investigation of Bombing, July 24–25," Spaatz Papers, box 168, LC (hereafter cited as Ohlke Report).

81. Ohlke Report.

82. Ohlke Report; Leigh-Mallory cited in Hoyt Vandenberg War Diary, 19 July 1944, Vandenberg Papers, LC.

83. Chester Hansen War Diary, 20 July 1944, USAMHI; Bradley, *A Soldier's Story*, 341; Collins' reaction related in Chester Hansen War Diary, 19 July 1944, USAMHI.

84. After Action Report, 30th Division, July 1944, box 3927, RG (Record Group) 407, NA; memo, "Report of Operations of 24 and 25 July 1944," RG 243, box 71, envelope 25, NA.

85. Collins cited in Sullivan, 104; Bradley cited in The Bradley Commentaries, The Clay Blair Collection, USAMHI.

86. Chester Hansen War Diary, 21 July 1944, USAMHI; Eisenhower cited in Chester Hansen War Diary, 20 July 1944, USAMHI.

87. Bradley cited in Chester Hansen War Diary, 23 July 1944.

88. In June, Marshall sent Generals Henry Aurand and Lucius Clay to improve Eisenhower's chaotic supply setup (Henry Aurand Papers, box 13, DDE).

89. Holt, "Column Cover," 13; IX TAC Air Corps Equipment Section History, Quesada Papers, LC; Craven and Cate, III, 589; IX TAC History, July and August 1944, 536.02, AFHRC; History, Sixth Airdrome Squadron, Quesada Papers, LC.

90. Rommel to Hitler, 17 July 1944, *The Rommel Papers*, and Hamilton, 742, citing Rommel's diary entry of 17 July 1944.

91. Eisenhower to Bradley, 25 July 1944, *The Public Papers of Dwight D. Eisenhower*.

Chapter Seven. Our Most Recent Effort Seems to Have Fallen Short

1. Chester Hansen War Diary, 24 July 1944, USAMHI.

2. Bradley, *A General's Life*, 278; Quesada interview 2; Chester Hansen War Diary, 25 July 1944, USAMHI. Unless otherwise cited, the following account is from Quesada interview 2.

3. Holt, "Column Cover."

4. Craven and Cate, III, 230; Ohlke report.

5. Chester Hansen War Diary, 24 July 1944, USAMHI.

6. Craven and Cate, III, 233; Kenneth Hechler, "VII Corps in Operation COBRA," Collins Papers, DDE (hereafter cited as Hechler Report).

7. Chester Hansen War Diary, 24 July 1944, USAMHI.

8. William Sylvan War Diary, 24 July 1944, USAMHI.

9. Unit History, Fourth Infantry Division, July 1944, SOR 304-0.3.0, box 6431, RG 407, NA.

10. Hechler Report; Hewitt, 36; Collins, 239.

11. Collins, 239; Omar Bradley memo, 25 July 1944, Chester Hansen Papers, USAMHI.

12. Hoyt Vandenberg War Diary, 24 July 1944, Vandenberg Papers, LC; Bradley memo, 25 July 1944, in Chester Hansen Papers, USAMHI.

13. The Bradley Commentaries, The Clair Blair Collection, USAMHI; Bradley, *A General's Life*.

14. Quesada interview 8.

15. Wings at War Series #2, *Sunday Punch in Normandy: The Tactical Use of Heavy Bombardment in the Normandy Invasion*, 16–17. OBOE was generally more accurate than H2X (H2S in British nomenclature), but radar stations could control only twelve OBOE aircraft an hour.

16. Bayerlein cited in German Seventh Army Diary, 186–188, box 74, Spaatz Papers, LC; Hechler Report.

17. Hastings, 253.

18. Holt, "Column Cover."

19. Quesada interview 8.

20. Ninth Division Commander cited in Bradley, *The Effects of Strategic and Tactical AirPower on Military Operations, ETO*, 215; Chester Hansen War Diary, 25 July 1944, USAMHI; pilot cited in IX TAC History, July 1944, 536.02, AFHRC.

21. Chester Hansen War Diary, 25 July 1944.

22. Unit History, Fourth Infantry Division, July, 1944, SOR 304-0.3., box 6431, RG 407, NA; Hechler Report.

23. Intelligence Summaries; "A Crack German Panzer Division and What Allied Air Power Did to It Between D-Day and VE Day," Spaatz Papers, box 134, LC (hereafter cited as Bayerlein interview).

24. Bayerlein interview; After Action Report, VII Corps, July 1944, RG 407, NA.

25. Hechler Report; Bayerlein interview; German soldiers cited in Hechler Report.

26. Bayerlein interview.

27. Craven and Cate, III, 234.

28. Pyle cited in Hastings, 254.

29. Soldiers cited in *History of the 120th Infantry Regiment*, by officers of the Regiment, Washington Infantry Journal Press, 1947, 36–37.

30. Cited in Hastings, 254.

31. Hechler Report; Hewitt, 36; Collins, 240.

32. Chester Hansen War Diary, 26 July 1944; William Sylvan War Diary, 25 July 1944; both in USAMHI.

33. Collins interview, USAMHI; Arnold quotation from Murray Green Collection, Index/Bibliography notes, box 43, USAFA.

34. Bradley to Eisenhower, 28 July 1944, Bradley Papers, USAMHI.
35. Hobbs cited in William Sylvan War Diary, 25 July 1944, USAMHI; Harrison cited in D. Bruce Lockerbie, *A Man Under Orders*, 79.
36. Quesada interview 8; Bradley, *A Soldier's Story*.
37. Craven and Cate, III, 233–34; Ohlke Report; Spaatz cited in Hoyt Vandenberg War Diary, 27 July 1944, Vandenberg Papers, LC.
38. Hechler Report.
39. Cited in Russell Weigley, *Eisenhower's Lieutenants*, 154; After Action Report, VII Corps, July, 1944, RG 407, NA; Hechler Report.
40. Chester Hansen War Diary, 25 July 1944; William Sylvan War Diary, 25 July 1944; both in USAMHI.
41. Eisenhower cited in Chester Hansen Diary, 25 July 1944, USAMHI; Eisenhower to Marshall, 28 July 1944, *The Public Papers of Dwight D. Eisenhower*.
42. Quesada to Momyer, 26 July 1944, Quesada Papers, LC.
43. Collins, 242–4; captain cited in *History of the 120th Infantry Regiment*.
44. Cited in Paul Carell, *Invasion—They're Coming*, 259.
45. Ninth Air Force Telephone Log, 533.305-3, AFHRC; Bayerlein Interview; Hechler Report.
46. Holt cited in Holt, "Column Cover," 241.
47. Cited in Holt, "Column Cover," 240.
48. Cited in Quentin Aanenson videotape, "A Fighter Pilot's Story."
49. "The Invasion Air Force," 533.306-1, AFHRC.
50. McLaughlin cited in Unit History, 70th Fighter Wing, July 1944, WG-70-HI, AFHRC; Nolte, *Thunder Monsters Over Europe*.
51. Officer cited in Hechler Report.
52. Report, "Armored Column Cover," Quesada Papers, LC; Rose cited in Hechler Report.
53. Aanenson letter quoted in Quentin Aanenson videotape, "A Fighter Pilot's Story;" Quesada's 27 July proclamation cited in IX TAC History, July 1944, 536.02, AFHRC.
54. Cited in Hastings, 256.
55. Bayerlein Interview.
56. Collins, 244; Bradley to Eisenhower, 28 July 1944, Principal File, Eisenhower Pre-Presidential Papers, box 16, DDE.
57. Chester Hansen War Diary, William Sylvan War Diary, 29 July 1944, both in USAMHI.
58. Cited in Unit History, Fourth Infantry Division, July 1944, SOR 304-0.3.0, box 6431, RG 407, NA, emphasis in original.
59. Nolte, *Thunder Monsters Over Europe*; Deputy Chief of Staff Journal, 28 July 1944, 533.305-4, AFHRC.
60. Wings at War Series #5, *"Air-Ground Teamwork on the Western Front: The Role of the XIX Tactical Air Command during August 1944."*

61. Pilot cited in IX TAC History, July 1944, 536.02, AFHRC; general cited in Craven and Cate, III, 242.

62. Collins cited in letter, no date, found in Hechler Report. As always, the question of actual claims is problematic. The numbers cited here represent a median average from reliable post-action sources and are confirmed by ground reports three days after the battle. The VIII Corps After Action Report for July states that "over eighty" tanks and "hundreds" of additional vehicles were destroyed; the VII Corps diarist states that careful examination revealed the estimate of 500 destroyed vehicles to be conservative; and internal IX TAC assessments claim over seventy tanks and 396 trucks destroyed.

63. Quesada cited in Unit History, 405th Fighter Group, July 1944, GP-405-HI, AFHRC; IX TAC History, July 1944, 536.02, AFHRC; Quesada to Walter and Carmen Kennedy, 3 August 1944, Quesada Papers, LC. The Hechler Report probably exaggerates the total tally of destruction; other historians deem claims of 362 tanks and assault guns destroyed and 1,337 other vehicles wrecked to be generally accurate (see Weigley, *Eisenhower's Lieutenants*, 165–166).

64. Hoyt Vandenberg War Diary, 28 July 1944, Vandenberg Papers, LC; memo found in Deputy Chief of Staff Journal, Ninth Air Force, 29 and 30 July 1944, 533.305-4, AFHRC.

65. Third Armored Division commander cited in Survey Answers; Bradley's convictions cited in Bradley, *The Effects of Strategic and Tactical Air Power on Military Operations, ETO*, 41.

66. Thirty-fifth Infantry Division commander and Collins both cited in Survey Answers.

67. Bradley, *A General's Life*, 388; Eisenhower to Doolittle, 2 August 1944, *The Public Papers of Dwight D. Eisenhower*.

68. Ernie Pyle, *Brave Men*, 432.

Chapter Eight. My Fondness for Buck Rogers Devices Is Beginning to Pay Off

1. Quesada interview 1; Stewart cited in Veteran Surveys, USAMHI.

2. Unit History, Fourth Infantry Division, July 1944, SOR 304-0.3.0, RG 407, NA; Collins Interview, USAMHI.

3. Quesada to Helen Quesada, 16 August 1944, Quesada Papers, LC.

4. Veteran Surveys, USAMHI; Division commander cited in Bradley, *The Effects of Strategic and Tactical Air Power on Military Operations, ETO*; 215.

5. Bradley cited in Bradley, *The Effects of Strategic and Tactical Air Power on*

Military Operations, ETO, 102, and The Bradley Commentaries, The Clair Blair Collection, USAMHI.

6. Garland interview, K239.0512-1332, AFHRC. Unless otherwise noted, the following account is based on this source.

7. Gerhardt and Quesada cited in Joseph Ewing, *29, Let's Go*, 112.

8. Ewing, 112.

9. Gerhardt cited in Ewing, 113; Quesada to Gerhardt, 13 August 1944, Quesada Papers, LC.

10. Quesada to Thomas Yawkey, 22 August 1944, Quesada Papers, LC.

11. Martin Blumenson, *Breakout and Pursuit*, 314.

12. Bradley, *A Soldier's Story*, 226.

13. Chester Hansen War Diary, 10 June and 27 July, 1944, USAMHI.

14. Garland interview, K239.0512-1332, AFHRC; Samuel Anderson interview, K239.0512-905, AFHRC. Anderson "really felt sorry for him [Brereton]. He was so stubborn, so sure of himself, and yet he was so mistaken. That's why he was relieved from the air force. No fooling—that's why."

15. Quesada interview 2. For Spaatz's promise to Vandenberg, see Hoyt Vandenberg War Diary, 16 July 1944, Vandenberg Papers, LC; and Eisenhower to Marshall and Arnold, 13, 15 July 1944, *The Public Papers of Dwight D. Eisenhower*.

16. For Vandenberg's background, see Phillip Meilinger, *Hoyt S. Vandenberg: The Life of a General*.

17. For evidence of Vandenberg's intrigue with Spaatz and Doolittle, see Hoyt Vandenberg War Diary, 3, 7 June 1944, Vandenberg Papers, LC.

18. Richard Hughes Memoir, 520.056-234, AFHRC; Meilinger, 50–51.

19. The Bradley Commentaries, The Clay Blair Collection, USAMHI; Chester Hansen War Diary, 26 November 1944, USAMHI.

20. Richard Hughes Memoir, 520.056-234, AFHRC.

21. Unit History, 367th Fighter Group, July 1944, GP-367-HI, AFHRC.

22. Hitler cited in Irving, *Hitler's War*, 683–684.

23. Chester Hansen War Diary, 5 August 1944, USAMHI.

24. Stewart cited in Veteran Surveys, USAMHI.

25. Collins interview, USAMHI.

26. Office of the Chief of Staff Journal, Ninth Air Force, 7 August 1944, 533.305-4, AFHRC; McLachan cited in "The Invasion Air Force," 324, 533.306-1, AFHRC; After Action Report, VII Corps, August 1944, RG 407, NA.

27. After Action Report, VIII Corp, August 1944, 208.-3, RG 407, NA; Generalmajor Rudolph von Gersdorff, Manuscript #A-921, German Report Series, USAMHI.

28. Unit History, Fourth Infantry Division, August 1944, SOR 304-0.3.0, box 6431, RG 407, NA; German officer cited in German Seventh Army Diary,

7 August 1944, Spaatz Papers, box 74, LC, and Carell, *Invasion—They're Coming*, 278.

29. U.S. soldier cited in Unit History, Fourth Infantry Division, August 1944, SOR 304-0.3.0, box 6431, RG 407, NA.

30. "The Story of the IX Tactical Air Command," 536.04, AFHRC; Nolan cited in "The Invasion Air Force, 533.306.1, AFHRC.

31. IX TAC History, August 1944, 536.02, AFHRC; Nolan cited in "The Invasion Air Force," 324, 533.306-1, AFHRC. As always, claims are problematic. The IX TAC believed it ruined 375 armored vehicles and over 1,800 motor transports; British Typhoons claimed an additional 135 tanks. The entire German force near Mortain was nowhere near that big, however, and the tallies here represent a figure closer to the numbers reached by post-action ground surveys.

32. Officer cited in "Special Projects File," SHAEF A-3, RG 331, NA; Bradley cited in The Bradley Commentaries, The Clay Blair Collection, USAMHI; Collins cited in Survey Answers and Collins, 255. The German assessment is drawn from German Seventh Army Diary, 533.55-3 AFHRC; and "Contributions of Air to the Defeat of Germany," Arnold Papers, box 257, LC.

33. Montgomery cited in Hamilton, 779; Bradley cited in Chester Hansen War Diary, 10 August 1944, USAMHI.

34. Raymond cited in Hastings, 298.

35. Bradley, *A Soldier's Story*, 367.

36. Office of Chief of Staff Journal, Ninth Air Force, 12 August 1994, 533.305-4, AFHRC; Red Line Messages, 12 August 1944, Vandenberg to Richard Nugent, Quesada Papers, LC.

37. Weyland interview, K239.0512-813, AFHRC.

38. Weyland interviews, K239.512-813, and K239.512-798, both in AFHRC.

39. Unit History, 367th Fighter Group, August 1944, GP-367-HI, AFHRC; IX TAC History, August 1944, 536.02, AFHRC; "The Invasion Air Force," 310, 533.306-1, AFHRC.

40. "The Invasion Air Force," 325, 533.306-1, AFHRC.

41. Frederick Burkhardt, *History in the Sky*.

42. Unit History, 367 Fighter Group, August 1944, GP-367-HI, AFHRC.

43. Figures from VII After Action Report, August 1944, RG 407, NA.

44. Patton cited in Chester Hansen War Diary, 12 August 1944, USAMHI.

45. Bradley, 337, 377.

46. Weyland interview, K239.512-813; Collins interview, USAMHI.

47. Ninth Air Force Telephone Log, 16 August 1944, 533.305-3, AFHRC; IX TAC History, August 1944, 536.02, AFHRC; soldier cited in VII Corps After Action Reports, August 1944, RG 407, NA; Hastings, 303.

48. Ninth Air Force Telephone Log, 16 August 1944, 533,305-3, AFHRC.

49. Consolidated POW Reports, 533.4501-9, AFHRC.

50. Figures are from Martin Blumenson, *The Battle of the Generals*, 21.
51. German soldiers cited in Wings At War Series #5: *Air Ground Teamwork on the Western Front*; and Hastings, 219.
52. Montgomery cited in Hamilton, 798; Eisenhower cited in Eisenhower, *Crusade in Europe*.
53. IX TAC History, August and September 1944, 536.02, AFHRC.
54. Quesada to Lovett, 21 August 1944, Quesada Papers, LC.
55. IX TAC History, August 1944, 536.02, AFHRC; Unit History, 555th Signal Aircraft Warning Battalion, BN-555-SU-HI, AFHRC.
56. Group commander cited in Holt, "Column Cover," 12. For more on these movements, see Craven and Cate, III, Chapter 16.
57. Pilot cited in Group History, 48th Fighter Group, August 1944, GP-48-HI, AFHRC; Quesada interview 2.
58. Hamilton, 796; Sheffield Edwards Papers, USAMHI. Joe Collins voiced best the minority view: "I believe disruption of enemy signal communications is of such great importance to us that it should be done irrespective of any delay that might be caused in our subsequent use of this system" (Bradley, *The Effects of Strategic and Tactical Air Power on Military Operations, ETO*, 209).
59. Quesada to Buddy Quesada, 30 August 1944; Quesada to Trubee Davison, 16 August 1944; Quesada to Helen Quesada, 16 August 1944; all in Quesada Papers, LC.
60. History, IX TAC Signal Section, Quesada Papers, LC.

Chapter Nine. We Have Slowed Down Here and Nothing We Try Seems to Help

1. Quesada interview 4.
2. Craven and Cate, III, 632.
3. Report, "Operation Queen and the Offensive by First and Ninth U.S. Armies," Courtney Hodges Papers, box 7, DDE. Hereafter cited as Queen Report.
4. Quesada interview 4.
5. Hodges to Bradley, 25 November 1944, Hodges Papers, box 7, DDE; Quesada, memo, "Operation Queen," 23 February 1945, Hodges Papers, box 7, DDE.
6. Queen Report; AAR, Third and 104th Divisions, November 1944, boxes 2524 and 3746, RG 407, NA.
7. Charles MacDonald, *The Siegfried Line Campaign*, map IX.
8. All predictions cited in Hamilton, 413–415, 418; "Updated Plans on the Invasion of Japan," 17 September 1944, War Plans Division, Army Air Forces, 287.76-12, AFHRC; Churchill cited in Hamilton, 327.

9. MacDonald, *The Siegfried Line Campaign*, 12–13; AAR, Eighteenth and Forty-Seventh Regiments, October 1944, boxes 987 and 3347, RG 407, NA.

10. MacDonald, *The Siegfried Line Campaign*, 27–39; cited in *History of the 16th Regiment*, 124.

11. MacDonald, *The Siegfried Line Campaign*, map I; for more on the Siegfried Line construction, see the same title, 30–34.

12. POW Reports, "Effects of Air Power," Edwards Papers, USAMHI.

13. Quesada to Jimmy Lee, 14 September 1944, Quesada Papers, LC.

14. Commanding General's Statistical Notebook, IX TAC, Quesada Papers, LC; Unit History, IX TAC, October 1944, 536.02, AFHRC; Unit History, 365th Fighter Group, October 1944, GP-365-HI, AFHRC; Unit History, 404th Fighter Group, October 1944, GP-404-HI, AFHRC.

15. "Reports of Staff Meetings," IX TAC, 5 October 1944, AFHRC; Operational Research Section Report #17, "Effects of Supply Shortages on Operations," in Unit History, IX TAC, December 1944, 536.02, AFHRC.

16. MacDonald, *The Siegfried Line Campaign*, 282.

17. AAR, Ninth Division, September 1944, box 2617, RG 407, NA; AAR, Third Armored Division, September 1944, box 2524, RG 407, NA; AAR, VII Corps, September 1944, box 1342, RG 407, NA.

18. Bill Sylvan War Diary, 21 September 1944, USAMHI; Unit History, IX TAC, September 1944, 536.02, AFHRC; MacDonald, 284; Quesada cited in "Reports of Staff Meetings, IX TAC, 23 November 1944, AFHRC.

19. Unit History, IX TAC, September 1944, 536.02, AFHRC; Holt to author, 17 March 1992.

20. Anderson to Tom Hughes, 17 March 1992.

21. Unit History, IX TAC, September 1944, 536.02, AFHRC; Memo, "Effect of Air Attacks on Aachen," 17 November 1944, Edwards Papers, USAMHI.

22. Soldier cited in POW Reports, "Effects of Air Power," Edwards Papers, USAMHI; Memo, "Effects of Air Attacks on Aachen," 17 November 1944, Edwards Papers, USAMHI.

23. Quesada interview 4.

24. MacDonald, 291; Weekly Intelligence Summaries, 1 October 1944, RG 331, NA; German commander cited in MacDonald, 315.

25. MacDonald, 297; Unit History, IX TAC, October 1944, 536.02, AFHRC.

26. Unit History, IX TAC, October 1944, 536.02, AFHRC; report, "Tactical Operation of the Eighth Air Force in the ETO," in 533.01, AFHRC; Unit History, IX TAC, October 1944, 536.02, AFHRC.

27. Quesada interview 4; Quesada cited in Generals' Telephone Logbook, 14 October 1944, 533.415-A, AFHRC; Unit History, IX TAC, October 1944, 536.02, AFHRC.

28. MacDonald, *The Siegfried Line Campaign*, 283, 316.

29. MacDonald, *The Siegfried Line Campaign*, 318; Collins, 269; Corlett Memoirs, USAMHI.

30. Unit Histories, IX TAC, September and October 1944, 536.02, AFHRC; Unit History, IX Bomber Command, October 1944, 534.02, AFHRC; Patton cited in Weyland interview, K239.0512-1421, AFHRC.

31. Unit History, IX TAC, October 1944, 536.02, AFHRC.

32. Memo, "Effects of Air Attacks on Aachen," 17 November 1944, Edwards Papers, USAMHI.

33. Report, "Conference of Group and Staff Commanders," 4, 6, 7 November 1944, 536.4501-2, AFHRC. Unless otherwise noted, all subsequent references and quotes from this conference are taken from this source.

34. Craven and Cate, III, 630.

35. Chickering to Tom Hughes, 28 February 1993.

36. Unit History, IX TAC, December 1944, 536.02, AFHRC; Unit Histories, 70th and 84th Fighter Wings, December 1944, WG-70 and 84-HI, AFHRC; Unit History, 555th Signal Aircraft Warning Battalion, November 1944, BN-555-HI, AFHRC.

37. Craven and Cate, III, 622; Operational Research Section Report, "Tactical Aviation in Close Air Support Roles," 17 December 1944, 533.4501-12, AFHRC; Quesada to Momyer, 2 December 1944, Quesada Papers, LC.

38. Memo, Allen to Edwards, 4 November 1944, Sheffield Edwards Papers, USAMHI; William Sylvan War Diary, 13 November 1944, USAMHI.

39. Quesada to Davison, 14 November 1944, Quesada Papers, LC.

40. Unit History, IX TAC, October 1944, 536.02, AFHRC; Unit History, XIX TAC, October 1944, 538.02, AFHRC.

41. Garland interview, K239.0512-1806; Craven and Cate, III, 639; Griggs to Quesada, 12 December 1944, and Griggs to Arnold, 18 November 1944, both in Quesada Papers, LC.

42. Eisenhower to Marshall, 28 and 30 November, Principal File, Eisenhower Pre-Presidential Papers, box 77, DDE; Craven and Cate, III, 639.

43. Hodges cited in William Sylvan War Diary, 1 November 1944, USAMHI. Eisenhower to Marshall, 3 November 1944, Principal File, Eisenhower Pre-Presidential Papers, box 77, DDE. Elsewhere, Sylvan referred to QUEEN as "COBRA-like" and "COBRA inspired."

44. IX TAC Operations Orders, Operation Queen, 9 November 1944, 536.4501-08, AFHRC.

45. First Army Letter of Instruction, AAA Marker Plan, 10 November 1944, Edwards Papers, USAMHI.

46. Unit History, IX TAC, November 1944, 536.02, AFHRC; Quesada cited in Blair Garland interview, K239.0512-1806, AFHRC.

47. Harold Holt to Tom Hughes, 17 March 1992; Craven and Cate, III, 632.

48. QUEEN Report; Unit History, IX TAC, November 1944, 536.02, AFHRC; General's Telephone Logbook, 16 November 1944, 533.415-A, AFHRC.

49. First Army Special Report, "Effects of Our Air Attacks of 16–30 November," 2 December 1944, Edwards Papers, USAMHI, hereafter cited as First Army Report; QUEEN Report.

50. German soldier cited in QUEEN Report; Craven and Cate, III, 633; First Army Report.

51. Unit History, IX TAC, November 1944, 536.02, AFHRC; First Army Report; QUEEN Report; Chickering to Tom Hughes, 28 February 1992.

52. First Army Report.

53. William Sylvan War Diary, 6 December 1944, USAMHI; Quesada to Momyer, 14 December 1944, Quesada Papers, LC; Quesada to Mills, 14 December 1944, Quesada Papers, LC; Arnold, *Global Mission*, 618.

Chapter Ten. We Took a Bit of a Beating on the Ground But Boy Did We Dish It Out in the Air

1. Parass cited in Nolte, 65.

2. Hugh M. Cole, *The Ardennes: Battle of the Bulge*, 611.

3. Cole, 611–612; David Eisenhower, *Eisenhower At War, 1943–1945*, 557; soldier cited in Cole, 199.

4. William Sylvan War Diary, 16 December 1944, USAMHI; memo of record by Dwight Eisenhower, 23 December 1944, *The Public Papers of Dwight D. Eisenhower*; Quesada interview 5; IX TAC History, December 1944, 536.02, AFHRC.

5. Officer cited in Fourth Infantry Division Unit History, 304.0.3.0 SOR, Box 6433, RG 607, NA; Cole, 238. The failure of Allied intelligence to foresee the German offensive is well described elsewhere; see Cole, 52–59, and Craven and Cate, III, 673–681. For more on the German preparations, see Cole, 48–71.

6. William Simpson interview, DDE; Richard Nugent War Diary, 17 December 1944, 533.13-2, AFHRC.

7. Motzenbacker cited in "The Invasion Air Force," 533.306-1, AFHRC.

8. Karl Laun War Diary, Edwards Papers, USAMHI; POW Reports, 533.454-2, AFHRC; "The Invasion Air Force," 533.306-1, AFHRC. These claims were later verified by ground forces.

9. Cole, 91–92.

10. Craven and Cate, III, 687; VII Corps After Action Report, December 1944, 56, RG 407, NA.

11. William Sylvan War Diary, 17 December 1944, USAMHI. Chester Hansen War Diary, 17 December 1944, USAMHI.

12. For Von Rundstedt's remarks on his shortage of fuel in the Battle of the Bulge, see Von Rundstedt interview, Edwards Papers, USAMHI.

13. William Sylvan War Diary, 17 and 18 December, 1944, USAMHI; Cole, 336.

14. Cassady cited in IX TAC History, "Achtung Jabos," 536.04, AFHRC.

15. Both Meyer and Stecker cited in "The Invasion Air Force," 533.306-1, AFHRC. The following account is from this source, 383–389.

16. Pilots cited in "The Invasion Air Force," 533.306-1, AFHRC.

17. Brooking cited in "The Invasion Air Force," 533.306-1, AFHRC.

18. "The Invasion Air Force," 533.306-1, AFHRC; Unit History, 365th Fighter Group, December 1944, GP-365-HI, AFHRC.

19. "The Invasion Air Force," 533.306-1, AFHRC; Craven and Cate, III, 688.

20. First Army Report cited in "The Invasion Air Force," 533.306-1, AFHRC.

21. Harmon cited in Ernest Harmon, "We Gambled in the Battle of the Bulge," *The Saturday Evening Post*, 2 October 1948.

22. Craven and Cate, III, 688; Quesada cited in Unit History, 70th Fighter Wing, December 1944, WG-70-HIST, AFHRC; Chester Hansen War Diary, 19 December 1944, USAMHI; IX TAC officer cited in "The Invasion Air Force," 390, 533.306-1, AFHRC.

23. Cole, 395; William Sylvan Way Diary, 21 December 1944, USAMHI.

24. Unit History, 555 Squadron, December 1944, SQ-555-HIST, AFHRC; Unit History, 70th Fighter Wing, December 1944, WG-70-HIST, AFHRC; Unit History, 365th Fighter Group, December 1944, GP-365-HIST, AFHRC; Unit History, 555 Signal Air Warning Battalion, Quesada Papers, LC.

25. Chester Hansen War Diary, 20 December 1944, USAMHI.

26. Memo "Concerning Allied Air Effort During the Battle of the Bulge," 28 September 1945, 533.4501-5, AFHRC.

27. Quesada interview 5.

28. For these movements of fighter groups among the TACS, see Quesada's redline messages of 22 and 23 December and Nugent's redline message of 27 December, both in 168.602-4-6, AFHRC; and IX TAC Movement History, Quesada Papers, LC.

29. IX TAC History "Achtung Jabos," 536.04, AFHRC; Bradley, *A Soldier's Story*, 479; Chester Hansen War Diary, 20 December 1944, USAMHI; Eisenhower to Truscott, 22 January 1944, *The Public Papers of Dwight D. Eisenhower*.

30. Unit History, 370th Fighter Group, December 1944, GP-370-HIST, AFHRC; Craven and Cate, III, 962; Cole, 468.

31. Craven and Cate, III, 962; Cole, 468.

32. Diary of Karl Luan, 24 December 1944, Edwards Papers, USAMHI; Cole, 567.

33. Craven and Cate, III, 694; Bayerlein interview in POW Reports, 533.454-2, AFHRC.

34. Chester Hansen War Diary, 23 and 24 December, 1944, USAMHI; Richard Nugent War Diary, 533.13-2, AFHRC; Quesada to Helen Quesada, 24 December 1944, Quesada Papers, LC.

35. Harmon, 68; "The Invasion Air Force," 533.306-1, AFHRC; 396; Collins cited in Collins, 291.

36. Unit History, 370th Fighter Group, December 1944, GP-370-HIST, AFHRC; Craven and Cate, III, 695; "The Invasion Air Force," 394, 533.306-1, AFHRC; Richard Nugent War Diary, 533.13-2, AFHRC; William Sylvan War Diary, 25 December 1944, USAMHI.

37. Harmon, 68. For more on the Celles pocket air strikes, see Cole, 566–574.

38. Cole, 553.

39. Report of Captain R.G. Crerie, G-3 Air, Tenth Armored Division, in envelope 317, box 166, RG 243, NA.

40. Remarks of Captain J.E. Parker, G-3 Air, 101st Airborne Division, in envelope 317, box 166, RG 243, NA.

41. For more on napalm in the Battle of the Bulge, see "Napalm Attack on Tanks in Woods," in envelope 317, box 166, RG 243, NA.

42. Cole, 481; McAuliffe to Vandenberg, 25 January 1944, 168.602-4-6, AFHRC; Ninth Air Force Telephone Log, 533.305-3, AFHRC.

43. Redline messages, 26 and 27 December, 1944, 168.602-4-5-6, AFHRC. For the medium bomber attacks near Malmédy, see Cole, 377.

44. Redline messages, 31 December 1944, 168.602-4-5-6, AFHRC. Chester Hansen War Diary, 31 December 1944, USAMHI.

45. "Report of POW Statements on the TAC Action in December 1944," Edwards Papers, USAMHI; Karl Luan Diary, 26 December 1944, Edwards Papers, USAMHI.

46. Unit History, IX TAC, December 1944 and January 1945, 536.02, AFHRC; Hart, *The German Generals Talk*, 292. For the Allied deliberations on this new offensive scheme, see Cole, 602–613.

47. "Report on POW Statements on the TAC Action in December 1944," Edwards Papers, USAMHI.

48. "Report on POW Statements on the TAC Action in December 1944," Edwards Papers, USAMHI.

49. Craven and Cate, III, 696–700.

50. "Contribution of Air to the Defeat of Germany," Report to Arnold, Arnold Papers, box 257, LC; Annual Report, 1945, Arnold to Secretary of War, 36, Arnold Papers, LC; Unit History, 363rd Fighter Group, December 1944, GP-363-HIST, AFHRC; Quesada to Major General H.R. Oldfield, 7 February 1944, Quesada Papers, LC.

51. William Sylvan War Diary, 1 January 1945, USAMHI.

52. Redline message, Nugent to Coningham, 23 January 1945, 168.602-4-6, AFHRC; IX Fighter Command A-4 History, Quesada Papers, LC; redline message, 28 January 1945, 168.602-4-6, AFHRC; Richard Nugent War Diary, 3 February 1945, 533.13-2, AFHRC; redline message, Nugent to Vandenberg, 17 January 1945, 168.602-4-6, AFHRC; Eisenhower to Hodges, 1 April 1945, Hodges Papers, DDE; redline message, Devers to Eisenhower, 12 April 1945, 373.5, box 67–68, RG 331, NA; Operations memo #10, Second Armored Division, 22 February 1945, After Action Report, Second Armored Division, 602-3, box 1439, RG 407, NA; Chester Hansen War Diary, 30 March 1945, USAMHI; Craven and Cate, III, 722; 703–705; After Action Report, VIII Corps and Second Armored Division, December 1944, RG 407, NA.

53. German soldiers cited in "POW Reports," Edwards Papers, USAMHI; Karl Luan Diary, Edwards Papers, USAMHI.

54. Karl Luan Diary, Edwards Papers, USAMHI.

55. Quesada cited in William Sylvan War Diary, 23 February 1945, USAMHI. See Cole for more on these last weeks in the battle.

56. Quesada to Cannon, 14 February 1945, Quesada Papers, DDE; Eisenhower to Churchill, 10 February 1945, Principal File, Pre-Presidential Papers, box 12, DDE; Chester Hansen War Diary, 13 January 1944, USAMHI; Quesada to Todd Sloane, 26 January 1944, Quesada Papers, LC.

57. Craven and Cate, III, 705; Report of Interdiction efforts in the Battle of the Bulge, Edwards Papers, USAMHI. Comment by Brigadier General Futch, Thirty-fifth Infantry Division commander, in Questionnaire.

58. *Impact: The Tactical Air War*, 48; Quesada to Jimmy Lee, 26 January 1945, Quesada Papers, LC. For division and corp commander comments, see Questionnaire.

59. Galland first cited in Arnold, *Global Mission*, 495; Adolf Galland, *The First and the Last*, 242.

60. Quesada to Momyer, 24 January 1945, Quesada Papers, LC.

61. Cited in IX TAC memo 100–57, "SCR-584 Controllers Handbook" 12 April 1945, Unit History, 70th Fighter Wing, April 1945, WI-70-HIST, AFHRC. For continuing innovations in bombing tactics and ordinance, see memo, "Report on Tests of the Operational Suitability of the Matagorda Method of Fighter Gunnery, Rocket Firing, and Dive Bombing," IX TAC, 6 April 1945, RG 18, 353.41, NA, and redline messages, Vandenberg to SHAEF and SHAEF to Vandenberg, 26, 27 March 1945, RG 331, 370-2, NA.

62. Quesada interview 4; Garland interview K239.0512-1306, AFHRC.

63. Memo of the C.G., IX TAC, 4 February 1945, Quesada Papers, LC.

64. Garland cited in Unit History, 70th Fighter Wing, February 1945, WG-70-

HIST, AFHRC; Unit History, 70th Fighter Wing, February 1945, WG-70-HIST, AFHRC; and Unit History, 555 Signal Air Warning Battalion, February 1945, BN-555-HIST-SU, AFHRC and Quesada Papers, LC.

65. Garland cited in Unit History, 70th Fighter Wing, February 1945, WG-70-HIST, AFHRC; Unit History, 70th Fighter Wing History, April 1945, WG-70-HIST, AFHRC. Clouds reduced operational sorties until the end of the war. The Ninth Air Force was grounded six days in February 1945 and eleven days in March 1945.

66. Ridgeway to Quesada, 14 February 1945, Quesada Papers, LC; Collins and Army Commanders cited in Questionnaire.

67. Eisenhower to Marshall, 15 April 1945, *The Public Papers of Dwight D. Eisenhower*.

68. Quesada cited in *Impact: The Tactical Air War*.

69. Commanding General's Statistical Notebook, Arnold Papers, box 78, LC; Eisenhower cited in Holt, *Column Cover*.

70. Richard Hughes Interview, 520-056-234, AFHRC. Unless otherwise noted, Hughes' words in the following paragraphs are taken from this source.

71. Redline message, 29 January 1945, 168.602-4-6, AFHRC.

72. SHAEF officer cited in Minutes to Weekly Air Meeting, SHAEF, 8 February 1945, 370-2, box 112, RG 331, NA.

73. Minutes, Ninth Air Force Commanders' Meetings, 7 February 1945, 533.142-1, AFHRC; Craven and Cate, III, 731–32.

74. Minutes, Ninth Air Force Commanders' Meetings, 7 February 1945, 533.142-1, AFHRC; Eaker to Doolittle, 10 February 1945, Eaker Papers, AFHRC; Craven and Cate, III, 733.

75. Craven and Cate, 734.

76. Redline Messages, Vandenberg to Spaatz, 22 February 1945, 533.819-A, AFHRC; *United States Strategic Bombing Survey, Summary Report*, August 1945, 16, hereafter cited as USSBS.

77. USSBS, 21; Craven and Cate, III, 735.

78. Omar Bradley, *Effects of Air Power on Military Operations*, 64; Allied Air Commanders Conference, 1 May 1945, Spaatz Papers, box 37, LC; Quesada interview 1.

79. William Sylvan War Diary, 14 March 1945, USAMHI; Craven and Cate, III, 772.

80. Chester Hansen War Diary, 30 March 1945, USAMHI; Quesada to Margaret McGee, 11 March 1945, Quesada Papers, DDE; Quesada to Helen Quesada, 6 April 1945, Quesada Papers, LC.

81. Von Rundstedt and Kesselring cited in POW Reports, Edwards Papers, USAMHI; Hermann Goering cited in Goering Interview, box 134, Spaatz Papers, LC.

82. Officer cited in 365th Fighter History, April 1945, GP-365-HI, AFHRC.

83. Quesada to Alice Mills, 22 February 1945, and Quesada to Davison, 10 March 1945, Quesada Papers, LC.
84. Chester Hansen War Diary, 14 April 1945, USAMHI.
85. Eisenhower Memo, 1 February 1945, *The Public Papers of Dwight D. Eisenhower*. For Bradley's list, see the Clay Blair Collection, USAMHI.

Chapter Eleven. There Was Great Arrogance in Victory

1. Quesada interview 5; Quesada to Eaker, 4 March 1951, Eaker Papers, AFHRC.
2. Quesada to Eaker, 4 March 1951, Eaker Papers, AFHRC.
3. Quesada to Eaker, 4 March 1951, Eaker Papers, AFHRC.
4. Vinson cited in *New York Times*, 13 October 1951, 1; Quesada interview 5.
5. Quesada interview 5.
6. *Philadelphia Inquirer*, 5 June 1945; Quesada 201 File, Quesada Papers, LC; Quesada to Jimmy Mills, 14 April 1945, Quesada Papers, LC.
7. Quesada to Helen Quesada, 14 April 1945, Quesada Papers, LC.
8. Arnold to Marshall, cited in Murray Green Collection, box 54, AFA; Annual Report, Arnold to Secretary of War, in Murray Green Collection, box 54, AFA; MacArthur cited by Tooey Spaatz, in Spaatz interview, K239.572–583, AFHRC.
9. Mark Clodfletter, *The Limits of Air Power: The American Bombing of North Vietnam*, 12.
10. De Seversky to Secretary of War, 4 October 1946, cited in Murray Green Collection, box 54, AFA.
11. Quesada interview 5.
12. Roosevelt to Arnold, 17 November 1944, Arnold Papers, LC.
13. Roosevelt to Spaatz, 9 November 1944 1943, Spaatz Papers, LC; Spaatz to D'Olier, 4 March 1944, Spaatz Papers, LC; Craven and Cate, III, 789.
14. USSBS, 7–10.
15. USSBS, 107.
16. Spaatz interview, K239.572–583, AFHRC; Quesada interview 5.
17. *Condensed Analysis of the Ninth Air Force in the European Theater of Operations*, 1, 107 (hereafter cited as Ninth Air Force Study).
18. Ninth Air Force Study, 43.
19. Meilinger, 90; Quesada interview 5.
20. Annual History, TAC, 1948, 417.01, AFHRC; Quesada interview 5.
21. Officer cited in Murray Green to Tom Hughes, 14 April 1992; Quesada interview 5.
22. Bradley, *A General's Life*, 654; Vandenberg to Quesada, 3 January 1949, Vandenberg Papers, LC; Quesada interview 1; Meilinger, 168.

23. Quesada interview 5.
24. Quesada to Eaker, 7 September 1949, Eaker Papers, AFHRC; Quesada to Finletter, 13 October 1949, Quesada Papers, LC.
25. For a good discussion of the post-World War II Air Force and its problems with close air support, see Mark Clodfletter, *The Limits of Air Power*.
26. Quesada interview 5.
27. *Wall Street Journal*, 22 January 1982.

Selected Bibliography

These are the major sources for this study. I have not enumerated here the correspondence I have had with hundreds of Quesada's contemporaries. Each correspondent specifically cited is adequately reflected in the text notes.

PRIMARY SOURCES

Air Force Academy Library, Air Force Academy, Colorado (AFA)

Frank Andrews Papers
Follett Bradley Papers
Claire Chennault Papers
James Doolittle Collection
The Murray Green Collection—Henry Arnold Papers
Haywood Hansell Papers
Larry Kuter Papers
James Parton Papers
Nathan Twining Papers

Air Force Historical Research Center, Maxwell Air Force Base, Alabama (AFHRC)

INTERVIEWS
Fred Anderson interview
Orville Anderson interview
Sam Anderson interview
Henry [Hap] Arnold interview

Herman Balck interview
Glen Barcus interview
Cleo Bishop interview
Joseph Caldara interview
Claire Chennault interview
Ben Chidlaw interview
Albert Clark interview
Fred Dean interview
Jacob Devers interview
William Dunn interview
Ira Eaker interviews
Benjamin Foulois interview
Blair Garland interview
Harold George interview
Barney Giles interviews
Haywood Hansell interview
Millard Harmon interview
Bruce Holloway interview
James Howard interview
Richard Hughes interview
Frank Hunter interview
William Jarvis interview
Leon Johnson interview
William Kepner interview
Hugh Knerr interview
Robert Lovett interview
Curtis LeMay interviews
Lawrence Kuter interview
Seth McKee interview
William Momyer interview
Elwood Quesada interviews
Louis Seth interview
William Simpson interview
Tooey Spaatz interview
Stuart Symington interview
Nathan Twining interview
O. P. Weyland interview
Thomas White interview

MANUSCRIPT COLLECTIONS

Air Corps Newsletter, 1926–1942
Air Service Newsletter, 1918–1926

Annual Reports, Army Chief of Staff, 1919–1945
Annual Reports, Chief of the Air Corps, 1927–1945
Annual Reports, Chief of the Air Service, 1911–1926
Division of Military Aeronautics Weekly Newsletter, 1920–1928
Lectures, Air Corps Tactical School, 1926–1938
Texts, Air Corps Tactical School, 1926–1938
Unit Histories
Uncatalogued material
John Cannon Papers
Ira Eaker Collection
Benjamin Foulois Collection
Nathan Glick Papers
Harry Halverson Papers
William Kepner Papers
Richard Nugent Papers
Gordon Saville Papers
Otto Paul Weyland Collection

U.S. Army Command and General Staff College, Fort Leavenworth, Kansas

TEXTS

G-1 course, 1936–1938
G-2 course, 1936–1938
G-3 course, 1936–1938
G-4 course, 1936–1938

Dwight D. Eisenhower Presidential Library, Abilene, Kansas (DDE)

Terry De La Mesa Allen Papers
Henry Aurand Papers
Lewis Brereton Papers
Harold Bull Papers
J. Lawton Collins [Lightning Joe Collins] Papers
Norman Cota Papers
Dwight Eisenhower Pre-Presidential Papers
Courtney Hodges Papers
Arthur Nevins Papers
Elwood R. Quesada Papers
Walter Bedell Smith Papers and Collection

Imperial War Museum, London, England

    J.L. Tizard Papers

Library of Congress, Washington, DC (LC)

    Henry [Hap] Arnold Papers
    Ira Eaker Papers
    Benjamin Foulois Papers
    William Mitchell Papers
    Carl Spaatz Papers
    Elwood R. Quesada Papers
    Paul Robinette Papers
    Charles Scott Papers
    Nathan Twining Papers
    Hoyt Vandenberg Papers
    Thomas White Papers

National Archives, Washington, DC (NA)

    Record Group 18: Records of the Army Air Forces
    Record Group 191: Records of the War Department Claims Board
    Record Group 225: Records of Joint Army and Navy Boards and Committees
    Record Group 243: Records of the United States Strategic Bombing Survey
    Record Group 331: Records of Allied Operational and Occupation Headquarters, World War II
    Record Group 332: Records of United States Theaters of War, World War II
    Record Group 407: Records of the Adjutant General's Office

Public Record Office, London, England (PRO)

    AIR 23: Overseas Commands
    AIR 25: Group Operations Record Books
    AIR 26: Wing Operations Record Books
    AIR 41: Narratives and Monographs

Royal Air Force Museum, Hendon, England

    William Douglas Papers
    Trafford Leigh-Mallory Papers

Hugh P. Lloyd Papers
Charles Robb Papers
John Slessor Papers
Arthur Tedder Papers
Hugh Trenchard Papers

*United States Army Military History Institute, Carlisle Barracks, Pennsylvania
(USAMHI)*

The Clay Blair Collection
Omar Bradley Papers
Charles Corlett Papers
Sheffield Edwards Papers
Charles Gerhardt Papers
Chester Hansen Papers
William Sylvan Papers
Veteran Questionnaires Project

PUBLISHED PRIMARY SOURCES

Andrews, Frank. "The GHQ Air Force as an Instrument of National Defense," *Army Ordnance Magazine*, 18:15–31 (November–December, 1937).
Arnold, Henry. *Global Mission*. New York: Harper & Brothers, 1949.
Bradley, Omar. *The Effects of Strategic and Tactical Air Power on Military Operations, ETO*. Washington DC: Government Printing Office, 1945.
———. *A Soldier's Story*. New York: Henry Holt & Co., 1951.
Bradley, Omar, and Clay Blair. *A General's Life*. New York: Harcourt, 1981.
Chandler, Alfred, ed. *The Public Papers of Dwight David Eisenhower, III–IV*. Baltimore: Johns Hopkins University Press, 1970.
Chennault, Claire. *Way of a Fighter: The Memoirs of Claire Lee Chennault*. New York: G.P. Putnam's Sons, 1949.
———. "Why Pursuit?" *The Coast Artillery Journal*, 15:1;15:2;15:3; (January–April, 1936).
Collins, J. Lawton. *Lightning Joe: An Autobiography*. Baton Rouge: Louisiana University Press, 1979.
DeGuinard, Francis. *Operation Victory*. New York: Scribner, 1947.
Foulois, Benjamin, and Carroll Glines. *From the Wright Brothers to the Astronauts: The Memoirs of Major General Benjamin D. Foulois*. New York: McGraw-Hill Book Co., 1968.
Frank, Anne. *The Diary of a Young Girl*. New York: Doubleday, 1952.

Harmon, Ernest. "We Gambled in the Battle of the Bulge." *The Saturday Evening Post*, 2 October 1948.

Hart, B. H. Liddell, ed. *The Rommel Papers*. New York: Harcourt Brace, 1953.

Holt, Harold. "Column Cover." *American Aviation Historical Society* (Fall/Winter 1983).

Kohn, Richard. *Air Superiority in World War II, Korea, and Vietnam: An Interview with General James Ferguson, General Robert Lee, General William Momyer, and Lieutenant General Elwood Quesada*. Washington, DC: Office of Air Force History, 1983.

Mitchell, Billy. *Winged Defense: The Development and Possibilities of Modern Air Power—Economic and Military*. New York: G.P. Putnam's Sons, 1925.

———. *Memories of World War I: From Start to Finish of our Greatest War*. New York: Random House, 1960.

Patrick, Mason. *The Unites States in the Air*. New York: Doubleday, 1928.

Roosevelt, Franklin. *The Public Papers of Franklin Delano Roosevelt, I–III*. New York: Random House, 1938–1950.

Turner, Richard. *Big Friend, Little Friend: Memoirs of a World War II Fighter Pilot*. New York: Doubleday, 1969.

OFFICIAL STUDIES

Ackerman, Robert. *The Employment of Strategic Bombers in a Tactical Role, 1941–1951*. Washington, DC: Office of Air Force History, 1953.

Army Air Forces Historical Study No. 6: Distribution of Air Materials to the Allies. Maxwell Air Force Base, Alabama, 1957.

Army Air Force Historical Studies No. 22: Legislation Relating to the AAF Material Program. Maxwell Air Force Base, Alabama, 1954.

Army Air Forces Historical Study No. 40: The Ferrying Command. Maxwell Air Force Base, Alabama, 1956.

Bald, Ralph. *Air Force Participation in Joint Army-Air Force Training Exercises, 1947–1950*. Washington, DC: Office of Air Force History, 1952.

Blumenson, Martin. *Breakout and Pursuit*. Washington, DC: Center for Military History, 1960.

Boylon, Robert. *Development of the Long Range Fighter Escort*. Maxwell Air Force Base, Alabama, 1955.

Cole, Hugh. *The Ardennes: Battle of the Bulge*. Washington, DC: Center for Military History, 1964.

Coles, Harry. *The Army Air Forces in Amphibious Landings in World War II*. Washington, DC: Office of Air Force History, 1953.

Craven, Wesley, and James Cate, Eds. *The Army Air Forces in World War II*, Vols. I–III. Chicago: University of Chicago Press, 1948–51.

Finney, Robert. *History of the Air Corps Tactical School, 1920–1940*. Maxwell Air Force Base, Alabama, 1955.

Futrell, Robert Frank. *Air Historical Study No. 139: Ideas, Concepts, Doctrines: A History of Basic Thinking in the United States Air Force, 1907–1964*. Maxwell Air Force Base, Alabama: Air University, 1971.

Garland, Albert, and Howard Smyth. *Sicily and the Surrender of Italy*. Washington, DC: Center for Military History, 1963.

George, Robert. *The Ninth Air Force, April to November 1944*. Washington, DC: Office of the Chief of Military History, 1945.

Greenfield, Kent. *Ground Forces and the Air-Ground Battle Team*. Washington, DC: Office of the Chief of Military History, 1948.

Greer, Thomas. *The Development of Air Doctrine in the Army Air Arm, 1917–1941*. Maxwell Air Force Base, Alabama, 1955.

Harrison, Gordon. *Cross-Channel Attack*. Washington, DC: Center for Military History, 1950.

Hennessy, Juliette. *Tactical Operations of the Eighth Air Force, 6 June 1944 to 8 May 1945*. Washington, DC: Office of the Chief of Military History, 1952.

Holley, Irving. *Buying Aircraft: Material Procurement for the Army Air Forces*. Office of the Chief of Military History, 1970.

Howe, George. *Northwest Africa: Seizing the Initiative in the West*. Washington, DC: Center for Military History, 1956.

MacDonald, Charles. *The Last Offensive*. Washington, DC: Center for Military History, 1972.

———. *The Siegfried Line Campaign*. Washington, DC: Center for Military History, 1961.

McClendon, R. Earl. *The Question of Autonomy for the U.S. Air Arm, 1907–1945*. Maxwell Air Force Base, Alabama: Documentary Research Division, Air University, 1950.

Mortensen, Daniel. *A Pattern for Joint Operations: World War II Close Air Support*. Washington DC: Office of Air Force History, 1987.

Mueller, Robert. *History of Air Force Installations*, I. Washington, DC: Office of Air Force History, 1989.

Ramsey, John. *Ninth Air Force in the ETO, 16 October 1943 to 16 April 1944*. Washington, DC: Office of the Chief of Military History, 1944.

Ravenstein, Charles. *The Organization and Lineage of the USAF*. Washington, DC: Office of Air Force History, Reference Series, 1986.

Reither, Joseph. *The Development of Tactical Doctrines at AAFSAT and AAFTAC*. Washington, DC: Office of the Chief of Military History, 1946.

Special Army Air Forces Historical Study: Review of Aerial Warfare for the Scientific Advisory Board. Washington, DC: Office of the Chief of Military History, 1945.

Stubbs, Mary Lee. *Armor-Cavalry*. Washington, DC: U.S. Government Printing Office, 1979.

Suchenwirth, Jack. *Development of the German Air Force, 1919–1939*. Maxwell Air Force Base, Alabama, 1968.

Terrett, Dulany. *The Signal Corps: The Emergency*. Washington, DC: Office of Chief of Military History, 1957.

The Unites States Bombing Survey, Overall Report: European War. Washington, DC: U.S. Government Printing Office, 1945.

USAF Historical Studies: No. 6: The Development of the Heavy Bomber. Maxwell Air Force Base, Alabama: USAF Historical Division, Research Studies Institute, Air University, 1951.

Watson, Mark. *Chief of Staff: Prewar Plans and Preparations*. Office of Chief of Military History, 1950.

SECONDARY SOURCES

Bechtold, B. Michael. "Close Air Support in Normandy: The Case of First United States Army and the IX Tactical Air Command. A Question of Doctrine, Training, and Experience." Masters Thesis, Wilfrid Laurier University, 1993.

Blumenson, Martin. The Battle of the Generals. New York: William Morrow, 1993.

Byrd, Martha. *Chennault: Giving Wings to the Tiger*. Birmingham: The University of Alabama Press, 1987.

Caddell, Joseph. "Orphan of Unification: The Development of United States Air Force Tactical Air Power Doctrine, 1945–1950." Ph.D. Dissertation, Duke University, 1988.

Caiden, Martin. *Flying Forts*. New York: Ballantine Books, 1969.

Calvocoressi, Peter. *Total War: Causes and Courses of the Second World War*. New York: Penguin Books, 1979.

Carell, Paul. *Invasion—They're Coming*. New York: Dutton, 1963.

Chandler, Alfred. *The Papers of Dwight David Eisenhower: The War Years*, III, IV. Baltimore: The Johns Hopkins University Press, 1970.

Clodfelter, Mark. *The Limits of Air Power*. New York: Free Press, 1989.

Coffey, Thomas. *Hap*. New York: Viking, 1982.

Coffman, Edward. *The War to End All Wars: The American Military Experience in World War I*. New York: Oxford University Press, 1968.

Cooling, Benjamin, Ed. *Case Studies in the Development of Close Air Support*. Washington, Office of Air Force History, 1989.

Cooper, Matthew. *The German Air Force, 1933–1945: Anatomy of Failure*. New York: Doubleday, 1981.

————. *The German Army, 1933–1945*. Chelsea, MI: Scarborough House, 1990.

Copp, DeWitt. *A Few Great Captains: The Men and Events that Shaped the Development of U.S. Air Power*. New York: Doubleday, 1980.

Cuff, Robert. *The War Industries Board*. Baltimore: Johns Hopkins University Press, 1974.

Davis, Eldon. "Army and the Air Mail," *Airpower Historian* IX, 35–51.

D'este, Carlos. *Decision in Normandy*. New York: Dutton, 1983.

Donovan, James. *The United States Marine Corps*. New York: Praeger, 1967.

Eastman, James. "The Development of Big Bombers," *Aerospace Historian*, 25:207–220 (December 1978).

Eisenhower, David. *Eisenhower at War*. New York: Random House, 1986.

Ewing, Joseph H. *29 Let's Go: A History of the 29th Infantry Division in World War II*. Washington, DC: Infantry Journal Press, 1948.

Frisbee, John, ed. *Makers of the United States Air Force*. Washington, DC: Office of Air Force History, 1987.

Goldberg, Alfred. *A History of the U.S. Air Force, 1907–1957*. New York: Arno Press, 1972.

Greenfield, K. R. *American Strategy in World War II: A Reconsideration*. Baltimore: Johns Hopkins University Press, 1963.

Haley, Edward. *Makers of U.S. Naval Policy*. Washington, DC: U.S. Government Printing Office, 1986.

Hamilton, Nigel. *Master of the Battlefield: Monty's War Years, 1942–1944*. New York: McGraw Hill, 1983.

Hastings, Max. *Overlord: D-Day and the Battle for Normandy*. New York: Simon & Schuster, 1984.

Hess, William. *B-17 Flying Fortress*. New York: Ballentine Books, 1974.

Holley, Irving. *Ideas and Weapons: Exploitation of the Aerial Weapon by the United States during World War I*. Washington, DC: Office of Air Force History, 1983.

Hough, Richard, and Denis Richards. *The Battle of Britain: The Greatest Air Battle of World War II*. New York: Norton, 1989.

Hurley, Alfred. *Billy Mitchell: Crusader for Air Power*. New York: Franklin Watts, 1964.

Hudson, James. *Hostile Skies: A Combat History of the American Air Service in World War I*. Syracuse: Syracuse University Press, 1968.

Irving, David. *Hitler's War*. New York: Avon Books, 1990.

Jablonski, Edward. *Doolittle: A Biography*. New York: Doubleday, 1976.

James, D. Clayton. *The Years of MacArthur*, I. Boston: Houghton Mifflin, 1970.

Killen, John. *A History of the Luftwaffe*. New York: Doubleday, 1968.

Killigrew, Frank. "Impact of the Great Depression on the Army," *Perspectives*, XIII, 1–12.

Lockerbie, D. Bruce. *A Man Under Orders: Lt. Gen. William K. Harrison, Jr.* San Francisco: Harper & Row, 1979.

MacIsaac, David. *Strategic Bombing in World War II: The Story of the U.S. Bombing Survey.* New York: Garland Publishing Co., 1976.

Martin, Jerome Vernon. "Reforging the Sword: United States Tactical Air Forces, Air Power Doctrine, and National Security Policy, 1945–1956." Ph.D. Dissertation, The Ohio State University, 1988.

Maurer, Maurer. *U.S. Army Aviation, 1919–1939.* Washington, DC: Office of Air Force History, 1988.

Meilinger, Phillip. *Hoyt S. Vandenberg: The Life of a General.* Bloomington: Indiana University Press, 1989.

Mets, David. *Master of Airpower: General Carl A. Spaatz.* Novota, California: Presidio Press, 1988.

Millis, Walter. *Arms and Men: A Study in American Military History.* New York: G.P. Putnam's Sons, 1954.

Moskin, J. Robert. *The U.S. Marine Corps Story.* New York: McGraw-Hill, 1977.

Nenninger, Timothy. *The Leavenworth School System and the Old Army.* Boston: Houghton Mifflin, 1978.

Nolte, Reginald. *Thunder Monsters Over Europe.* Manhattan, Kansas: Sunflower University Press, no date.

Paret, Peter. *Makers of Modern Strategy: From Machiavelli to the Nuclear Age.* Princeton: Princeton University Press, 1986.

Pogue, Forrest. *George C. Marshall: Education of a General.* New York: The Viking Press, 1963.

———. *George C. Marshall: Ordeal and Hope.* New York: The Viking Press, 1966.

Pyle, Ernie. *Brave Men.* New York: Grosset and Dunlap, 1945.

Sampson, Jack. *Chennault.* New York: Doubleday, 1987.

Shiner, John. *Foulois and the U.S. Army Air Corps, 1931–1935.* Washington, DC: Office of Air Force History, 1982.

———. *The Army Flies the Mails.* Boston: Houghton Mifflin, 1980.

Sullivan, John. "The Botched Air Support of Operation Cobra." *Parameters* (March 1988).

Swanborough, Gordon, and Peter Bowers. *United States Military Aircraft Since 1909.* Washington, DC: Smithsonian Institution Press, 1989.

Weigley, Russell. *The American Way of War.* Bloomington: Indiana University Press, 1973.

———. *Eisenhower's Lieutenants.* Bloomington: Indiana University Press, 1980.

White, Paul Andrew. "Silent Force: The Contribution of Air Force Combat

Teams to Airborne Operations, 1944–1991. Masters Thesis, Central Missouri University, 1993.

Ziemke, Caroline Frieda. "In the Shadow of the Giant: USAF Tactical Air Command in the Era of Strategic Bombing, 1945–1955." Ph.D. Dissertation, The Ohio State University, 1989.

Index